Kandice Chuh and Karen Shimakawa,

Editors

ORIENTATIONS

Mapping Studies in the Asian Diaspora

Duke University Press

Durham and London

2001

"The Eclipse of Kuan-yin and Rahu" in "Creating Performative Communities: Through Text, Time, and Space" by Russell Leong appears as "Eclipse" in *Phoenix Eyes and Other Stories* by Russell Leong (Seattle and London: the University of Washington Press, 2000) 101–111. Reprinted by permission of the University of Washington Press.

"Notes toward a Conversation between Area Studies and Diasporic Studies" by Dipesh Chakrabarty appears in *Public Culture* 10, no. 3 (1998).

"Modelling the Nation: the Asian/American Split" by David Palumbo-Liu appears as "Pacific America: Introjection and the Beginnings of Modern Asian America" in *Asian/American: Historical Crossings of a Racial Frontier* by David Palumbo-Liu (Stanford: Stanford University Press, 1999) 17–42. Reprinted with the permission of Stanford University Press.

"Leading Questions" by Rey Chow appears as "Introduction: Leading Questions" in *Writing Diaspora: Tactics of Intervention in Contemporary Cultural Studies* by Rey Chow (Bloomington and Indianapolis: Indiana University Press, 1993) 1–26. Reprinted with the permission of Indiana University Press.

Typeset in Monotype Garamond by
Tseng Information Systems, Inc.
Library of Congress Cataloging-in-Publication Data appear
on the last printed page of this book.

We dedicate this book to our teacher, Susan Jeffords.
Thank you.

Contents

Acknowledgments

This book quite literally would not exist had it not been for the support we received from many people along the way. Our first thanks go to Susan Jeffords, to whom this work is dedicated, for pushing us to "think big." We are equally grateful to Ken Wissoker of Duke University Press, whose faith in this project was instrumental in its completion, and to this volume's contributors for their exceptional patience and commitment. Katie Courtland and Justin Faerber, also at Duke University Press, have our thanks as well for their knowledgeable guidance, especially toward this project's completion.

Orientations is the culmination of work begun at a colloquium entitled "Disciplining Asia: Theorizing Studies in the Asia Diaspora," at the University of Washington in Seattle, 2–3 May 1996. For both material and less tangible but equally important support, many at the University of Washington have our gratitude: The colloquium itself was sponsored by the Department of English, The Graduate School, the Office of the Dean of Arts & Sciences, The Center for the Humanities, The Hilen Endowment, The Department of Anthropology, and The Jackson School for International Studies and its China, Korea, South Asia, and International Studies Programs, with additional support from the Departments of American Ethnic Studies, Asian Languages & Literatures, History, and Women Studies. We are particularly grateful to Ross Posnock, Thomas Lockwood, Shawn Wong, Leroy Searle, and especially, Tani Barlow, for their generous efforts on our behalf. Susan Williams and the other members of the Department of English's main office provided instrumental administrative support.

We would be remiss were we not also to thank participants in the colloquium itself, some of whom ultimately do not have pieces in this anthology but whose participation at that stage helped to shape this work. Thus, our thanks go to Oscar Campomanes, Chungmoo Choi, Inderpal Grewal, Yukiko Hanawa, Shu-Mei Shih, and Shawn Wong. Ann Anagnost, Stevan Harrell, and Connie So were gracious moderators at the colloquium. Rebecca Aanerud, Jane Adam, Tamara Kaplan, and Karen Kuo were vital in pulling the colloquium together and have our sincerest gratitude. Cathy Davidson has been an important source of both personal and professional support, and our thanks go to her as well.

In addition, Karen Shimakawa would like to thank her students, colleagues, and friends in the English Department at Vanderbilt University and the Theatre and Dance Department and Asian American Studies Program at the University of California at Davis, including Myriam Chancy, Barbara Sellers-Young, and Kent Ono, and David Román at the University of Southern California, for their intellectual generosity and support. Special thanks go to crack research assistant Hope Medina. This project was in part made possible through the support of the Robert Penn Warren Center for the Humanities at Vanderbilt University, and the Davis Humanities Institute at U. C. Davis. Finally, heartfelt thanks go to her family for their encouragement, faith, and above all, patience.

Kandice Chuh would like to thank her colleagues and friends in the Department of English at the University of Maryland, including William Sherman and Jonathan Auerbach, who have respectively endured with graciousness the physical challenges of anthology production in shared office space; and Nicole King, Robert Levine, and Sangeeta Ray, for providing vital collegial support and friendship. William Cohen deserves especial mention for his excellent critical assistance with the volume's introduction in addition to sustaining friendship: thank you. And finally, deepest thanks to her family—Young, Alice, and Patricia Chuh, and Josh Green—who make everything possible.

Orientations

Introduction:

Mapping Studies in the Asian Diaspora

KANDICE CHUH AND KAREN SHIMAKAWA

In the past decade, we in the United States have witnessed what Neil Gotanda has described as a "distinct[ly] anti-Chinese turn" in anti-immigrant sentiment. Consider the campaign finance scandal in which the Clinton administration was accused of accepting donations from Chinese officials, and the implication that these "suspect Chinese donations would somehow undermine the American political system" (1999, 1). More recently, the indictment of Wen Ho Lee, a Chinese American research scientist, on nuclear weapons spy charges, has garnered the mainstream media's attention, again raising the specter of possible infiltration of the U. S. government by Chinese forces. Lee's subsequent release from prison and the revelation of impropriety in the government's conduct in pursuing its case against him, highlights the ways that anti-Chinese sentiment can gain hold in the U.S. imagination despite evidentiary weaknesses. This is not surprising, for it is but a contemporary manifestation of what Gotanda has called "Asiatic racialization," a process characterized by "[a] group of related yet distinct ideas—Asiatic unassimilability, the conflation of Asian Americans with Asian citizens, and the perception of Asians as a threat to the American nation" (1999, 1–2).

These are ideas that have effected violence against, and exclusion, disenfranchisement, and internment of, Asians in the United States over the years. They describe a historic and ongoing portrayal of "Asia" as an immutably foreign entity, always somehow threatening to America.[1] Especially notable in this particular iteration of Asiatic racialization—in the form of charges of espionage—is its concern with governmental infiltration as intersected by finance and technology. While money and techno-logical ability have arguably always preoccupied and motivated the United States, in the present moment, the booming health of the U.S. economy and its wealth of technological resources, both in terms of internet capa-bilities and the more traditional areas of military power, have made finance and technology key words in popular discourse about the nation. This it-eration of Asiatic racialization, in other words, taps into and implicitly ref-erences present conditions. Why has Asia, especially in the figure of China, become so visible and important to contemporary U.S. national identity formation?

This question presents a crucial challenge for current (especially U.S.-based) practitioners engaged in studies of Asia and of "Asianness." This is a challenge to understand the historical and political particularities that enable Asiatic racialization to continue apace. The multiple spheres through which Asiatic racialization works—politics, law, culture, eco-nomics—speak to the complexity of what it means to "know Asia," to gauge the significance of particular formulations of the cultures, peoples, and politics imagined under the name "Asia." *Orientations* offers critical tools that can help us understand what it means that anti-Chinese sentiment (as an instantiation of Asiatic racialization) has (re)emerged so forcefully. This vol-ume is concerned with locating this inquiry in the U.S. academic realm, and the essays collected here accordingly excavate certain practices of producing knowledge about "Asia." What are the constitutive elements of and critical influences on such practices and the resultant knowledges produced? How might such practices be deployed to disrupt Asiatic racialization?

The campaign finance scandal and the Wen Ho Lee case unfold as we move from the "American Century" to the next. The later part of the 1900s has seen the end of the Cold War, the "collapse" of the Soviet Union, the in-creasing globalization of capital, and related (sometimes coerced) flows of people and products, as well as the emergence of technologies that facilitate rapid communication and information-sharing. Globalization fundamen-tally references the interpenetration of economies, political and otherwise, across regions and as enabled by available technologies.[2] It is a phenome-non aggressively advanced by U.S. capitalist ideology. As Bruce Cumings has explained, the absence of the Soviet Union and the Cold War does not mark a change in the world itself so much as the revelation of the global structure created by Americans in the middle of the century: "Our 1990s world is an anticipated consequence, the liberal capitalist world order that was the ultimate goal of American planners in the 1940s" (1999, 15).[3] From this perspective, the world exists by American design, dominated by U.S. hegemony. Yet this "new world order" poses a set of problems for the United

States, for a level of anxiety accompanies this interrelation of economies. What does a national identity look like, what kind of coherence can it sustain, in the face of such porousness? Against whom do we define ourselves, now that the ultimate Other of the Cold War is no longer?

Enter China. China, still "remote and encapsulated" (Cumings 1999) in the U.S. imagination, is a market as yet not open to the world (read: U.S.) economy. Figured through the liberal discourse of human rights violations, China thus easily becomes a market that *needs* opening in order that (American) democracy may prevail. It is important to note here the distinction between China-as-government and China-as-people central to this imagining. China-as-government is the bad other: the force of Communist repression through violation of human rights. China-as-people registers through the images of the student protestors during the Tiananmen Square event of 1989, those attempting to change the social and political arrangements structuring the nation, as well as through the images of the men and women suffering transport in cargo holds in attempts to migrate to the United States. Perennial debates in the U.S. Congress over the granting of Most Favored Nation trade status to China speak to the tensions arising from this double-faceted idea of China. As yet unresolved, these tensions have resulted in the partial "opening" of China to the United States; the United States's hesitancy to commit fully to trade relations with China is arguably a symptom of the paradox between the universalist humanism and sectarian economics characteristic of U.S. capitalist ideology.[4] The distinction between people and government is a crucial component in justifying U.S. efforts to tap into the vast potential of the Chinese market: we rationalize our profit-based efforts at infiltration and control by recourse to an ethical/moral motivation. As Susan Koshy has argued, the deployment of human rights discourse is a rhetorical strategy of contemporary neocolonial power that works "less through military force than through economic domination" (1999, 1). These conditions enable, and perhaps even—in their logic—necessitate, the figuration of a Chinese threat exemplified and embodied by suspect campaign contributors and Wen Ho Lee.

Of course other factors are at play here. The prominence of China-as-threat is conditioned by the post-World War II emergence of various Asian nations as (developing) technological and economic powers, and as (potentially) nuclear weapons-equipped. American recognition of these conditions is signalled by the growth of "Pacific Rim" discourse in the latter decades of the 20th century, a rhetoric that moves the United States into, or consolidates America with, Asia. This discourse is, as Christopher Connery explains, a kind of internationalism that among other things reveals the contingency of "America" on "Asia" (1995). It explicitly recognizes the significance of Asia to U.S. economic/military interests as well as to American culture. It posits a kind of sameness, or contiguity, between Asia and America that makes it possible to imagine compatibility as economic partners. The rise of "Japan bashing" in the 1980s marks the recession of this rhetoric, and this pattern of dominance and recession illuminates the uneven but everpresent construction and deployment of "Asia" in the U.S. imaginary.[5] That Asia consistently has been a significant determinant in the formation of U.S. national identity since this nation's inception has been well-established, if not yet popularized.[6] The consolidation of a phantasmatic "Asia" continues to undergird the solidity and imagined wholeness of a U.S. identity that is (among other things) not-Asian. What "Asia" means in and for the U.S. imagination, and how those meanings are deployed, are inquiries that lead us toward understanding the nature and effects of U.S. nationalist and internationalist practices and discourses. For, the "meaning" of Asia responds to the exigencies governing U.S. (inter)national self-fashioning at a given moment: "Asia" is the threatening rival to U.S. technological dominance, the untapped natural and labor resource for U.S. industry, the limitless consumer market for U.S. goods and culture, the mysterious and feminized territory awaiting and in need of U.S. military protection.

If we accept Cumings's assertion that what is different about now versus then is a matter of re-cognizing the world structure plotted decades ago by Americans, the understanding of the present sketched above brings us precisely to the issue of knowledge production. *Orientations* offers a critical approach to analyzing the contemporary phenomenon of globalization driven by U.S. ideology as it is articulated through and against "Asia." How do Asian and Asian American studies, two realms of intellectual practice engaged with the project of understanding "Asia," constitute their objects of study? What do "Asian" and "Asianness" come to mean for practitioners in these areas? In what ways can understanding the overlaps and distinctions among these meanings inaugurate new epistemologies or critiques that might productively further the work of Asian and Asian American studies, thereby enlightening understanding of the contemporary moment? *Orientations* identifies these questions as central to a critical engagement with the epistemological and institutional practices giving rise to knowledge production about "Asia," especially as that knowledge is constituted in and by the U.S. political and cultural imaginary. *Orientations* urges a recognition of the ways in which particular configurations of Asianness in specific Asian diasporic studies are embedded in institutional economies that are ideologically implicated and valued. That is, this volume argues in toto not merely for recognizing the multiple meanings of Asianness in Asian and

Asian American studies and the historical conditions that give rise to them. Instead, it calls for recognizing the dimensions of a newly emergent field of inquiry, situated *around* and *between* those disciplinary formations, that takes as its focus precisely the differences among those meanings as a way of exposing the ideologies that affiliate particular kinds of value (political, institutional, cultural, historical) to epistemological objects and practices. This process of thinking through "Asia" as epistemological object from various ec-centric positions illuminates the ideologies and material conditions characterizing the present. The approach advanced here suggests that those engaged in the production of knowledge about Asia and Asianness reflexively situate their work within an institutional network larger than any individual disciplinary or areal formation. In order to understand the phenomenon of globalization, it is necessary to "globalize" academic practices by thinking across disciplinary and areal boundaries.

Critical Contexts

Such academic globalization is well under way, propelled by, among others, the discourses of postcolonialism and transnationalism, which have in their respective, sometimes overlapping ways, required the recognition of interpenetration across boundaries. Postcolonialism's interrogation of the consequences of imperialism for both the (formerly) colonized and the metropole has effectively undermined binary epistemologies that give rise to essentialist conceptions of East/Other and West/Self. As scholars like Gayatri Spivak, Edward Said, and Homi Bhabha have demonstrated, the figure of the Oriental Other has been integral to maintaining the semblance of coherence of the Western Self within imperialist symbolic, psychological, and political economies. They and others have made clear that to be excolonial is to be neither precolonial nor free of colonialism's effects.[7] The "post" of postcolonialism marks not a discrete end to colonialism but instead signals a configuration of global relations characterized by both continuities with and disjunctures from colonialism's practices. Likewise, transnationalism exposes the apparatuses through which such ideologies continue to be deployed and reveals how these contemporary deployments are shaped by available technologies. Transnationalism is grounded in recognition of global movements of capital and related migration of peoples; as a theory, it both describes and interrogates the possibilities for inhabiting and coopting this cross-border mobility for the sake of envisioning communities bounded not principally by national identifications and investments. These complementary discourses have decisively undermined the stability of the Three Worlds model of global organization inherited from the Cold

War era. *Orientations* works from and within this understanding of global relations made available through postcolonialist and transnationalist paradigms.

At the same time, this volume engages with U.S. minority discourse in a particularized form. Minority discourse describes a critical practice of valuing the epistemologies emergent from minoritized (disempowered, disenfranchised) perspectives, for the sake of working toward the realization of social justice.[8] Like postcolonialism and transnationalism, U.S. minority discourse attends to differential power relations in the processes and material conditions of subject and social formation. Such studies as Michael Omi and Howard Winant's *Racial Formation in the United States* (1994) show how minorities come into being through the interplay between an international economic system and national cultures and ideologies. Susan Koshy describes the current international economic system cogently: "What we are witnessing in our time is the scramble among developed countries (which now no longer refers exclusively to the former colonial powers) not for territory but for the competitive edge in trade and commerce, especially through monopolistic control over vital sectors of profitability (information, biotechnology, and technological innovations)" (1999, 1–2). What we have called academic globalization is a process that tracks and keeps pace with these changes. Transected and substantively informed by feminism and gay and lesbian studies, contemporary academic discourse attempts to produce Jameson's "cognitive map" of the postmodern world. *Orientations* likewise takes up a similar project of charting the contours of what it means to study "Asia" from critical perspectives that axiomatically recognize globalization. For this reason, we adopt the "Asian diaspora" as anchoring this field of inquiry. The concept of the Asian diaspora evokes multiple locations and movements and hesitates to fix itself as a static epistemological object.

Areas, Relations, and Objects of Knowledge

This new field of inquiry both corresponds with and goes beyond established disciplinary and areal boundaries. The history of this volume's development describes this condition. This project was initially conceived around three central questions: What is at stake (culturally/politically/intellectually) in maintaining the distinction(s) between Asian Americanness and Asianness? What historical shifts, if any, have taken place that necessitate or facilitate a reassessment of the constitutive bases of Asian and Asian American studies? How are the specific fields of study within these disciplines (i.e., history, literature, sociology, etcetera) affected by a (critical) crossing or (uncritical) blurring of the distinction between Asian and Asian American studies?

As these questions suggest, *disciplinarity* initially functioned as our organizing principle. The project's original title, "Disciplining Asia: Theorizing Studies in the Asian Diaspora," was intended to provoke multiple trajectories of thought, including a critique of institutional practices, Foucauldian notions of power, the histories of U.S. and European imperialisms giving rise to the imaginary figure of "Asia," and so on. Several of the essays included here analyze the ramifications of this organizing trope and make clear that, as Kuan-Hsing Chen argues, at issue fundamentally is the identity of the subject who is doing the "disciplining."[9] Thus, this volume does not finally focus on disciplinarity itself, but instead maps multiple iterations of Asianness as epistemological objects in their relationships to specific disciplinary and institutional areas and practices. "Orientations" obviously plays on this sense of relationality, refering to exchange and interaction among object, location, and understanding. Rooted by "orient," it simultaneously connotes the histories through which the Orient, the East, and Asia have been configured through variegated practices of locating self against other. The Asian diaspora as an alternative epistemological object (alternative, that is, to "Asia" and "Asian America") is itself a relation, and makes reference to a kind of conceptual ratio comparing origins and present locations. Metonymic rather than metaphoric, this comparison focuses on movement itself, on the literal circulation of peoples and cultures, and on the figurative meanings of those movements. It describes a conceptual space where attention is drawn to *how* "Asia" materializes through historically specific institutional and symbolic economies. Mindful of Foucault's insight into the function of academic disciplines in the *creation* (rather than mere investigation) of objects of knowledge, *Orientations* seeks to examine this process and its implications — both liberatory and repressive — by working from the eccentric perspective of the Asian diaspora.

To be sure, neither "Asia" and "Asian America" nor their corollary fields of study are exactly parallel as comparative terms. The emergence of area studies, of which Asian studies is a part, within the context of and driven by Cold War politics and U.S. foreign relations interests, contrasts against the establishment of Asian American studies consequent to the Third World Movement of the 1960s — a movement arguably specifically opposed to those interests.[10] Area Studies gained a foothold in American universities partly as a consequence of U.S. participation in World War II. During the war, many universities provided "various types of area instruction demanded by military forces" (Hall 1947, iii). As Robert Hall, chairman of the Exploratory Committee on World Area Research (formed immediately following the war) explains in his 1947 report on the committee's findings, this wartime experience made clear that "the scholarship of this country was found wanting when put to the test of war—wanting in precise knowledge of different areas and their peoples, and wanting in the accumulation of materials which would have made sound research or analysis possible" (22). Without such knowledge, the argument goes, it is impossible to achieve lasting peace—that is, to conduct war effectively. "Those who hold most strongly to this view contend that the universities have an obligation to the nation. National welfare in the postwar period more than ever before requires a citizenry well informed as to other peoples, and the creation of a vast body of knowledge about them" (22).

A second part of the argument for area studies "develops around the criticism that research, especially in the social sciences and certain of the humanities, has failed to yield complete or reliable results because they lack universality" (23). We cannot, in other words, know if we are right: "We need the data of other areas to check our assumptions" (24). The cross disciplinary approach of area studies would be better suited to meeting these needs because it can provide "whole knowledge" of an area not available through the vertical approach of individual disciplines (25). Thus, studies of such "large and important" areas as China are justified as being in the national interest—for the preservation of our peace, for the confirmation of our knowledge. As Vicente Rafael (1994) summarizes in his analysis of Hall's report, "just as the humanities were meant to cultivate a self that was authorized to transmit the legacy of the past, area studies would develop a body of elite scholars capable of producing knowledge about other nations to the benefit of 'our' nation" (93). Rafael extends this critique,

> What is significant about area studies . . . is not so much the unsurprising point that they are tied to Orientalist legacies; rather, it is that since the end of World War II, area studies have been integrated into larger institutional networks, ranging from universities to foundations, that have made possible the reproduction of a North American style of knowing, one that is ordered toward the proliferation and containment of Orientalisms and their critiques. Furthermore, it is a style of knowing that is fundamentally dependent on, precisely to the extent that it is critical of, the conjunction of corporate funding, state support, and the flexible management systems of university governance characteristic of liberal pluralism (91).

"Asia," as an epistemological object of area studies, thus emerges out of American modernity's characteristic imperialist ideology and concomitant belief in the possibility of objective knowledge.[11] Rafael's description of area studies as a *style of knowing* usefully emphasizes the practical dimensions of this field of knowledge production. Institutionally embedded, corporately funded, and state-validated, this emphasis makes clear the ways in which area studies may be complicit in the reification of Asiatic racialization.

It would be tempting to identify Asian American studies as an alternative style of knowing, and hence as a palliative, to Asian studies.[12] Established as part of the institutionalization of U.S. ethnic studies in universities in the 1960s and 70s, Asian American studies carries the histories of the Civil Rights Movement, the Third World Peoples Movement, and the protests against U.S. involvement in the Vietnam War. As Russell Leong summarizes in his essay in the present volume, "the formation of Asian American Studies is linked directly with the struggles and movements of self determination by Asian American students in response to their exclusion from the educational curriculum. Asians in the 1960s and 70s, together with African, Latino, and Native Americans, saw their lives and communities as part of the American experience, yet recognized that their histories had not been adequately studied, fairly taught, or widely disseminated. . . . The Asian American movement in a broader sense struggled to develop longer-term strategies toward the inclusion of people of color in the social fabric and political transformation of the United States."

Even as Asian American studies has gained, though unevenly, legitimacy within many American universities, struggles to establish and maintain such programs at other institutions continue today. Incorporation into university curricula has often localized the oppositional energies Leong describes, such that institutionalization itself is deemed a successful effect of Asian American studies' politics. From "within," Asian Americanists have mounted effective critiques of the mythology of American greatness. Yet, the liberal humanist ideology of pluralism/multiculturalism driving academic institutionalization that is equally a part of the history of Asian American studies functions as a strategy of containment. Like area studies, ethnic studies is materially supported by corporate and state investments; its institutionalization in the university system ensures that resistance will always be complemented with complicity. The intellectual and pedagogical work of ethnic studies scholars has been instrumental in dislodging racist, sexist, and, more recently, homophobic renderings of minoritized U.S. social subjects. Yet, simultaneously, as George Lipsitz succinctly explains in his essay presented here, "while Ethnic Studies is doing very well, ethnic people are faring very badly." There is a growing disjuncture between the "success" of ethnic studies and the impoverished conditions in which many of the presumed subjects of those studies live. Liberatory intentions and rhetoric must be considered in light of this gap. The politics embedded in the term "Asian American," a politics of claiming legitimacy and rights as Americans, is clearly not wholly effective in establishing social justice.

Even these abbreviated histories make clear the need for a joint consideration of Asian and Asian American studies. By recognizing that the styles of knowing characterizing each field emerge out of the demands of American modernity, we see as well that a continued insistence on their separation participates in furthering the Asiatic racialization that is also a part of modern America's character. We are not positing some putatively common object ("Asia") as the rationale for yoking these fields of practice together. Instead, this volume asks what happens when we identify American modernity as a common genealogical location for fields involved in the investigation of multiple forms of "Asia": what happens to our understandings of Asianesses, in the U.S. frame and elsewhere, by working from this point of departure?

The wealth of critical scholarship that has emerged from this eccentric position testifies to the gains made through *this* style of knowing. The appearance of progressively inclined journals like *positions: east asia cultures critique, Diaspora,* and *public culture;* the work of scholars represented in the volume edited by David Eng and Alice Hom, *Q&A: Queer in Asian America* (1998); and the marked impact of recently consolidating South Asian American studies, are exemplary of the kind of academic globalization we are here describing, as is the turn toward attending explicitly to globalization and epistemological object formation characterizing contemporary issues of such longstanding journals as *Amerasia*.[13] Though reaching in different, multiple directions, this work has eccentricity in common: presumed objects of knowledge are revisited and recast, such that the disciplines creating and undergirding those objects shudder by being exposed as unstable. *Orientations* attempts to capture and examine the anatomy of such discourses, attending to and going beyond disciplinary boundaries in the process.

Four axes of investigation organize this study. First, Part One of *Orientations* considers anatomy literally, illuminating the relationship between the different kinds of personal and intellectual investments and material consequences embedded in studies of Asia, and the embodiment of practice and experience in such studies. By focusing on "the Asian diaspora" through the lens of embodiment, new modes of academic and cultural practice become visible or visualizable. A second way in which Asian and Asian American studies may be refocused is by modelling what Naoki Sakai (1997) terms "translation as a social relation." Part Two extends the concept of translation beyond its linguistic usage to consider how cultures, epistemological objects, and disciplinary practices participate in the act of translation at the level of the social. In Part Three, *Orientations* examines the constitution (or sedimentation) of boundaries themselves, both academic and otherwise, to address how academic disciplines come into being, and what it means politically and ideologically to work both within and beyond them. This study concludes by explicitly triangulating Asian diaspora studies and American studies with (post)modernity in order to illuminate the continuing impact of "America" on knowledge production about "Asia." Globalization, after all, works in multiple directions; while much critical work examines the effects of that process "elsewhere" (or on our conceptions of that "elsewhere"), we end by considering these effects within American studies, which takes as its object that from which, ostensibly, "global" effects flow—but on which the effects of globalization have rarely been taken seriously.

Part 1. Investments and Interventions

The body is crucial for thinking about discourse and epistemology, for it locates the stakes involved in the production of knowledge. As Arjun Appadurai (1998) has argued, the uncertainty wrought by the destabilizing forces of globalization has produced new tensions, anxieties, and even brutalities, which "fix" the fluid formations of "ethnicity." If, as he asserts, "there is a growing sense of radical social uncertainty about people, situations, events, norms, and even cosmologies" produced by the ascendance of (economic) transnationalism, "the ethnic body can be a theatre for the engagement of uncertainty under the special circumstances of globalization" (906). While Appadurai's concern here with ethnic violence as a brutal and extreme mode of establishing an ethnic/national "truth" in the body, Part One of this volume considers the question of diasporic or transnational embodiment in a broader sense, one more specifically tied to academic disciplinarity.

Dorinne Kondo's essay, "(Un)Disciplined Subjects: (De)Colonizing the Academy?" uses the format of "autobiographical political history" to map her own trajectory, "from the epistemologies of anthropology and East Asian studies to those of Asian American studies, minority discourse, cultural studies, and performance studies." That Kondo's academic trajectory toward performance studies and Asian American studies is fueled by "feelings . . . that are in and of the body in ways that are difficult to describe in words" thus illustrates that the instability of racial and cultural taxonomies described by Appadurai is not only apprehended by those seeking to fix the racial/ethnic "other"; it can be a material, bodily experience of the self that produces new modes of academic praxis. There are, she reminds us, significant material differences between Asian Americanness (which must be further particularized by ethnicity, gender/sex, sexuality, class, etcetera) and Asianness (another fictive monolith comprised of similarly disparate identities); we must be attentive to these specificities, including how they are embodied and where their/our interests diverge and conflict. This mutually constitutive connection, between what we do as academics and what we experience as marked and embodied subjects, is arguably one of the driving forces behind this collection: theorizing the relation between the self and the epistemological object is a first-order project necessary to engagement with questions of disciplinarity and practice.

That Kondo's self-problematizing gaze should shift her focus toward performance is not surprising given her interest in embodiment. Appadurai's discussion of ethnic violence is also framed in terms of staging ethnic identity on the "theatre of the body"; racial, ethnic, and diasporic identities are not only felt but actively scripted, performed, and read. Karen Shimakawa's "(Re)Viewing an Asian Diaspora: Multiculturalism, Interculturalism, and the Northwest Asian American Theatre" examines one Asian American theater company's strategic engagement with Asian diasporic issues. Caught between economic "multicultural" and "intercultural" theatre trends and historically committed to an Asian American focus, NWAAT responds to global reorganization through "a resignification of the [Asian] body in global/diasporic terms that nevertheless resists the pull of biological-racial essentialism." Shimakawa argues that NWAAT's innovative program, which combines Asian and Asian American theatre artists in ways that highlight dialogue and self-reflection, "calls into critical question the ways in which we 'read' raced bodies in terms of their perceived positions within national, international or (post)colonial frameworks." Complex and potentially contradictory meanings, scripted onto Asian and Asian American performers' bodies, have the potential to destabilize the already muddled concepts of multiculturalism, interculturalism, and transnationalism; the Asian/Asian American body on stage thus may serve as a text, an informant, and a model for new forms of academic cross- or interdisciplinarity.

Like Kondo's and Shimakawa's contributions, Russell Leong's essay/performance text underscores the consequences of redefining Asianness. New bodily materialities—what it means, literally and figuratively, to embody Asianness—necessitate new academic practices that affiliate meanings to bodies in explicitly ideological ways. Kondo's and Shimakawa's crossings between the disciplines of the academy and of the theatre interrupt uncritical celebrations of multiculturalism or border crossing by exposing their consequences on bodies. Leong's piece, "Creating Performative Communities: Through Text, Time, and Space," extends that project, demonstrating the intimate relationship between questions of embodiment (be it theatrical or quotidian) and questions of disciplinarity and academic professionalization. Leong's recounting of the histories of Asian America through the histories of Asian American studies and *Amerasia Journal*, which he edits, suggests that the relationship of Asian American studies to Asian studies has been complex from its inception in the 1960s. Leong's remembering of the international and cross-racial activist roots of Asian American studies narrates an embodied, materially grounded, politically activist model for academic work, which is situated in both U.S. and global politics. Moreover, the second section of his essay, a performance text titled "The Eclipse of Kuan-Yin and Rahu," reenacts precisely that kind of embodied criticism. Taken together, the two sections model the genre/disciplinary transgression that Leong sees as the future of Asian and Asian American studies: the characters in "Eclipse" must negotiate differences in ethnicity, sexuality, gender, race, class, and more; they cannot be considered within discrete boxes, but are defined by their interactions with one another. By illustrating the multiplication of generic forms that academic writing may assume, Leong expands conventional notions of how scholarly work in the fields of Asian and Asian American studies may be accomplished, and how the objects of those studies may be rendered knowable.

Sharon Hom's essay, "Cross-Discipline Trafficking: What's Justice Got to Do With It?" approaches the question of embodiment raised by the intersection of Asian and Asian American studies "in a law register," considering effects of such intersections on human rights law. Asian American critical jurisprudence has exposed implicit assumptions of social inequalities that constitute U.S. political-legal systems of governance; on the "international law" side, China figures prominently in human rights scholarship. "These two legal subfields," she notes, "reflect different genealogies, demographics, institutional locations, methodologies, and political projects," yet Hom charts her own personal and professional position between these two discourses, including "current debates over the rapprochement or tensions between area and ethnic studies" and how law might be a force in that negotiation. By developing the concepts of "ethico-political" praxis and "interdisciplinary raiding," Hom argues for "micropolitical projects" through which the Asian/Asian American subject/scholar may move beyond the "area studies versus ethnic studies" impasse. "The daily choices we make," writes Hom, "in a variety of institutional contexts—work, education, family, and politics—are concrete, site-specific opportunities for doing justice . . . in the here and now." Hom's call, to reframe seemingly "academic" questions of globalization and international human rights in terms of lived experience and individual responsibility challenges us to be mindful of such questions' consequences for the bodies that are our objects of study.

Part 2. Translating Knowledge

The essays in the second section explore the translation of knowledge across discourse communities—knowledge not as mere information, but as structuring worldviews, as expressions and reflections of larger epistemological systems. This section uses the concept of translation to understand academic globalization as a way of pointing to the social relations embedded in and produced through thinking across boundaries. In so doing, it identifies the ways in which academic globalization may exclude certain voices, or in other words, how academic discourses represent only certain kinds of subjects and subject formations, importantly reminding us of the limits and partiality of knowledges produced. Practitioners of academic globalization must remember that globalization is not always liberatory: movement may be compelled or prohibited by economic and/or political necessity. This recognition requires a careful, materially grounded deployment of boundary crossing paradigms.

In contemplating the ramifications of writing for multiple linguistic audiences, Naoki Sakai suggests that "translation structures the situation in which it is performed," and asks, "what sort of social relation is translation in the first place?" (1997, 3). It is a social relation, Sakai argues, because translation posits a fixed relation between two discourse communities, fleeting though that stability may be. Drawing a distinction between "homolingual" and "heterolingual" address, Sakai argues that "the homolingual address assumes the normalcy of reciprocal and transparent communication," whereas the heterolingual address "assumes that every utterance can fail to communicate because heterogeneity is inherent in any medium, linguistic or otherwise." Dipesh Chakrabarty's "Notes toward a Conversation between Area Studies and Diasporic Studies" takes up the problem of literal and figurative translation across a diaspora. He begins by situating area studies within larger projects addressing "the problems of knowledge and . . . the challenges of citizenly education" in the United States, providing a genealogy of U.S. area studies as situated in both liberal humanist and Cold War contexts. He then raises "the problem of different reading communities" resulting from the proliferation of these academic discourses, in order to consider how the journal *Subaltern Studies* locates itself within that "problem." Chakrabarty sees the journal, whose focus is "South Asia" and whose editorial board is globally dispersed, as operating under the rubric of heterolinguistics: writing to and for a transnational audience, the editors of *Subaltern Studies* must attend to the nontransparency of communication across differently constituted, differentially empowered sites.

Sau-ling Wong's contribution, "The Stakes of Textual Border Crossing: Hualing Nieh's *Mulberry and Peach* in Sinocentric, Asian American, and Feminist Critical Practices," traces the journey of "a literary text of 'Asian' provenance [as it] crosses national, political, linguistic, and cultural borders" to demonstrate the difficulties posed by translation and heterolinguistic pedagogy. Wong reflects upon "the novel's protean nature, its radical uncontainability" and its ability to produce radically varied translations in different institutional settings. Despite its heterolingual potential to communicate across these differences, the novel and the readings it produced point out some obstacles to an uncritical application of transnationalism. Arguing for "historical situatedness" and cautioning against an overeager "valorization of border-bursting multiplicity," Wong's essay suggests that texts such as Nieh's can be translated across disciplinary borders — but only with care, and at a cost.

Chakrabarty and Wong both examine translations across academic disciplines and the social relations circumscribing such communication. Martin Manalansan IV and Kuan-Hsing Chen expand this inquiry, examining translation beyond the academy. Manalansan's "*Biyuti* in Everyday Life: Performance, Citizenship, and Survival among Filipinos in the United States" argues for "the strategic importance of the commonplace and the quotidian" in facilitating translation for Filipino immigrant communities. Using the concept of "positioned performance" to analyze everyday rituals, Manalansan describes acts by Filipino "transmigrants," who experience "diasporic consciousness" day-to-day as well as in their cultural histories. According to Manalansan, quotidian (rather than academic) configurations of Asianness are transgressive of national and disciplinary borders. Developing diasporic rituals as a means of translating between cultures, Manalansan argues, these transmigrant communities produce new knowledges, new ways of being Asian in a global context.

Manalansan's insistence on the importance of the quotidian contrasts sharply against Chen's attention to U.S. imperialisms on a global scale. In "Missile Internationalism," Chen casts a skeptical eye on "the current vogue of 'globalization,'" and suggests that it "provides an all too easy answer" to the question of how to understand contemporary cultural and political formations. Positioned "outside the geopolitical space of U.S. academia," Chen accounts for this vogue, as well as the glossing-over of U.S. imperialism, in analyzing their effects in Taiwan. Invoking the "pan-class based politics of internationalism," Chen deciphers traces of U.S. imperialism implicit in U.S.-based East Asian studies, which are rarely acknowledged. The ostentatious avoidance of the question of U.S. imperialism, moreover, has effects beyond U.S. academia, which are felt within Asian political spheres. Whereas Manalansan's transmigrant translates the life-worlds of U.S. and Filipino cultures and produces a heterolingual, diasporic praxis at the level of quotidian ritual, Chen suggests that the oppressively homolingual address of U.S. imperialism effectively precludes the possibility of meaningful dialogue. Chen reminds us that the academic/discursive questions raised in this volume must be thought in terms of their realpolitik effects, and challenges us to engage in cross-disciplinary, cross-national academic work in ways that resist the imperialist pull of traditional area (and ethnic) studies.

Part 3. Para-Sites, Or, Constituting Borders

Part Three turns to a consideration of how disciplinary formations come into being. For, as Sakai points out, "[w]e might remind ourselves of a Foucauldian insight: It is not because the objects of knowledge are preparatorily given that certain disciplines are formed to investigate them; on the contrary the objects are engendered because the disciplines are in place" (1997, 40–41). The constitution of academic disciplines is neither preordained nor arbitrary; as this section shows, the fields of Asian and Asian American studies have formed along specific historical, racial, and political trajectories, which in turn produce specific historicized, racialized, and politicized objects of study. Recognizing emergent scholarship that works both within and beyond disciplinary boundaries precipitates this section's examination of boundaries themselves.

Rey Chow's contribution begins this section's focus on border construction. "Leading Questions," which first appeared in *Writing Diaspora: Tactics of Intervention in Contemporary Cultural Studies* (1993), considers the "orientalist melancholia" plaguing much scholarship in Asian studies, and traces it back to the " 'colonial situation' that lies at the origin" of Asian studies in the West, hidden and unacknowledged. Chow enjoins cultural theorists "to think primarily in terms of borders—of borders, that is, as para-sites that never take over a field in its entirety but erode it slowly and tactically." By focusing the task of Asian studies as the study of "imperialism as ideological domination," Chow offers Asian studies a path out of its mired melancholia, and in so doing, suggests possible links to or models for Asian American studies as well. For recognition of the impact of U.S. imperialisms on disciplinary production also draws attention to the complicity of American domestic formations, and hence pressures celebratory conceptions of even—or perhaps especially—ethnicized Americannesses, by revealing the limits and contradictions of practices attending only to conditions in the domestic sphere.

16   Kandice Chuh and Karen Shimakawa

The essays by David Palumbo-Liu and Yoshikuni Igarashi exemplify different ways of taking up this strategy. In "Modelling the Nation: the Asian/American Split," Palumbo-Liu examines the contribution of global politics to the construction(s) of Asian Americanness in the Cold War era. Analyzing the strategic deployment of the "model minority" myth in U.S. Cold War politics, he concludes that the U.S. nation-state grounds its stability in large part on the successful drawing of the Asian/American line; and to the extent Japanese Americans are/were perceived to constitute a potential threat to the integrity of that line, they have been anxiously situated, at various historical moments, on one side or the other. Within the parameters of a study of Asian/Americanness, that is, Palumbo-Liu's consideration of U.S. imperialism reveals the complex history of the production of that identity category as imbricated with international power dynamics.

Igarashi's essay provides a correlative study of popular discourse on Japanese Americans in the production of Japanese national identity. As Igarashi notes in "In-Betweens in a Hybrid Nation: Construction of Japanese American Identity in Postwar Japan," "to discuss Japanese American experiences uncritically within the context of Japanese studies is an appropriation of Japanese American identity back within the boundaries of Japan," and as a result, "it is by now commonsensical that Japanese American experiences do not belong to the field of Japanese studies." According to Igarashi, there remain good reasons to acknowledge an analytic distinction between Japaneseness and Japanese Americanness (in Japan); yet, while Japanese American experiences might not be appropriately claimed as objects of study for Japan scholars, "the strategies deployed in representing Japanese Americans in 1950s Japan" are important to Japan scholars, for what these representations suggest about conceptualizations of the Japanese nation-state after World War II. Just as Palumbo-Liu suggests that Japanese Americans functioned as the limit-case, the racial-cultural marker at which the limits of citizenship were set in U.S. (post-)Cold War rhetoric, Igarashi argues that much the same process took place in postwar Japan, using precisely the same border figures. In both cases, a renewed focus on the formulation of the "essential" characteristics of traditional objects of study—Japaneseness and Asian Americanness—in the context of U.S. imperialism and international relations during the Cold War era allow us, in Chow's formulation, to "rethink . . . the solidarities themselves."

"Conjunctural Identities, Academic Adjacencies," R. Radhakrishnan's essay here, takes a more expansive or metadiscursive approach to boundary formations. Taking as his focus the "fraught relationship of identity to methodology" in Asian American and in Diaspora studies, and in turn the connections between methodology and disciplinarity, Radhakrishnan argues for "a critical deployment of double-consciousness" within Asian

American studies as a way to negotiate its current and historical linkages and delinkages to Asian studies, and to domestic identity politics. "The *hyphen as such* in Asian-America," he writes, "has to do double duty and coordinate the Asian experience with the American experience without resort to hierarchical maneuvers or identity coups" (emphasis added). Radhakrishnan's crucial observation, that "the interests that inform Asian studies and Asian American studies are different," seems self-evident, but is obvious only in retrospect: "Built into the Asian American experience of Asia," he suggests, "is the diasporan context, the diasporan perspective: if you will, the historicity of the diaspora as well as the historicity of hybridity." This fundamental difference in perspective argues for self-consciously particularized engagements among Asian American, Asian, and American studies and identities in academic-professional contexts.

Part 4. Asian/American Epistemologies

The final section places the preceding essays and issues explicitly in conversation with U.S. American studies. For, as Palumbo-Liu puts it in his recent study of Asian American racial formation (from which his contribution here is drawn), "modern Asian America should be read within a context of multiple subjectivities whose multiplicity can be depathologized through a close and critical reading of Asian, American, and Asian/American history" (1999, 389). Specifically, he argues that "the unity presumed to be enjoyed by 'America' is in fact better read as a set of adjustments and reformations that disclose the fact that America is always in process itself" (389). Accordingly, the effects of globalization on the dominant construction of "America" as the object of "American studies," and specific consideration of the function and potential of "Asian Americanness" within that construction, are considered in this section in tandem with a critique of U.S. imperialist emanations of "globalization." New faultlines are traced and new possibilities for advancing a social justice agenda mined. Essays by Lisa Lowe, George Lipsitz, and Kandice Chuh, respectively, consider academic globalization's ability to dislodge historically dominant constructions of "Americanness" that have not only infused American studies, but have actively contributed to the racist, capitalist, practices of U.S. imperialism at home and abroad.

Lisa Lowe's "Epistemological Shifts: National Ontology and the New Asian Immigrant," continues the investigation begun in *Immigrant Acts: On Asian American Cultural Politics* (1996), foregrounding the constitutive role of "the (new) Asian immigrant" in the current and historical processes of U.S. American racialization. The post-1965 " 'new' Asian American," forces practitioners in all of these fields to reckon with a newly organized, newly "globalized" future and to reconceptualize narratives of their pasts: "the critical force of the new Asian immigrant," Lowe writes, "reveals the area 'Asia' to be highly unstable," even as it "rewrites the history of the United States as a complex racial history." Perhaps most provocatively, Lowe offers a new model for area studies, one which focuses on the "truly necessary inquiry into the comparative history of racialization" that becomes visible only by focusing our disciplinary lens on "different Asian formations within the global or neocolonial framework of transnational capitalism." Lowe's envisioning of Asian American studies as an explicitly politicized and culturally engaged project challenges us to think about "Asian Americanness" in specific, historicized, and materially grounded relations to both "Asianness" and "Americanness," and to consider the implicitly politicized subjects of area studies more generally as well.

Kandice Chuh's "Imaginary Borders" carries this project forward, by explicitly articulating how the intersection(s) of Asian and Asian American studies are bound up with the question of what and who gets to be considered "American," thus setting forth the unavoidability of triangulating American studies to Asian and Asian American studies. The segregation of "Asian American" literature as a subcategory of "American" literature highlights tensions among the conceptual categories of "Asian," "American," and "Asian American." In much the same way that Chow enjoins us to think "primarily in terms of borders," Chuh suggests that foregrounding these seemingly aesthetic-literary distinctions brings to the surface the historico-political negotiations that created them. Chuh reminds us that national identities are produced in and through particularly structured narratives; and that to acknowledge the narrative structures that produce Asian American identity is to call into question the adequacy or coherence of those that purportedly produce "Asian" and "American" identities. Thus, Chuh argues for "understanding that Asian Americanist studies is a nodal point not only in the studies of U.S. Americanness, but in those of Asianness as well."

A different triangulation of Asian and Asian American Studies takes place in George Lipsitz's " 'To Tell the Truth and Not Get Trapped': Why Interethnic Antiracism Matters Now," in which Lipsitz considers the question of (academic) globalization and the concept of an Asian diaspora in relation to ethnic studies. Contrasting the gradual institutionalization and legitimation of ethnic studies and/or some form of "multiculturalism" within U.S. curricula with the continued oppression of "ethnic people" under the twin burdens of the domestic attack on racialized populations within the U.S. and the "global" exploitation of labor, Lipsitz argues for a socially and politically engaged ethnic studies. Lipsitz issues a call for cross-ethnic, antiracist coalition: "[t]he panethnic concept of 'Asian American' identity offers the quintessential model for interethnic antiracism in both activism and scholarship"; thus, he argues, Asian American studies is ideally situated to contribute to an intellectual agenda committed to transnational, interethnic social justice. The socio-historical, juridical, and cultural forces that have brought Asian and Asian American studies into conversation in this volume (and elsewhere) are precisely those forces that now place ethnic studies scholars "in an advantageous position . . . to play an active role in transforming social relations by helping build the forms of knowledge and action capable of creating quite different kinds of social relations." Thus, Lipsitz sees in the advent of globalization an opportunity to reshape racial, ethnic, and national coalitions to achieve new and different forms of social and political activism. The value of such coalitional work, Lipsitz argues, lies in "its epistemological value in enabling us to understand how power actually works in the world." Along with Lowe, Chuh, and, indeed, *Orientations* as a whole, Lipsitz envisions — for the purpose of working toward the realization of social justice on a broad scale — a renegotiation of epistemologies as a means of revisioning what it is that "area studies" do and study; and conversely, of reorienting area studies as a means of renegotiating epistemological values.

Notes

1 We follow Marilyn Ivy's explanation as to the function of the quotation marks framing the term "Asia": "The quotation marks . . . are meant to indicate (as such marks do) the unstable identities that . . . proper names signify. By claiming that 'Japan' [or in our context, "Asia"] is as much a discursive construct as an objective referent . . . I merely want to emphasize the imaginative and historical dimensions of what we commonly call 'Japan' [or "Asia"]" (1995, 1, n.1).

2 Arjun Appadurai (1998) provides an illuminating summary: "Globalization (both as a socioeconomic formation and as a term of folk ideology in journalism and in the corporate world) marks a set of transitions in the global political economy since the 1970s, in which multinational forms of capitalist organization began to be replaced by transnational, flexible, and irregular forms of organization, as labour, finance, technology, and technological capital began to be assembled in ways that treated national boundaries as mere constraints or fictions. In contrast with the multinational corporations of the middle of the [20th] century which sought to transcend national boundaries while working within existing national frameworks of law, commerce, and sovereignty, the transnational corporations of the last three decades have increasingly begun to produce recombinant arrangements of labour, capital, and technical expertise which produce new forms of law, management, and distribution. In both phases global capital and national states have sought to exploit each other, but in the most recent decades it is possible to see a secular decline in the sovereignty of national states in respect to the workings of global capital." (907–8).

3 Cumings explains: "The stunning events from 1989 to 1991 . . . [laid] bare the hegemonic role that Roosevelt grasped for in 1941 and that Truman and Acheson consum-
mated in 1950: a hegemony that substituted for Great Britain's role as leader of last resort
in the world system, a hegemony never explained to the American people but instead
rationalized by pointing to an enemy the more fearsome for being remote and encapsulated, whether abroad or at home—an enemy of which we were abruptly deprived by
Gorbachev, thus terminating the counter-system that justified it all and finally making
conspicuous the other name of the cold war game: world economy" (1999, 16).

4 See Balibar & Wallerstein (1992) on precisely this issue of the paradoxes embedded in
and characteristic of capitalism. See also Omi & Winant (1994).

5 Connery (1995) provides incisive overview and analysis of the development of Pacific Rim
discourse. He identifies multiple discursive trajectories as genealogies for this discourse,
including Orientalism, modernization theory, left-liberal humanist internationalism,
and Cold War discourse (33). Connery explains that "Pacific Rim Discourse is an imagining of U.S. multinational capitalism in an era when the 'socialist' bloc still existed, and
it is the socialist bloc that is the principle and discursive Other. Pacific Rim Discourse,
though is a *non*-othering discourse. Unlike Orientalism, which Edward Said delineates
genealogically as a discursive formation centered on a fundamental othering . . . Pacific
Rim Discourse presumes a kind of metonymic equivalence. Its world is an interpene-
trating complex of interrelationships with no center: neither the center of a hegemonic
power nor the imagined fulcrum of a 'balance of power' " (31–32).

6 Palumbo-Liu (1999) is especially thorough in demonstrating how this figurative "Asia"
has centrally informed the development of American modernity. See also Connery 1995;
Leon W. 1995; Lowe 1996; and Okihiro 1994.

7 See especially Shohat 1992 and McClintock 1992.

8 See Ferguson 1990 and JanMohamed and Lloyd 1991.

9 See Messer-Davidow, Shumway, and Sylvan 1993 for discussion of disciplines and disciplinarity.

10 For histories of and information about the development of area studies, see Bennett 1951,
Hall 1947 and Steward 1950; see also the report by the Association of American Colleges
(1964) on "non-Western studies in the liberal arts college." For contemporary critique,
see Rafael 1994; see also Dipesh Chakrabarty's contribution to this volume. On the history of the development of Asian American studies, see Aguilar-San Juan 1994; Okihiro
et al. 1988; Omatsu 1989; and Wei 1993. See also Russell Leong's and George Lipsitz's
respective contributions to this volume.

11 See Chakrabarty's and Chow's respective essays in this volume for further consideration
of area studies' genealogy.

12 In one sense, this kind of oppositional positioning has occurred, creating the lack of
conversation between Asian and Asian American studies. From the latter perspective,
self-serving rhetoric as to the Orientalism of Asian studies has made it easy to ignore
the ways in which such binary divisions facilitate problematic practices characteristic of
both fields.

13 See, e.g., *A Part, Yet Apart,* edited by Lavina Shankar and Rajini Srikanth (1998).

I INVESTMENTS AND INTERVENTIONS

(Un)Disciplined Subjects:
(De)Colonizing the Academy?

DORINNE KONDO

The editors of this volume have asked me to write an autobiographical political history, a reflection on the ways my career trajectory traces larger social and political transformations. Despite my engagement with reflexive writing practices, such an endeavor feels risky. Yet, as one of the few Asian Americans to begin in Asian studies and then move to Asian American studies, perhaps this "retrospective" can indeed address larger issues: a political history of the academy, the possibilities for intervention in disciplinary regimes, and the relation of Asian and Asian American studies. Though the direction of this movement is rhetorically overstated, one could read this trajectory as the unlearning of formative disciplines: from the epistemologies of anthropology and East Asian studies to those of Asian American studies, minority discourse, cultural studies, and performance studies; and from the academy narrowly defined to work in creative, artistic registers and to work that blurs the artistic and the critical. These movements are themselves enabled by demographic transformations within the academy, in which people who were formerly the objects of representation by the dominant are ourselves entering the academy and the arts in order to "represent ourselves," however problematic that enterprise might be. This in turn describes a political and historical horizon that is simultaneously shaped by the dominant and alive with possibilities for continued transformation. My account, then, instantiates certain shifts in epistemological regimes over the last twenty years and articulates the contradictory formation of one particular Asian American subject constituted by and moving within particular institutional and disciplinary histories. This movement articulates positions from which to reflect upon the relationship of Asian to Asian American studies.

The 1970s: Feminist Anthropology, Asian Studies, Political Critique

My choice of anthropology as a discipline in retrospect seems the result of eminently political concerns: the allure of feminist anthropology and the presence of a vibrant, exciting feminist faculty at Stanford, where I was an undergraduate; the ways that Japanese and the anthropology of Japan became a vehicle for understanding aspects of Japanese American historical experience. Both the feminist project and the anti-Eurocentric deployment of anthropology offered an edge of political critique.[1]

From anthropology, I took concerns I could now label phenomenological, existential, political, interpretivist: the focus on the experiential and the everyday, the linguistic/historical/cultural construction of subjectivity, a sensitivity to difference and to the ways language could articulate a world, and a skepticism toward the academy's bias toward textuality. Further, anthropology's reputation as a discipline for marginal people made it a comfortable place to be. For me, anthropology opened the question of racial difference via the trope of cultural difference.[2] The discipline's liberal humanist imperative, to show that there are multiple and equally valid ways of "being human" — that category we cannot not want — was at that historical moment compelling given my position as a racially marginalized subject. At that early stage, anthropology and Asian studies represented self-discovery with an edge of political critique. Given a certain formation as a racialized subject, it is perhaps no surprise that I found attractive a discipline whose point of departure was cultural difference, experience, and everday life and that has historically been relatively open to "marginalized" people: ethnics, racial minorities, women. It now strikes me as especially ironic that this sense of possibility occurred at an institution whose founder, Leland Stanford, headed an organization that employed and exploited thousands of Asian Americans; indeed, both of my grandfathers worked for the Union Pacific Railroad for a brief period during their lives in the United States.

Disciplines

Graduate school is designed to create disciplined subjects, properly differentiated and socialized members of "the profession." My graduate school training and my first teaching position occurred within the context of the Department of Anthropology and an association with East Asian studies at Harvard, where I spent the years 1975–1989.

The contradictions of being an Asian American subject "doing" Asia (the sexual connotations of masculine penetration are apposite here) emerge starkly. East Asian studies in the United States is inescapably linked to the geopolitical histories of U.S.-Japan relations. Like many in my generation, my first three years of graduate education were funded by the National Defense Foreign Language fellowship, an eloquent articulation of the strategic political importance accorded research on Japan. Many of the "Japan hands" who were my teachers came to the field through the legacy of the Pacific War as members of the Occupation or as children of missionaries. Whatever the intentions of any individuals involved, at the institutional and geopolitical levels there can be no denying our area studies enmeshment in a geopolitics that inevitably involves a long Orientalist legacy. Still, Foucault reminds us that disciplinary regimes are productive as well as coercive; those of us who "did" Japan were the beneficiaries of considerable resources and Harvard's impressive amassing of "knowledge" of East Asia.

The late seventies and early eighties witnessed another fundamental challenge to disciplinary conventions: the reflexive turn, or what some have infelicitously called "postmodern" anthropology. The critique of fieldwork as enabled by colonialism, the scrutiny of the conventions of ethnographic writing, a focus on power relations constructing the ethnographic encounter—all were emergent at that moment. Much like the ferment caused by feminist anthropology, the problematizing of foundational concepts and conventions fostered the sense that an important disciplinary shift was in process.

My fieldwork experiences, dissertation, and first book instantiate a transition from the epistemologies of British social anthropology and East Asian studies to a reflexive, power-sensitive critique of ethnography. My own subject position as a Japanese American working in Japan overdetermined this shift, for almost inevitably my analytic attention was drawn to the power-laden, shifting processes of identity formation in everyday life. By the mid-1980s, a full-blown critique of the discipline from within had emerged. For me, this critical turn involved a close scrutiny of the ethnographer's positioning in fieldwork, incorporating the process by which an ethnographic problem emerges, and clarifying my stakes in the project as an Asian American. Rather than the "objective," dispassionate panoptical gaze, I sought to locate my angles of vision in specific, power-laden interactions. Movements of decolonization in anthropology were beginning to occur from within. Finally, the influence of poststructuralist feminist theory was generative. My first book, *Crafting Selves* (1990), is part of a discursive formation that arose in the seminar on gender run by Joan Scott at the Institute for Advanced Study. Through the presence of feminist scholars such as Judith Butler and Donna Haraway, and the notions of gender performativity/performance, the work transformed from an interpretivist study of meaning to a poststructuralist analysis of the performance of gendered work identities, enacted within larger discursive fields of power.

Multi-, Inter-, Postdisciplinary Spaces

In different ways, challenges to the notion of a singular "culture" in the form of transnationalism, an experiential history as an Asian American subject, and feminist articulations of performance and performativity have shaped the research that formed the basis for my book *About Face: Performing "Race" in Fashion and Theater* (1997). One analytic axis pivots around the fabrication of difference—race, nation, gender, class, sexuality—in the globally dispersed, commodity capitalist world of international high fashion, especially the work of the so-called "Japanese avant-garde" designers who are credited with the all-black, loose-fitting, unisex fashion aesthetic of the early 1980s. Orientalisms, counter-Orientalisms, and autoexoticizing practices create complex, contradictory racial/national/gendered discourses in this industry that could be considered emblematic of our capitalist regime of truth. The fashion industry becomes a privileged site from which to problematize the notion of a singular "culture" via the notions of transnationalism and the global assembly line. For example, the fabrication of "Japan" and the work of the "Japanese" designers reverberates in the construction and performance of Asian American racial and gender identities.

A second site, Asian American theater, examines the challenges and reinscriptions of Orientalisms as they bear on the lives of Asian Americans. I view Asian American and multiracial theater as arenas for the performance and production of coalition and new political identities such as "people of color" that can contest our figuration as "Orientals." Inevitably problematic yet replete with possibility, theater compels passionate commitment as an ongoing political, artistic, and intellectual project.

This passion for theater arises from lived experiences as an Asian American subject. In long years on the East Coast, Asian American theater offered political sustenance and the vision of cultural and political possibility I rarely saw elsewhere. It is this vision that urgently requires documentation and a writing into history in both academic and popular registers. In such a context, critique becomes a political intervention, a way to make things better collectively. A physical move to Los Angeles locates me in a major center of Asian American cultural production, enabling me to write about and for performance. Since then, my work has continued to move toward spaces in and between the artistic and the critical, and in/ between disciplines. For example, playwriting classes at East West Players, the Odyssey Theater, and Moving Arts Theater—initially a fieldwork "participant observation" technique—have opened possibilities of contributing to this collective project in voices other than our customary academese.

Further, my work as a dramaturge at the Mark Taper Forum for Anna Deavere Smith's play *Twilight: Los Angeles 1992,* a play based on the L. A. uprisings, has also fostered an equally inspiring sense of the political possibilities of multiracial collaboration. Using methods familiar to ethnographers, Smith created *Twilight* from over 200 interviews she did with Angelenos and others, recreating and performing these people and their words onstage. The play went from Los Angeles to productions at the New York Shakespeare Festival and then on to Broadway. Working on *Twilight* awakened me to the position of artists of color in mainstream theater and the constraints under which they must operate. It also highlighted the tense, contentious, yet utopian process of multiracial collaboration, in which sometimes difficult and painful disputes about race and attempts to be responsible to multiple and often conflicting communities resulted in an inevitably imperfect yet critically important intervention in mainstream theater. In moving toward theater, my work has shifted from studying an "Other" as an anthropologist to joining Asian American artists and artists of color as a partner in struggle, to help as best we can to intervene to aid in the social transformation of structures of power. Here, theater enables the creation and performance of emergent, heterogeneous, contentious, and politically necessary coalitions such as "Asian American" and "people of color." These productions in turn can become articulations of political empowerment that constitute always already complicitous critiques of the dominant.

Roughly, then, the movement I describe is one from disciplines to increasingly interdisciplinary spaces, from academic "study" to artistic "creation," from anthropology and East Asian studies to feminist theory, minority discourse, cultural studies, performance studies, and to performance itself. Perhaps the editors are right in seeing this as a movement—uneven, incomplete, and always complicit—toward decolonization. In thus seeking some overall direction to this path, however, I do not wish to imply that I have abandoned "my" discipline altogether. Indeed, such an abandonment would be impossible for any of us. Yet even as we are aware of the political baggage of our disciplinary training, there should be ways of bringing its useful aspects into interdisciplinary spaces.

For example, at first glance anthropology and East Asian studies are among the most obviously problematic academic locations in terms of their enmeshment in colonialism and the perpetuation of Orientalism. The critiques of anthropology from within and without are well-known and need no repetition here. Yet the discipline's (relative) openness to autocritique makes it for me a far more comfortable space than the more confidently positivistic or Eurocentrically humanistic disciplines. Ethnographic practices open themselves to critique; for example, the process of fieldwork invites a scrutiny of textualizing practices and power relations. Anyone who must somehow render the chaos and indeterminacy of everyday life into a patterned understanding in an "ethnography" must somehow come to terms with the obvious power relations involved in the imposition of our understandings on this indeterminacy. I would argue that similar indeterminacies are present in other disciplinary sites, but are more effectively masked or silenced. Moreover, the anthropological master trope, "culture," proves to be as useful as it is problematic. On the one hand, reified and monolithic notions of culture all too often elide power relations and history. Culture can be a less threatening, liberal humanist way of domesticating the more power-laden issue of race. Yet anthropology's attention to cultural difference as both taken-for-granted and interesting rather than threatening, has become all the more welcome to me the more time I spend in (often Eurocentric) interdisciplinary spaces such as cultural studies and feminist theory. Furthermore, the anthropological emphasis on everyday life rather than simply textual or Cultural (with a capital "C") artifacts, arises from a (liberal humanist) democratic impulse behind the more expansive notion of culture (small "c"). These disciplinary proclivities I carry through into my new work. Even though "theater" can be seen as Cultural, my attraction is to performance rather than to textual analysis, whether of the script or of our new texts: film and video. The ephemerality of performance, its implication of audiences, its resistance of fixity, make it more continuous with the anthropological focus on the contextual and on the practice of everyday life.

For all of us involved in the production of knowledge, the point is to be open to problematizing our own positions, regardless of the disciplinary space one occupies. Anthropology has long been engaged in processes of autocritique, and I have been one of those practitioners. Yet it is disturbing to note that one effect of this autocritique has been to install anthropology as emblematic of all problems of knowledge production in the academy. Far from leading practitioners from other disciplines to scrutinize their own complicities, anthropology's reflexive scrutiny can be taken (in such "American" fashion!) as a sign of weakness, an admission of disciplinary failure. Of course its enmeshment in colonialism and imperialism make this critique an especially urgent one. Yet each discipline has its complicities. In the social sciences, anthropology and sociology are divided at least partially along the lines of "external" versus "internal" colonialism, with sociology retaining a more positivistic bias. Psychology and political science, likewise, enshrine an unproblematized positivism. Further, these disciplinary boundaries create reified spaces that reinscribe conventional definitions of public/private, social/individual, and the political as an autonomous domain. Similarly, literature, art, and music inevitably reify a category of "art" or "culture" that reproduces elitist notions of Culture as refinement and as universal or transcendent. Here, the battles over canonicity illustrate the workings of power relations in adjudicating what can count as "great" art. The textual biases of literature and philosophy, among other disciplines, often leave larger political, historical, and cultural contexts unexamined. Philosophy, especially, enshrines certain European canonical works and conventional notions of what counts as theory, but literary theory is also highly complicit in this regard.

While none of us can escape our institutional legacies, epistemologies, and disciplinary formations, we can try to utilize the critical tools our disciplines provide, while working to stretch, unlearn, and challenge those formations. The institutionalization of different, inter-, or multidisciplinary spaces, such as ethnic and women's studies, cultural studies, postcolonial theory, and minority discourse are one such aid. Yet we should be sure that we do not make the mistake of believing that we have therefore left behind our intellectual/political disciplinary baggage. For instance, like many people of color, I find it disturbing that cultural studies has won such quick acceptance in comparison to ethnic and women's studies; in some cases, like the discourses of postmodernism, one suspects that it functions as a (last?) refuge for white men.[3] In the United States at least, cultural studies has enabled important and exciting work while reproducing notions of Culture as a domain tenuously linked to production and to the material, such as text, film, television, music, performance, dance: "art," in a word. It has also, often under the name of postmodernism, given rise to superficial analyses of contemporary phenomena viewed with a panoptical gaze that skips over surfaces and ignores long-term familiarity and specificity: the stuff of ethnography. Thus the postmodern panopticon reinscribes conventional notions of what counts as theoretical. My argument here is for a far more self-problematizing gaze, animated by the sense that all knowledge production is inseparable from relations of power. Part of our task as analysts, then, is to clarify and specify the ways those power relations animate our own work.

Asian/American Studies

That said, how can we analyze more specifically the relation of Asian to Asian American studies? When considering the arguments and positionalities of various critics, one must ask what battles are being fought and what the stakes are. For me, the relocation of Japanese Americans remains definitive and generative. Speaking about it at any length provokes profound feelings of rage and sorrow and defiance that are in and of the body in ways that are difficult to describe in words. That which heightens the possibility of the confusion of Asian with Asian American raises for me the spectre of relocation in truly visceral terms. Japan-bashing in any form does so even more obviously. Inevitably, my own political antennae are highly attuned to any of these discursive modes.

On the one hand, then, I am deeply invested in keeping separate "Asian" and "Asian American," for the confusion of these terms has produced some of the most egregious incidents of racism in this country's history, events that touch the lives of all Asian Americans. But precisely because there is an elision of Asian with Asian American, *About Face* centers around the ways hegemonic representations, mostly of Asia, reverberate in Asian American lives. The Orientalisms deployed at one site produce effects in others. For this particular authorial subject, the stakes are clear. As I stated in *Crafting Selves,* arguing for the humanity of "the Japanese" is in some sense arguing for "my own" humanity, the humanity of Asian American subjects. No matter how problematic the liberal notion of "the human" might be, it remains—in certain contexts—strategically necessary.

My impassioned view as an Asian American subject deploying feminist theory and minority discourse in Asian and Asian American studies marks but one position in a much larger discursive field. Hegemonic East Asian studies, for example, stands as heir to an Orientalist legacy, permeated by an unproblematized empiricism hostile to "theory," yet blind to its own theoretical presuppositions and its conservative politics. In Japanese area studies are many who would challenge such a hegemony. One could deploy the label "progressive" to describe the formations of various impassioned and incisive critics who speak from different, sometimes highly disparate, sites of enunciation. It is important to underline our common projects and solidarities, particularly our challenges to "traditional" area studies. Within the general rubric "progressive," however, different positionalities produce different investments, different stakes, and different contexts of argument. Generally, I would argue that the major oppositional stance in Japanese studies focuses on sharply incisive critiques of the Japanese state, of Japanese imperialism and colonialism, and of multinational capitalism, informed by a variety of Continental theorists including the Frankfurt School, the Lyotard/Baudrillard axis of postmodernism, postcolonial theory, and the Marxism of analysts such as Fredric Jameson. Such perspectives are crucially important.

While I share these concerns and perspectives to some degree, my uneasiness arises from an Asian American position that focuses on the politics of reception in the United States. Japan presents us with a constitutive theoretical/political dilemma when we ponder the politics of reception, for it is a First World, capitalist nation with imperialist histories and ambitions that is nonetheless racially marked. My surmise is that the nuances and *positionalities* of such critiques are scarcely noticed by an American public all too willing to believe in the juggernaut of Japanese capitalism and imperialism. Given a centuries-long history of exclusion, penetration, interimperial rivalry, war, incarceration, even genocide, of Asian Americans and people of color, I would argue that the dominant deploys the critique of Japan or of any other racially marked nation *in order to buttress a sense of U.S. superiority.*

Consequently, I want to highlight what is at stake for *Asian Americans* when we consider the politics of reception in a North American context. Here, racial marking bristles with significance, for, like it or not, all Asian Americans are profoundly affected by Japan-bashing discourses, including its more subtle forms—what Yoneyama calls the discourse of "benevolence and assimilation." Certainly, worries about the politics of reception should not entail a silencing of critique, particularly from those who have been colonized by Japanese imperialism. But it does suggest, to this Asian American subject, the necessity for *strategic* deployment of certain kinds of arguments with an eye to the politics of reception in a nation with a long history of anti-Asian sentiment and racist practice, a legacy that remains all too vigorous. Admittedly, the intentional fallacy tells us that we cannot guarantee how those arguments will be appropriated by others; Michael Crichton's recasting of my critique of hegemonic "Western" individualism in *Crafting Selves* in his book *Rising Sun* is one personally salient example. Yet this should not preclude attempts to account for certain kinds of predictable readings. Such attempts are all too rare, but they still vibrate with urgency as long as the dominant fails to differentiate Asians from Asian Americans and various Asian American groups from each other. The racist perception that "we all look alike" seems still to be alive and well. Of course my position, like any other, is by definition interested and partial. If the primary mode of progressive critique in Japanese studies seems to me to be insufficiently attentive to its potential reverberations in Asian American lives, then no doubt my stance seems in their terms to be insufficiently critical of the Japanese state and of transnational capitalism.

Perhaps the most disturbing tendency, however, comes from work that takes its primary inspiration from the Frankfurt School, Jameson, and canonical forms of postmodernism. Generally, such work is animated by an elitist pessimism about "the masses" and about the pervasiveness of transnational/commodity capitalism. This leads to a fatalistic stance that sees efforts at contestation always already recuperated through processes of commodification and the reinscription of power relations. Stuart Hall aptly notes the ways this approach figures cultural politics as a zero-sum game; I would add that it lacks any notion of complicitous critique. Even though nothing is beyond the dominant, every attempt at contestation is not thereby completely vitiated. Furthermore, the elitist pessimism of this strain of social theory positions the critic above "the masses," failing to problematize his/her always already problematic site of enunciation. Fredric Jameson, for instance, clearly mourns for the days when history could be History, with its telos and its certainty; his analyses of postmodernism are suffused with this mournful nostalgia.[4] Where such perspectives are brought to bear on so-called popular culture, these are critiques of popular culture uttered by those who remain impervious to its potential pleasures or who certainly have little stake in actively *producing* more contestatory forms of popular culture. Skepticism and nihilism can always look more politically hip, for it is easy to dismiss more optimistic visions as merely naive. Such critics, to their credit, do the important work of pointing out the dangers of an overly celebratory enshrining of "the people." But when one is attempting to create more contestatory cultural work, it is *constructive* critique that matters, and constructive critique is all too rare. What David Román terms "critical generosities" in his work on plays about AIDS must be brought to bear when discussing aesthetic/political interventions.

Attesting to the power of interventions like those mounted by Asian American artists must be part of a critical project — even if those interventions are never beyond complicity. If we can breathe more easily for a moment, if lives are subtly empowered, if institutions shift even modestly, then these moves count as what Stuart Hall calls "cultural strategies that can make a difference" (Hall 1992, 24). Nihilism and elitist pessimism are luxuries some of us cannot afford. Rather, critical consciousness must be mobilized in order to recognize the important work that is being done, while subjecting it to thoroughgoing critique in order to make more effective interventions. The Asian and Asian American artists and activists who are the subjects of my work are attempting to do precisely that, even if their/our efforts can never be pristine or beyond the dominant.

Since we are speaking of positionalities, then, what of the premise that animates this very anthology in which I am writing? Like several new exemplars of diaspora and transnationalism in print culture, including *positions, Diaspora,* and *Public Culture,* this volume turns on a constitutive ambivalence in the relations between Asian and Asian American studies. On the one hand, it is absolutely necessary to begin to reappraise the sharp distinctions made between the two. Demographic shifts due to changes in immigration laws, especially the Immigration Act of 1965, and to geopolitical upheavals have meant that increasing numbers of "Asian Americans" are recent immigrants whose identifications and histories may not lie within the political collectivity "Asian American." These new kinds of diasporic identities require new analytic tools; certainly their complexity exceeds the boundaries of "Asian" or "Asian American" studies as presently constituted. Within the Asian studies field, moreover, there are increasing numbers of analysts who are *Asian Americans* studying Asia. In the Japan field alone, the number of Sansei scholars is striking, and there are growing numbers of Asian American scholars like myself who write both on Asia and on Asian Americans.[5]

Yet there are reasons to be wary of too unconsidered an alliance between Asian/Asian American studies. The worry is one of appropriation. Certainly, the genesis of the two fields—in Orientalism on the one hand, and in the struggles of the 1960s, in the case of Asian American studies— could not be more opposed. All of us who are in the Asian studies field are to some degree the beneficiaries of an Orientalist geopolitical legacy. Asian American studies, on the other hand, was born of 1960s student and antiwar activism, and along with Chicano studies, Afro-American studies, Gay and Lesbian studies, Women's studies, Asian American studies constitutes the academic arm of progressive political movements. Often existing in relatively marginal institutional positions, if it exists at all, Asian American studies has little access to the resources and endowments that come easily for long-established fields such as Asian studies. Given these different histories, institutional positionings, and available resources, a hasty marriage between the two surely augurs ill for the autonomy of Asian American studies.

Consequently, one must be wary of the implications of such a conjoining. Do elisions of the boundaries between Asian American studies and Asian studies work in fact to "deliver" Asian American studies to the Asianists? In *Orientations,* the implications of blurring the boundaries are thematized and analyzed from various positions, and both celebratory and cautionary voices emerge strongly; indeed, the two are not mutually exclusive. Yet, such a nod to intellectual developments cannot erase the greater resources, power, and visibility represented in Asian studies. Here, one must be especially suspicious of a vanguardist stance. For example, within the field of Asian studies, the journal *positions* provides an urgently needed, welcome alternative to the official instrument of the Association for Asian Studies, *The Journal of Asian Studies.* A reaction to the empiricism and de facto political conservatism of the field, *positions* is theoretically and politically informed; I myself endorse its project by sitting on its editorial board.

Yet one wonders whether the vanguardism emblematized in *positions* is not overstated—and perhaps one might utter the same cautions to all of us

Asianists who have contributed to *Orientations*. Is our own enmeshment in Orientalism sufficiently scrutinized? What is at stake for some of the "new guard" of Asian Studies in their/ our embracing of the latest forms of Continental theory and cultural studies? Are the positionalities and the stakes for differently located analysts sufficiently clear? For example, among "Asians" and "Asian Americans," differences along lines of class, immigration history, nationality, can produce quite different stances on issues of power and identity. I think here of the ways that "authenticity" or "purity" can be deployed by more recent Asian immigrants or by Asian scholars, implying that Asian Americans longer resident in the United States are too white, too assimilated, and/or too blind to the workings of transnational capital. From Asian American perspectives of Chinese and Japanese Americans who came in the first waves of immigration, authenticity is a problematic notion; rather, "Asian American" is precisely about heterogeneity, hybridity, creating emergent and unprecedented historical identities (cf. Lowe 1991b). For white analysts—and there are multiple positions within this category, of course—the stakes must also be clarified. What are their/ your investments in Asia, in women, in socialism, in aesthetics, in the "trade wars," in sexuality, in the critique of (Asian) capitalism; how much hard work of problematizing race are they/you willing to do? Without more clearly specifying our sites of enunciation and problematizing our own complicities, this avowed progressive theoretical and political stance is in danger of merely signifying political hipness, and its claim for a progressive politics could become merely a case of "the changing same."

A similar note of caution could be directed at other sites of the production of the "transnational"; for example, the journals *Public Culture* and *Diaspora*. The focus on movement and of global flows carries out the important work of challenging essentialist definitions of nation and culture, and journals such as these have provided some of the most interesting contemporary writing in cultural studies and in anthropology. Yet at times the focus on the public, the transnational, and the cosmopolitan can and has come at the price of the local, the domestic, the out-of-the-way, and elides the continuing salience and occasional political necessity for essentialist identities, including the "nation." Moreover, this writing sometimes presupposes gender and class privilege. Kamala Visweswaran, citing Caren Kaplan's work on deterritorialization and feminist theory, utters a cogent critique of the work of Arjun Appadurai, one of the founders of *Public Culture* and a major theoretician of transnationalism:

> Uncritically theorized notions of deterritorialization project too comprehensively a 'global homelessness' and displacement, trivializing the political particularities of the phenomenon and erasing the 'resolutely

local' homesites necessary both for First World anthropologists to interrogate their own privilege and for less privileged subjects to claim home as a place of nurturance and protection. Is it coincidence, then, that while many feminist theorists identify home as the site of theory, male critics write to eradicate it? (Visweswaran 1994: 110, 111)

Similarly, I have argued (1997) that the work of Appadurai and others presumes an always already masculine, elite diasporic subject.

A related difference among "progressives" arises from the diverse immigration histories among those who might be labeled "Asian American." One could argue that the Asian American Studies field has from its inception been dominated primarily by narratives of Chinese American and Japanese American immigration, marginalizing the histories of other groups. Changes in immigration policy, especially post-1965, have produced far-reaching transformations in Asian American identity, and in the kinds of analytic tools necessary to describe this transformation. Diaspora and transnationalism offer themselves as particularly helpful concepts to think through these shifts, and postcolonial theory provides potentially valuable methodologies for analyzing some kinds of Asian American formations, and they offer profound insights into the histories of particular groups. Yet the emphasis on case-by-case specificity must be asserted strongly, lest another kind of hegemony emerge.

The recent attacks on affirmative action highlight one political consequence of differences in immigration histories. Just as there has been a "retreat from race," to use Dana Takagi's eloquent phrase, to class-based considerations in admissions rhetoric and policy, so has the valorization of class *at the expense* of race occurred on occasion among analysts of diaspora, global capitalism, and the postcolonial.[6] For example, for those born abroad and accustomed to being a dominant racial presence in their own societies, race politics in the United States may seem to be mere "identity politics," obscuring the supposedly more important and more truly political issues of class, transnational capital, and imperialism. Of course these issues are crucially important and eminently political. It is disturbing, however, to see those unconnected with the civil rights struggles in the United States and the very real and continuing racial oppression here, dismiss politics based on race as merely epiphenomenal. Instead, I would want to mark the specificities of different axes of oppression in particular locations and historical contexts, advocating a politics that would take account of those specificities. As Lata Mani notes:

Not having grown up as the Other of my society, I do not expect to be positioned as such. Indeed, this fundamental difference in life experience has led to my own sense of the importance of specifying the differences between those of us from the geographical Third World and those of us who came to adulthood as people of color in the West. Attention to such differences is crucial if we are not to falsely equalize groups with very different relations to the U.S. power structure. We need to be wary of the possibility that university affirmative action or diversity agendas might be met by filling positions with people trained elsewhere. (Frankenberg and Mani 1996, 351–52)

Mani and Ruth Frankenberg propose a notion of feminist conjuncturalism that would attend carefully to such "uneven, unequal relations" (1996, 361), yet leave room for alliance and political solidarity.

In light of such cautions, one can only note that to this point journals such as *positions* and *Public Culture* have been far more receptive to "postcolonial" theorizing than to analyses that emerge from the histories and situations of Asian American populations longer resident in the United States. Legitimizing such institutional sites as the most theoretically/politically hip venues in which to publish in Asian American studies could marginalize, perhaps obscure, those earlier geopolitical formations and labor histories. The situation of Asian Americans resident for three, four, five or more generations in the United States will not be adequately described by the present articulations of diaspora, transnationalism, and postcoloniality now circulating in journals of scholarly theory. Given the resources available to these new journals *premised* on their salience, the exclusive privileging of these forms of theory could potentially subvert the analysis of Asian American identities in their multiplicity and diversity. Indeed, specific histories may be in danger of elision—paradoxically—by these forms of transnationalism and postcolonial theory. Instead, one might seek an overall trajectory for the journal that would see such forces as *coconstructed* and as operating unevenly and unequally with these and other axes of oppression in specific contexts.

In sum, perhaps we can extend this analysis more generally to the role of transnationalism in Asian/Asian American studies. What of the different immigration histories and class positions of those who speak from Asian American and diasporic or postcolonial Asian positions, and how might this shape what is at stake in particular scholarly projects? Here, Anna Tsing (1993) argues that postcolonial theorists, as those speaking from spaces between nation-states, have urgent political stakes in decentering nationalist/colonialist essentialisms. I would add that, as those excluded from the Eurocentric definitions of the human, postcolonial theorists often write to erase the markings of difference, either claiming a more universally human category or subsuming difference within some larger theoretical frame, such as neo-Marxism or psychoanalysis.[7] Someone speaking from a position of racial exclusion within a nation-state, however, has a different agenda. In part, this involves the *assertion* of racial and other markings, to destabilize the category of the universally human—that which always already marks a site of race, gender, class, and sexual privilege. Consequently, could an emphasis on celebrating diaspora and transnationalism divert necessary attention from the need for multiple and contextually specific strategies, *including* the assertion of seemingly essentialist identities such as "Asian American"? Vanguardism and celebration of diaspora, then, can all too easily occlude other positions. Nor can we simply jettison the overdetermined historical contexts and particular institutional formations that shape the formation of the journals and volumes in which we write. I want, then, to acknowledge and to applaud the very real institutional changes that such volumes represent, but I also worry that an uncritical or self-congratulatory celebration of our progressivism could become a form of nouvelle Orientalism, class privilege, or reinscription of the autonomous Master Subject. These dangers would be all the more insidious for remaining unrecognized as such.

Cautionary remarks aside, however, one cannot but work from particular sites of enunciation, and ultimately, multiple kinds of interventions are urgently necessary on multiple fronts. The point is to specify those sites and our stakes in them, and to intervene, while remaining cognizant of the partial and located nature of our attempts at transformation. In my own case, I see these occurring on multiple fronts: through teaching students, especially those from racial, gender, class, and sexual margins; through "artistic" practice: playwriting, dramaturgy, and performance; in academic work; and through community and political organizations. An activist mode of inquiry pervades both the scholarship and the creative work, as I join with Asian American artists and artists of color as a partner in struggle. For those of us who occupy one or more marginal sites, work in the academy, in community organizations, on stage and screen, in the streets, continues a legacy of guerilla warfare, where there is no position beyond complicity or enmeshment in the dominant. Knowing this, we must still try to shift and dis-orient existing networks of power, using the means at our disposal. At stake is the hope that these interventions, however small, will enable subversions that matter.

Notes

1   At that moment, Michelle Rosaldo and Louise Lamphere were just finishing their pathbreaking anthology *Woman, Culture, and Society.* Clearly, a critical transformation was occurring, and clearly, it was the young women in the department who were responsible, including, at that moment, Bridget O'Laughlin, Harriet Whitehead, Rosaldo, and Collier.

The refiguration of "Man" from feminist perspectives seemed to open historically unprecedented theoretical and political possibility.

2   Kamala Visweswaran has argued that the anthropological privileging of culture has preempted a more thoroughgoing discussion of race within the discipline.

3   Cf. Renato Rosaldo 1994; and Newton and Shapiro 1995.

4   David Palumbo-Liu (1999) offers a cogent critique of Jameson's (and Richard Rorty's) disease around issues of race.

5   Elaine Kim, Takashi Fujitani, Aihwa Ong, David Palumbo-Liu, among others.

6   See, e.g., Lye 1995.

7   See, e.g., Chow 1995.

(Re)Viewing an Asian American Diaspora:
Multiculturalism, Interculturalism, and the
Northwest Asian American Theatre

KAREN SHIMAKAWA

Two signal events that are often held to have catalyzed the formation and development of Asian American studies as an academic discipline are the 1968–69 student protests that led to the establishment of Asian American studies programs at San Francisco State University and the University of California at Berkeley, and the 1974 publication of *Aiiieeeee! An Anthology of Asian-American Writers,* a collection of short stories, poems, excerpts from novels, plays, and memoirs, all by Asian American writers.[1] Social and political activism was intimately connected to, and in some cases fostered by, both academic legitimation and artistic expression by and about Asian Americans.[2] This (post-) civil rights-era wave of Asian American artistic endeavor took various forms, including the development of several Asian American theater companies and the attendant emergence of new Asian American playwrights, performers and other theater artists and technicians.[3]

The historical associations of Asian American studies with (and arguably its continuing focus on) primarily domestic concerns have been well-rehearsed by now, and this "indigenization model" (in Sau-ling Wong's terms) is reflected in the inception and shaping of these theater companies as well (Wong 1995: 4). According to its founder and first artistic director, the establishment of the first (permanent) Asian American theater company, Los Angeles' East West Players, in 1965, for instance, emerged out of the dissatisfaction of Asian American performers tired of the limited range of roles available to them—all of which were either Asian or "Fresh Off the Boat," and in either case, were distinctly un-American and concomitantly ignoble (Mako 1995). The Northwest Asian American Theatre of Seattle similarly cites the prevalence of "such one dimensional characters as Charlie Chan, Fu Manchu, Lotus Blossom, and Susie Wong" as a motivating factor in its formation (Iwamoto 1993, 6). One of NWAAT's original members, Ken Mochizuki, recalls that he was drawn to Asian American theater after having worked in mainstream film and television, because, in his experience, "the most stereotypically 'foreign' looking actors got all the work, and rarely did we get to portray the Americans that we are—those who have lived, worked and died in this country. That only happened on the stage of an Asian American theatre" (Mochizuki 1993, 22).

Interestingly, this version of "indigenization" gave rise to two separate (and sometimes bitterly conflicting) impulses: a desire to "tell our stories"—to create and perform roles that would reflect the heretofore buried or erased histories and experiences of Asian Americans as American—and another to fill traditionally white roles with Asian American actors. "I dreamt that an Asian American actor could portray leading roles," writes Tisa Chang, founding member and artistic director of the New York-based Pan Asian Repertory, founded in 1976, "unlimited by misconception and stereotype. That we, too, could be accepted as Clytemnestra, a Blanche Dubois, the Manchu Empress Dowager" (Chang 1995, 2). The relationship between these two positions is complex, but in the context of the current discussion about disciplinarity and Asian/Asian American studies and their (respective and/or mutual) objects of study, suffice it to say that both reflect different yet equally indigenizing strategies of representing Asian Americanness on stage.

Playwright Philip Kan Gotanda cites "the late '60s" as a major creative influence: "It [my creative inspiration] is in concert with the whole Asian-American creation," he has stated, noting the importance of "Asian-American" as a "political" construct (Seyd 1987, 172). Gotanda described his initial responses to coming to a politicized ethnic consciousness during this period as "very discouraging," in part due to his subject matter:

> I was . . . very interested in writing works, creating art that dealt with what I was discovering about myself being Asian American, having this face and living in America. At the time I was writing music . . . [and] trying to break into the larger recording industry and my songs were like, "The Ballad of the Issei," "The Asian American Dream," things like that, and there was just no interest in that sort of thing whatsoever. (Gotanda 1995)

Gotanda eventually gave up on music (at least temporarily), and went on to write a musical drama (*The Avocado Kid, or Zen and the Art of Guacamole*) that was produced in 1979 by the East West Players, a company "where I found I could do exactly what I wanted to—in my own voice" (Seyd 1987, 172). Gotanda was only one of several Asian American writers who found(ed) their way to East West and other Asian American theaters during this period: Frank Chin, Wakako Yamauchi, Momoko Iko and many other now prominent Asian American playwrights were first produced there in the late 1970s and early 1980s.

Why should theater prove so amenable a form for such expression? Gotanda has speculated that, in the political climate of the 1970s, theater presented itself to Asian American activists as an attractive medium because "it's cheap and it's immediate and . . . there are aspects of it that are really symbolic—the agitprop aspect of it, where you can very quickly put out political and cultural ideas, you can do kind of a guerrilla theatre. . . . It's all so out there: you're out in front" (Gotanda 1995). His initial response suggests that theater emerged as a dynamic site of representation and political activism through sheer expedience, but his last comment indicates that there were more than merely pragmatic or material concerns at play, which again raises the question: Why theater?

Out in Front

Anthony Kubiak's conceptualization of theater as "terror" and his suggestion that "theatre is the site in which cultural consciousness and identity come into being through *fear*" provides a possible explanation for Gotanda's (and other Asian American activists') choice. Kubiak's articulation of theater as that which "displaces the terror of chaos with form or structure (plot), while simultaneously indicating the possibilities of that lurking chaos as coercive threat" positions the medium of theater prominently within a cultural identity-formation process (Kubiak 1991, 6–7).[4] "The essential performative circumstance of theatre," he argues,

> is the alienation of self in the locus of the Other [which] eventually causes what Lacan calls aphanisis, or disappearance, as "I" am displaced outside the locus of "my" self, and seem to vanish into the Other. . . . The threat of disappearance in/by the presence of the Other generates this kind of terror out of the differentiating space, the rupture in consciousness that displaces the self into the power of an other. This is the same terror that either defines or conceals the ruptures or disunities that characterize culture itself. (Kubiak 1991, 13)

In other words, the "chaos" that Kubiak identifies as a source of terror—the knowledge that individual identity is a fluid construction, the result of a constant process of radical differentiation, and is constantly besieged by that which is designated Other, the very grounds of 1970s civil rights discourse and activism—is a prerequisite of theater. An audience to a live theatrical performance must accept the conditions under which that performance takes place. If for Kubiak the "terror" of theater is a perceived erosion of "the split between . . . reality and appearance, inside and outside," that is also theater's strength: the dramatic form can provide a bounded space in which those borders may be crossed (relatively) safely (Kubiak 1991, 7). The actor's bodily identity is necessarily doubled or layered with that of the character or role (Kubiak uses the term "unarticulated"), and in order simply to make diegetic sense of the actions taking place on stage an audience must necessarily and voluntarily accept that process of disarticulation by (partially) suspending the process of identity-construction that establishes individual consciousness and subjectivity as "natural" to particular, nationalized, raced individual bodies.

Insofar as it takes place within and arises from this tension between inside and outside, theater is a medium that arguably depends on both the functioning and dysfunctioning of (racial/national) identity. "Theatre hinges on the partial occlusion of the presentational by the representational," writes Stanton Garner, "the actual by the virtual, the solidness of self-coincidency by internal difference" (Garner 1994, 39). Neither Garner, one surmises, nor I would want to claim that theater achieves a *total* occlusion, however, and it is in that partiality that the potential for a dynamic engagement with social construction/perception lies. The dynamic tension between the body of the actor and that of the character—or perhaps more precisely, the process by which an audience experiences and reconciles that tension—is achieved through the self-conscious (albeit partial) disabling of the "reading" process by which we "know" ourselves and others (racially, nationally, sexually, etc.) in order to facilitate "partial occlusion." It is not simply that audiences are somehow "fooled" into believing the illusion they see before them on stage, but that on some level, they *will* themselves to, if not believe the illusion, then to behave and respond (in limited measure) as if they did. Because this process requires some proactivity on the part of the audience (not to mention that of the performer), I would argue that it is in fact a positive attribute of dramatic performance that the layeredness of the actor's/character's body is always apparent. As Garner points out, for better or worse, it is unavoidable:

> Considered one way, the actor's body is eclipsed, de-naturalized by the character's fictional presence. . . . And yet the actor's body never ceases asserting itself in its material, physiological facticity. On one level, of course, it does so by endowing the character-body with "borrowed" physicality. . . . But the body inserts a much more fundamental and in-

trusive actuality into the field of dramatic representation. . . . A point of independent sentience, the body represents a rootedness in the biological present that always, to some extent, escapes transformation into the virtual realm. (Garner 1994, 44)

This "facticity" of the body, however, does not necessarily imply a particular "meaning," reading, or construction of that body's identity. I am not arguing for an essential or true identity of the body (i.e., that of the actor), merely that the material presence of an actor's body forces an awareness that the character's identity (which is the product of a written, re-existing text and can be embodied by other actors) is not coextensive with that of a given performer. In order to make sense of a dramatic performance, an audience must contend with this corporeal actuality of the actor's body (in tension with that of the character) on the one hand, and reliance on the integrity of the categories "inside" and "outside" that generate subjective identity on the other; and what distinguishes theater as a medium, I would argue, is that an audience is required (or at least invited) to negotiate between these two positions.[5]

Peggy Phelan sums up this complex relation by pointing out its circularity: "Corporeal bodies amid real objects; realistic theatre employs properties which reproduce the effects of the real. . . . These props index the failure of representation to reproduce the real. The real inhabits the space that representation cannot reproduce" (Phelan 1993, 126). Yet part of theater's power, she argues, is in its capacity to induce audiences to (attempt to) ameliorate that failure: "Theatrical spectators . . . see what they believe to be false—and in attempting to account for that falsity, they see the truth of disguise and discover the need to augment the theory of the real itself" (Phelan 1993, 116). The possibility of this augmentation, finally, is what positions theater as an ideal site in which to examine and confront the "domestic vs. foreign" divide that largely structures Asian American theater. Moreover, as Garner points out (following Sartre), "The appearance of the performer-as-Other represents the permanent possibility of my being seen in turn; this appearance establishes my own position as visual object in another individual's perceptual field" (Garner 1994, 48). The "real" that may emerge as a product of this engagement with dramatic illusion, then, is not merely a means of addition or accumulation: alteration to the "real" that lies within one's perceptual field necessarily implies a concomitant alteration to the perceptual fields of others, in which one may be an object. That is, the very act of "reading" a character/actor on an Asian American stage (or, for that matter, any stage) necessarily involves setting up a phantasmatic relation between that body and one's own—a relation oriented not only by race, sex, or gender, but often by (imputed or inferred) national indices as well.

Theater is thus a medium both less and more embodied than others—less, in the sense of the ephemerality of a given performance; and more, in that it requires the presentation of live bodies for its full textual exposition. Theater's presentational layering was consistent with the political agenda that provided the cultural context for the development of these first Asian American theater companies. For activists whose involvement with Asian American theater was tied to their antiracist politics, then, theater offered itself as a means of creating (albeit on stage) a new and different reality—one that adamantly and prominently located Asian Americans in U.S. culture and society, and often radically differentiated "us" from "foreign" Asians. On the stages of Asian American theaters, Mochizuki points out, it was possible to see a kind of Americanness that was visible nowhere else in U.S. popular representation—and thereby to see oneself within or in relation to that national identity differently.

The Dance That's Happening—
Multicultural and Intercultural Theater

Recent developments have called the continued viability of such an agenda into question. The forces that have given rise to this anthology and that have brought pressure to bear on the academic, cultural, ideological, and economic distinctions between Asianness and Asian Americanness have also impacted the U.S. theater industry and Asian American theater artists and companies in particular. This process has manifested itself in two distinct but intricately related trends: an attempt, by mainstream theater companies to "multiculturalize" their repertoires with the addition of works written and (sometimes) performed by minority artists; and the vogue of intercultural productions of Western theater works.

In recent years, as funding for the arts has come under fire in the popular/political media and subsequently dwindled, and theater subscriptions (in most cases) have dropped or leveled off, competition for the resources that do remain has grown fierce; and nowhere is this phenomenon more acutely felt than in small to mid-size nonprofit theaters. In its annual survey of U.S. nonprofit theaters, *American Theater* reported that, in general, as foundation and federal funding have decreased over the past five years, that slack has been only partially taken up by state and local funds. Similarly, whereas season ticket purchases have declined, individual and group ticket sales have increased—but not enough to fully compensate for the loss of subscriptions (Samuels and Tonsic 1996, 1–15). Attacks on the NEA from prominent politicians such as Jesse Helms have cast a pall over future prospects for reversal of these trends and, as a result, the report concludes, "the country's theatres have begun to prepare for losses in public and private funding," particularly at the national level. Ironically, the cries from federal politicians about the erosion of public morals attributed to "offensive" art, and from theater critics lamenting "the balkanization of the arts" represented by the inflection of multiculturalism in professional, for-profit theater, have conspired to impel some smaller, nonprofit theaters—whose community identities, audiences, and repertoires were heretofore predominantly white—to cultivate new and broader bases of local funding by incorporating (some form of) multiculturalism into their seasons, if not their institutional structures (Bernstein 1990, H1).

In recent conversations with several Asian American playwrights and performers, the importance of visibility, both for Asian Americans seeing themselves reflected on stage and for non-Asian American audiences learning to see Asian Americans in their "Americanness," was a concern stressed by nearly every artist interviewed. It would follow, then, that these recent efforts on the part of so-called mainstream theater companies to make their seasons more "diverse" should be a cause for celebration—yet when I asked these Asian American playwrights and performers about their early and ongoing investment(s) in Asian American theater as an institution, in each case and without prompting, virtually every interviewee commented on this "diversification" phenomenon, with reactions ranging from mild concern to deep skepticism. The problem, as they explained it, is that mainstream theater companies have made efforts to add works by playwrights of color, utilizing ethnic minority performers in plays on "ethnic" themes solely in a bid for (especially public and foundation/grant) support, and to widen their subscriber bases to include demographic groups newly-deemed desirable. "The theatres here [in Seattle] are just now beginning to create multicultural seasons," observes Judith Nihei, former artistic director of NWAAT, and while she is quick to add, "which I think is wonderful, which is what we wanted," she also expresses some "curiosity" at the political sincerity and artistic competence of such companies in producing these works:

> I believe, personally, that you have to have some sort of cultural basis, a cultural perspective within which to present the show. . . . If you don't, it's not just that you're not going to show sociologically or anthropologically the way that it should be shown; but as an artist you're cutting yourself off at the knees because you're missing some dramatic little moments in there. . . . If you're going to do Shakespeare, for instance, you'll do all this research, you'll learn the language, you'll learn the body language, and you'll use all that in order to put your play up. And it seems to me, or I am really curious to see, who's going to do that with Asian American drama? (Nihei 1995)

Nihei expresses a concern that, to the extent that Asian American plays are interpreted as purely "universal" works in which the emotional, psychological, or social significance of a given action or interaction is measured against a nonspecific (or perhaps generic "American") standard, subtle aesthetic and political cues will be overlooked. "What does it mean to have a conversation with your father with no one else home?" asks Nihei. "What that means in 'American' culture is one thing. What that means in a Chinese American, or Korean American, or Filipino American family is something completely other" (Nihei 1995). Gotanda expresses similar concerns about having his work produced outside Asian American theater companies, despite the fact that he more often than not produces his new works there.

> You have to be really aware of to what degree racism is happening at that particular theatre company, and it could be in the most sophisticated, subtle form, where no one is even aware of the dance that's happening. I think that's what you really find now . . . [For new playwrights of color, the theatre will say,] "we'll give you a certain director," and if you're new, you have to accept that. Now I come in and . . . I demand that they have a certain level of sophistication about what I'm doing, my world . . . He or she doesn't necessarily have to be Asian, but she better know my world. (Gotanda 1995)

Even David Henry Hwang, who is widely credited with bringing Asian American drama to the "mainstream," and who has taken the position that "the future is not in monoethnic theatre, but in multicultural theatres that will do a black play, an Asian play, a white play, whatever," warns that that future is not yet here, and that before it arrives, the entire institution of commercial theater needs to be rethought: "I think that we, as citizens of this country, of many different cultures and ethnicities would have to essentially coopt the major structures as they exist now" (Hwang 1995).[6] Hwang deems many of the misguided attempts at multiculturalism now evident in mainstream theater as well-intentioned (if ill-conceived): "I think actually in terms of trying to discover new theatre forms and attract new audiences there is some genuine interest there, but I don't know that they necessarily know how to do it. So I think there's this attempt, by a lot of white male artistic directors to bring in ethnic shows, but not with the degree of understanding that is necessary to do them well" (Hwang 1995). He, like Nihei and Gotanda, expresses some concern that any director who wants to put up a play, in any venue, has the responsibility to familiarize herself with the play's cultural milieu.[7]

These artists, in other words, suddenly find themselves arguing against not only the portrayal of Asian American characters authored by non-

Asian Americans, but even the production of Asian American plays, in non-racially-specific theaters; in some sense, then, this represents a conflict with these institutions' earlier expressed objective of integrating Asian Americans into the fabric of U.S. culture. In another sense, though, this is the logical extension of their original aims in that it reflects a desire for self-representation, autonomy, and recognition. Of course, there is also an obvious pragmatic concern: these economically driven efforts toward multiculturalism on the part of mainstream theaters could effectively put Asian American theaters out of business before their (political/pedagogical) work is done.

Clearly, the connections between the trajectory of multiculturalism in these theater companies is not unlike (and, I would argue, not unrelated to) the force and effect(s) of multiculturalism in the context of the U.S. academy and Ethnic and American Studies programs in particular. That is, there is a tension between those two (when they are conceived as two) programs in that a multicultural agenda argues for the annexation, inclusion, or (re)absorption of the former into the latter as an integral component of it, aided perhaps by the adamant declaration of indigeneity (and self-differentiation from foreignness) on the part of some Ethnic studies scholars; such inclusion can represent legitimation, recognition, and material support for scholars of U.S. minority literatures and cultures. Yet as my earlier qualifier "or (re)absorption" indicates, such inclusion may also represent erasure, a surrender to traditional (Euro-American-centered) academic canonicity.

Perhaps more significantly, the emergence of the discourses of postcoloniality, diaspora, and "global" economics also thwart such attempts at merging Asian American studies with American studies in such a way as to deny the continuities between Asianness and (Asian) Americanness. This last shift, too, has made its mark in the theater as well, in the form of "interculturalism" as an aesthetic/artistic trend. Western theater artists have long been interested in Near and Far East performance theory and practice — Brecht's fascination with "Chinese acting" constitutes merely a revisitation of a frequently sounded theme — but in the late 1980s and 1990s, this interest (combined with postmodernist theory as well as shifts in global political and economic relations) found new expression in the work of such prominent avant-garde theater artists as Ariane Mnouchkine, Lee Breuer, Peter Sellars, and Peter Brook. Mnouchkine's ten-hour cycle of four plays (Euripides' *Iphigenia* in Aulis followed by Aeschylus' *Agamemnon, The Libation Bearers,* and *The Eumenides*) titled *Les Atreides* was originally conceived and performed in Mnouchkine's Paris performance space, La Cartoucherie, but in 1992 was brought to New York's 14th Regiment Armory by the Brooklyn Academy of

Music, where it sold out its entire run. In his review of the New York production, Frank Rich observed that "the performers appear in opulent ceremonial costumes of vaguely Asian provenance . . . the stagehands are Kabuki-ish while the chorus's choreography emulates the Kathakali dance dramas of Southern India" (Rich 1992, C1). Describing the musical accompaniment, Michael Ratcliffe dubbed composer Jean-Jacques Lemêtre "the samurai of European musical theatre," producing a "wild tapestry . . . [of] Greek and Asia Minor mountain music . . . Balinese dance music, Indian Kathakali (the stutter step) music, Kabuki aragoto, and for good measure he uses as a motif the small fragment of music that we have extant from the [Greek] ancient period" (Ratcliffe 1991, H5). *Les Atreides,* which was generally enthusiastically received by critics and scholars, was only one of the more prominent works in a series of recent productions evidencing the director's interest in Eastern theater aesthetics and techniques; since the 1980s Mnouchkine, a white French woman, has experimented with various Eastern movement and presentation theories, often using Western dramatic texts — including a series of Shakespeare plays produced in 1981–2 that referenced Noh and Kabuki, as well as commedia dell'arte.

It was also during this period that Peter Brook (a white Englishman working primarily in Paris) collaborated with Jean-Claude Carrière on an adaptation of *The Mahabharata* for the stage. Probably the most oft-cited exemplar of intercultural theater, the Brook-Carrière nine-hour play (and four-hour film), like Mnouchkine's "Greek" cycle, enjoyed international, high-profile (and generally positive) attention from Western theater critics and scholars. In this case, however, some critics voiced some concerns about the "smorgasbord" approach to the text, which resulted in a quasi-Homeric, quasi-Shakespearean epic drained of theological or socio-historical specificity: "Brooks' *Mahabharata* falls short of the essential Indianness of the epic," surmises Gautam Dasgupta, "by staging predominantly its major [martial] incidents and failing to adequately emphasize its coterminous philosophical precepts" (Marranca and Dasgupta 1991, 81).

If the phrase "essential Indianness" causes one to stop short, it is worth thinking for a moment about the causes and effects of intercultural theater. Because as Bonnie Marranca observes of intercultural theater, "[t]hat some of the most suggestive work comes out of the intersection of British (or French) culture and a former colony is in no small measure a decisive factor in the discussion" (Marranca and Dasgupta 1991, 13). Daryl Chin puts it even more bluntly: "The idea of interculturalism as simply a way of joining disparate cultural artifacts has a hidden agenda of imperialism" (Chin 1991, 87). These cultural samplings, performed almost exclusively under white Euro-American directors simultaneously erase and concretize cultural, racial, and/or national essences and differences through radical de-historicization. Many of its proponents claim alliegance to some form of postmodern aesthetics, and while it may be characterized more directly as a response to, or a form of, postcolonial discourse, the critique of (some forms of) postmodern discourse holds true here as well. As Chin formulates it, "the Eurocentric ego is making a declaration, which is: if it can no longer claim dominance and superiority, if equity must be awarded, if the Eurocentric ego can no longer presume on self-importance, then nothing is important. Hidden in the agenda of postmodernism is, I think, a rebuke, an insult, a devaluation" (Chin 1991, 85). Intercultural performance (as Chin imagines it here) is in some sense the quintessential postmodern, late-capitalist product: commenting somewhat cynically on the "transculturation business" transacted via international theater and performance festivals that function as the primary conduit for these productions, Carl Weber surmises that

> quite inevitably, any "transcultural" experiment will be traded as a device that employs exotic ingredients to make the product more palatable, i.e., marketable. . . . What [the economic exigencies of international festivals] lead to is that a great number of transcultural products, trying to combine, fuse, blend—or whatever you'd like to call it—features of the indigenous with those of an alien culture, arrive at performances which use the alien component as a spicy sauce to make some old familiar gruel palatable again. (Weber 1991, 29–30)

Unlike the multicultural phenomenon I discussed earlier that takes place primarily in small to mid-size nonprofit regional theaters, these intercultural productions are, as I indicated, extremely high-profile. The genre has generated numerous nationally circulated reviews, articles, anthologies, and full-length studies—and, predictably this coverage often translates into economic support in the forms of corporate and grant funding and enhanced ticket sales, arguably to the detriment of the smaller, more locally funded theaters discussed above, both Asian American and "multicultural." Moreover, in the case of Asian American theaters, this rush toward the exotic foreign other erases not only the distance between "them" and "us" (the distinction these theaters were instituted to highlight), but also those who somehow reside in neither and both of those camps. In other words, Asian Americanness is recognizable within the intercultural field only insofar as it is continuous with (foreign) Asianness—and then only as a diluted, degraded, or contaminated form thereof.

Asian American theater companies are thus caught between a political and economic Scylla and Charibdis: the domestic deconstruction, erasure or appropriation of racial, national, and ethnic differences represented by multicultural theater on the one hand and the transnational deconstruction, erasure, or appropriation thereof by intercultural theater on the other—both threaten to drain away audience and other material support. The crossroads at which Asian American theaters now find themselves thus not only resembles, but is intimately connected to, that which gives rise to this anthology: for as an Asian American institution, emerging from and heir to an aggressively domestic U.S.-identified stance posed in opposition to (some construction of) foreign "Asianness," these theater companies are beginning to reexamine those seemingly definitional tenets in light of shifting immigration/emigration patterns, "global" politics and economics, and the attendant theories and/or discourses attempting to address them.

The Northwest Asian American Theater and Diasporic Performance

One particularly interesting instance of this reassessment is NWAAT's current undertaking, funded by a private foundation, whose objective is "to foster and produce a multidisciplinary collaborative project that: 1) involves artists of developing countries of Asia and American artists and 2) serves the Asian American community through youth involvement or community presentations" (NWAAT 1996, 1). The company recently embarked on an ambitious, multiyear project that is not only the product of the trends and forces alluded to above, but that actively engages those forces and is consciously, deliberately, and self-reflexively attempting to intervene in and reap the benefit of these movements.

The project spans multiple years, involving from two to five artists per year in a series of residences (in the United States and Asia), during which the artists conduct workshops with Seattle Asian Pacific American artists and youths and collaborate on a new performance work. The "American" artists must include "Asia-based, Asian/Pacific Islander (API) American and Asian immigrant (newcomer) artists" (NWAAT 1996, 8). In its inaugural year, this International Artists Program (IAP) brought together five artists: a Filipino American choreographer, a Japanese American vocalist, a Singaporean choreographer, a Malaysian choreographer, and a Singaporean American playwright. The resulting performance piece, "Home: Places Between Asia and America" (a multimedia performance piece inspired by the murder of Susana Blackwell, a "Filipina mail order bride who was shot to death by her American husband in the King County Courthouse," according to the show's program) premiered at NWAAT in 1998. The second collaboration, which premiered January 2000, was a multimedia dance theater work entitled "Traces," created by Malaysian chore-ographer/performer Mew Chang Tsing and Chinese American filmmaker John Pai, and was inspired by a series of conversations between the artists, during which they explored the similarities and differences in their relations to "Chineseness" (both are ethnically Chinese, although their parents immi-grated to Malaysia and the United States). For this project, both artists did residencies in the other's country (though Tsing's visit to the United States was more extensive). The stated criteria and goals for these works (according to their grant proposal project description) are that they should be "derived from more than one Asian culture which utilizes the talents of Asia-based, and API artists and newcomer immigrant community members. Eventually, the pieces created will add to the global repertoire of creative work that reflects the experience of the Asian Diaspora" (NWAAT 1996, 11–12).

On a cynically pragmatic basis, the project may be seen as NWAAT's attempt to "jump on the intercultural bandwagon" and reap the material benefits associated with this artistic trend; as former artistic director Nihei sardonically puts it, "why is it that those other theatres get to play with the Thai dance instructors, and we can't?" (Nihei 1995). As noted in the project proposal itself, corporate sponsorship might well be enhanced as a result of this collaboration, "if artists were brought from countries they [the corpo-rations] were seeking improved trade relations with, for example Vietnam and Indonesia" (NWAAT 1996, 3).

Another (and potentially more damning) critique lies in the political interests and strategies implied by such a project in light of the genealogy of Asian American theater previously posited. "The history of the Northwest Asian American Theatre," proclaims even this proposal, "evolved out of a vision, need and dedication to celebrate and explore the many cultures and voices of our diverse *nation*" (NWAAT 1996, 4, emphasis added), highlight-ing the domestic (indigenized?) agenda that informed its establishment. A project that may address the continuities between Asianness and Asian Americanness, the argument runs, could conflate those two identities and encourage the perception of Asian Americans as less legitimate U.S. citi-zens and therefore less entitled to the rights and privileges that citizenship should afford.

What I want to suggest, though, is that in conceiving and structuring this project, NWAAT has negotiated this uncharted territory with precisely these objections in mind. "The residency is designed to elicit dialogue and creative expression about a number of topics facing the Asian Diaspora," declares the project description, and this initial statement might suggest a problematic blurring of distinctions or disregard of material specifici-ties, thus exhibiting the worst transgressions of the intercultural theater discussed above. The statement goes on to list "aspects" by which members of an Asian diaspora are related, including racism, sexism, religious intolerance and "colonization of Asian countries and of U.S. communities of color" (NWAAT 1996, 9). The combination of these last two factors into one "aspect" on a bulleted list similarly suggests (or at least affords the possibility for) an uncritical equation and even conflation of the two populations without regard for the ways in which they are not coextensive and whose interests at times may be, in fact, actively opposed. Yet the statement continues: "This global population is similar and dissimilar and varied in their relationships with the United States. Some Asians have immigrated to, [or] were born or have relatives in the U.S.; some have been affected directly by U.S. economic or military policies and actions" (NWAAT 1996, 8). Thus, the proposal acknowledges and articulates grounds for both identification and disidentification, and allows for the possibility that the resident artists may choose to focus on one, the other, or both poles of experience — or perhaps to reconfigure them as something other than "poles" altogether.

Moreover, as the preceding description of the project demonstrates, in addition to the development of original collaborative works by Asian and Asian American artists, an equally prominent component of the program is its focus on local Asian American communities, fostering (in the mode of multicultural theater programming development) Asian American audiences — especially young people — conducting classes and performing works that address their specific "domestic" experiences — "the API immigrant community's experiences *living in the United States*" (NWAAT 1996, 11, emphasis added). That contemporary Asia-based artists might have something to offer such a project is in itself a radical departure from the governing, rigidly indigenized model of Asian American creative production prior to this project. The stated criteria for selecting the resident artists similarly reflects this dialectic approach: as stated above, the group would include "Asia-based artists . . . in collaboration with Asian or Pacific Islander American artists . . . and newcomer artists, [all of whom] would be chosen for both artistic skills and for their willingness to work in residency with both youth and adults *from the community*" (NWAAT, 1996, 11, emphasis added). The Theater's insistence on cross-participation between Asians and Asian Americans, between more and less established Asian Americans (hence the separable category of "recent immigrant artists"), between the "Theater" and "the community," between adults and children, all position this project to enable a synthesis of intercultural and multicultural impulses, and suggest that any distinction between those two concepts, particularly in the case of Asians and Asian Americans, is arbitrary and (at best) fluid.

Earlier, I suggested that theater as a medium is both less and more embodied than other media, and that this (in part) explained the emergence of theater as a dynamic site in the movement for Asian American civil rights by creating an opportunity for a radical resignification of the Asian American body, on an experiential level, in measures both subtle and profound, in order to resignify the Oriental body as Asian American. Yet despite over twenty years of resignification on the stages of Asian American theaters, the "other" body that cannot be experientially or visually differentiated from it, the Asian body, has continued to shadow it. If the possibility of such successful differentiation is smaller than ever (if in fact such possibilities ever existed), perhaps what NWAAT offers is another alternative: a resignification of the body in global/diasporic terms that nevertheless resist the pull of biological-racial essentialism and that call into critical question the ways in which we "read" raced bodies in terms of their perceived positions within national, international or (post)colonial frameworks. The very fact that audiences are presented with Asian bodies and Asian American bodies sharing the same theatrical space, making visible aspects of sameness and difference, poses a challenge to any construction of national (foreign and/or domestic) bodies in terms of biologically raced essentialism—even when it seems to offer those bodies up to such an enterprise.

Notes

1   See Chan et al. 1974.
2   Needless to say, there were numerous other historical conditions/events that contributed to this process, and I would not want to argue for the real causal primacy of these two; nevertheless, these occurrences are often prominently discussed in histories of Asian American studies, and I single them out for recognition here in order to point out the mutually productive relationship shared by the (community-based) political, academic, and artistic branches of this social movement. On the relationship between the student protests at SFSU and UC Berkeley and Asian American studies and an "Asian American movement," see, for instance, Wei, 1993, especially chapter 5, "Activists and the Development of Asian American Studies," 132–61. On the connections between social and political activism and aesthetic production in the formation of Asian American studies, see Chan 1991, 181. See also Russell Leong's contribution to this volume.
3   While a relatively small number of performers (and an even smaller number of nonperforming theater artists and technicians) were working in mainstream (or other) venues prior to this, I am referring here to theater artists whose work contributed directly, self-consciously, and deliberately to the establishment of Asian American theater companies such as the East West Players, the Asian American Theatre Workshop of San Francisco, the Northwest Asian American Theatre and Pan Asian Repertory—companies with more or less explicit agendas to cultivate a social, political, and aesthetic "Asian American" identity and community.
4   Emphasis in original. I note that Kubiak carefully distinguishes "theatre" as he uses the term here as distinct from "drama, from the theatre that exists as text/criticism and not

as spectacle" (1991, 12). My focus, however, is on the link between performance/spectacle and the development of literary/aesthetic texts (along with their attendant criticism).

5 I would not venture to posit a monolithic audience whose responses I can definitively predict (or even describe); however, to the extent that a dramatic text designates roles to be performed by actors, I would argue that in performance some degree of layering is unavoidable, as is the potential for tensions between those layers of identity.

6 It is worth quoting the entire passage, in fairness to Hwang:

The Asian-American theatre movement has been important to me . . . if you grow up as a minority in this country there's a residual negativism that you take into your system, simply because of the racism in the air. You get to a point where you feel a certain amount of self-loathing and wonder if you don't measure up to certain things. One of the only ways to remedy that is for minority people to get together, segregate themselves for a while, and realize that they all have common experiences. You can sort of repair the damage that way. But once that's done I believe there's an obligation, at least if one is going to remain engaged in the American experiment, to reintegrate yourself into the larger society. In the long run, if ethnic theatres do their jobs properly, they should phase themselves out of their own existence. I think the future is not in monoethnic theatre, but in multicultural theatres. . . . (Berson 1990, 95)

7 I do not believe, however, that he, or the other Asian American artists I questioned on this topic, would argue for the tyranny of "authenticity" in this regard. All of them expressed an interest in seeing Asian American plays done in non-Asian American theaters, and all saw a value in making cross-cultural connections through such productions. Yet such crossings, all seemed to agree, must be made carefully, knowledgeably, and responsibly.

Creating Performative Communities:
Through Text, Time, and Space

RUSSELL LEONG

Amerasia Journal/ Spaces of Asian American Studies

The spaces of "Asian American studies" have become even more complex with time. The term itself encompasses at least four overlapping and sometimes conflicting "spaces": *political space*—ideological formulation based upon the history and ideas of the Asian American movement of the 1960s and continuing to the present; *discursive space*—analytical and disciplinary approaches within the field itself; *designated space*—institutional units and programs; and *local space*—within diasporic or transnational studies frameworks, Asian American studies as a "local" subsection of global "Pacific" or "Asian" diasporic formations. These four spaces include both ideological and disciplinary approaches as well as various institutional, research, and publishing locations. Within Asian American studies, the *Amerasia Journal* occupies a unique position as the interdisciplinary journal that has helped to actively shape the field for thirty years, reflecting the evolution and spaces of the field itself—political, discursive, designated, and local.[1]

In political terms, the formation of Asian American studies is linked directly with the struggles and movements of self-determination by Asian American students in response to their exclusion from the educational curriculum. Asians in the 1960s and 1970s, together with African, Latino, and Native Americans, saw their lives and communities as part of the American experience, yet recognized that their histories had not been adequately studied, fairly taught, or widely disseminated. While this reclamation of a neglected history was important, in a broader sense the Asian American movement struggled to develop longer-term strategies toward the inclusion of people of color in the social fabric and political transformation of the United States. At the same time, according to Takagi and Omi, "attention centered on Asian American communities as sites for political mobilization, the building of alternative institutions, and the creation of an oppositional culture" (Omi and Takagi 1995, xii).[2]

By the time that Don T. Nakanishi and I surveyed Asian American studies programs in California, Washington, Colorado, New York, and Hawaii in 1978, a decade after the establishment of the first programs, we found that much energy was expended in maintaining programmatic and institutional resources, as well as undergraduate programs. Research, a major concern, tended to be historical in the form of oral histories or policy studies for government agencies. Teaching and program survival, due to administrative constraints, were the overriding concerns of all Asian American studies programs during this period. Maintaining the material base of the programs took tremendous energy, but, at least by this time, some programs had obtained a designated space within institutions of higher learning (Nakanishi and Leong 1978).

By the second decade of the 1980s Asian American studies programs were grudgingly recognized by universities and colleges especially on the East and West coasts as interdisciplinary endeavors. Accordingly, time and money were invested to train undergraduate and graduate students, and the recruitment of faculty to teach within these programs appeared to flourish at many schools. But in the twentieth anniversary commemorative issue of *Amerasia*, Glenn Omatsu referred to the state of the field as "two steps forward, and one step back" pointing out a history of gains and losses (1989). For at the same time that Omatsu along with Mary Kao were revisiting community sites of struggle and garnering the voices of Asian American activists for the journal, tenure struggles, such as Nakanishi's, were occurring on the UCLA campus.[3] University administrators at UCLA and elsewhere continue to criticize Asian American scholars for producing irrelevant or nontraditional scholarly research. Debates over educational philosophy, multiculturalism and curriculum revision were occurring throughout the nation. At the same time, placed in a defensive posture by colleagues, and under pressure to "publish or perish," young Asian American academics believed that they had to justify their work through the production of articles and monographs published in traditional disciplinary—not interdisciplinary, Asian American, or community-based—publications. Themes and theories of social transformation, based on the philosophy and practices of such thinkers as Mao Zedong, Paulo Freire, Karl Marx, Frantz Fanon, Malcolm X, and Grace and James Lee Boggs, and others were studiously avoided by these academics, who retreated "to more mainstream, discipline-based paradigmatic orientations," according to Dana Takagi and Michael Omi in their introduction to "Thinking Theory," a revisionist *Amerasia* edition on theoretical developments in the field. As Takagi and Omi state:

> Contributing to this trend was the increasing "professionalisation" of the field in academic settings, the demands of tenure and promotion for faculty members, and the entrance of newcomers to the field trained in specific disciplines who had not participated in the new social movements of the previous decades. The result of this has been the contraction of a space for dialogue across the disciplines—one which could have critically interrogated disciplinary boundaries and fostered cross-disciplinary perspectives. (Omi and Takagi 1995, xi–xv)

While the ability of scholars to focus their attention on a particular research topic was often useful, the utilization of social and political theories—along with cultural, postmodern, or structural analyses—would have helped to bridge the gap between theory and practice. While this professionalization continued throughout the late 1980s and into the 1990s, the institutionalization of Asian American studies and the training of undergraduate and graduate students also provided stability and opportunities for linking students with community issues. Students, with others, involved themselves in struggles around unpaid Chinese garment workers in the Jessica McClintock case in San Francisco; the struggle over urban redevelopment and Parcel C in Boston's Chinatown; the case of seventy-two imprisoned Thai garment workers in El Monte, California; and the New Otani Hotel workers' struggle in Los Angeles. Students not only helped to organize campaigns, letter-writing, petitions, and demonstrations, but wrote and published reports, and, with faculty, organized study groups and classes around such issues. Learning from workers, students were able to discern linkages between the local and global. In the case of the New Otani, for instance, local exploitation of Japanese and Latino workers in Los Angeles' Little Tokyo by the Japan-based Kajima Corporation was linked with its past exploitation of Chinese slave labor in Northern China during World War II.[4]

Meanwhile, on campuses throughout the United States, students renewed their long-time demands for Asian American courses and faculty at Northwestern, UC Irvine, Princeton, Columbia University, and elsewhere. Despite the institutionalization, professionalization, and progress of Asian American studies, each gain has required struggle and sacrifice on the part of students, workers, and community activists in order to transform both college curriculum and public consciousness.

What lesson of the writing of culture is spoken through affective inscription at the point of human enunciation?—Homi K. Bhaba

During the first decade of the journal, its editors—Lowell Chun-Hoon, Megumi Dick Osumi, and Carolyn Yee—published articles, essays, and reviews that expanded on the themes of immigration, race relations, civil rights, identity, and the literary and artistic exploration of Asian American sensibilities that characterized the interdisciplinary content of Asian American studies.[5] According to Don I. Nakanishi, *Amerasia Journal*'s founding publisher, "the journal, as an active participant rather than a passive spectator in the creation of a new field, had to vigorously search for, encourage the writing of, and probably play an inordinate editorial role in developing material, be it in the form of a research article, a short story, an engaging interview, or a book review."

During the 1977–1987 period when I became editor, the journal continued to focus on groups: particularly Chinese, Korean, Filipino, and Japanese American history, with special issues devoted to the writings of Carlos Bulosan, to the Chinese in America, and to Filipino Americans. *Amerasia* also addressed community issues such as the Japanese American movement for redress and reparations, and the emergence of contemporary Korean American communities.[6] By the mid-1980s, however, those who taught Asian American studies found they needed materials to meet the demands of the changing demographics of their own students—Vietnamese, Cambodian, Hmong, and 1.5 generation (those who immigrated as young children) South Asian, Korean, Chinese and Filipino students.

The years 1989 and 1990 were pivotal for *Amerasia,* portending its current agenda of covering transcultural Asian communities within both local and global multidisciplinary contexts. By 1989, the journal found itself both commemorating the local—the twentieth anniversary of the San Francisco State University Strike and the beginnings of ethnic studies, followed by an issue that same year on the Asian diaspora in the Americas—with articles on Asians in Trinidad, Peru, and Canada.[7] As Shirley Hune stated in the introduction to her guest-edited volume of *Amerasia* on "Asians in the Americas": "One can gain a more complete understanding of both the Asian American experience and the Asian diaspora by incorporating the international dimension of the Asian American experience and comparative studies approach into our framework of analysis" (Hune 1989, xix–xxiv).

The 1990 volume attempted to link issues within and outside the university and Asian American studies to broader, revisionist conceptualizations of the field. The first issue of volume sixteen, for example, highlighted scholar and activist Haunani-Kay Trask's essay, "Politics in the Pacific Islands: Imperialism and Native Self-Determination." In the same issue (16:1[1990]), Glenn Omatsu edited a special section on the Don T. Nakanishi tenure struggle at UCLA. In the following issue (16:2[1990]), the journal published an acrimonious debate among leading scholars in Asian American studies over Ronald Takaki's *Strangers from a Different Shore.* The writers included L. Ling-chi Wang, Sucheng Chan, Elaine Kim, Ronald Takaki, Paul Wong, Frank Chin, and Karen Leonard. In 1991, *Amerasia* published three issues per year to meet the increased number of article submissions, reviews, and special issues planned by members of its editorial board and staff. Building upon its history of fostering multidisciplinary perspectives, the *Amerasia Journal* and the UCLA Asian American Studies Center began a collaborative publications series with the University of Hawaii Press entitled: "Intersections: Transcultural Asian and Pacific American Studies."

During the past thirty years, *Amerasia Journal* has established fruitful critical relationships with both the activist practitioners and those operating within the field of Asian American studies itself: presenting perspectives that reflected current developments and debates in the field—i.e., the Takaki debate, new historiography, and publishing articles that pushed the field further—with special volumes on Asian American grassroots labor organizing, Southeast Asian identity, gay and lesbian sexuality, war and Asian Americans, transnationalism and media, and Asian-descent multiracial peoples.[8]

The influence of postcolonial and diasporic studies on Asian American studies was beginning to be felt: authors delved into the relationship between large Asian corporations and local migrant workers, the creolization of local Trinidadians by Britain, Asia, and Africa, or the effects of Western imperialism on Samoa and Hawaii, for example. As an Asian American journal, we chose not to subsume ourselves under East Asian studies or Asian Diasporic studies, but rather to position ourselves as a publication concerned with the multiple articulations and roots of the racial, ethnic, and gendered identities of the peoples of the Americas.

The "Thinking Theory" issue of *Amerasia Journal* (21:1,2[1995]), guest edited by Dana Takagi and Michael Omi, generated a great deal of debate around the perceived "split" between academics and community, between "intellectuals" and "nonintellectuals." Omi and Takagi believed that "the dichotomy kaleidoscopes an interrelated series of issues and debates about the subject, theory, method, and history, arguing for transdisciplinary approaches (1995, xi–xv). Since then, a number of scholars have attempted to clarify the nature and linkage to theory and practice, among them, R. Radhakrishnan:

For too long a time, theory has been the executor of such a colonialist and imperialist will. But theory can work very differently . . . The theory that we require is a nonobjectifying and connecting theory that in honoring "subjectivity" will honor the "subject" in each group or constituency. . . . The historical bonding between such a theory and ethnicity is to make possible a generous but critical articulation between a purely local sense of ethnicity and a common and global heritage within a shared and simultaneous history. (Radhakrishnan 1996, 92–93)

It is this "honoring of the subject" and "critical articulation" between the local and the global that are revealed in *Amerasia Journal* issues of the 1990s, in volumes that address specific racial, gendered, or religious subjects within Asian American groups. For example, a special issue (19:2[1993]) on postrebellion Los Angeles not only published articles by Asians, but had sections devoted to African American and Latino perceptions and observations on the event. "Dimensions of Desire" (20:1[1994]), which explored the gay and lesbian experience, focused on many subjects: from Pacific Islanders to Filipino transvestites to Vietnamese lesbian artists, and 1970s activists.[9] Such interrogation into realms of difference within both public and personal subjects linking the local and global can perhaps be seen most clearly in a recent *Amerasia* issue, "Racial Spirits: Race and Religion in Asian America" (22:1[1996]) that melded scholarly research, interview, and experimental literary works. A number of articles linked transnational religious movements and issues in the Philippines, India, China, and Korea to the lives of Asians living in the United States.

As the editor of UCLA's *Amerasia Journal* for more than two decades, I have been privileged to work with scholars, writers, journalists, and artists in their probing into the Asian American experience and its implications for both the individual and the body politic. It would be simplistic, however, to view the scholarly project of *Amerasia Journal*'s thirty-year history as merely an additive one, an accrual of information or statistics or publication of an article on the latest immigrant or refugee group. Working with, and inspired by, the staff of the journal, I have been as much concerned with "the writing of culture" and how ideas are enunciated through textual formation and visual imagery. This concern is most apparent in the attention we pay, within each issue, to juxtaposing textual and visual material, scholarly essay, and literary expression against one another. For example, in the issue on "Thinking Theory," the articles were placed, by designer Mary Kao, against black and white photographs of community activism and "practice," such as a photo commemorating the "Greensboro Five"—organizers of garment workers slain by the Ku Klux Klan in 1979 in Greensboro, North

Carolina. Distinctive formations of language and reformulations of image, often by computer, present opportunities to explore ideological differences, to trangress textual boundaries, and to present ways of seeing in alternative and multiple dimensions. *Amerasia Journal* continues to create provocative spaces in Asian American studies: presenting challenging scholarship and offering primary materials including interviews, translations, fiction, memoirs, and bibliographies in its quest to interrogate society, politics, and culture. Recent (1999/2000) volumes focused on "Satyagraha in America: The Political Culture of South Asian Americans" (25:3) and "Crossing the Color Line: The End of the 20th Century" (25:2) that focused on Detroit social philosopher and activist, Grace Lee Boggs.

Poetics of the Personal and the Political

As an editor of books on Asian American filmmaking, sexuality, and literature—and as a writer and filmmaker—I have sought to probe more deeply into what Dipesh Chakrabarty calls "interactive multiculturalism": "a politics of multiculturalism which goes beyond the usual liberal—pluralist stances of seeing the culture of public life as one and homogeneous (i.e., the dominant culture) and allowing for a politics of representation of difference by defining difference as so many instances of the same, and by consigning all problematic differences to the so-called sphere of privacy" (Chakrabarty 1996).[10]

The "Disciplining Asia" project, as this volume was initially called and conceived, thus gave me a chance to diverge, for a moment, from my role as editor of the journal to explore new ways of discussing subjectivities, especially those that dealt with the integration of private and public culture, with notions of heterogeneity and homogeneity and the politics of difference. I was eager to see whether I could find ways in which to articulate the themes I had been working on for the last decade within and outside of Asian American studies, and to form strategies by which individuals from diverse backgrounds could enter into new, dialogic spaces.[11] Moreover, I wanted to move away from the jargon-ridden language of postmodernism and to incorporate a sensuous vernacular language still capable of carrying ideas on: racialized sexuality and mixed-blood cultures; transsexuality and transnationalism; and the symbiotic relationship between the researcher and the researched, the speaker and those spoken to.

What is the relationship between the speaker and those who are spoken about, or spoken to? In a recent issue of *Amerasia Journal,* "Racial Spirits: Religion and Race in Asian American Communities," Ruth Y. Hsu describes Joy Kogawa's series of readings in Hawai'i in 1994. Instead of reading from her novels, Kogawa "switched from reading to talking with the audience. . . ." Hsu continues:

> In "performing" the literary event the way she had, Kogawa, inadvertently perhaps, had also set up the conditions for a critique of the traditional model of such events, in which information is passed on unilaterally, in which the audience is passive and the author is constructed as the ultimate law. Instead, she attempted to substitute circularity, reciprocity, and interchange. She reminded us that any artistic event is for the community and has to be done with the community. (Hsu 1996, 200)

In developing *The Eclipse of Kwan-yin and Rahu* for an academic meeting, I sought to collapse, overlap, and eclipse notions of transgendered sexuality, transnationalism, transgressive spoken dialects, and to contrast the traditional methodology of field research with the performance of the protagonists. For the formal presentation, volunteers from the audience and panel read from a prepared dramatic script. Through this strategy, the performance piece also worked in a concrete way to allow individuals to transcend their usual scripted roles as students, scholars, and to become a part of, and contribute to, a spoken word performance. My notion of community was inclusive of the mainly straight academic audience; rather than estrangement, participants and listeners were part of a new performative community during the reading and subsequent discussion. Within this performance, roles became transgressive—heterosexual, transsexual, gay, academic, actor, performer, and/or listener.

Who Is Crossing, from What, and to Where?

In discussing the making of female masculinity, Judith Halberstam states that "we are all transsexuals except that the referent of the trans becomes less and less clear (and more and more queer)" (Halberstam 1994, 212). I thus see the transgressive aspects of sexuality, and *The Eclipse of Kwan-yin and Rahu* as a metaphor for locating Asian American studies and Asian studies in a more transgressive arena. Thus, I ask the question: "Who is crossing, from what, and to where?" No longer is Asian American studies merely the "crossing" of the Pacific from the ancestral country or nation to the continental Americas—a one-way stream that excludes the island nations of the Pacific. No longer is Asian studies the study of Asia—without accounting for the global migration, settlement, and intermarriage of immigrants, and the circulatory paths of its peoples, ideas, cultures, capital, and technologies. At the same time, no longer can Asian American history be confined to the history of a Western frontier bluntly shaped by heterosexual male hands alone. The voices of women, gays and lesbians, youth, and persons of mixed racial ancestry must be included in the formation of a richer, radical, heterodox interpretation of Asian American and Pacific Islanders based not only on ideologies of "development," but on diverse iconographies of "desire" (Leong 1996).

To develop interactive ways of seeing and reading means that we must participate in formulating cultural practices at a local level, based on the recognition of human emotion, enunciation, and difference. Note the eclipse, the passing into shadow of what formerly was clear, patriarchal, linear, binary, and straight. During this moment, when the sun is eclipsed by the moon, when the sky darkens at dawn and birds fly back to their nest during daylight, we pause and grasp the potential for new roles. We may choose to transcend the roles of academic and actor or to transgress the boundaries between artist and scholar. We may choose to enunciate differently than before, to inscribe our gender and ethnicity in new ways. Creating spaces for performative communities, we cross the lines of home, history, and nation.

The Eclipse of Kwan-yin and Rahu

All characters in this piece are fictional. This is an earlier version published in *Phoenix Eyes and Other Stories* (2000).

LETA HUNTER is a transgendered, pre-op Afro-Asian American, mid-twenties. Olive-skinned, with expressive eyes and hands. A dancer's body.

DANTE WOO is a muscular Chinese male, shaved head, with a combination of rough good looks and street smarts. Artist/occasional hustler.

PROFESSOR RICHARD "DICK" KUSAI is a New York University professor of anthropology, Japanese American. Closeted, in his late-thirties. He is doing a study on sexual self-representation among Asian Americans, a comparison between straight, gay, and transgendered individuals. "Kusai" means "stinky" in Japanese—a pun.

10:30 P.M. The Cafe Mou-Mou, a popular vegetarian cafe in the East Village. The cafe is usually slow until after midnight, a few patrons talk, read books, write in their notepads.

PROFESSOR: Another ginseng tea, iced.
WAITRESS: It'll keep you concentrating on those notes!
PROFESSOR: Ah, yes. It's for a research project. Thanks. How about some of your wildflower honey?
WAITRESS: Certainly.

Through the wooden door, DANTE WOO *steps in. He is wearing a black T-shirt and baggy grey wool slacks. A small gold Buddha hangs around his neck on a red silk cord. He smiles at the waitress and she points to a table, two tables away from the* PROFESSOR. PROFESSOR KUSAI *cannot help staring at the young man.* DANTE *smiles back;* DICK *averts his head, nervously.*

DANTE: (to WAITRESS) I'll have the same thing — is it iced ginseng or loquat tea?

WAITRESS: Ginseng. You've tried the loquat. Ginseng is drier, with a bitter undertone, almost.

DANTE: Okay. And a plate of tortilla chips.

As DANTE *wolfs down the chips,* PROFESSOR KUSAI *studies the young man's face and body, noticing a tattoo on the man's forearm. It is the character "nan," meaning "man" in Chinese (the same "otoko" in Japanese kanji). The* PROFESSOR *is tempted to walk over, but instead, tears a sheet of notebook paper in half, then in half again. With his Montblanc pen, he writes: "Hi! I'm Professor Richard Kusai, New York University, Anthropology. I'm doing a survey on Asian Americans. May we talk?"*

DANTE *and the* PROFESSOR *glance at each other. Placing the paper on a small plate,* PROFESSOR KUSAI *looks directly at* DANTE, *who returns his look and reaches for the small white dish that is thrust toward him. After unfolding the note,* DANTE *motions with a nod of his head for the* PROFESSOR *to come over.*

PROFESSOR: It's brazen of me. But I couldn't help noticing you as you walked in the door.

DANTE: And why me?

PROFESSOR: Because you must be an artist, or a dancer. The way you walk and dress yourself.

DANTE: You could say I'm in the arts. I work in a frame store part time. I just frame the art, that's all. Lift heavy paintings. (He pulls up a sleeve to show off a bicep.)

PROFESSOR: I may be able to offer you a small job.

DANTE: (laughs) Whadda you think I am! I'm not lookin' for a one-night stand, man. I came in to freshen my lips.

PROFESSOR: No, you've got it wrong. I'm a professor at NYU. I am doing a study on Asian Americans — on sexuality and self-representation.

DANTE: Representing what?

PROFESSOR: Oh, it's just how people — man or woman, straight or gay or transgendered — view themselves. How they express their sexuality through speech, body language, dress . . .

DANTE: And you're doing a study on it?

PROFESSOR: Yes, so far I've interviewed about twenty people. I'm actually going over some notes now. Here's how it goes. An interview, maybe in my office—or even here—for about an hour. I ask a few questions, you get fifty dollars. You want to answer, okay. If you don't like the questions, you remain silent!

DANTE: Sounds easy enough. Am I what you're looking for? For the record, I am Asian. Asian American, whatever that is. I am sexual. And I love men. And I love women. Whomever.

PROFESSOR: Perfect. Tomorrow afternoon?

DANTE: How about meeting here? It's not busy around two o'clock.

PROFESSOR: A deal.

DANTE: How about if I bring a friend? A girlfriend.

PROFESSOR: Fine.

DANTE: Fifty for her, too?

PROFESSOR: I haven't met her.

DANTE: You'll love her. She's transgendered. Asian. Not the usual hang-ups. Beautiful.

PROFESSOR: I'll take your word for it. I'm a good sport. Now tell me about yourself, what you're doing here.

DANTE: It's personal. Maybe we can save the chit-chat for later. For tomorrow. You can ask me anything, within the hour! Besides having good taste in men, and a job at NYU, what are you here for?

PROFESSOR: I get tired of seeing all the nannies from India wheeling the white babies of those NYU professors in Washington Square. They may be liberal, but I think their ideology stops at the cradle. I come here to escape them.

DANTE: Yeah, the world is full of contradictions. For instance: what's a nice-looking man like you doing with your head buried in these notes and books?

PROFESSOR: Oh, just trying to escape myself, as academics are wont to do. When I look at you and think of my lost youth. Don't lose your . . .

DANTE: Nothing is lost, unless you let it go, man. See my Buddha—he's always reminding me that I could be reborn—better or worse. You can keep it or you can lose it, but ya gotta use it.

PROFESSOR: What do you mean?

DANTE: Tomorrow, all the answers, okay? Ciao.

The next day. The Cafe Mou-Mou.

DANTE: Dante Woo. So we meet again. This is Leta.

LETA: Leta Hunter. And you must be Professor Richard . . .

PROFESSOR: Dick Kusai, NYU. Thanks for coming. Eh, do you mind if I use this microcassette recorder? You understand that everything is confidential. And at the end of this session, I do have checks for you. A small token for your time. Let me reiterate: you are part of my universe of informants. But I look at each one of you as individuals with unique voices.

LETA: No problem. But just call me Leta and ditto for Dante here, my boy toy.

PROFESSOR: Hmmn, that's an interesting term.

LETA: He's pretty, don't you think? That pout. Those long long lashes. Those pecs. Much too pretty. That's why he's my boy toy.

DANTE: What do you think it all means?

PROFESSOR: That you two are going together, perhaps?

LETA: (laughs) We're the same sex, how could that be possible, Professor!

PROFESSOR: But as I understand it, you're transgendered, right? And . . .

LETA: And have I cut it off? No. I haven't cut it off. Yet. I just swallow it between my legs, like everything else.

DANTE: She is my spore whore—my partner in crime.

LETA: That means wherever I lay myself, my body, something sprouts up.

PROFESSOR: What do you mean?

LETA: Whatever. Love or hate. Ecstasy or whatever. But no man can leave me without feeling something primal in his guts.

DANTE: Yeah. They can't get her out of their nose for two days.

LETA: Two weeks. At least.

WAITRESS: We have a special Wednesday veggie plate. Braised eggplant, turnips, and baked brown rice. It comes with two kinds of salted pickles.

DANTE: For me, the Yokohama veggie burger and iced ginseng tea.

PROFESSOR: Give me my usual California roll, thanks. And a Diet Coke.

LETA: I'll try the special. With a mango shake. Can you add bee pollen and wheat germ?

WAITRESS: Certainly.

PROFESSOR: Tell me something about yourself, your background, Leta. What led you to want to become a female?

LETA: You can't generalize, Professor, though I know NYU is a good school. My background? First, I'm not the color you think is black.

DANTE: She considers herself the twenty-third descendent of Nefertiti.

LETA: Shush. You see, I was born in Okinawa. To a black soldier and an Okinawan woman. My father and my mother. Oliver Norbett Hunter the Third. He was handsome, with smooth black skin. Miyumi Kiya. She was beautiful, as pale as he was black, with wavy dark hair. But I wasn't raised by them. After father died, when I was around five, my mother sent me back to Oakland, and I was raised Afro-American by his sister. I haven't seen my mother since.

PROFESSOR: Do you miss her?

LETA: Sometimes I dream of her. Other times I curse her. But in real life, no. I don't have time to miss the past. I don't even know if she's alive. Do you want to see a picture of us?

PROFESSOR: Yes.

From her purse, she withdraws a small photograph of a black soldier and an Asian woman, and a boy clutching onto his mother's hand. There is part of a wall and a sago palm in the background.

LETA: This is the only photo I have.

DANTE: They were hot, babe. You inherited their looks. And intelligence. Fusion, man.

LETA: Fusion may be good for music. But it hasn't always been good for me. If it weren't for my aunt I'd be dead. She taught me to love who I was, no matter what.

PROFESSOR: Hmmn.

LETA: She told me, "God has his reasons for mixing and meddling, child. Now don't you go on messin' things up!" My skin may be smooth. No pores. No acne. But in some circles I'm too dark. In other circles, I'm too light. I got black lips and those tight Chinese eyes.

DANTE: And cheekbones. And a black ass. Men die for that. Shit, I'd trade my ass any day for that.

LETA: But baby, I have traded my ass. And look how much trouble I've gotten myself into!

PROFESSOR: Getting back to. . . . What did your aunt think of your desire to be . . .

LETA: Female? Oh, yes. My femininity, as it were. Why are you interested in the subject, professor? I'm just as curious as you are.

PROFESSOR: You're the subject, Leta. And Dante. I am just the transmitter. I listen. I record. I interpret.

DANTE: Are you gay, professor?

PROFESSOR: That's not relevant. But let's just say, for the sake of our little discussion, that I'm open. I'm exploring bisexuality. It's part of my work. Trying to define race, gender, and sexuality in terms of Freudian repression and desire. My Ford Foundation grant.

DANTE: I see. You won't cop to getting a hard on when you first saw me in the restaurant. Leta here and I could teach you a few tricks, Dick.

PROFESSOR: I'm sure you could. But getting back to . . .

LETA: Oh! I'm not what you might assume. I used to lift weights. See these muscles? *Flexes her well-toned biceps.* And I'm very well-hung. But, one day, I just decided that women's clothing and makeup were more natural for me. Even my features seemed to glow more as a woman. Sexuality is like an eclipse. Shadow over light. Moon over the sun. Interconnected electrons.

DANTE: Sexual poetry. She's an X-rated poet.

PROFESSOR: But what is a woman to you, Leta? Only a matter of clothes, makeup, drag, performance?

LETA: Only? My, but you are naive for a professor. Pay attention! My aunt, for instance. She said: "Man or woman. Either or neither. That's God's will. Who am I to interfere?"

PROFESSOR: So it didn't phase her. . . .

LETA: Listen. I went to Oakland High, West Coast. The prom. I had no date. No female, that is. That's when me and Hansel—he's Black—decided to go as a couple. My first time in drag. No one knew. No one guessed. I dressed discreetly, elegantly. High neck, but very low-backed. A long string of pearls. My hair was pulled back and tied with a matching silk scarf, forties-style. My aunt sewed it up. We looked like a couple right out of the Harlem Renaissance.

DANTE: The essence of essence.

LETA: Then we drove to Lake Merritt, under the moon.

PROFESSOR: And after that time?

LETA: I just grew into womanhood. When I used to look in the mirror, I felt raw, naked, vulnerable as a man. Especially being of mixed blood. But as a woman, I could blossom, come into myself. Despite my blood. Being a woman, I learned to touch things. My thighs. Forehead. Hair. Ears. They felt differently, as a woman. With another hand almost. I knew how my aunt or Ma felt.

DANTE: Girl, even Kwan-yin, I heard, was a man in India. By the time she got to China and Japan, she put on those jewels and robes and shaved off her little mustachio. My Ma prays to her every day.

LETA: So I started experimenting with make-up, hair conditioners, clothes. Clothes are like feathers are to a bird. They protect, warm, warn. They're delicate and dangerous. Me.

PROFESSOR: And emotionally, did you have satisfying relationships with other men? Did they know you were a man?

LETA: Some did and some didn't. Most didn't care. Front door or back door. They came and they went.

PROFESSOR: Oh, I see. But were you satisfied?

LETA: You sound like a Catholic priest—and I'm confessing!

DANTE: I bet those priests get all hot and bothered under those thick robes. They probably ain't even wearing underwear. The better to get themselves off.

LETA: Who ever is completely satisfied? I take them as they come. But I don't fake it. I am Leta. She is me. My dick—bad word choice!—is not the dividing line between male and female. Neither are my breasts or hips or my ass. Though for most folks, that's the line between heaven and earth.

DANTE: Yeah. Sometimes she is a he acting like a she.

LETA: Or a he acting like a she acting a he.

DANTE: Did ya see *Heaven and Earth,* Dick?

PROFESSOR: (flustered) I'm confused. No, I'm not. Yes, yes, I did see it. Oliver Stone, wasn't it? Now Dante, you're definitely a he acting like a he. Whew! How long have you known each other?

DANTE: Me? Why, about seven years, since she was fifteen.

LETA: Fourteen-and-a-half.

DANTE: Okay. Whatever you say, babe.

PROFESSOR: And what is your relationship?

DANTE: Then? Now? We messed around when we first met. Leta hadn't come out as a woman yet. Yep. Just two guys suckin' and fuckin.' But I lost track of her for a couple a years.

PROFESSOR: And now?

DANTE: She is my sister. My main woman. I protect her. And she protects me. I am her shaman. She is my Miss Shasha Man.

LETA: I like that, Dante.

PROFESSOR: Tell me a little about yourself.

DANTE: Not much to tell. Second generation. Born in the projects. San Francisco. Ping Yuen. Peaceful Garden housing projects. Guys used to beat the shit out of each other. I could fight men. I could whip their asses. But then I decided that loving them was better. For me. I can't speak for others.

PROFESSOR: And how did you first come out?

DANTE: I didn't come out. It just came out.

PROFESSOR: What do you mean?

DANTE: The ME out of the me, man. Fluids and juices and semen and tears and sweat exchanging and changing and charging up my world.

PROFESSOR: Can you be more prosaic? A little less poetic? More specific.

DANTE: You're a sociologist.

PROFESSOR: Anthropologist.

DANTE: Forgot! Lemme see. Hmmn. I didn't respect the other yellows who were hanging onto the arms of old white guys. Or even the young white guys, for that matter. I had more self-respect than that. So I started hanging around in Oakland. A black jazz club. Thunder Alley. I grew a beard, so I could get in the door. My first lover was black. He played bass. Man, he could seduce a sunset.

LETA: And you have loved that blackness ever since!

DANTE: Could say that I found the blackness in me. Under my yellow skin. Under these oblique lids here, here was a darker man waiting to be born. A dark man desiring a darker man. That is, until you came along.

LETA: And I did come, honey.

DANTE: Yeah. The perfect combination. The eclipse of male and female.

Friend and companion. The most beautiful being my tight eyes had ever seen. I had to put on my shades otherwise I would be blinded. I offered my body to her. Every muscle of my 150 pounds. Like burning black incense and offering black foods to Rahu, the four-armed dragon.

PROFESSOR: What's that?

DANTE: It's a Hindu god I think. Maybe Thai. Who burns in a chariot of fire. Who tries to eat the sun and the moon. Like during an eclipse.

PROFESSOR: I see.

DANTE: Me and Leta have this word chanting we do. I'm Rahu. She's Kwan-yin. Wanna hear it?

LETA: That'll be twenty bucks extra.

PROFESSOR: I see.

Before the professor can make up his mind, DANTE *and* LETA *push two empty tables together. Other patrons turn and stop talking as the two scramble onto the tabletop.* DANTE *strips off his T-shirt to reveal a solid physique. They begin chanting;* Dante *taps his booted foot on the table. The waitress rushes over but stops as the two appear to mesmerize the audience with their bodies and voices.* LETA *bends her arms in a slow, sinuous movement; in contrast,* DANTE *continues tapping the table and slowly running his hands over his throat, chest, and stomach. The two, trance-like, begin to recite, in alternating lines, beginning with* LETA:

LETA: From the thigh of Tehran,
> The moon's shadow unfurls.

DANTE: Racing to reach the belly of Calcutta,
> To touch the forehead of Bangkok.

LETA: To clasp the ears of Phnom Penh.
> Seventy-seven seconds to go.

DANTE: This is the color you think is black.
> But I am not it.

LETA: Sky darkens at dawn.
> Already, sparrows wing back to their nests.

DANTE: Sun suffers. Soothe it, soothe it.
> Walk full circle. Start a fire in the hearth.

LETA: Light flames in the temple.
> Toss roots, herbs, nuts, rice, sugar, dried almonds,
> Apricots, peaches and millet into the flames!

DANTE *jumps off the table, bends his waist, looks directly into the eyes of* PROFESSOR KUSAI, *who is sweating with excitement.*

DANTE: *If you are pregnant, remain indoors.*

LETA: Burn black incense and offer black foods.
> Appease Rahu, the four-armed dragon.

DANTE: Who burns in a chariot of fire.

 Who tries to eat the sun and the moon.

LETA: If you believe that the moon can hide the sun,

 Then bathe and chant holy hymns.

DANTE: Blow conch shells and ring brass bells.

 Fire your pistol at the sky.

LETA: Wear your shades, boys and girls.

 Race your bikes to the beach. Look up.

DANTE: This is me. Dark as you are light.

 The one you think is black.

Patrons and professor applaud. Waitresses rush over and admonish them. DANTE *and* LETA *smile and rearrange the tables.*

DANTE: So that is how Leta and I became friends. She started as a he. I lost track of him for a couple of years, but I found Leta—as a woman—later. But as I said, she and he are the same to me. The same in my eyes. I look for structure. Had I gone to school I would have been an architect, I think.

LETA: He brings out the structure in me. Like I feel like I am whole, a man and a woman fused when we are hanging out together.

DANTE: Simple. Like a temple. Or a house. A house is not a home.

LETA: Not a home unless you have a bed.

DANTE: And a window. A wall. A step. A toilet. A yard. You can't separate them. Otherwise you don't have a house.

LETA: We share a one-bedroom closet. Brooklyn.

PROFESSOR: Hmmn. Let's backtrack a bit. Now, you and Leta are just platonic friends. But Dante, tell me a bit about your relationships with other men—as lovers, friends.

DANTE: We're telling this priest here a whole lot for fifty bucks. Even if he is so damn sincere and searching so hard for enlightenment. Shit, even those Times Square booths don't give that much detail, honey. I don't think we can talk much more, can we babe?

LETA: Unless we get a little more. Rent's due tomorrow.

PROFESSOR: Well, that's the standard fee I'm paying for informants on the project. That's what was budgeted on the grant.

DANTE: So how much are you getting paid?

PROFESSOR: As an academic, nothing. Of course, I have two research assistants to process and transcribe the interviews, a travel budget, miscellaneous expenses, a computer, conference monies, that kind of thing. All standard.

LETA: Where are you going?

PROFESSOR: This is a four-city study, maybe I didn't explain. I am interviewing people in San Francisco, Los Angeles, Chicago, and New York.

DANTE: Professor Dickhead—understand we are not standard. We are boy toy and a spore whore. Or, call us Kwan-yin and Rahu Woo. We know our names. We are a team. We are talent. And we will talk no more to you before we talk to our agent.

PROFESSOR: I am sorry. You misunderstood. I can't pay informants differently, that might bias my sample.

DANTE: Cut this crap. We're not gonna sign any release form.

LETA: Forget it, Dante.

PROFESSOR: You know, I do have good intentions. My study, if published in a reputable referred journal, will help gays, lesbians, and transgendered individuals. Like yourselves.

DANTE: It will help you. I don't know how it'll help us. Will it help us get laid? Will it make money for us? Will it help our parents so they can quit their fuckin' shit pay jobs?

PROFESSOR: The academic world is really a terrain of ideas. Hardly a metropole of desire and desperation. It's hardly the street. Now, I've spent a good two hours with you. Most of my informant interviews are an hour-and-a half—at most. I have been very patient with you two. Trying to translate your—lingo.

DANTE: Lingo! Take your flat ass home, boy. Now. Fifty for me and fifty for her.

LETA: Plus twenty for our little ditty!

PROFESSOR: I'm afraid I need your social security number, address, and phone. Just fill out this release form.

DANTE *takes the microcassette recorder and throws it to the painted concrete floor where it shatters in gleaming, black plastic shards.* DICK *quickly takes out the cash he has from his pocket and places a couple of twenty dollar bills on the table.* LETA *picks them up and counts the bills.*

DANTE: Fuck you. C'mon, Leta, let's split.

The two flee into the dark night air. PROFESSOR KUSAI *morosely begins to pick up the pieces of his tape recorder from the floor.*

Notes

The author would like to thank Sharon K. Hom, Don T. Nakanishi, and Glenn Omatsu for reading previous drafts of the essay, and the Asian Pacific AIDS Intervention Team, Los Angeles, where I taught a writing workshop, for inspiring me to write on the subject of Kwan-yin and Rahu. Participants of the Disciplining Asia Symposium, especially R. Radhakrishnan, Dipesh Chakrabarty, Karen Shimakawa, and Kandice Chuh, provided sensitive and critical feedback for the performance piece.
1 See "Linkages and Boundaries Commemorative Issue—Twenty-Five Years of Asian

American Studies," *Amerasia Journal* 21:2 (1995–1996). See *Amerasia* at www.sscnet.ucla. edu/aasc.

2 See Omatsu 1989 and Umemoto 1989.

3 See "Power to the People: The Don Nakanishi Tenure Case at UCLA," compiled by Glenn Omatsu, in *Amerasia Journal* 16:1(1990), 63–159, with articles by Dale Minami, Mary Katayama, John W. Chien, M. Dick Osumi, Karen Umemoto, Don T. Nakanishi, Glenn Omatsu, and Gann Matsuda.

4 See McDonnel 1996; Kim and McClintock 1993; and Nakagawa 1995. For an update on transnationalism and Asian Americans, see Dirlik 1996.

5 See articles from the journal's early period including Ichioka 1971 and Okihiro 1973. See also Nakanishi 1973 and Chung and Valparaiso 1973. See special issues of *Amerasia*, 2:2 (1974) and 3:1(1975) on "Civil Rights and the Law," edited by Megumi Dick Osumi, with pathbreaking articles including Ling-chi Wang's "Lau v. Nichols: The Right of Limited English Speaking Students"; Judy Chu's "Prison and the Asian American: From the Inside and Outside"; and "Campaign to Repeal the Emergency Detention Act" by Raymond Okamura, Robert Takasugi, Hiroshi Kanno, Edison Uno, Arthur A. Hansen, and David A. Hacker.

Under Osumi's editorship, the Stanley Sue/Benjamin Tong debate on personality, mental health, and Chinese American culture also debuted in *Amerasia*. Volume 3:2 (1976) was a special Asian American literature issue developed by Osumi and coeditor Carolyn Yee, with selections by Lonny Kaneko, Hisaye Yamamoto, Jeffrey Chan, Paul Stephen Lim, Wakako Yamauchi, Toshio Mori, Deng Ming-Dao, Tomas Santos, Alan Chong Lau, Janice Mirikitani, Lawson Inada, and Carlos Bulosan. Volume 4:1 (1977) had historical and contemporary articles on emergent groups, including "Ameyuki-san: Japanese Prostitutes in Nineteenth Century America" by Yuji Ichioka; "Korean Nationalist Activities in Hawaii and the Continental United States, 1900–1945" by Kingsley R. Lyu; "Asian Wives of U.S. Servicemen: Women in Shadows" by Bok-Lim C. Kim; "Koreans in America: An Emerging Ethnic Minority" by Eui-Young Yu; and "Selected Statistics on the Status of Asian-American Women" by Carolyn Yee.

6 See for instance DeWitt 1978; Uyeda 1978; and *Amerasia* 6:1 (1979). See also Hellwig 1979. Special-topic issues of the journal during this period include "Hawaii: Issues and Perspectives" (7:2[1980]); "The Chinese of America" (8:2[1981]); and "The Korean American Experience: 1980s" (10:2[1983]).

7 See *Amerasia* 15:1 (1989), "Salute to the 60s and 70s Legacy of the San Francisco State Strike"; and 15:2 (1989), "Asians in the Americas."

8 Topic issues in the 1990s include "The Asian American Subject: Vietnamese, Hmong, Filipino and South Asian texts" (19:3[1993]); "The Asian Pacific American Worker: Issues in the Labor Movement" (18:1[1992]); "Asian American Panethnicity" (22:2[1996]); "Transnationalism, Media, and Asian Americans" (22:2[1996]); and "No Passing Zone: The Artistic and Discursive Voices of Asian-descent Multiracials" (23:1[1997]).

9 This volume, in expanded form, was published as *Asian American Sexualities: Dimensions of the Gay and Lesbian Experience* (Leong 1996).

10 See Leong 1990 and Leong 1991; see also Leong 1996.

11 Published creative work deals with themes of sexuality, race, and nationalism, including "Rough Notes for Mantos" (Leong 1974); "Geography One" (Leong 1993); *The Country of Dreams and Dust* (Leong 1993); "Paper Houses" (Leong 1996); and "Phoenix Eyes" (Leong 1996).

Cross-Discipline Trafficking:
What's Justice Got to Do With It?

SHARON K. HOM

—————+—————

Never does one open the discussion by coming right to the heart of the matter. For the heart of the matter is always somewhere else than where it is supposed to be. — Trinh T. Minh-ha (1989)

Locations, Disclosures, and Questions

I would like to raise some "trafficking" questions in a law register, and explore their implications for the current reassessments and theorizing of the relationship between Asian and Asian American studies, and more generally for our role as intellectuals and academics. In its general usage, "traffic" as a noun refers to commercial activity, involving import and trade; as a verb, to carry on negotiation or communication, to deal, bargain, to pass to and fro, to journey over. Lurking in the margins of the deal, is the shadow of possible illegal or disreputable activity.[1] The current circulation of "traffic" as both noun and verb in cultural studies discourses on the production and disruption of specialized bodies of (or disembodied) knowledges, also references trade, negotiation, and border crossings. With its transgressive poststructuralist appeal, this appropriation of "traffic" into cultural studies discourse, however, often elides the human exploitation and suffering that "trafficking" in a law context must account for. In a law register, trafficking calls up pervasive human rights violations and abuses of women and children, through exploitative domestic labor, bonded labor, sexual exploitation, forced prostitution, and servile forms of marriage. Yet, in light of the substantial economic profits that this human exploitation generates for individuals and national economies, the enforcement of existing international human rights norms is largely ineffective and marginal (Farrior 1997). Trafficking in a law register thus necessarily invokes structural and ethico-political questions that implicate not only the border guards of various academic disciplines, but the policing power of the state and domestic and international regulatory regimes; that is, a world beyond the walls of the academy. Like the political ambiguity of "disciplining," the discursive formulations of current cross-discipline reconfiguration debates, or discursive trafficking, thus take on a peculiar (self-)critical and complicitous resonance in law.[2]

More starkly than literary interpretation, as Robert Cover elegantly and passionately pointed out, "legal interpretation takes place in a field of pain and death. . . . When the interpreters have finished their work, they frequently leave behind victims whose lives have been torn apart by these organized, social practices of violence" (Minow et al. 1995, 203).[3] Law must answer for the violence it inflicts and account for increasing social disparities in power and resources if it is to claim institutional legitimacy, and this violence includes not only the violence of legal categorizations and the devaluation of human complexity, dignity, and empowerment as values and goals. Law's violence also includes the legitimation and enabling of daily microaggressions through administrative, legislative, judicial, social, and ideological processes and institutions. Through immigration and citizenship narratives, a system of state-sanctioned death, and an impoverished and partial vision of welfare and social security, law and legal discourses define community and belonging, dignity and survival, and life and death. In readings of immigration law and policy, race, gender, sexuality, and class, critical legal and cultural studies theorists share this recognition and social justice concerns with law's constitutive power, the ideological operations of the processes of knowledge formation, and the interrogation of geopolitical, discipline, and discursive borders across a global terrain. "In the [post]modern cultural moment of late capitalism, the work of the critic becomes trans-disciplinary and global" (Leonard 1995, 10).

At the same time, critical legal scholars working across critical race theory, Asian American critical jurisprudence, and feminism(s) are increasingly speaking in the post-accented discourses of postmodernism and post-structuralism.[4] Self-consciously adopting cultural studies postures, the work of many critical legal scholars reflects cultural studies practices such as the experiential approach of stories and narrative, the turn to textual readings and deconstruction and counter readings, and the effort to situate and theorize "texts" like cases and statutes, within precise historical and social formations (Leonard 1995). These discursive cross-discipline conversations problematize the constitutive presence of law in the formation of social relations and various academic disciplines.[5] Yet justice, however defined, disputed, or contested, is by and large not the normative referent for assessing the institutional legitimacy of other disciplines. In this essay, I build upon this constitutive presence of law already implicated across and within multiple disciplines, but I suggest that law, viewed more broadly, might generate critical insights and challenges for a more inclusive micropolitical project of social justice. By a broader approach to law, I am referring to law as an academic formation, a profession, a system of coimplicated legal institutions, and as competing legal discourses and metadiscourses that are constitutive of multiple social spheres.

In exploring the possible productive interventions that law might make to the current theoretical project of this volume, any intervention must also be situated institutionally, discursively, materially, and politically. As Arif Dirlik (1996) reminds us, in any inquiry regarding power relationships, paradigms, and knowledge production, it is *positioned* human beings who engage in the construction of the paradigms that guide the inquiry. Thus law's intervention in these discipline debates is not as an agentless abstract body of knowledge, rules, or discourses. Rather, law's intervention in this project of theorizing area/ethnic studies implicates not only the usual elite suspects implicated in knowledge production—academics, public intellectuals, theorists, and scholars—but also other nonacademic actors. These judges, lawyers, prosecutors, legislators, and activists are located within a self-regulated profession that has a specific relationship to and material impact on the lives of communities and individuals beyond the academy's walls. Law as a profession has been analyzed and explored, but with a tendency toward an occupationalist orientation and a focus on questions of stratification, hierarchy, power, and social stature. Yet "lawyers and law work are deeply imbricated within the web of class, gender and ethnic relations which structure the social world and its legal rules. This fact, of course, greatly affects the possibilities for legal work to transform oppressive social relations" (Cain and Harrington 1994, xi).

As Rey Chow has also vigilantly pointed out, the disclosure of one's location in these discursive debates, particularly for Third World intellectuals, also requires "a scrupulous declaration of self-interest" (1993). So I offer a brief disclosure of my own uneasy location in law as preface and intellectual caveat, an autobiographical riff as it were. Growing up in an immigrant family, belonging to a class of poor people, outsiders, aliens, I never wanted to be a lawyer and had no interest in law prior to my single application to one law school, NYU, because of its public interest Root-Tilden scholars program. Unsupported by empirical or experiential evidence, my trajectory into law was not inspired by any particular heroic models of radical law practice or justice. Perhaps it was an intuitive sense of the instrumentalist role of law coupled with the transformative potential embedded in the inherent contingency of any perceived order, that engendered an inchoate vision that law could be a tool for fairness, for structural change, for a transformative project of social justice. Yet, my law experience in the past two decades was and continues to be a sobering struggle to resist the deforming pressures of law practice and hold onto some vision of law as justice.

Like many critical theorists and practitioners, I have attempted in my own work to unmask law's numerous betrayals of justice, and at the same time not to give up on law's potential to be an instrument of justice.[6] In my China and human rights scholarship, I have also attempted to negotiate both the demands of an international focus and some of the domestic debates in which Asian Americans are clearly implicated. Choosing law as a professional life, I had to attempt, though never really got the hang of, a gendered, raced autoventriloquism of the languages of white masculinist power. That I am able to speak at all, and without "accent," is a source of amazement and interrogation for some law students, professors, and others whom I professionally encounter. I am also discovering that perhaps I have been cognitively rewired by my law training in ways not clearly marked or obvious, even to myself. My recent call for jury service, as a result of the institution of new rules in New York State that eliminated automatic exemptions, provided insight into this process of becoming a lawyer. During the *voir dire* (the questioning by the lawyers as part of the impaneling of a jury), I was repeatedly questioned about whether I thought I could make a judgment solely "as a juror" and not as a result of "thinking like a lawyer." I was genuinely stumped by this question. The phrases, "a juror" and "thinking like a lawyer," simply did not describe simple oppositional exclusive categories for me. After more than twenty years of struggling with the "foreign" languages of law and legal analysis, I realized that I could not honestly say whether and where the lines could be drawn. It is out of this location of collapsed and rewired cognitive borders marked by formal professional training that I would like to engage in a cross-discipline conversation with multiple academic "speech communities." Yet despite or because of my uneasy relationship with law, I find my explorations here suggesting the possible usefulness of law's intervention in these cross-discipline conversations somewhat ironic.

There are two levels of cross-disciplinary questions that interest me. The first arises from the rather limited role of law, generally, in current debates over the rapprochement or tensions between area and ethnic studies. What theoretical insights and political questions would emerge from bringing law into the project of theorizing these shifts, fault-lines, and reconfigurations in Asian/Asian American studies? What challenges might be generated by law's inclusion, in relationship to the current reassessment of the rapprochement (or not) between area studies/ethnic studies? The overarching question that informs these questions is "so what"? Would an expanded intervention by law in these debates make a difference? And to whom? What are the institutional interests implicated? What questions do these questions invoke regarding accountability, constituency, and the role of intellectuals for social justice? These questions might be understood as ethico-political questions.

By "ethico-political," I am suggesting the rescue of moral judgment from a historical modernist project of truth with a capital "T" retrieved though objective illusions. I locate "ethico-political" in a hyphenated relationship between moral philosophy and power, in the conjunction of an awareness of potential moral conflicts, the exercise of human agency to make moral judgments, and the taking of political responsibility for the consequences of these choices. This conceptual location perhaps reflects an implicit rejection of an "engineering ethics model," in which problems are presented, problem-solving is the goal of applied ethics, and problems are "solved" by subsuming the "facts" under a moral theory (Caplan 1992). That is, I am not suggesting ethics as reference to preexisting foundational standards, or guidelines. Instead, my essay concludes with a series of questions that outline an invitation to the reader to join in theorizing, generating, and acting upon frameworks that problematize the institutional contexts in which we live and work. The political part of the conjunctive project implicates the exercise of human agency to respond to distributive and equitable justice claims through the individual micropolitical choices we negotiate on a daily basis, and the constant interrogation of the complex multiple ways we empower and disempower each other.

These ethico-political concerns also raise other questions regarding the very condition of law itself at the end of the twentieth century, questions that I name under the label of (un)disciplining law. That is, law does not enter these debates as a coherent discursive or disciplining voice. Destabilized by a self-perceived professional crisis with a capital "C" and the challenges posed by a range of competing discourses and politics, law as academic discipline and as profession is undergoing its own millennial angst. I imagine other disciplines may not view destabilization or incoherence as necessarily problematic. Poststructuralist discourses would be intellectually embarrassed by a claim to such a pre-postmodernist (pre-posterous) project as a total(izing) coherence. But law is normatively accountable to justice as its rationale, and should be concerned about the increasing ethico-political incoherence surrounding its millennial crisis of professional identity and role. The potential value of law's intervention in these area studies/ethnic studies reassessments is thus as a normative intervention grounded in mining this moment of professional crisis.

The second level of cross-disciplinary questions concerns the area studies/ethnic studies debates in a law register filtered through two specific "subfield" examples. Despite claims of increasing porousness between disciplines and fields of study, the history and institutional locations, and the respective specialized methodologies engendered by different academic speech communities, Asian American studies and Asian studies have developed separate (although sometimes overlapping) agendas and concerns. In terms of academic formations, one might identify Chinese legal studies as an example of area studies and Asian Americans and the Law studies as an example of legal ethnic studies. Yet, a focus on academic formations might be too narrow to include the activist, social transformation agenda of many Asian American legal scholars, teachers, and activists. For this essay, I will use the term Asian American critical jurisprudence to refer to a growing, diverse, and contested body of Asian American legal scholarship, emerging critical legal discourses, and collective progressive political projects.[7] These two legal subfields reflect different genealogies, demographics, institutional locations, methodologies, and political projects. What are some of the consequences of these separate trajectories? Despite the increasing traffic in other disciplines focused on by current ethnic and area studies cross-disciplinary debates, and some limited "crossovers," the "traffic" between these two legal subfields is barely audible. I suggest that more interdisciplinary "raiding" and greater traffic might be usefully encouraged, but in the face of the considerable obstacles, am skeptical that much crossover activity is possible in the immediate future.

Even without arguing for more explicit traffic between these two legal subfields, or establishing that indeed these are two distinct subfields, I want to suggest that the general intervention of law into current area/ethnic studies reassessments may still produce some useful insights, questions, and reminders of the complex social roles of the academy, and expand the range of questions raised by critical voices across the self-investments of academic disciplines. This limited essay does not aim to set forth a prescriptive analysis of the questions raised here, but rather to suggest prefigurative ways that legal perspectives might challenge and enrich the conversation. In the final part of this essay, I suggest the exploration of a reconstructive agenda embedded in an explicitly ethico-political project that I refer to as "trafficking justice." This project would exploit the subversive utility of border transgressions even as it critically names the embedded privileges such valorization of transgression enables, legitimizes, and at the same time, masks. I urge the exploration of possible multiple mutual interrogations in spaces enabled by a proliferation, and subversion, of, and respect for, boundaries. This imagining of possible interventions is mediated and problematized by the coimplicated layers of disciplinary boundaries, legal professional self-perceptions, and metadiscourses. I am, however, suggesting not another master theoretical project, but the exploration of micropolitical projects in which each individual can get into the act of "trafficking justice." Borrowing from analyses of postmodern political agency (Mann 1994), I suggest that the daily choices we make as human agents in a variety of institutional con-texts—work, education, family, and politics—are concrete, site-specific opportunities for doing justice. Thus trafficking justice operates along tem-poral and spatial axes of possibilities—that is, in the here-and-now.

My primary aim is not, however, to join or contribute to merely a discursive remapping of the academic world, or even to move the polic-ing markers at the edges of discursive and institutional borders. I am not suggesting that discursive moves are irrelevant to an activist agenda. As the international women's human rights movement has demonstrated, chal-lenging and enlarging existing human rights concepts and practices has re-sulted in the gradual understanding that violence against women is a human rights violation and not simply a private matter, for example. Discursive shifts and battles are extremely critical to exposing the inadequacies of exist-ing discourses and creating new languages of power and empowerment, but as academics and critical intellectuals, we also need to foreground a human global/local material terrain, or, in Chandra Talpade Mohanty's phrase, "a material cartography," in our discursive and theoretical struggles (1991). This material cartography is marked by uneven development and underdevelopment and gross disparities in wealth, education, and health resources (UNDP 1995; World Bank 1995), ethnic conflicts and massive dis-locations of peoples (Jean 1995, Gilbert Loescher 1993; Deng 1993), per-vasive gender-based violence in family and in "public" spaces (Bunch and Reilly 1994), and environmental degradation and destruction (Brecher and Costello 1994; Sachs 1992). In the United States, there is an increasingly mean, ugly, and dangerous xenophobic spirit that is fueling attacks on poor people, on immigrants, on the environment, on women and children, and on so-called minorities (who are soon to comprise the majority of the U.S. population of the 21st century). Conservative politicians, newspapers, and anti-immigrant groups like Americans for Immigration Reform and gov-ernment agencies like the Immigration and Naturalization Service circu-late dominant narratives that scapegoat immigrants for economic problems and portray them as aliens and foreigners who freeload and drain public resources (Hondagneu-Sotelo 1995).

In the face of brutal global human realities and a vicious conservative backlash in our own backyard, academics and critical intellectuals need to remind ourselves that discursive shifts and remappings do not necessarily result in material shifts or a remapping of the micropolitical or of macropolitical systems of privilege and material power.[8] In the project of social transformation that justice demands, perhaps only a privileged few have the luxury of (and vested interest in) marginalizing these local and global material realities.

(Un)Disciplining Law and Mining
Professional Crisis

In the television show, *The Practice,* a scruffy, passionate Dylan McDermott, playing a scruffy, passionate lawyer with a small, similarly committed and appropriately diverse staff, takes on big, bad tobacco companies, hard district attorneys interested only in convictions not innocence, and tries to pay the rent. In comparison, a show that received much "serious" attention in the law reviews, and even in some law classrooms, *L.A. Law,* depicted a law firm with a committed and appropriately diverse staff that takes on big, bad companies, hard district attorneys interested only in convictions, but that does not appear to have difficulties paying rent or supporting the expensive fashion statements made by its lawyers each week. In *Law and Order,* committed and carefully dispassionate law enforcement officials and district attorneys battle to put the "guilty" behind bars. In these popular shows, the fictionalized representations of the lives of lawyers, the legal system, and the often misleadingly clear demarcations between guilt and innocence play simultaneously against the sensationalized glued-to-the-television-set appeal of televised real criminal trials, one of the most sensationalized being the O.J. Simpson trial. The American public's view and understanding of lawyers, law, and the legal profession is mediated by these media-generated and mediated fictions.[9] Yet, "of the forces that are contending for the soul of the legal profession, only a select few will be seen on prime time" (Glendon 1994, 262).

Against the backdrop of mass-mediated images of "lawyers in perpetual attack mode," or as soulless ambulance chasers, romanticized champions for justice, or literally as the devil himself, the self-perception of the legal profession today is marked by a language of crisis and discontent. Despite high salaries and powerful positions, lawyers are among the most unhappy and frustrated professionals, demoralized by pervasive professional dissatisfaction and negative public and self-images. The adoption of a technical assembly line model of legal work promoted by early industrialists, the law firms, and corporate pressure to generate billable hours, results in the degradation of law work and contributes to this high level of dissatis-faction among lawyers (Waire-Post 1994). Volumes assessing and lamenting the current state of the legal profession carry titles that echo loss, betrayal, and law out of control.[10] Instead of being simply part of the general discur-sive end-of-the-millennium business as usual, this current crisis is actually part of an ongoing professional self-reflexivity about its problematic role as a "public" calling, and the tensions between our duty to represent our clients zealously, our simultaneous role as officers of the court, accountable for ensuring the integrity and fairness of the legal system, and the complex shifting demographics of the profession and U.S. society.[11]

The analysis of this predicament facing law and the profession includes a range of perspectives regarding the causes of the crisis, the issues facing it, and what we should be doing in response. Mary Ann Glendon argues that the United States has become "one vast school of law," reflected in the culture and popular speech ("law talk") invoking a language of rights. She suggests that the problem, however, is not too much law, too many lawyers, or too much litigation, but the quality of the law produced, the way law-yers imagine their new roles, and the peculiar uses to which courts are put (1994, 272–274). David Luban and Michael Milleman have approached this crisis from the perspective of clinical teaching about ethics. They suggest that the crisis has actually been with us for perhaps fifteen years, though this one might be "The Big One," arising from a widespread perception of lost professional values and wholesale public disapproval and lawyer-bashing (Luban and Milleman 1995).

Yet amidst the debates and the sense of crisis, still, "law is ultimately a purposive and judgmental discipline, laying down rules for real people and solving real conflicts with real consequences in real time" (Kandel 1993, 21). This involves representation, a foundational concept in literary theory, that is for lawyers also both an aesthetic and a political act (Lentricchia and McLaughlin 1990, 11–22). Like the representation problematic for literature, law both "stands for" other things (justice, order, social control) and in-vokes a political process of representation in which one person, the law-yer, "acts for" other persons. Patricia Williams has identified three features of "theoretical legal understanding" as characterized in Anglo-American jurisprudence: "the hypostatization of exclusive categories and definitional polarities, the drawing of bright lines and clear taxonomies that purport to make life simpler in the face of life's complication: rights/needs, moral/immoral, pubic/private, white/black. (2) the existence of transcendent, acontextual, universal legal truths or pure procedures . . . [and] (3) the exis-tence of objective, 'unmediated' voices by which these transcendent, univer-sal truths find their expression" (Williams 1991, 8–9). Lawyering consists in large part of representing via interpretation "the best interests of the client" within the categories, processes, and institutions of existing substantive law. To put this more critically, the only way a client can get legal redress is for her lawyer to misrepresent or reduce the human complexities of the client's problem to legal fictions, or to create new fictions.

Against the largely domestic sense of professional crisis described above, there is also a reassessment of the role of American law, the legal profession, and legal education within the frame of an increasingly globalized world.[12] There are references to human rights practice but clearly the non-lucrative public interest areas of practice are not the main attractions of the professional opportunities created by globalization or the "MacDonaldization" of the legal landscape. These global visions tend to view the role of legal education as instrumentalist handmaidens of a transnational corporate order, to train the next generation of American lawyers with an understanding of global perspectives, to serve better the needs of corporate enterprise in a pluralistic and diverse world (Gordon 1994). However, as David Palumbo-Liu has argued within the project of a critical multiculturalism, "one way to understand the recent interest in diversity is to see it as a mode of managing a crisis of race, ethnicity, gender, and labor in the First World and its relations with the Third as late capitalism has fostered the uneven flow of capital, products, materials, and labor across more porous borders" (1995, 6). This warning of the dangers of cooptation and racialized conflict management presented by this kind of instrumentalist multiculturalism also provides a useful critical perspective on current globalization discourses in law.

What do the demographic characteristics of the legal profession add to this picture? First, the number of lawyers is staggering compared to the total population. Today in the United States, with a population of over 264.6 million people (1996 U.S. Census), there are over 800,000 lawyers, projected to reach more than one million lawyers by the year 2000, perhaps too many for those who can afford them and not enough for the poor and underrepresented. Second, the presence of Asian Americans in the legal profession, especially on law faculties, is a relatively recent phenomenon, and our numbers are minuscule and underscore the limits of working within/against a larger system from a minority position. Of the 800,000 lawyers in 1991, Asian Pacific Americans constitute 1.5 percent of the total.[13] Each year, the over 180 American Bar Association-accredited law schools enroll over 120,000 law students. The number of Asian Pacific American applicants to ABA law schools increased from 2.1 percent (1984–85) to 3.4 percent (1988–89) (Balaoing 1994: 8–9). A substantial percentage of Asian American law faculty have entered the profession recently: 70 percent since 1980, and 40 percent since 1986. Asian American male faculty (72 percent) substantially outnumber Asian American female faculty (28 percent) (Chew 1996, 18–19). In 1990, Asian Americans comprised 2.9 percent of the American population, but only 1.4 percent of all law faculty.

In a study of the impact of perceptions of racial identity on law school hiring programs, Yen suggests that Asian Americans are often excluded from affirmative action programs and viewed as not "true" faculty of color. In 1990–1993, the period when affirmative action programs were initiated, the success rates for finding teaching jobs for Asian Americans (13.42 percent) was much lower than for African Americans (21.89 percent) and Latinos (29.89 percent) (Yen 1996, 47). Beneath these statistics suggesting complex racialized dynamics, additional complicated debates play out across vast highly contested professional internal discourses about the direction and goals of legal education more generally.[14] For the more limited purposes of this essay, I will reference some of the various aspects of these debates to underscore the impact that institutional locations have on discursive debates and on any efforts to reframe these debates and the political projects engendered.

The ethico-political commitments of diversity, inclusion, and service that the profession is wrestling with are reflected in the legal struggles around affirmative action, diversity on law faculties and in law schools and law firms, and the demands of public service for each member of the profession encoded in model rules of ethics and conduct.[15] Although the majority of American lawyers in private practice work in small firms (fewer than six lawyers), the dominant model of law practice, education, and legal culture is the hierarchy, elitism, and profit focus of large corporate law firms, and this practice hierarchy is replicated within and between law schools (Kennedy 1983). It is precisely this professional institutional struggle to negotiate the demands of an inclusive justice that mirrors or echoes broader debates about the role of the university or the academy in today's world. When research institutions are heavily funded by corporate and government sources, the image of "pure" research institutions constituted by independent scholars in pursuit of knowledge is complicated by questions regarding their choice of research agendas as well as their priorities (Soley 1995). Law's professional and discipline crisis is thus compounded by the larger crisis that academia and intellectuals are facing or have been facing for hundreds of years. On another front, all this millennial crisis talk may also be, to borrow from Upendra Baxi's elegantly coined phrases, simply another manifestation of an epistemic epidemic, *endomania,* produced by the "philosophical cottage industries of the North" to proclaim the end of, among other endings, history, the subject, metanarratives, the author, the book, ethics, justice, human rights, and politics.[16]

86   Sharon K. Hom

Viewed within a more historicized frame, the proclamations of the end of history notwithstanding, this present crisis also has deep roots in a racist and sexist institutional history marked by formal discrimination against women and minorities by the courts, the professional associations, and encoded in substantive laws. The American Bar Association (ABA), founded in 1878, explicitly prohibited African Americans from joining. In 1873, the Supreme Court of the United States in *Bradwell v. Illinois,* 83 U.S. (16 Wall.) 130, rejected Myra Bradwell's assertion of her right to practice law, and stated "the paramount destiny and mission of woman are to fulfill the noble and benign offices of wife and mother." Since the nineteenth century, when the first Asians arrived in substantial numbers, U.S. law has served as gatekeeper and enforcer of racial stereotypes through laws imposing racial restrictions on immigration, such as the Chinese Exclusion Act of 1882, or racially based bars on citizenship. Jan C. Ting and others have exposed the anti-Asian bias in U.S. immigration law that reflects a protracted policy to exclude Asians (Ting 1995). As Gabriel Chin, Sumi Cho, Jerry Kang, and Frank Wu point out, "all Americans should be shocked to learn that naturalization rights were granted to Asians only in the mid-twentieth century; in 1943 for Chinese, 1946 for Asian Indians, and 1952 for all other Asians" (1996, 14). The detention during World War II of over 110,000 persons of Japanese descent, two-thirds of whom were American citizens, based solely on race, was found to be a "tragic wartime mistake" by a government commission that investigated the internment. Against this history of discrimination, racism, and violence against Asians, groups of Asian Americans, like the Chinese, have resisted unfair laws, brought lawsuits, lobbied the government, and organized their communities since the turn of the century (Ong Hing 1993; McClain 1996).

Thus law enters the debates around area studies/ethnic studies as a deeply troubled profession, embedded in contested internal discourses and political visions, and burdened with a less than honorable historical record in rendering justice for all members of society. Although the legal profession has failed at realizing many of its liberal ideals of access, inclusion, and civil/human rights—it is significant that these are the aspirational norms and values that the profession continues to claim as its vision for the next millennium. In a project to rethink the ethics of lawyering and to reclaim the transformative potential of law, Allan Hutchinson has described four versions of lawyering. In the traditional modernist model, lawyers as neutral super technocrats function as hired-hands, accepting their clients' values and agendas as their own. As a "proud, unapologetic and loyal defense of The Rule of Law" (1995, 771), Hutchinson argues that this image fails theoretically in its formalism, empirically in relation of the actual practice of law, and ideologically as a political defense that serves to undermine its definite ideological commitments (1995, 771). Emerging from a realist critique of law, the lawyer-as-civic engineer imagines lawyers as paternalistic and patronizing drivers on the road to civic redemption. Still a member of the Rule of Law family, lawyers-as-civic engineers function as creative constitutors who work the indeterminate relation between lawyers and clients for progressive effect (1995, 774). The skeptical anti-image of lawyering-as-lost cause views law as an inherently corrupt cooptive enterprise, and radical lawyering as an oxymoronic pursuit (1995, 776). Instead of these discredited versions of lawyering, Hutchinson argues for a postmodern vision of lawyering in which a program of progressive politics must be constantly negotiated and renegotiated, and urges the adoption of guerrilla-like tactics of utilizing different strategies and interventions at different times and in different ways (1995, 778–80).

As feminist, critical legal studies and critical race theorists have argued, in order for law to respond to complex socially situated human problems, it must be released from narrow legal fictions of objectivity and neutrality and categories that constrain legal analysis, procedure, and substantive areas of law (Crenshaw et al. 1995; Wing 1997). Law as substantive rules and processes, as a discourse of power, and as an institutional mechanism of social control, social engineering, and dispute settlement must be (un)disciplined. I suspect competing visions and self-images of lawyering will remain under negotiation well into the next century. At present, ethical lawyering suggests that each lawyer must take responsibility for the clients she represents, the causes she fights for, and the tactics she uses in working toward notions of justice that are concrete, individual, site-specific, and that engender group based empowerment (Hutchinson 1995, 782–785). The sharp moral discomfort that law is not doing well in response to the demands of justice should bleed into other academic disciplines and beyond discursive debates.

Cross Interventions: Law, Chinese Legal Studies,
and Asian American Critical Jurisprudence

At a past conference of Asian Pacific American law teachers, I was faced with the not uncommon dilemma of choosing between competing workshops and presentations: a paper on Chinese sovereignty by a Chinese scholar, and a paper on affirmative action by an Asian American scholar. As my own work has been in the field of contemporary Chinese legal studies, I finally decided to attend the Chinese presentation. Due to the small size of the group, the organizers decided to consolidate the presentations of the comparative and international papers. The Chinese scholar rushed through an outline of more than 2,000 years of Chinese history as "background" for his fifteen-minute international law argument in support of a Chinese assertion of sovereignty over some disputed islands. A Filipino scholar reflected upon his training experience in Europe and criticized the parochial and U.S.-centric tendencies in U.S. legal scholarship. I speculated silently to myself about the discussion that might have been if the speakers in the affirmative action debates in the United States were also in the same room. As a number of domestic civil rights and critical legal scholars are beginning to recognize, international human rights norms and practice are underutilized and undertheorized resources for developing domestic antisubordination analysis and strategies (Deale 1996; Hom and Yamamoto 2000).

In retrospect, this seemingly insignificant conference moment, in addition to revealing differences in style and analysis on the part of U.S.-, European-, and China-trained scholars, thus suggested more was possibly at stake than the simple logistics that diverted "international" and "domestic" discussions to separate "rooms." Although an international focus should not be conflated with area studies, nor domestic debates conflated with ethnic studies, area studies and ethnic studies both reflect to some degree perceived demarcations between the global and local, the international and domestic, even as these configurations are being reconfigured.[17] But what would further enabling such an exchange require? What would such an exchange enable? The reconceptualizations of our roles, our fields, our methodologies? Or perhaps these subfield separations are useful and necessary as an efficient allocation of critical progressive intellectual labor? These questions do not mean to suggest that there is a clear division historically between domestic and global configurations and concerns. The international history and genesis of Asian American studies has been pointed out by scholars arguing for new paradigms that locate the history of twentieth-century Asian Americans within the twentieth-century global history of imperialism, colonialism, and of capitalism (Mazumdar 1991). Don T. Nakanishi has described the ways that minority groups have historically transcended domestic political systems evidenced in phenomena such as secessionist movements, identification with the "homeland," support for antiapartheid struggles, sending goods, money, or other resources to homelands and other states, and appealing to international organizations and bodies for assistance (Nakanishi 1976). Traffic between the disciplines of area and ethnic studies, however, has been and continues to be discursively and institutionally discouraged in part by different political projects and competition for institutional resources and legitimacy.

In the following discussion, I listen to the barely audible traffic between two specific subfields of area and ethnic studies, Chinese legal studies and Critical Asian American jurisprudence, to surface possible benefits for mutual transdisciplinary raiding as well as inventory some of the considerable obstacles. This discussion is complicated by the peripheral disciplinary location of law generally within an Asian studies field largely dominated by anthropology, history, and literature.[18] Although more audible in immigration and civil rights narratives, Asian American critical jurisprudence is also a minor within the dominant American law school curriculum. So to some extent, any discussion of traffic between these two legal subfields is also about a conversation between two minors. I begin with brief mappings of these two subfields focusing on the scholars and the foci of the work, and offer some critical comparative observations.

Like the Cold War mission of area studies, Chinese legal studies also has focused and continues to focus on the provision of experts on a specific region of the world. Since China's reopening to the West in the late seventies and the ambitious economic reforms implemented since 1980, there has been a proliferation of research and scholarly work by Chinese legal studies scholars in the United States about Chinese law, economic, and political reform. Contemporary Chinese legal studies scholars have focused on legal reform and modernization in China, with a primary emphasis on constitutionalism, criminal law, private law areas such as private economic law and forms of doing business in China, intellectual property (Lee 1997; Wang and Zhang 1997; Potter 1994; and Lubman 1996), and, more recently, human rights (Davis 1995; Hom and Xin 1995; Woo 1993). Like other area studies scholars, Chinese legal studies scholars also bring their expertise to bear in arenas beyond the U.S. academy. Chinese legal studies practitioners operate as consultants and provide technical assistance on Chinese law reform initiatives, training of personnel, and development of legal exchange programs through Chinese and U.S. government, foundation, or privately funded efforts (Hom 1994). Like area studies scholars, Chinese legal studies scholars have also focused on the study of the "other" — suggesting some "distance" between the primarily non-Asian, non-Chinese "investigators," and the "native" subjects/objects of research.[19] Against an implicit narrative of situated modernity, law (read: Western democratic liberal models) operates as both a measure of progress and the referential norm for assessing the development of a rule of law.

I have argued elsewhere that research, writing, and teaching about Chinese law in the United States reflects inadequate critical attention to the gendered dimensions of each area of work; that this marginalization of gender analysis results in inaccurate, incomplete analysis of legal and social reforms underway in China; and that when used as a basis for policy formulation, it politically serves to reinforce an unjust status quo. I then suggested some not-so-scary strategies for engendering Chinese legal studies in the area of exchange work, curriculum, and research methodologies and theoretical paradigms adopted (Hom 1994). In attempting this intervention, I was in the rather illegitimate position of being a Chinese woman "native" writing on gender issues in China, that is, one who lacked the "distance" and objectivity of an "outsider." At the same time, as many Chinese feminists working in the West have noted, we are viewed by Western feminists as not truly "authentic," not Chinese, and often by Chinese women as not "Chinese," tainted by our Western training and experience. This is not a lead-in to arguments about or for authenticity, but rather is to suggest some of the very complicated negotiations that an individual critical scholar faces in attempting critical interventions that bridge different subfields from the perspective of being "inside" and "outside" simultaneously.

In contrast, in a developing Asian American critical jurisprudence, "we" are both anthropologists and native informants, as the investigators and parts of communities who are collectively the object and subject of research, theorizing, and sites of activism. In contrast to Chinese legal studies scholars generally, Asian American legal scholars are relative newcomers to the law field and are implicated in domestic political debates within the profession whether we choose or not. Within critical Asian American legal discourses, law in the formal texts and processes of law is deconstructed as an exclusionary and racist instrument and simultaneously is asserted as a source for the protection of rights. Strongly influenced by narratives of citizenship, the nation, and minoritized oppression, Asian American critical scholars have addressed affirmative action, violence against Asians, immigration history, law and policy, civil rights, and many substantive areas of law.[20] In contrast to the predominantly modernist projects of Chinese legal studies, Asian American critical scholars have drawn upon, enriched, and have been critical of critical race theory, law and narrative debates, and questioned the relationship of theory and the intellectual to communities beyond the academy. This expectation of individual and institutional accountability to a larger community resonates with the historical and political roots of Asian American studies—the activist demands for accountability and involvement in the community.[21] These concerns also resonate with the commitment of Chinese legal studies scholars who have focused on human rights work to contribute through international exchanges to Chinese legal reform efforts.

Area studies scholars in general might contribute to the understanding of the interplay between domestic and international human rights discourses and practices. Civil rights might be understood at one level domestically as referring to the rights of equality, equity, and empowerment demanded in the historical movements and social struggles of African Americans, other ethnic minorities, and women in the United States. In international human rights theory and practice, civil rights, as in civil and political rights, refers to specific rights such as freedom of expression, freedom of religion, right to be free from torture. Constrained by an international human rights regime that is largely statist in theory and practice, the primary interplay between domestic and international regimes of rights is at the level of implementation and norm building. I have argued elsewhere that this statist human rights regime needs to be reconceptualized to include other powerful actors who have impact on the conditions of human rights, such as transnational corporations, and nonstate actors such as nongovernmental organizations (NGOs). I have also argued for more nuanced and problematized attention to the contexts of human rights articulation and implementation, such as culture and language, but not as an intervention captured by current (and in my view impoverished) debates about universalism and cultural relativism (Hom 1996). In the difficult challenges of theorizing these tensions and conflicts, both Chinese legal studies scholars and Asian American critical legal theorists have useful expertise and insights to contribute to ongoing human rights discourses and debates (Hom and Yamamoto 2000).

There are several levels at which we might examine crossover activity or its lack between Chinese legal studies and critical Asian American jurisprudence: at an individual level, at an institutional level, and at a discursive level. On the individual level, there are a few scholars who cross over, and write on both Asian American issues and Chinese law (Hom 1999; Woo in press). Yet I must confess that the labels "Asianists" and "Asian Americanists" seem somewhat constraining to my (un)disciplined ears. This is not to disown any professional affiliations, but only to remark on the odd way (it seems to me) academic disciplines have of creating labels of belonging and exclusion. I think of the numerous instances in which I as a Chinese American scholar, law teacher, and human rights activist found myself in a room where I experienced myself as (il)legal interloper. Rather than back out of these foreign and often disempowering spaces, I try to listen to various languages of power and sometimes attempt to speak across these differences and tensions and raise additional questions that gesture toward the potential value of allowing oneself such destabilizing intellectual discomfort.

In terms of cross-discipline traffic at the institutional level in law curriculum, research programs, or faculty hiring, there is virtually no significant crossover between Chinese legal studies and Asian American critical jurisprudence. This may be due in part to the distinctions between the international law/comparative law programs (within which Chinese legal studies tend to belong) and ethnic studies-type courses, such as Asian Americans and the Law, and Race and the Law. The institutional commitments to both of these areas vary from institution to institution but it would be safe to say that in the overwhelming majority of American law schools, Chinese legal studies (or more broadly an international component for training law students) and Asian American and the Law courses are nonexistent. Whitmore Gray estimates that only 10 percent of U.S. law schools offer one Asian law course and enrollment is small for these courses. He cites the need for preparation in Asian languages and cultures to increase the demand and improve the quantity and variety of such courses. Gray argues as well for the preparation of students to participate in Asian legal practice, creation of an accessible and sophisticated literature about Asian law and legal systems, and contribution to the development and modernization of legal systems in Asia (Gray 1995). These arguments echo the instrumentalist ones for the inclusion of more international law and globalization perspectives and programs in the law school curriculum. Despite the initial interest and push for Asian American and the Law courses in the early 1970s developed at UC Berkeley, UCLA, and San Francisco State, these courses are also not visible or included in most law school offerings (Gotanda 1995).[22] Without adequate bases of support for scholarship, faculty hiring, or curriculum development for each subfield, the exploration of cross-discipline traffic is perhaps somewhat premature.

At the same time that each discipline maintains an apparatus of legitimation and control over its practitioners, the institutional histories of different disciplines are also marked by patterns of mutual infiltrations. Manual Utset (1995) has analyzed the ways in which economics have moved into "contiguous" disciplines such as politics, sociology, linguistics, education, and law. He identifies three forms of production across disciplines: an imperial production in which one acts as a "peer, a knower, a sayer in another discipline" (1995, 1094); interdisciplinary poaching, in which one looks to contiguous disciplines for advice, techniques, data, and new insights; and cross-discipline or joint production, which parallels a joint venture or a relational contract. Yet the impediments to this last approach, such as tenure requirements and path dependence within disciplines, make this unrealistically costly for some academics (1995, 1085). In terms of cross-discipline production between area and ethnic studies, the considerable obstacles to the creation of joint intellectual and programmatic spaces suggest that while some interdisciplinary poaching may take place, joint production and exchange is largely nonexistent and discouraged.

On the level of the individual scholar, take for example the costs of professional memberships necessary for grounding in multiple areas of specialized expertise and methodologies for a critical scholar and teacher working in law, Asian studies, Asian American studies, and women's studies. The time alone that one would have to invest in such multiple memberships would be a disincentive for anyone who wanted a life beyond an endless round of conferences. The prohibitive costs of attending several annual meetings alone, or the additional membership fees, or journal subscriptions, underscore the inherent built-in class bias and institutional hierarchies that such multiple membership and cross-border travel encode. For those for whom these questions are too insignificant, this dismissal simply underscores the privilege of material location and class, and masks the questions of just who is enabled to participate in the construction of these cross-border sites and the power of the policing mechanisms. A young untenured scholar who attempts to write across disciplinary spaces will probably also be caught between clear categories for tenure scholarship review, standards for evaluating scholarship, assignments based upon teaching expertise, or competing demands for establishing the requisite professional service record (i.e., recognition within one of these membership bodies). That is, each discipline has erected the licensing, legitimation, and control mechanisms that discourage cross-disciplinary work. Despite these obstacles, scholars continue to borrow and raid other discourses and methods and infiltrate across their own disciplines.

Yet even as we imagine greater traffic across local borders, Asian American as a hyphenated minority sign does not travel well beyond the cultural borders of the United States. Growing up in the United States, I was acutely aware of my status as a "minority," as a Chinese American, never just an American. When I was living in Beijing, I had the odd destabilizing experience of suddenly being part of the "majority." In China, where there are over fifty-six ethnic groups comprising only about 5 or 6 percent of the total population, as a Han Chinese I am part of the statistically overwhelming majority. Vis-à-vis my Tibetan friends in China, I was uncomfortably not only a Chinese American, but also a member of the ethnic group that was controlling and oppressing their people. What Eric Yamamoto (1995) calls simultaneity, in which we can be both victim and perpetrator of racial oppression, takes on another layer of complexity and complicity in the transnational field.

Trafficking Justice

In this brief essay, I have explored the intervention of a broader institutionally and discursively situated conception of law into the current debates regarding Asian/Asian American studies, the intervention of Asian

American critical jurisprudence into law, and the barely audible cross-interventions between Chinese legal studies and American critical jurisprudence. Yet ultimately we must come back to my earlier "so what?" that calls forth a host of ethico-political challenges. What is the point of these discursive interventions? Manuel Utset asks, "If all academics were to step out of their disciplines at the same time, what would they step into?"[23] It seems to me this question might be reframed thus: what are the purposes of these boundary transgressions? What values are embedded in these formulations? If transgression were itself valorized, does this lead to greater human empowerment and/or the amelioration of the terrible human suffering and pervasive injustice in the world? Does the valorization of transgression also suggest the valorization of fluid subjectivity and cultural world citizenship? Who is (can be) included in this new citizenry? What is the nexus of local/regional citizenship? What are the embedded material conditions that limit, shape, and enable these transgressions and applications for multiple citizenship? Ultimately, whether drawn by a nation-state, the law, or the disciplinary guardians of the academy who preside over what constitutes legitimate crossing, and determines the value of border transgressions, the response to borders must be more than the granting of travel visas to those powerful, rich, chic, or clever enough to play the fields.

In warning against the dangers of a vocabulary of infinite interpretations underlying the allure of postmodernism and poststructuralism, Sau-ling Wong points out that "the infinity of layers of self and community inevitably shrinks when one attempts to translate the claim into reality" (1995, 12). That is, time and energy are infinite and political struggles are defined in terms of national borders and across international borders, or, as an international women's human rights slogan suggests — think globally, act locally. In cross-discipline and antipolicing debates, perhaps it is also necessary to be wary of uncritically embracing borderlessness. Since transgression is very much in poststructuralist vogue, the notion of accepting and working within limits goes against the grain of the discourse of limitless possibility posited by postmodernism. Yet, this tension between limits and borderlessness plays out along complex race, class, and ethnic lines.[24] One example of this in law is a tension between rights-based discourses as a discourse of limits (e.g., limits of state power in relation to the individual, or limits of each individual's power in relation to other individuals to the society), and communitarian discourses viewed as a discourse of possibility, marked by a suspicion of formal rights (Williams 1991). It is perhaps not coincidental that disenfranchised and disempowered groups feel more comfortable demanding the protections of rights, that is, invoking a discourse of limits. As Patricia Williams observes, "one's sense of empowerment defines one's relation to the law, in terms of trust/distrust, formality/informality, or rights/no-rights ('needs')" (1991, 148).

In law, critical Asian American scholars and activists have offered markers for individual and collective empowerment.[25] Maggie Chon (1995) has written eloquently of the need to tell our stories and in doing so creating the space for empowering ourselves and others. Robert Chang (1993) proclaimed an Asian American moment and called upon Asian American scholars to produce a distinctive body of scholarship that "speaks our oppression into existence . . . [and] by so doing creates an opportunity to erase this oppression" (1245). Mari Matsuda (1995) urges a jurisprudential method of "looking to the bottom," grounding critical legal theory in the real experiences of oppression, and asking the "other question" to discover our responsibility and complicity for gender-, race-, and sexuality-based oppressions of others and to build coalitions across differences. Keith Aoki (1996) cites Angela Harris's call for a "chastened Reconstruction scholarship, that reflects both sophistication and disenchantment, that commitment to building intellectual structures that are strong, complex and capacious, sound, and knowledge that reason and logic alone will never break down the barriers between ourselves and those we seek to persuade" (Aoki 1996). Drawing upon the work of critical race theorists and the experience of grassroots coalition building, Eric Yamamoto (1995) suggests a commitment to interracial justice as a way beyond the traditional bipolar black/white paradigm of race relations. In light of the changing demographics and the complexity of power relations among racial groups, Yamamoto argues that interracial justice moves us beyond legally defined notions of racial justice and histories, and particularizes contemporary interracial conflict and healing (Yamamoto 1999). The project of interracial justice thus avoids highly abstract universalized notions of justice, decenters "whiteness" as the referent for determining racial group identities and relations, and clears space for fresh examination of complex race relations amid changing demographics (1995, 33–37).

The work of activist Asian American lawyers like Julie Su also underscores the transformative potential of engaging in the difficult work of coalition-building across race, class, and ethnic lines. Su has spoken powerfully of her experience as a lawyer for Thai and Latino workers in the sweatshops of El Monte, California, workers who were forced to work for about 60 cents an hour during 18–20 hour days under substandard conditions and who suffered daily abuse and harassment. She suggests that we struggle to work in coalitions even though it's often difficult, painful, nasty, and contentious, because coalition-building work "shows us who we are, lets us define ourselves, and challenges us to be more than we thought we were." [26]

She challenges critical theorists to make their work accessible without compromising its integrity, to send the work to not just one another, but to community and legal activists, to develop theoretical bases and research for court arguments and foundation proposals. Her call to theorists for "translations" of theoretical projects into useful tools for front-line activism, such as sound bites, media pieces, press releases, position papers, summaries, indices, and community education flyers identifies some contributions that activist scholars might make in daily struggles against human exploitation and suffering.

An effective example of such activist scholarship by Asian American law professors is the collaborative project by law professors Gabriel Chin, Sumi Cho, Jerry Kang, and Frank Wu, *Beyond Self-Interest: Asian Pacific Americans Toward a Community of Justice, A Policy Analysis of Affirmative Action* (1996). Located at four different institutions, they bring different styles and perspectives to bear on developing a critique of attacks on affirmative action by exposing the weaknesses, fallacies, and ideological agendas of so-called merit-based approaches, the gratuitousness of colorblindness in an era of judicial retrenchment, and the model minority myth. As important as the content of the analysis are its framing and presentation in clear, accessible terms, the identification of concrete ways in which it could be used in a range of settings, and the circulation of the policy paper beyond the limited law review readership through the internet and to broader community audiences.

These voices that reflect an emerging critical Asian American jurisprudence point not to *a* way, however, but to multiple ways simultaneously. These markers set out by Asian American activists, lawyers, and scholars do not suggest the building of a monolithic edifice, activist movement, or a vision of a project for hegemonic justice (a political oxymoron). Rather, they suggest the rich strands of struggle, thinking, and work that Asian Americans can draw upon, and are engaged in. Rather than calling for an Asian American critical political project or a single project invoking some grand master narrative even if claiming hybrid heterogeneous complexity, we need to figure out ways to support multiple projects, making necessary judgments and knowing when not to judge. To these multiple voices, I add this modest intervention: the suggestion of a micropolitical project that I call "trafficking justice," a project that is prefigurative, performative, and ethico-political. By gesturing toward practices that envision alternative power relations and that articulate new social meanings, trafficking justice is prefigurative (Cain and Harrington 1994, 8). In the sense that "the performative says and does, saying what it does by doing what it says," it is performative by saying and doing justice, through discourse and praxis (Douzinas and Warrington 1995, 221). Enabled by postmodernism's project of multiplicity, this trafficking justice project hopefully may also engender "a multiplication of justices" arising from multiple social spheres, such as the communal, the economic, the cultural, and the civic (Murphy 1991, 124).

In this project of justice, law has a role—those of us in the legal profession have a challenge to mine our moment of professional crisis and take the self-critical reflections seriously. We are part of a profession that is being pushed from within and without to reimagine who we are, who we can become, and how we can move toward a more just, inclusive society. If lawyers are "the enlisted guardians of the *status quo*," is ethical and radical lawyering "merely oxymoronic in its expression or actually moronic in its aspiration?" (Hutchinson 1995, 773; 769; emphasis in original). After more than sixteen years of being part of a special committed public interest law community at CUNY School of Law, I have come to realize that attempting to build institutional alternatives that would seriously accept the challenges of transformative lawyering is frustratingly limited, less by the nature of the enterprise as by the selves we bring to the enterprise. Instead of acceptance of a dead-end nihilism, radical lawyers can be both deconstructive pessimists and reconstructive optimists, who accept and utilize enduring indeterminacy and inescapable politics for progressive ends. In the present, lawyering can be an occasion for resistance through empowerment, and must remain piecemeal, situated, responsible, and humble (Hutchinson 1995).

Yet it is not only lawyers, law teachers, and judges who are called to do the work of justice. Everyone can get into the act of trafficking. Vassilis Lambropoulos proposes a definition of justice not as the eternal truth to be revealed, but as "a valid account to be rendered" (1996, 873). "Justice is the reinstitution of proportional (as opposed to Hegel's symmetrical) reciprocity where an inequitable and unrepresentative apportioning has occurred" (1996, 874). Justice is a task for each of us irrespective of the "fields" we find ourselves in. By appropriating "trafficking," a noun and verb of abuse, exploitation, and violence, and reenvisioning it as metaphor for a prefigurative vision of justice, everyone can traffic justice. Struggling against oppression and subordination shaped by the dynamics and ideologies of gender, race, ethnicity, and sexualities may take place in myriad micropolitical arenas of social life. At the level of micropolitical struggle, each individual can negotiate and create the community conditions, the institutions, the relationships, that are fair, nonviolent, respectful, and that honor each person's place in the multiple communities to which each of us belong. At the institutional level, within our educational institutions, in the marketplace, and the workplaces inside and outside the home, each one can work to make these institutions breathe justice. I recognize these suggestions encode a valorization of substantive norms and value choices, such as peace, economic justice, and respect for the natural and human world. Yet one lesson that international human rights debates and practice suggest is that avoidance of the hard tasks of making value choices in the name of inclusiveness or cultural relativism runs the risk of masking a moral bankruptcy.

Clearly, what is at stake is more than a discursive rewriting of the world that creates new intellectual capital for career advancement for an elite. Ethico-political accountability thus also invokes an affirmative governance aspect along the lines of Lambropoulos's proposed reorientation of the humanities under the name of nomoscopy (from the noun *nomos,* customary practice, and the verb, *scopein,* to examine closely). Urging the political urgency of theory beyond deconstructive fatigue, Lambropoulos suggests that nomoscopy challenges us to become constructive legislators again, to participate voluntarily in governance, to envision how a community should be "democratically assembled, organized, and run—in the here and now" (1996, 853–879, 878). Reclaiming the moral urgency of theory, we might move beyond oppositional stances to respond to the suffering, inequities, and injustice that surround us in whatever ways our intellects and hearts teach us. Some days, I simply despair that one cannot act without doing more damage in the world. It is very difficult to act consistently. These micropolitical questions of reconstructing justice may not necessarily be the questions that formal intellectuals ask across different disciplines, but these should be questions that we ask as ethical beings in the world.

I am always struck that when I do women's rights or human rights training workshops, as opposed to academic presentations, the piece that touches and makes immediate connections with the audience is this attention to the micropolitical. Across class, race, language and cultural differences, I often talk about raising a teenage son as a single mother and how I see this as an opportunity for micropolitical struggle against racism, sexism, and the incredible violence that splatters across video games and movies, and I say how this struggle is teaching me that humor, patience, and love are possible and necessary. And I see eyes and smiles, nodding heads, embracing the numerous questions that I cannot answer. The details and micropolitical negotiations of daily living may not have the cachet of postisms (poststructuralism, postmodernism), but they are the human instantiations of oppressive discursive formations that critical interventions seek to dismantle.

In an analysis of the difficult ethical questions raised by the allocation of organs for transplantation, Caplan suggests fairness in distribution requires critical attention to the reasons (criteria, policies, and procedures) for the present distribution, the values reflected, the means for challenging existing distributions (Caplan 1992, 158–77). In the stark context of who gets, say, a heart transplant—who gets to live and at what costs—the accountability for distributive consequences is frighteningly unmediated. We need to figure out ways to reach beyond the often mediated realities that numb us and ask questions that might get to the heart of the matter of living. What are our daily relationships with our colleagues, students, family, and friends—relationships that all encode the negotiations of power and privilege of macropolitical struggles? What are the working conditions for the support staff who enable our intellectual production as academics? What is the impact of our academic institutions on the surrounding or larger communities around them? Are our academic institutions slum landlords? What are our institutional pension funds investing in to the tune of billions of dollars to ensure the security of our retirement? In what ways can we encourage and nurture our students to intervene in the various communities of which they choose to be part? How do we balance the different demands and priorities of "teaching" versus "research" and revalue the teaching enterprise? In the face of pervasive cyber video street violence, how are we raising our children? What are we eating? What are we throwing in the garbage cans? Whose backyard is the garbage dump for the toxic remains of the day? Simple questions. Difficult questions. Material questions. Questions that invoke challenges to a throwaway society created by consumer capitalism. Questions we ask to get to the heart of social justice, to traffick justice. Paraphrasing Marian Edelman Wright that service is the rent we pay for living, ethico-political engagement with our times is also the rent we pay.[27] Indeed, there is no free lunch.

Notes

I thank my colleagues and friends, Penny Andrews, Keith Aoki, Bob Chang, Pamela Goldberg, Ruthann Robson, and Eric Yamamoto for their helpful comments and suggestions on drafts; Russell Leong for his support and encouragement for this project; Lisa Carbone for her calm secretarial assistance; and Kandice Chuh and Karen Shimakawa for their critical editorial input, and much patience and prodding. I dedicate this essay to my CUNY law students—for their many gifts of the heart and mind, and for their struggles to breathe justice.

1 See *OED* 1989, s.v. "traffic."

2 While referencing or invoking academic disciplines as sites of theorizing work/crossings, the "ing" of disciplining invoked by the original title of this collection encodes many other questions. Are we bringing to the surface further enclosures or demarcations, as in a disciplining act? Are we suggesting the limits/resistance to act(s) of disciplining? The locution "disciplining Asia," in a law register also invokes geopolitical power

moves at the juncture of human rights and trade policy, usually with human rights as pawn and hostage.

3 Cover was specifically referring to the violence of judicial interpretative acts, but his analysis of the relationship between the violent side of the law and interpretation and rhetoric is relevant here for its reminder of the human suffering caused by any interpretive act.

4 During the late 19th century, founders of modern legal education like Christopher Columbus Langdell aligned law study with "science" in attempts to establish legal expertise as an objective, rigorous, and scientific field. The recent cultural studies turn of many critical legal scholars to embrace the very humanities disciplines that this early institutional genesis rejected is thus somewhat ironic.

5 In addition to law's constitutive presence, as law and society scholars have suggested, there has been a long tradition of interdisciplinary approaches to law, beginning in earnest with the empirical studies of legal realists, and the interest of anthropologists, political scientists, and psychologists in rules and norms, legal decision making, deviance, and social control (Abel 1995).

6 I reflect upon this trajectory toward and away from law in *(Per)forming Law: Deformations and Transformations* in Hom (1999). I suggest a number of my starting premises regarding law as disciplinary formation and as a political (transformative) project. Drawing upon personal narratives, I deploy polyvocality and cross-dressing as both metaphor and as strategy to suggest the transformative possibilities in a life in-/outside of law.

7 Some other terms that are used to refer to this body of work are Asian American legal studies or scholarship, Asian Americans and the Law, and Asian American jurisprudence. As a comprehensive survey of the Asian American legal scholarly literature is not my goal in this limited essay, I focus on the critical strands of this body of work as theoretical resources for social transformative strategies.

8 I have also attempted to address cross-cultural linguistic and political translation issues embedded in international and local women's human's rights work in the development of a Chinese-English lexicon (Hom and Xin 1995). By micropolitical, I am referring to an individual, local level of analysis. Some examples are the daily human negotiations and interactions in the home, the outside workplace, and in multiple communities of belonging.

9 A large body of legal literature examines popular conceptions of law in literature, films, and the media. See for instance the special symposium issues, "Symposium: Popular Legal Culture," *Yale Law Journal* 98 (June 1989) and "Symposium: Picturing Justice: Images of Law and Lawyers in the Visual Media," *University of San Francisco Law Review* 30 (Summer 1996).

10 See, for example, *The Lost Lawyer* (Kronman 1993), and *The Betrayed Profession* (Linowitz 1994).

11 In the area of ethics teaching in law (an oxymoron for the more cynical), there have been ongoing calls for more integration of the teaching of professional responsibility throughout the law school curriculum, and a more rigorous attention to the twin obligations lawyers owe as officers of the court to the administration of justice as well as lawyers for clients. See *Symposium Proceedings: Teaching and Learning Professionalism* (1996).

12 While globalization can mean many different things in different contexts, it may be useful to begin with a working definition of globalization as encompassing complex, dynamic legal and social processes that can be intensely local or regional, but processes that are not necessarily synonymous with universality nor homogeneity (Aman 1993, 1).

13   The statistics follow the terminology (e.g., Asian Pacific American, Asian American), of the articles cited.

14   For example, to look briefly at the legal education perspective, the Section of Legal Education and Admissions to the Bar of the American Bar Association (ABA) implement the ABA accreditation standards. These standards and the accrediting procedures have been subjected to increasing professional criticism and legal scrutiny. See "Symposium on Accreditation," *Journal of Legal Education* 45:3 (September 1995): 415–456. Law school deans have criticized the process and the standards as "overly intrusive, inflexible, concerned with details not relevant to school quality . . . , terribly costly in administrative time as well as actual costs to the schools" (415). Furthermore, the ABA has had to defend itself in investigations by the Antitrust Division of the Department of Justice for possible anticompetitive effects that flow from the accreditation process and standards. On June 27, 1995, the ABA and the Justice Department entered into a consent decree that requires the ABA to reexamine its standards and interpretations regarding faculty teaching loads; leaves of absence; the calculation of the faculty component of the student-faculty ratio; physical facilities; the allocation of resources by the law school or its parent university; and bar preparation courses.

15   The Bylaws of the Association of American Law Schools §6–4c states that "a member school shall seek to have a faculty, staff, and student body, which are diverse with respect to race, color and sex." The stated reasons for affirmative action hiring include remedial action for underrepresentation, remedial action for past discrimination against persons of color, and the provision of role models for students of color. Yet Asian Americans have been excluded from these initiatives (Yen 1996, 40–41).

16   Upendra Baxi, "The Unreason of Globalization and the Reason of Human Rights." Revised paper version of the First A.R. Desai Memorial Lecture delivered at the University of Bombay, 7 February, 1996. On file with author.

17   See for example the colloquium on LatCrit theory that explores the productive interventions that LatCrit theory might make to international human rights discourse and practice and the strategic value and insights that an international move will have for domestic anti subordination struggles. *Inter-American Law Review* 28:2 (winter 1996–97).

18   As attendance at the annual meeting of the main professional body, the Association for Asian Studies, indicates law professors and scholars are definitely in the minority. For example, at the 1997 Annual AAS meeting, registration by discipline reveals that out of a total paid registration of 2,715, twenty (20) were in law. This small number can be compared to the numbers registered for history (585), literature (315), political science (200), and anthropology (198). 1997 Annual Meeting Report. *Asian Studies Newsletter* 42:2 (spring 1997): 39.

19   I should note, however, that with the growing number of Chinese scholars trained in the PRC who stay in the United States after a visiting scholar's stint or after completing advanced degree work, there appears to be a growing body of collaborative work between U.S. and Chinese legal scholars as well as publications in English-language law journals by Chinese scholars. It will be interesting to follow the development of these collaborations and mutual influences.

20   The body of scholarship is growing so fast and is so extensive that a bibliographic project is in progress, led by Julie Lim, as part of the development of shared resources for the Fourth Annual Conference of Asian Pacific American Law Professors, 10–11 October 1997, hosted by CUNY School of Law.

21   This is not, however, to suggest a monolithic critical jurisprudence or literature. Within

emerging Asian American law literature, there are also tensions and intense debates about ideology, politics, identity, methodology, and our roles. See for instance Jim Chen's response to Robert Chang's call for an Asian American jurisprudence (Chang 1993). Chen accuses Chang of racial fundamentalism and offers a vision of a Creole Republic, formed through multiracial families as the key to racial conflict (Chen 1994). This article reads as an example of neoconservative "tough love" and backlash, and provoked a whole colloquy of intense reactions, joined by a response from Chen (Aoki 1996).

22   With the resurgence of law student activism, however, demands for greater inclusion of Asian American perspectives, courses, and faculty hiring, it remains to be seen what impact these interventions will have. Law students have initiated campaigns for faculty hiring at Columbia, Harvard, and other schools, organized Asian American jurisprudence courses, or contributed to the organization of clinics (Leong 1994).

23   Utset suggests that the boundaries between academic disciplines help to identify particular issues and provide a confine from which to deploy modes of knowledge to address these issues. He argues that we need a notion of boundaries as stepping stones to get a better view of both what lurks within and without academic disciplines. "Back to School with Ronald Coase." *Boston University Law Review*: 1096.

24   For example, in her analysis of denationalization, the easing of culturalist nationalist concerns, and the growing permeability between Asian Americans and "Asian Asians," Sau-ling Wong (1995) has pointed out that we need to be careful of the dangers of decontextualization, the erasure of class in the privileging of transnational mobility, and the glamorization of nonpolitical stances.

25   I have learned from so many of these scholars that naming a few runs the risk of leaving out many. I trust that my many acknowledgments of their work through the years will stand in addition to these citations.

26   After the eighty Thai workers and about seventy Latino workers were freed, they filed a federal civil rights lawsuit against the manufacturers and retailers for whom they sewed, including Dayton Hudson, Miller's Outpost, Montgomery Ward, and B.U.M. Equipment. After two years of litigation, the suit was settled in 1997 and five manufacturers and retailers paid the workers over $2 million. Remarks of Julie A. Su, Critical Race Theory Conference Plenary Session: "Critical Coalitions." Yale Law School, 13 November 1997.

27   A graduate of Yale Law School, Marian Edelman Wright is the first Black woman admitted to the Mississippi bar and is the founder of the Children's Defense Fund.

II   TRANSLATING KNOWLEDGE

Notes toward a Conversation
between Area Studies and Diasporic Studies

DIPESH CHAKRABARTY

Arjun Appadurai recently suggested that postcolonial and post-Orientalist studies of non-Western societies conducted in the United States have a crucial role to play in developing a self-reflexive liberal education that does not simply reproduce the Eurocentric assumptions of "old" liberal political philosophy. He writes: "More [of diversity in curricula] may be better, but it is not good enough. It is not good enough *for the university* unless the commitment to diversity transforms the way in which knowledge is sought and transmitted" (1996a, 26, original emphasis). For, as he puts it, "the cosmopolitan self which is the object of humanistic pedagogy is tied up with a series of political, cultural, and social assumptions that might cause unease among some of us in an era in which liberalism has to be critically reconstructed and not just passively enjoyed" (33). This essay may be read as an extended commentary on Appadurai's remark, but I have a more limited focus. The task of how liberalism may be critically reconstructed is addressed here mainly from the point of view of those scholars who have some autobiographical ties to South Asia. In thus limiting my focus, I do not in any way intend to deny the value—to this discussion—of the critical and committed scholarship of those who study a non-Western area without having any prior autobiographical ties to it; witness the conversation being carried out in journals such as *positions: east asia cultures critique, Public Culture,* and *Social Text.* I acknowledge it to be a serious limitation of this essay that it does not have a wider and more general focus. I hope it will be read as a first tentative step toward a more wide-ranging conversation.

Appadurai's ideas could not be more apt, in part because the origins of area studies in this country go back to certain issues in the history of

American liberal education, and Appadurai's suggestion nicely revisits that site of origin and yet spirals out from it. After all, "area studies" arose in the United States as a response to the question of what might constitute general/liberal education for Americans in the postwar period. The question itself arose from an American reading of an older connection between liberal education and empire. The United States, it was argued, could not take over the global responsibilities of Great Britain without possessing an enlightened citizenry. In his preface to a Social Sciences Research Council pamphlet (Hall 1947, 1), Wendell C. Bennett of Yale University cited John Stuart Mill's advice about the imperial British needing to destroy their own provincial attitudes by " 'frequently using the differently colored glasses of other people' " and asked: "Is not there a similarity in our own position today? Do we [not] need 'those differently colored glasses' to live wisely in our new 'one world'?" Area studies were critical to this effort of "general education." As Milton Singer (1976, 193), the noted South Asianist from the University of Chicago, once said, discussing his colleague Robert Redfield's contributions to the development of "area studies": "When we have carried on long and intensive study of the economics, government, sociology, history, and arts of Russia, China, India and Latin America . . . then we shall have in our understanding of these other parts of the world a basis for general education comparable with what is provided by our knowledge of Western Europe and some of its offshoots." Redfield himself defined this "general education" as something that helped "the mind and spirit of each one of us be liberated from the narrowness of the particular into the interests and excitements of the general" (Sartori, forthcoming).[1]

The older concept of a "general education" spoke to yet another idea gaining in popularity in the 1940s: that of a "universal social science." At a conference on the study of "world areas" in 1948, Charles Wagley of Columbia University defined the intellectual objective of "area studies" as the development of a "universal social science" that would be cognizant of "cultural differences" (Social Science Research Council 1948, 7–8). A certain kind of Eurocentrism, however—or even an idea of "white supremacy"—was never far from this conception of a universal social science. Consider the following quotation from J.C. Furnas with which Redfield, an ardent advocate of area studies, closed his well-known 1953 book on "the primitive world":

> For generations the western world has bitterly blamed western man for the crime of not understanding the savage. It never seems to occur to anybody that, other things being equal, it could be equally fair to blame the savage for not understanding western man. Since that would obviously be absurd, the two sets of cultures are unmistakably on dif-

ferent levels, a statement that can be made without specifying higher and lower. Western man has something which neither the preliterate nor any of his ancestors possess or ever did possess, something that imposes the privilege and complicating duty of intellectual integrity, self-criticism, and generalized disinterestedness. If there is such a thing as the white man's burden, this is it. (Furnas 1937, 488)[2]

What made these Eurocentric assumptions invisible was in part the fact that area studies were still a matter of studying cultures that were considered "foreign." Postwar immigration of Asian professionals and peoples into the Western democracies, as well as the impact of postcolonial nationalisms in the politics and production of social science scholarship in the Asian countries themselves, have fundamentally altered the scene of area studies. Many scholars dealing today with cultural practices of peoples in and from Asia have lived and complicated relationships to their objects of study. Recent debates over the very status of theory itself—in effect, a reexamination of the project of a universal social science, what Furnas described as the "white man's burden"—have given rise to two propositions somewhat in tension with each other: (a) that Asia (or the non-West generally) is not exotic and can be studied with the same set of tools as those with which we study European formations; but also (b) that the existing theories, while indispensable, are often inadequate in that their Eurocentric and masculinist biases need to be contested and challenged. Contemporary journals such as *positions: east asia cultures critique, Public Culture,* and *Social Text* exemplify this double concern with the need to avoid both exoticism and Eurocentrism in studying areas that may be broadly regarded as non-Western. Tensions between nationalist scholarship back in the Asian countries and scholarship produced in the Asian diaspora in the West, by contrast, have given rise to debates about "location" (as exemplified in the debates over Aijaz Ahmad's book *In Theory*).[3]

In other words, the field is now complicated enough to encourage a critical discussion of its inheritances, including the legacy of liberalism. That is why Appadurai's call for such a discussion is timely. To facilitate a focused and coherent discussion, however, and for reasons of familiarity, I will in the main stick to the area of South Asian studies, but I hope that the argument I develop will have a more general import.

Bilinguality, Transnationality, and the Politics of Location in Area Studies: The Case of Subaltern Studies

I will use the example and experience of the Indian series *Subaltern Studies* to illustrate some of these tensions, as well as to discuss—at the very end of this piece—the possibilities that exist for productive conversations between a project such as *Subaltern Studies* (which is a mutant of area studies) and theoretical-empirical positions that arise from one's engagement with diasporic life forms. An anecdote highlights the discontinuities in the various reading communities within which *Subaltern Studies* circulates. A review of the American anthology *Selected Subaltern Studies* (1988) edited by Ranajit Guha and Gayatri Chakravorty Spivak was published in the respected Indian journal *Contributions to Indian Sociology*. It was written by Sujata Patel, a well-known Indian historian then based in Delhi. Patel made the point in her review that while it was a welcome development that Oxford University Press should now endeavor to "introduce *Subaltern Studies* to the American audience," the introduction by Gayatri Chakravorty Spivak did not add much "substantially to the volume." She went on to express the hope that "American readers [would] be shrewd enough to proceed [beyond the introduction] . . . in spite of the heavy demands of reading through Chakravorty Spivak's somewhat tendentious, pedantic and abstruse prose" (Patel 1990, 137–38).

Leaving aside the question of how she read Spivak's "Introduction" to *Selected Subaltern Studies,* Patel, one can say in hindsight, could not have been more wrong. "American readers" did not do what Patel thought they should. Most North American scholars, particularly those constituting the reading publics in university and college English departments, read only Spivak and ignored the rest of the volume for quite some time. The best-known contribution of that volume to seminar-speak for a long time remained the phrase "strategic essentialism." This, I must make it very clear, was not by any means Spivak's fault—if anything, one can safely attribute the later popularity of *Subaltern Studies* in the U.S. academy to a whole constellation of forces among which Spivak's own energetic advocacy on behalf of *Subaltern Studies* must be given a very prominent place. The anecdote refers us to the problem of different reading communities. In the United States Spivak was a larger presence than the rest of the volume; in India, for reasons beyond anybody's control, her work did not have the same appeal. We can even surmise from Patel's comments that the two reading communities did not intersect, not at least at that time. Of course it remains possible that Patel later on realized how far off the mark her initial reactions were. I simply use the episode to point to the very different locations that both Spivak (herself an icon) and *Subaltern Studies,* the series, enjoy in India and the United States.

Subaltern Studies is marked by certain noticeable processes of both globalization and localization in its operations. It is a series that comes out of Delhi; in fact, in the past the editorial collective has resisted invitations by U.S.-based publishers to (re)locate it in the United States. Within India, however, critics often label it as "NRI" (or nonresident Indian) scholarship.[4] Yet the editorial collective of the group has steadfastly refused to give much prominence in the pages of *Subaltern Studies* to issues that concern South Asians in the Western democracies, primarily to retain the claim that *Subaltern Studies* is about South Asia. What kind of South Asia? The South Asia we live in? The answer is complicated, for the production of *Subaltern Studies* is, whether or not we like it, transnational: the editorial board is distributed over four continents—Europe, North America, India, and, until very recently, Australia. Even the India-based editors are sought-after visitors to universities around the world. Lately, there have been links formed with Sri Lankan scholars and one can visualize similar forging of links with scholars in other countries of South Asia. Within India, *Subaltern Studies* has, on the whole, led a contested existence. Many prominent feminist groups have been critical of it (while some equally prominent feminists are now on the editorial collective); many Marxists have criticized the series on account of its intellectual proximity to the currents of poststructuralist and postmodern thought; nationalist Marxists of an older generation have seen in it the work of fads and fashions when they have not seen it as part of a larger CIA conspiracy; one-time fellow-travelers, Sumit Sarkar and Ramachandra Guha, have deplored the "decline of the subaltern in *Subaltern Studies*," seeing in the "Saidian moment" an unfortunate turn that replaced diligent search for the subaltern voice in the archives and in the fields by lazy, deskbound textual analyses.[5] The debates are not always friendly or even reasonable. Whether or not one agrees with these criticisms of *Subaltern Studies,* it is clear that those of us involved with the series would have made life easier for ourselves if we had given up the stance of speaking from and about South Asia. At least we would not have been open to the charge of having fallen for "Western fads" (for it must be more excusable for scholars in the West to go for fads that are "Western"), and we would have been more consistent with the actual mode of production. That is, we would have acknowledged what in any case is a reality about the production of *Subaltern Studies:* it is produced through a process that can be best described in terms of the various kinds of "flows" that Appadurai (1996b) has recognized as marking the disjunctures and conjunctures of globalization.

Here then is one of the fundamental contradictions of *Subaltern Studies* that I want to reflect on while investigating possible relationships between *Subaltern Studies* and diasporic South Asian studies. Clearly, the editorial collective of *Subaltern Studies* feels attached to the stance that the series claims, primarily, to speak for and to the region called India (if not for South Asia). Ranajit Guha, the founding editor, used to enjoin us to "think through the specificities of Indian history," to make that archive central to our thought. The injunction was no less paradoxical in his own case: By the time he started editing *Subaltern Studies,* Guha had spent about three decades in the West (in the United Kingdom, the United States, and Australia), and yet there was this insistence to think through a life form one had physically left behind, to think through memories, or, more precisely, a blend of archives and memories, in order to arrive at the kind of scholarship *Subaltern Studies* produced. Why this attachment to a region in one's thought? Why this apparent denial of the multifarious ways in which living in the West had undoubtedly changed both one's questions and one's mode of answering them? Was *Subaltern Studies,* then, simply yet another instance of scholarship pretending that life did not exist? Wasn't this attachment to a region peculiar for a project that was known for its critique of both nationalism and nationalist historiography?

The paradox becomes somewhat understandable if we pursue the difference between, say, *Public Culture* and *Subaltern Studies. Public Culture* is committed to a space that is produced by the interstices between nations and territories, by the economic and cultural processes of globalization. The political imagination invested in both *Subaltern Studies* and *Public Culture* visualizes an international solidarity of scholars and activists against global and regional forces of injustice and inequalities. But with one difference. Both Carol Breckenridge and Arjun Appadurai, the two founding editors of *Public Culture,* have expressed the need to "think ourselves beyond the nation." [6] *Subaltern Studies,* by contrast, it seems to me, is committed to operating, intellectually at least, within a framework for which the nation—though perhaps not the nation-state—is still a salient and resilient category. Given the critique of nationalism and nationalist historiography on which *Subaltern Studies* was founded, however, this commitment to the idea of the nation can only operate with interesting and significant differences from old nationalism. If the old nationalism imagined the nation as a political body with an identifiable center to it, the primary tendency of *Subaltern Studies* is to challenge the idea of this center and to try to examine Indian history to see how the picture of a variegated, many-centered India might emerge—and, indeed, how each of these "centers" could in turn be destabilized.

The lesson of this difference between *Subaltern Studies* and a project such as *Public Culture* seems to be this: Critical scholarship requires us to imagine and locate a site where we can effectively intervene; hence one might argue that critical scholarship is committed to the production of a space within which it situates itself. *Public Culture* helps us see and (re)produce spaces that are already decentered and framed by the multidirectional processes of globalization; both *positions* and *Public Culture* promote a variety of "critical internationalism" while sharing the desire to bring area studies in conversation with cultural studies and social theory. Tani Barlow's (1995, vi) introduction to the "Marxism" issue of *positions* clearly says: "In editing this volume, I sought to reinforce the complex connections that in my view already exist and that could, Derrida's recent polemic on Marx not withstanding, cautiously be called a New Internationalism."[7] *Subaltern Studies* intervenes in the space that the nation-state has made available but only with the aim of being able to imagine this space differently and in a radically decentered manner (which is why scholarship committed to the present shape and structure of the Indian nation-state finds fault with us).

This choice of site is what has primarily dictated the relationship between *Subaltern Studies* scholarship and the globalized conditions under which it is produced. It is important to understand, however, that such a choice of site, while inevitable, is never a deliberate and completely rational choice; it arises from historical constellations of shared life forms, memories, desires, and fantasies, not all of which could be accounted for. Also, the differences between *Subaltern Studies* and *Public Culture* or *positions* cannot be considered absolute, for scholarship by its very nature—and moreso today for reasons that Appadurai addresses in his work—is also influenced by the fact of a certain global time that structures academia in such a way that we all, regardless of which part of the world we study, struggle with the same issues at the same time (which is why South Asianist, East Asianist, Central Asianist, and Southeast Asianist panels at the annual conferences of the American Association for Asian Studies are devoted to topics that all seem the same!). This phenomenon of academic global time is not independent of questions of domination and hegemony in academic institutions, but its pressures often ensure that there is a convergence of aims between projects situated in seemingly dispersed parts of the world.[8] So intellectual solidarity arises from both local and global factors. Forming bonds of solidarity with East Asian Studies, Middle Eastern Studies, African Studies, Latin American Studies, Irish Studies, and others has primarily been our way—in the project of *Subaltern Studies*—of garnering resources in order to fight battles the ultimate location of which, for us, was in South Asia.

One important weapon in this struggle has been the engagement that *Subaltern Studies* has had with various reading communities at the same time. This is true both within India and outside. The reason is not difficult to seek. As you may imagine, a nation like India is literally more represented in the capital city of Delhi than elsewhere. The current construction of a "national" life in India has a strong centralizing pull working on it (though recent formations of coalition governments in Delhi may be indicative of changes to this tendency). A legacy of colonialism, the imagination of India has remained somewhat empire-like.[9] This is, of course, as you would expect, reflected in museums, in the construction of ethnic villages, in regional emporia, and so on.[10] This is also true for intellectual life: Delhi boasts the best universities, some of the best libraries, the "national" (i.e., the central government's) archives, and it enjoys a lion's share of funding agencies for research. Delhi is thus set up to dominate Indian intellectual life and to set the intellectual agenda for the country. Indeed, this is how it all happened in the 1970s and is still largely the nature of what happens. To struggle against the domination of Delhi, we have to prove that significant intellectual conversation can take place about India in which Delhi is just one partner among many and no longer in an exclusive position of deciding the agenda. In this, the development of a readership outside of Delhi and sometimes outside of India (in the United States, for example) has been critical for *Subaltern Studies*. An additional and welcome factor has been what Ranajit Guha has called "convergences": the Latin Americanists in the United States have set up their own subaltern studies project; translations of selections in Spanish and French have come out of Bolivia and Senegal; there is a Japanese selection under preparation. These all globalize the project in ways never originally anticipated.

Increasing globalization of scholarship produces some interesting anomalies in the debate on *Subaltern Studies* that goes on in India. For instance, a popular argument often advanced by Indian nationalist-Marxists against *Subaltern Studies,* and in order to explain the latter's popularity in the West, is that since the Westerners do not have any real patience for the details and complexities of Indian history, efforts such as *Subaltern Studies* succeed by making it all available in short, simple, schematic theoretical packages that do violence to the complexities of history, but are more easily digestible for a Western audience with a weak stomach for the details of non-Western pasts. Once this was said inside India to an Indian audience and perhaps sounded to some quite convincing. Now our critics make the point in what they themselves publish in the West. Tanika Sarkar put the argument thus— with a thinly veiled reference to Partha Chatterjee's *Nationalist Thought and the Colonial World: A Derivative Discourse?* (1986):

> Most recent works on cultural developments in the colonial period [in India] tend to assume the operations of a single, monolithic colonial discourse with fully hegemonistic capabilities. All that Indians could possibly do was to . . . form a secondary, derivative discourse. . . . I think the acceptability of these readings in the First World owes a lot to an unstated conviction there that historical processes in the Third World have been without much depth or thickness and an understand-

ing can be easily managed by positing a single binary opposition as the only axis around which they revolve. (1993, 61)

It is a tribute to the power the West wields on the Indian imagination that these kinds of criticisms of *Subaltern Studies* have begun to be exported out of India. A strange contradiction necessarily begins to inhabit this gesture that both globalizes a debate and at the same time claims security in not having to address the "unstated convictions" of the First World. For, if the original argument that Westerners do not have the stomach for the details and complexities of Indian history and culture is true, then this turning to the West must have the same effect on the substance of what the critics of *Subaltern Studies* have to say. That is, they must also, in order for their writings to appeal to audiences in the West, empty these writings at the same time of all detail and complexities. In the end, then, the authors would be guilty of the same crime with which they charge us! If this is not so, then something must be wrong with their original argument. The irony of the situation is usually lost on our earnest-minded adversaries, but I just mention this to show how globalization of scholarship leads to an Indian debate in which a purely nationalist argument or an attempt to completely separate the local from the global becomes self-defeating.

Apart from engaging with the scholarly community in North America, there is another way in which we have tried to make the reading publics for *Subaltern Studies* heterogeneous. This is by writing in the regional languages of India at the same time as we write in English. So far, one Hindi anthology of *Subaltern Studies* has come out and another is in press; there is a Bengali one on its way, and a Tamil anthology is under preparation. This move toward the regional languages of India has several advantages. It diversifies and makes heterogeneous the agenda for subaltern history-writing in a way that no amount of talking about plurality in any one language can ever achieve. It is hard, if not impossible, for writers in one region or language in India to control the cultural politics of another region. Within the regions, again, there exist specific debates on local, national, and global issues, all inflected by local histories and traditions of critical thinking. *Subaltern Studies* enjoys no hegemonic position in these locations; what we write is often subject to disputation, though not on the same terms as those mobilized in the metropolitan centers, including Delhi. One of the interesting commitments of *Subaltern Studies* comes out of this bilinguality of most members of the editorial collective. Our commitment to decentering India is ultimately our commitment to expressing the many different ways the world can be imagined and experienced in the different Indian languages (including English), and it thus constitutes a gesture of defying the hegemonic claims of the descriptions available in any one of them. A most recent instance of this is Shahid Amin's book *Event, Metaphor, Memory* (1995), a study of peasant nationalism and memories in colonial and postcolonial India. In many places, Amin has let stand the peasant speech in the dialect of the region studied, resisting the temptation to translate. (Of course, he has to translate enough for the book to qualify as a teachable text in the English language.)

If I could be a little personal on this point, I could elaborate the implications of this politics of bi- or multilingual writing with reference to my own efforts, every year, to write at least one academic essay in Bangla (Bengali), my first language. An important value of the exercise is intellectual. I know that the world, when imagined in Bangla, has a different feel to it, different from the way it comes across in English. This difference does not mean consensus within Bengali culture — far from it. The Bengali speech-community is as riven by the debates of status, class, and gender as any other community, and we have the additional burden of having to debate and negotiate the divisive legacies of modern Hindu and Muslim nationalisms (two-thirds of what was once the British-Indian province of Bengal have now become Bangladesh). Yet writing in Bangla makes me more aware of the politics and the problems of cross-cultural and cross-categorial translation. It also helps me maintain a perspective on all universalist claims, including some of the hasty strictures that come out of certain versions of left-liberal U.S. campus radicalism.

Consider the following statement by a U.S.-based academic philosopher trying, legitimately from his own point of view, to give Heidegger's philosophy an acceptable shape for the present (the question of whose present and where is a moot point; I will come to that in a moment) by ridding it of its "fascistic" elements. John D. Caputo's (1993, 97) critique is informed by a vision of the world that he thinks Heidegger, the man, would abhor: "It is a multilingual, multicultural, miscegenated, polymorphic, pluralistic world without national-ethnic unity, *without the unity of a single language or a deep monolinguistic tradition*" (emphasis added).

My engagement with the Bengali cultural practices and their histories suggests to me that Caputo's hostility to any "deep monolinguistic tradition" is hastily conceived and is probably itself a particular form of prejudice. For whom would this world "without the unity of a single language" be a home? For anybody and everybody? Having a language other than a European language as my first language means that I have an everyday lived access to imaginations of the world, aesthetics, personhood, sensibilities, practices of civility and the good life that are not necessarily universal but that do challenge someone else's version of a universal world constructed without any regard for differences in the histories of subject formation in different parts of the globe. Forget about Heidegger abhorring the world that Caputo wants to live in; his strident hostility to any "deep monolinguistic tradition" may make it inhospitable for even a Shakespeare or an E.P. Thompson, not to speak of the Bengali national poet Rabindranath Tagore.

There is perhaps no language in the world that is already not plural, but this fact does not mean that there cannot be any legitimate pleasures of so-called deep monolinguality. The modernization of the "vernacular" languages in India under colonial rule resulted in the emergence or invention of some "deeply monolinguistic traditions." The emergence of modern Bengali, Assamese, Tamil, Oriya, Hindi, Gujarati, Telugu, Malayalam, among others, as modern literary languages was critical to nationality formations in those regions. People learned to take pleasure in being able to think the world through their language, which increasingly took on the character of a "deep monolinguistic tradition." The tradition was no doubt an "invented" one, as indeed many traditions often are. Yet this does not mean that the pleasures it produced within the modern Bengali middle-class life form were unreal. Bengali writers like Rabindranath Tagore, Bankimchandra Chattopadhyay, or Kazi Nazrul Islam embodied the capacity for this pleasure. Their claim to the pleasures of "monolingualism"—they often criticized, for instance, Bengalis who used English as their main means of self-expression—was not a claim about the purity of the Bengali language. As they themselves knew better than others, Bengali would not have acquired its modern shape or character without Bengalis being exposed to the pleasures and charms of the English language, and they themselves often deliberately and self-consciously borrowed and translated from other languages and cultures, both Indian and foreign, but this only added to their pleasures and practices of monolingualism.

If anything, translations and borrowings, one could argue, were their way of making the "monolinguistic tradition" deep, for Bangla now became an object with a rich and diverse history. In spite of all the "multi-"s, "poly-"s, and "plural-"s that litter the sentence I have quoted from Caputo, it seems to me that the conception of "monolingualism" he takes for granted is not one that would speak to the Bengali historical experience of literary modernity and anticolonial nationalism. What would we do in India if we had to live by Caputo's strictures? Would we have to unlearn our love of Tagore (for this happens within a capacity to enjoy Bengali as a monolinguistic tradition)? The answer surely is in making our critiques more situated, in engaging with the differences in our histories and not prescribing positions from on high.

Bilinguality, or even multilinguality, is thus a critical weapon in the struggle for many-centered worlds, provided we realize that there is no inherent contradiction between being able to imagine the world in many different languages and engaging with the "deep tradition" that each of these languages may claim to embody. By "bilinguality" or "multilinguality" on the part of academic intellectuals, however, I do not simply refer to the acquisition of a second or third language for professional reasons. This many academics do and do very well, indeed. Anthropologists, for instance, do it all the time and in a sense that does make them "bilingual," but not in the sense in which I am using the word here. By "bilinguality" I mean the capacity to experience, and equally important, the capacity to *express* the world in the two languages concerned (that is, to be able to participate in the life forms to which the languages belong). It is hard to set up any fixed standards here, for obviously one's capacity to be creative in a language is not crucially dependent on one's mastery of it. I am talking of literary — though not necessarily canonized — creativity, the capacity to engage affectionately with the poetics of a language (which, I may add, is not necessarily an elite activity). In this sense, and only in this sense, Salman Rushdie, for instance, is not a bilingual intellectual, for I do not know that he can bring the world alive in Urdu, although he obviously has a feel for Urdu and is quite a genius at making it murmur audibly just below the surface of his English prose.

Let me note it as an aside, however, before I continue with this discussion of bilinguality, that the example of Rushdie may with justice appear to cut both ways. While I think Rushdie does help to illustrate what I mean by bilinguality — the capacity to express oneself creatively in two languages — he is precisely a writer who also makes us see what is hybrid in a language and thus calls into question the pleasures of monolinguality. For instance, he makes the syntactic structure of Hindi or Urdu shine through the grammar of his English, thereby prefiguring in his performance some of the political resources that can be generated in the diaspora. Rushdie is an effective and sharp reminder that the English language is itself plural, that there is no one model of right English with respect to which other forms of English may be judged deficient. Now one can imagine many occasions where one has to hang on to that insight, especially if monolinguism came in the form of a claim of the dominant, a position that denied the undeniable plurality that each language contained within itself. The argument about hybridity, one might say, is most effective when purity has become the ideology of the oppressor.[11]

Here I have to walk a tightrope to explain my position. One could argue against me by pointing out that it was the construction of Bangla as one unified and unitary language that relegated certain forms of speech and writing to the status of "dialects," and this criticism would have a point.

Surely, the rise of modern vernaculars in colonial India—and subaltern studies scholarship is admittedly still dominated by members of language groups that modernized and produced "nationalist" fiction in the nineteenth and early twentieth centuries—came at some price. Part of that price was paid by language elements and speech communities that got marginalized in the process. Considered in that context, the claim of being a "monolinguistic tradition" can sound like the voice of the oppressor. But "purity," "monolinguality," and related concepts are not always the argument of the dominant. After all, it was the British in India who told the Indians that they, the Indians, were too plural to have anything in common, so that the nationalist project of achieving Indian political and cultural unity, while an oppressive factor in some other contexts, had to win its followers in the face of strenuous British attempts to reject its veracity or validity. The pleasures of "monolingual traditions"—traditions that enabled Bengalis, Tamils, and others to feel the emotions of devotion, love, and loyalty toward their languages—was part of a historical process through which one found in the emerging identity of the Bengali or the Tamil a sense of belonging (Ramaswamy 1997). A "deep sense of monolingualism" was part of that process. The liberation war in Bangladesh in 1971 came out of a movement that saw Bangladeshis express tremendous love for a language that they claimed was one: Bangla. To see this history as simply oppressive would be to ignore the many contradictory truths of that historical experience.

My point about bilinguality and the bilingual intellectual's capacity to take pleasure in each of the languages under question, by treating them as though they belonged to "deep monolingual traditions," does not entail any assumptions of the purity of languages. My argument is about the recognition of differences without essentializing them into insurmountable barriers to communication. It is a matter of recognizing that, while conversation increasingly becomes global and one's sense of space, as Appadurai argues, unstable and fluid, we do not automatically all get delivered into the same world by the shared processes that globalize and hybridize us. Conversing across differences is the art we have to learn.

Conversing across Differences

The question of productive conversations between a project of area studies (*Subaltern Studies* is my example) and projects that come out of lives and practices in the South Asian diaspora in the United States and other Western democracies strikes me as an important site where we can practice and learn this art of conversing across differences.[12]

Language is sometimes a problem in this conversation. The students we get from the diaspora are, on the whole, English-speaking (i.e., their first language is English), although this is slowly changing among the graduate students. Yet as an area-studies person and without trying to be exhaustive, I see the following as areas where the concerns in the diaspora raise new questions for area studies (my reference remains South Asia):

1. The history of power and oppression in the dynamics of the family — that is, histories of sexuality, gender, aging, and bodily practices. Feminist scholarship has done much within India to highlight these problems, yet there is a peculiar way in which movements in the diaspora give us new archives and insights. Histories of domesticity in India cannot be written out of official archives, as the area was beyond their concerns. Standard textbooks on modern Indian history have nothing on the family, "history" being equated to public life and the life of the nation. When interested in this material, one depends on autobiographies and prescriptive, regulative literature. Some amount of domestic violence these days, thanks to feminist activism, gets reported to the police and becomes subject to disputation under criminal law. The material is hard to access, however, and comes with all the normal problems of police reports in South Asia. But imagine the networks of shelter for battered South Asian women that have been built up by the hard and dedicated work of feminist activists in the United States, United Kingdom, Canada, Australia, and elsewhere. As a result of this work, these activists have built up an archive of histories of South Asian familial lives and relationships that could provide insights to any academic working on South Asian cultures.

2. Reflecting on the problem, what is a "generation"? This is, once again, an underthought problem of South Asian history. It is there in every description of cultural change under colonial rule. The history of English or Western education in colonial India is often written about as though it embodied conflicts of generations. Yet the term *generations,* a modern expression in South Asia, is taken as a natural, given category and left unquestioned even when the category *youth* is put under the microscope. But this is a lively, charged, and contested category in the diaspora, and it offers us an opportunity to unpack and reflect on it. Mainstream South Asian studies do not offer quite the same opportunity.

3. Memory. Tied to the question of generation is the question of memory. Issues in diasporic life forms highlight this question, which is often suppressed by the theme of an assumed unity of all Indians that nationalist historiography celebrates. "Generation," however, remains a key organizing principle in the diaspora because diasporas are internally differentiated around constellations of shared memories. What is a pure pleasure of remembering to one generation comes across as "pathological nostalgia" to

another that does not share the same memories. Diasporic life forms cannot avoid the politics of memory and must be rich in material that lends itself to the study of what memory is.

4. Politics of the identity of being "South Asian" in the Western democracies. In the worst cases, this can lead to Hindu or Islamic chauvinism, but I am more heartened by my experiences at the University of Chicago. We are beginning to get students—young Americans born to parents from South Asia, people whom their cousins back home would affectionately and teasingly call the ABCDS (American-born confused *desis*—the word *desi* meaning "indigenous")—whose interest in the intellectual traditions of South Asia is deep and who consciously want to move away (I am merely quoting here from an application for admission to my home department) from models of postcolonial theorizing that entail no serious engagement with a South Asian language. This development is at a very embryonic stage, yet there are already a few graduate students whom I would describe as belonging to this group or type. These students, if they seriously pursue the project of bi- or multilinguality, may one day contribute substantially to the question of how to live and perform human diversity in the democracies of the West that are fundamentally structured by the life-philosophies of European peoples. This point connects with what I say next.

5. Globalization of South Asian class formations and cultures. This is something on which the area studies and/or *Subaltern Studies* scholarship is weak. Some aspects of the working class's "globalization" have been studied under the rubric of "migration of labor." Yet there are no cultural histories that I am aware of on, say, the Pakistani taxi drivers in New York or Chicago and on how their lives here might be impacting on lives back in Pakistan.[13] We have not yet begun to think about the implications of a middle class that is forming itself in the age of a media that is globalized and that, sociologically speaking, is now distributed all over the globe. It is now common for many South Asian families to expect to have relatives in other countries. We do not know how these families manage to sustain—or lose, as the case may be—their sense of being a network of connections. Films, literature, and other creative arts are far ahead of the social sciences in these areas. Interesting work is beginning to be done on the sociological and political aspects of this globalization; this is an area where area studies and diasporic studies can productively come together.[14]

Additionally, there are *two* areas at least where diasporic studies may use area studies material as resources and where we, the scholars in area studies departments, have a lot to learn without necessarily contributing anything directly to battles that are located in the here and now of the United States, Canada, the United Kingdom, or Australia.

First is the struggle for "interactive multiculturalism" in which Asian Americans and Asian American studies, I assume, have to engage. By interactive multiculturalism I mean a politics of multiculturalism that goes beyond the usual liberal-pluralist stances of seeing the culture of public life as one and homogeneous (i.e., the dominant culture). The latter allows for a politics of representation of difference by defining "manageable" differences as so many instances of the same, and by consigning all problematic differences to the so-called sphere of the private. Against this is the struggle for changing legal structures, institutional practices, and government policies so that, as far as possible, practical (but not essentialized) cultural differences are recognized and a process allowing negotiation for such recognition is built into the procedures of public life. Here, of course, the struggle gets manifold as one also fights simultaneously against those oppressive forces within the diaspora that have their own vested interests in defining particular immigrant cultures as single and homogeneous. Here I can imagine being of use—as a subaltern studies and area studies scholar— to some of these struggles.

The second is a very exciting field of development—the area of creative and performance arts within the diaspora: films, painting, writing, dance, plays, and music, among others. Here I have to draw on whatever little experience I have had in the Australian scene, although I am sure there will be similar examples in abundant number from other places, in particular observing the creative work of a dance group called Kailash Dance Company in Canberra, run by Padma Menon. This is cultural practice at a microlevel—one person's bodily experiences, one observer's private consumption of emotions—affecting many and affecting them deeply. Menon's cast is multiethnic, not just South Asian. Watching them at work, I have often wondered, what does it mean for a Greek-Australian woman or a man to try to express through her or his bodily movements the particular South Asian idiom of some sentiment—say, of submission, or of love, or of modesty? The sentiment may be in its substance universally available, but the idiom of expression, which gives it all its specificity, is South Asian. I do not know the answer, but I do know that Menon is transforming both herself and others in ways that academics will seldom be able to do. Here I think both the limits of the *Subaltern Studies* project and the possibilities of diasporic lives become visible.

The reader will have noticed that all of the issues I have mentioned as coming out of diasporic life forms have one thing in common: They move us away from the conception of centers. Area studies scholarship has been focused on centers—cultural, statist, bureaucratic, familial. Diasporic studies, the politics of multiculturalism, and the writings of theorists such as

Homi Bhabha and Arjun Appadurai—all lead us away from the imagination of centralizing structures. That is their strength. Bhabha's and Appadurai's work in particular reminds us that there are many forms of life and human bonding that can only be thought and appreciated if we learn to inhabit and theorize what is in-between, interstitial, neither here nor there.[15]

At the same time and all over the world there are life-practices that focus more on centers than on the in-between. It would be wrong to think that centers simply represent some profound error of thought. The nation-state, the centralizing bureaucracies, the integrative mechanisms that bring the different parts of the world together are not just illustrations of human greed and folly. They are there because we, in our contradictory ways that are at once common and divisive, need and want them. The conversation between area studies and diasporic studies is then a matter of communication between the politics of different life-worlds: on the one side are life-worlds produced by travel, (im)migration, battles for cultural recognition, and survival in capitalist-consumerist democracies and in postnationalist structures; on the other side are life-practices fashioned in the shadow of nationalist struggles against imperialism and in the context of the oppressions that nationalisms, in spite of their liberating potential, also are.

Of course, nobody belongs to any one particular life-world exclusively; life-worlds are worlds in and through which we both reside and travel, in greater or lesser degrees. But the politics of generations that is structural to the politics of diaspora means that we have to distinguish between different types of immigrants and their descendants. The memories of so-called first-generation immigrants—I say "so-called" because, technically, an immigrant is by definition first-generation in relationship to his or her children who are born in the country their parents adopted—may not be as self-consciously tied to the themes of travel and mobility as those of their descendants. Both formations of memories are valid. Communications from within practices that are made different by the fact of their belonging to different life-worlds require us to make our theorizing sensitive to the question of diversity in this world. I conclude by illustrating through some anecdotes what I mean by this.

Diversity of Life-Worlds and Their Implications for Theory

I want to share two anecdotes from my own experience that brought home to me the importance of the question I address in the concluding sections of this essay. Although storytelling may sound like personalizing, to use anecdotes is not necessarily to personalize: I use anecdotes merely to present the ethnographic evidence one inevitably collects from life. I could have used somebody else's study, but often the study you need is just not available. These anecdotes, I submit, relate to a larger question. Theories in the social sciences—including those of liberalism or Marxism—usually carry with them a normative vision that is universal. Lives, on the other hand, are spent in worlds, life-worlds, that are specific and different, although never completely insulated from one another. How do we, in being universal-theoretical, negotiate the differences that are also part of our being? I cannot, of course, give a general, universally valid answer to this question—that would be contrary to my argument—but my anecdotes, I hope, will offer a particular answer. It is that answer that helps me to return to Appadurai's question with which I began this essay: What does it mean today to "critically reconstruct liberalism"?

Both anecdotes here refer to the relationship between my academic/critical/theoretical practices and those pertaining to the context of my kinship. My first story comes from Australia, where an Australian friend who works on the politics of health issues in aboriginal communities once told me—with a feeling of satisfaction that was understandable in a politically committed person—that he was now obliged to write without jargon as he had discovered that his mother and his aunts read what he wrote. His point, obviously, was about writing for a larger and nonacademic audience. He was glad that his work had reached beyond the narrow confines of academia, forcing him to reconsider the use of specialist language. The incident made me remember that my parents and family do not read what I write as an academic, nor do they engage with the substance of my argument even when they look at my writings out of curiosity or parental/familial pride. I also realized that I felt a certain sense of relief and comfort in that knowledge.

The second story helps explain this sense of relief. Once I was back in Calcutta watching television with my parents and a cousin and his wife who were visiting. All of us sat, Indian-style, on my parents' bed. A young Bengali academic was discussing contemporary Bengali short stories on the state-owned television channel. This academic person also happened to be the newly married wife of a relative. I soon found myself having to strain hard to listen to what she had to say, for my parents, my cousin, and his wife—none of them academics or with any academic interests, though they all had university degrees, my mother being a teacher of literature herself—were discussing, volubly and vigorously, this woman's looks: if she was wearing a good sari, whether she made a suitable wife to her husband, whether she was a good addition to the family, and so on. I felt amused and irritated, but recognized that my parents and I were viewing different objects, after all. My academic interests were of no concern to them. My parents could look at and relate to this woman on television without engaging with what she was saying—filtering out, that is, the academic matter.

My sense of relief comes from knowing that the very fact that my parents do not read what I write about Bengali history and culture is what actually frees me to develop a "critical" academic-theoretical voice, to say things about my culture and history and about my ancestors that, in a Bengali kinship context, could come across as "bad form," if not downright rude. More generally, however, it gives me peculiar, if somewhat perverse, feelings of hope and humility to know that there are people like my parents who can live adequately, meaningfully, and purposefully without engaging with academic work in the social sciences. For it tells me that lives can be adequate—or inadequate—without academic criticism being a prominent part of them.

Why do I find this humbling experience important? Because it fundamentally has to do with my reading of Appadurai's question: What do we do with the once-European, now-universal heritage of liberal thought that underpins all conversation in academia in the democracies? Appadurai says: Let's use the study of non-Western peoples and practices to reconstruct a "critical liberalism." I agree with the goal but must also submit that the reconstruction of liberalism, in order to bring it into a serious engagement with the question of human difference, is, frankly, the hardest thing to do, for when we are faced with practices we genuinely do not approve of, our (by which I mean most left-liberal social scientists) instinct is to revert to the classical tenets of liberalism and thereby, in spite of all our talk against them, to binaries that redivide the world into two: good and bad, white and black, liberal and illiberal.

Let me make a cautionary tale here out of an essay by the well-known British multiculturalist playwright and filmmaker Hanif Kureishi. "The Rainbow Sign," an essay that moves between Kureishi's life in England and his visits to Pakistan, where some of his relatives live, carries all the marks of Kureishi's commitment to struggles against racism in British cultural life. Every paragraph in the essay dealing with England, one might say, is dedicated to fighting the likes of Enoch Powell and Duncan Sandys. Kureishi is clear that there could not be a simple assimilation of differences into a pregiven identity—to the attitude that says, "I want you to be exactly the way I am"—in the history of race relations in Britain. He writes: "The British complained incessantly that the Pakistanis wouldn't assimilate. This meant they wanted the Pakistanis to be exactly like them. But of course even then they would have rejected them. The British were doing the assimilating: they assimilated Pakistanis to their world view. They saw them as dirty, ignorant and less than human—worthy of abuse and violence" (1986, 12).

Yet there are moments in this essay where Kureishi's resistance to the politics of assimilation in the context of cultural politics in Britain gives way to an assimilationist political philosophy, especially when he is confronted with choices made by human beings elsewhere with whom he genuinely finds no room for agreement. Faced with the Nation of Islam movement among some African Americans in the United States or so-called Islamic fundamentalist attitudes among some of his acquaintances in Pakistan, Kureishi's world suddenly collapses into a series of familiar twofold oppositions: the modern and the medieval, reason and unreason, the liberal and the illiberal. Regarding the Nation of Islam, he writes: "Elijah's disciple Malcolm X, admirer of Gandhi and self-confessed anti-Semite, accepted in prison that 'the key to a Muslim is submission, the attunement of one towards Allah.' . . . I saw racism as unreason and prejudice, ignorance and a failure of sense. . . . That the men I wanted to admire had liberated themselves only to take to unreason, to the abdication of intelligence was shocking to me" (14). Of a Pakistani Islamacist lawyer, he says: "The entire recognizable rhetoric of freedom and struggle, ends in the lawyer's mind with the country on its knees, at prayer. Having started to look for itself it finds itself . . . in the eighth century. . . . The many medieval monologues of mullahs I listened to. So much talk, theory and Byzantine analysis" (26–27). Kureishi is within his rights—as indeed we all would be—to disagree strongly with the Nation of Islam or with the mullahs in Pakistan. But why should the binaries of reason and unreason and medieval and modern be any truer than the binaries an Enoch Powell or the contemporary race-mongering Australian politician Pauline Hanson would employ?

I do not mean to suggest that there are any simple solutions to Kureishi's problem. For it is true that we do not, in modernity and as yet, know of *desirable* institutional arrangements in public life that could be seriously built on principles other than those of liberalism. Yet the fact that we cannot do this is a failure of our collective intellectual imagination, and a failure of the imagination must not be made to look like an achievement, as though it were something for which to claim credit! Acknowledging that we academics cannot find or imagine institutional arrangements better than those dictated by the premises of liberal political philosophy does not mean that other nonliberal life-worlds—with all the richness and contradictions of human existence—do not exist. Kureishi's own understanding of modern Pakistan as "medieval" and "eighth-century" sits side by side with this sensitive description of a Muslim servant woman in his uncle's house. The very subtlety of Kureishi's prose allows one to hear the half-audible stirrings of another understanding of life, something that a secular and liberal political philosophy would never fully comprehend:

I strode into a room in my uncle's house. Half-hidden by a curtain, on a verandah, was an aged woman wearing my cousin's old clothes, praying. I stopped and watched her. In the morning as I lay in bed, she swept the floor of my room with some twigs bound together. She was at least sixty. Now, on the shabby prayer mat, she was tiny and around her the universe was endless, immense, but God was above her. I felt she was acknowledging that which was larger than her, humbling herself before the infinite, knowing and feeling her own insignificance. It was a truthful moment, not empty ritual. I wished I could do it. (27)

Notice the "half-hidden" figure of this woman. By the side of the other women of Pakistan whom Kureishi quotes and with whose complaints about the patriarchy of the clergy and the officialdom one can easily sympathize, this woman remains "half-hidden," not just literally "by a curtain" but by the very prose of Kureishi's text. In disparate turns, the passage resorts to (Kureishi's) ideas of Christian spirituality, of divinity, even to the unrealistic image of a social structure that is built on a unitary and complete consensus around opposition to a "liberal melange"—all in order to make sense of this half-visible figure of the old Muslim woman seated on her prayer mat: "Perhaps she did not want a society in which [only] her particular moral and religious beliefs were mirrored, and no others, instead of some plural, liberal melange; a society in which her own cast of mind, her customs, way of life and obedience to God were established with full legal and constituted authority. But it wasn't as if anyone had asked her" (27). Kureishi knows that he will never get to know this woman and her desires. She will remain forever "half-hidden." Yet Kureishi can vaguely but certainly feel—in that half-darkness that will always remain the non-knowledge of everyday life—the movements of another life-world, a "truthful moment," faced with which a mood of self-doubt and self-inadequacy comes upon him. A mood that will soon transform itself into the desire to become the other, an impossible desire. Faced with it, Kureishi can only experience the limits of the life form, from within which he speaks: "I wished I could do it."

This episode in Kureishi's experience of Pakistan—a crisscrossing between his diasporic life-practices and those of someone firmly embedded in another world, a meeting marked by both different forms of relating to each other, but never by full, mutual recognition and comprehension—illustrates for me something of how I envisage the conversation to go between area studies and diasporic studies. They are forms of studies that speak to different life-worlds, connected but different. The task of critically reconstructing liberalism, to go back to the problematic broached by Appadurai, is in effect the task of producing knowledge that begins from

Kureishi's position of humility and not from the old premise of liberalism where what was good for everybody was known and given from the very outset. The old servant woman exemplifies a possible third position in Kureishi's text, a position in the gap between the big divide of reason and unreason, a position that cannot be fully comprehended from either side of the divide. To stay with that which I do not fully comprehend—not in the hope that one day I will wake up in the dawn of a knowledge that renders the world transparent, but rather in the hope that my failure to comprehend will make visible to me the limits of my apparatus of comprehension and by the same token challenge and stretch the capacities of that apparatus— that is the optimism to which I look for a principle with which to animate what I have called the art of conversing across differences.[16]

Notes

Thanks are due to the participants at the *Disciplining Asia* conference at Seattle in 1996 where the original draft of this paper was presented, to Kandice Chuh for a generous but critical reading of that draft, and to Tani Barlow for longstanding conversations in a spirit of solidarity across areas in area studies. I am grateful to Sheldon Pollock, Kamala Visweswaran, Faisal Devji, Homi Bhabha, Uday Mehta, Arjun Appadurai, and Carol Breckenridge for ongoing and illuminating discussions on several of the issues broached in this essay, and to Andrew Sartori for allowing me to read and use an unpublished essay of his. My continuing indebtedness to my colleagues in *Subaltern Studies* and in the editorial committee of *Public Culture* scarcely needs mention.

1 That a liberal education was critical for the development of an enlightened citizenry was a point to be explicitly repeated by Robert Hall (1947, 37–38) of the University of Michigan: "Area studies are regarded by many as an important and highly desirable step in educating a better citizenry. . . . It is possible and, in our time, highly desirable that we have diffused through our population large numbers of citizens who know relatively much of the character, aspirations, resources, and problems of at least one foreign area and its people. . . . These people should have great influence in the moulding of enlightened public opinion concerning our foreign relations. They should do much to break down the barriers of ignorance, mistrust and prejudice, and the provincial orientation of public thinking."

2 I am grateful to Andrew Sartori for bringing this passage to my attention. He discusses it in his forthcoming essay.

3 See *Public Culture* 6, no.1 (1993).

4 Non-resident Indian" is a category invented by the government of India for the purpose of attracting to India financial and capital investment by businessmen and professional people of Indian origin now settled outside the country.

5 See Sarkar 1994. The fallacies in Guha's (1995) critique of subaltern studies were pointed out in Chakravarty 1995.

6 See Appadurai, "Patriotism and Its Futures" (1993) 158; Breckenridge, "The Global Modern," *Public Culture* (forthcoming).

7 See also Robbins 1997 and Lee 1995.

8 I owe this particular use of the word "convergence" to Ranajit Guha, who pointed out

to me in conversations the advantages of thinking through the idea of "convergence" rather than through that of "comparison" or "comparative histories," the latter framework often giving rise to a false and ungenerous spirit of competition among scholars working on different sites of the third world.

9   I deal with this theme in my own "Modernity and Ethnicity in India" (forthcoming).

10 See Greenough 1995.

11 This is how I read Bhabha's (1994) strategy of making "hybridity"—the idea of a "difference within"—a weapon of the oppressed. My discussion here owes much to Kandice Chuh's gentle but searching criticisms of an earlier draft.

12 The question of Indians in places such as Fiji, Mauritius, South Africa, the West Indies, and so on would require a separate treatment.

13 We do not yet have anything on South Asian immigrant workers that compares, for instance, with Roger Rouse's 1992 work on Mexican immigrants in the United States.

14 The New York-based magazine *Samar* provides concrete example of this opportunity.

15 See in particular Bhabha's introduction to *The Location of Culture* (1994).

16 These thoughts owe much to discussions I have had with Uday Mehta while he has been engaged in writing his book *Liberalism and Empire*. See also his "Liberal Strategies of Exclusion" (1997).

The Stakes of Textual Border-Crossing:
Hualing Nieh's Mulberry and Peach *in Sinocentric,*
Asian American, and Feminist Critical Practices

SAU-LING C. WONG

In an era when, in Elaine H. Kim's succinct formulation, "the lines between Asian and Asian American . . . are increasingly being blurred" (Kim 1992, xiii), what happens when a literary text of "Asian" provenance crosses national, political, linguistic, and cultural borders and ends up being claimed by a variety of critical (and pedagogical) practices, including but not limited to those in Asian studies and Asian American studies? What stakes are involved in such claims? How are feminist concerns inserted, if at all, in these processes? To explore these questions, this essay examines the protean publication and reception history of the novel known in Chinese as *Sangqing yu Taohong* and in English as *Mulberry and Peach: Two Women of China,* by the writer known in Chinese as Nieh Hualing and in English as Hualing Nieh.[1]

This last sentence, deliberately awkward, is meant to underscore the inherent instability of the subjects ("persons" as well as "subject matter") implicated in transnational practices. As Shu-mei Shih remarks on the multiple name changes undergone by border-crossing women like herself, Nieh, or Theresa Hak Kyung Cha, author of *Dictée,* "Each name and each language evok[e] a different aspect of one's self, a different life, a different story, a different time and space. And yet the contradiction is that they also coexist at the same time" (Shih 1992, 3).[2] Shih's statement is a truism, but one that, far from conferring comfort because of its familiarity, compels constant, often distressing, negotiations of meaning. As such, it provides a thought-provoking induction into the problematics of Asian/Asian American crossing.

A Synopsis and Brief Publication History of
Sangqing yu Taohong/Mulberry and Peach

In the synoptic convention favored by book reviewers, one could say that Nieh's novel is "about" a woman who lives through some of the most harrowing traumas in recent Chinese history and ends up suffering from what is clinically known as multiple personality disorder or dissociative identity disorder: she is split into Sangqing, or Mulberry, and Taohong, or Peach.[3] Her story begins in 1945, when she is 16, and ends (textually, at least) in 1970. During this period she traces a geographical trajectory evoking the political upheavals that have dislocated numerous Chinese. Because the protagonist's journey originates in China and continues on to the United States, even by the most mechanical criterion of "physical setting," the novel could be understood as a text spanning the Chinese and the Chinese American, the Asian and the Asian American.

In part 1 of the novel, on the eve of China's victory over the Japanese invaders, Mulberry is stranded in a boat along with other refugees in a Yangtze River gorge. In part 2, on the eve of Communist victory over the Nationalists in 1949, Mulberry enters the besieged city of Beijing to marry Shen Chia-kang, the man to whom she has been betrothed since childhood. In part 3, covering 1957 to 1959, Mulberry is in Taiwan, hiding out in an attic with Chia-kang, now a fugitive from the law for embezzlement, and with Sang-wa, their daughter. In part 4, the protagonist is alone in the United States as an illegal alien; she is pregnant from an affair with a Chinese professor and cannot decide whether or not to have an abortion. By now the identity dissociation has occurred; there is evidence that Peach has been wandering across the American continent and eventually "kills off" her primary identity. Each of the four sections is supposed to be an excerpt from Mulberry's diary, introduced by a letter to the U.S. immigration service written by a mocking, teasing, and defiant Peach. Framing all this are a *xiezi* or prologue and a *ba* or epilogue.

The above bare-bones account can, I think, be agreed upon by readers in both languages, but its simplicity is achieved by eliding details of the novel's many textual metamorphoses. The book's tortuous publication history resonates uncannily with the physical and psychological traversals experienced by the protagonist, which in turn echo the author's own ordeals, not so much in biographical detail as in spirit.

Born in Wuhan in 1925, Nieh was uprooted numerous times during her formative years as a result of the Japanese invasion and the unremitting Nationalist-Communist strife. After fleeing to Taiwan in 1949, Nieh became the literary editor of a dissident publication. When her superiors were arrested in 1960 for criticizing Chiang Kai-Shek's repressive rule, she had to flee again, this time to the United States. *Sangqing yu Taohong* was written in Iowa.[4] It was first serialized in Taiwan's *United Daily News* in 1970, but had, by part 3, drawn such vicious political and moralistic attacks (for veiled satire of the Nationalist regime and for "pornographic" accounts of Peach's sex life) that the editors were forced to terminate the serialization. The ban on *Sangqing yu Taohong* was not lifted until after the death of Chiang Ching-kuo, Chiang Kai-shek's son and successor.[5]

It was left to Hong Kong, then a British colony caught in but not committed to either side of the Nationalist-Communist conflict, to provide the relative neutrality needed for *Sangqing yu Taohong* to first see the light of day in its entirety. Hong Kong's *Ming Pao Monthly* took up the serialization, and the novel finally appeared in book form in 1976, published by Youlian chubanshe.[6] The second edition was published by Zhongguo qingnian chubanshe in Beijing in 1980, after the resumption of diplomatic relations between the People's Republic of China and the United States. But this is a drastically expurgated version, with a number of changes, including the deletion of part 4, initiated by the press but acceded to by the author.[7] On the mainland, the unexpurgated version appeared in 1989 and again in 1996.[8]

As for the English version, in 1981, an English translation by Jane Parish Yang and Linda Lappin, *Mulberry and Peach: Two Women of China,* was simultaneously published by New World Press in Beijing and Sino Publishing Company in New York. New World Press unilaterally made some changes to the typescript, despite reassurances to the author that the project, being intended for non-Chinese audiences, was politically safe.[9] The altered version appeared in Great Britain in 1986, published by The Women's Press in London. In 1988 Beacon Press of Boston, using the original typescript, reissued *Mulberry and Peach* as part of its "Asian Voices" series (which included titles by both Asian and Asian American authors). Beacon later dropped the title for unsatisfactory sales, but in 1998 the Feminist Press at the City University of New York republished it.[10]

As can be seen even from this brief factual account, it is impossible—quite simply, inaccurate—to talk about Nieh's novel as if it were a single text. The unauthorized changes in English are relatively minor, but in Chinese the unexpurgated and expurgated editions of *Sangqing yu Taohong* diverge drastically. When the censor's "suggestions" were acquiesced to by the author, however reluctantly, the cut version cannot simply be placed outside the "true intentions" of the author. For the author's desire to see her book published on the Chinese mainland, which was strong enough to override protectiveness toward her creation, was one of her "intentions," too. Add to this the fact that Nieh implemented certain changes to the English translation to assist the Anglophone reader, such as the subtitle, *Two Women of China,* a well-intentioned but misleading misnomer, or "dramatis personae"-type lists summarizing the main characters in each section.[11] Thus the questions of fidelity and equivalence usually obtaining with translations are raised exponentially. In short, Nieh's novel must be recognized as an unstable textual complex that traverses multiple national, political, linguistic, and cultural borders.[12]

While it is safe to say that contemporary works of literature seldom generate variants matching *Sangqing yu Taohong/Mulberry and Peach* in convolution, I suggest that Nieh's textual choices, where they existed, are not merely "idiosyncratic." In other words, I don't believe that her authorial decisions can be reduced to matters of individual personality, much less of artistic integrity. Rather, if Nieh endorsed or at least tolerated changes to her novel, she did so in response to certain historical circumstances that have irreversibly problematized the notion of the Chinese subject. It is precisely such historical circumstances that have made for the current surge of interest in the Chinese diaspora.[13] At the same time, the case of the unauthorized alterations points to the ways in which Nieh's novel itself problematizes the notion of the Chinese subject. Hence its distinctly unwelcoming reception by Chinese authorities on both sides of the Taiwan Straits which relaxed only very recently.

Assignment of Discursive Locations

In a thoughtful review of the Beacon edition of *Mulberry and Peach,* Kirk Denton raises the question of how to classify the novel and its author, given their extensive border-crossings:

> The genesis of *Mulberry and Peach* raises some questions about literary hermeneutics. . . . For those of us who study modern Chinese literature, the question begs: is Nieh Hualing a Chinese writer, a Taiwanese writer, or an overseas Chinese writer? Drawing from such diverse literary traditions as she does, based on which tradition are we to view her novel? . . . But perhaps we should see her novel in a larger context [of the literature of exile]. (Denton 1989, 137)

Denton poses his questions as scholarly and disciplinary ones, but his query is predicated on a broader understanding: that classification is never innocent. As David Perkins has observed with regard to literary taxonomies, "a classification is also an orientation, an act of criticism" (Perkins 1992, 62). Each classificatory label not only brings forth expectation-setting contexts and intertexts, but also signals a discursive location constituted by recognizable political and cultural assumptions and underwritten by interested institutions (universities, publishers, etc.). Reading practices will differ according to where one places the text. While Denton's terms are understood to function in a U.S. academic context, their implications are generalizable.

The label "modern Chinese literature" leaves the nation-state unspecified; however subliminally, this label hints that cultural commonalities could (and should?) transcend political differences. Thus what appears to be a "national" label ("Chinese") could in geopolitical terms be already "transnational," involving, just as the publication history of Nieh's novel does, three political entities, of which two have the full trappings of the nation-state. Denton's loose usage of "Taiwanese writer" to cover both transplanted mainlanders and native-born Taiwanese would be more vehemently contested today, given the growing strength of Taiwanese nativism. Still, this label recognizes not only the powerful presence of mainland-origin writers of Nieh's generation and beyond, but also the peculiarities of the island's post-1949 cultural development.[14] Depending on one's purposes, the label could be "regional" or incipiently "national." The term "overseas Chinese writer," privileging shared origin over the specificities of current locations, connotes centripetalism. The defining distinction is between *guonei* ("within the country"—nation-state again unspecified) and *haiwai* ("overseas"). The "literature of exile" label places Nieh's novel in a "world literature" location; while the concept of exile appears to be centrifugal and border-transcending, it actually recuperates the notion of a legitimating political and cultural center, as I will presently argue.

Even without addressing the issues of expurgation and translingualism, Denton has been struck by the range of discursive locations that Nieh's novel could occupy. I would like to further the analysis initiated by Denton by adding two items to his list: Anglo-American feminist literature and Asian American literature. The relevance of the former is evident from the sponsorship of feminist publishers in both Britain and the United States;[15] the germaneness of the label "Asian American" is less obvious, perhaps even farfetched to many, yet could certainly be established "empirically" beyond the matter of chapter setting.[16] In the following section, outlining my evolving relationship with *Sangqing yu taohong/ Mulberry and Peach* as a teacher and analyzing the critical scholarship on the novel, I will tease apart questions raised when these two additional discourses are taken into account.

Critical (and Pedagogical) Practices

Born and raised in Hong Kong until I came to study in the United States at age 20, I first read *Sangqing yu Taohong* in Chinese when it appeared in Hong

Kong's *Ming Pao Monthly*. In the early 1980s, I began a "professional relationship" with Nieh's novel, using excerpts (the Prologue and part 4, both set in the United States) in an undergraduate course on Chinese immigrant literature offered by the Asian American Studies Program, Department of Ethnic Studies, at the University of California, Berkeley. "Chinese immigrant literature" here refers to writings in Chinese by first-generation writers about their life in the United States; the course was designed to serve Chinese-literate, recent immigrant students.[17]

The fact that such a course was initiated by the Asian American Studies Program is, in itself, significant. As a discipline under the ethnic studies rubric, Asian American studies began with an activist commitment to "local" (as opposed to "homeland," i.e., "Asian in Asia") politics; an emphasis on the experiences of American-born, Anglophone Asians; and a strong anti-Orientalist agenda that, in extreme cases, led to a studied avoidance of Asian connections by cultural critics. By the late 1970s and early 1980s, however, the numbers of first-generation Asian students at UC Berkeley had become large enough to prompt greater attention to their curricular needs; hence the immigrant literature course. This was one of the first signs of the blurring of Asian and Asian American that has become such a part of the intellectual climate of the 1990s. Tellingly, Chinese immigrant literature did not attract the interest of East Asian studies at the time, perhaps because of the former's marginality to the Sinological core of "great traditions."[18]

The English translation of Nieh's novel, in the meantime, made its appearance elsewhere in my teaching and research, the majority of which has been in Anglophone Asian American literature.[19] I have used *Mulberry and Peach* in an introductory course on Asian American literature and, most recently, in a seminar on transnational narratives by Asian American women. In addition, some of my graduate students specializing in Asian American literature have developed an interest in the novel, some discovering it on their own or from other courses taught by non-Chinese colleagues, others giving it a closer look upon my suggestion.[20] The majority of these students, unlike my undergraduates in the Chinese immigrant literature class, are U.S.-born, typically non-Chinese literate and often non-Chinese.

Throughout over a decade of teaching and discussing *Sangqing yu Taohong/Mulberry and Peach* in various institutional environments, I have come to be struck more and more forcefully by the novel's protean nature, its radical uncontainability. The same book has been claimed by different critical and pedagogical practices in the same institution—in my case, by the same person—and each time it was taught or read in a new setting, something different about it emerged into the foreground. The potential for contradiction in such a situation is immense, and it all came to a head for me when, after years of interpreting *Sangqing yu Taohong* as a coherent allegory on the tragic fate of the modern Chinese and teaching it as such in my Chinese immigrant literature course, I was presented with persuasive readings of *Mulberry and Peach* in papers, conversations, and in-class remarks, by Asian American graduate students who expressed little interest in the "Chinese" aspects of the text.[21]

It is true that, before being confronted with these readings, I had already reflected on a possible Asian American discursive location for *Mulberry and Peach,* over and above what my adoption of the text in an Asian American studies class would prompt. I took encouragement from King-Kok Cheung's and Stan Yogi's annotated bibliography of Asian American literature, which espouses a comprehensive definition of the term. As the bibliographers note, arguing against "cultural nationalist" prescriptivism:

> The influence of overseas Asians—be they sojourners or immigrants with American-born offspring—cannot be ignored in a study of Asian American literary history. There are also authors who may regard themselves as expatriates or as regional writers rather than as Asian Americans. We choose to list them because national and regional allegiances, which often vary with time, cannot easily be determined. (Cheung and Yogi 1988, v)[22]

There are a number of well-known precedents in Asian American literature for a Chinese-language text entering the Asian American canon upon translation, such as *Island* (Lai et al. 1980) and *Songs of Gold Mountain* (Hom 1987).[23] Based on these precedents, I have done some preliminary theorizing on incorporating Asian-language immigrant writing into Asian American literature as well as analysis of specific texts from that perspective (Wong 1987; 1988a; 1988b; 1989; 1991; 1992). In a 1993 book-length study of the Asian American literary tradition, I read *Mulberry and Peach* intertextually against English-language works that engage the mobility myth of America; thus Peach's wanderings were read parodically, against the idea of "westering" as liberation and renewal for American national subjects (Wong 1993, 120; 127). But that critical move performed on Nieh's novel, part of a larger motifs-study project that argues for an Asian American reading practice, was but a minor element in that framework, and I was not compelled to pursue its full implications.

It took the defamiliarizing discomfort of some major conceptual disruptions for me to realize that my biliteracy did not necessarily give me privileged access to the "true" or "intended" meaning of Nieh's novel. The picture has proven to be vastly, confoundingly more complicated than that. Part of it is, of course, the characteristic inexhaustibility of powerful literature, but more importantly, I have come to learn that the discursive locations to which *Sangqing yu Taohong/Mulberry and Peach* has been assigned entail a range of critical practice (that in academe extends into pedagogical practices), each with its own institutional history, ideological axioms, analytic vocabulary, aesthetic framework, intertexts, and thematic concerns.

"Chineseness": The Chinese Nation and/or Chinese Peoplehood

I was in good company when I taught *Sangqing yu Taohong* to my immigrant students as an allegory about "the tragic fate of the modern Chinese." The overwhelming majority of published criticism (in both Chinese and English) on Nieh's novel treats it as an allegory of the Chinese nation and/or Chinese peoplehood, with Leo Ou-fan Lee's reading of the deconstructive potential of diaspora being a notable exception (Lee 1994, 229–31).[24]

The ambiguity of "and/or" in the above statement arises from the novel itself, which shifts focus ceaselessly, often barely perceptibly, from one to the other. We might say that, artistically, "Chineseness" is a richly productive, if painful, concept for Nieh. Perhaps the productiveness comes precisely from the pain — from the impossibly snarled relationships between the Chinese nation-state (of course, the immediate question is "which?"), the "Chinese people" or *zhonghua minzu* (how far and how long can this already ineffable entity be stretched under diasporic conditions?), and the *zhongguoren,* the individual onto whom "Chineseness" has been indelibly inscribed, to her endless grief. In what I call Sinocentric allegorical readings of the novel, the "Chineseness" of the protagonist is regarded as the most crucial determinant of her life; the tragedies of the modern Chinese nation-state (chief among them internal strife ending in political division) as either responsible for or symbolized by her personal calamities; and dislocation from China proper as an irreparable trauma.[25]

Such readings are easy to support. For one thing, Nieh herself has offered explicit suggestions on how to read her novel as a symbolic enactment of injuries sustained by the modern Chinese nation and a lamentation over the Jew-like fate of the diasporic Chinese. In her preface to the 1980 edition in Chinese, tellingly entitled "*Langzi de beige*" ["The wanderer's lament"], she draws attention to the recurrent images of imprisonment in the four parts of the novel, each marking a crisis in recent Chinese history. Even specific characters and textual details are carefully explicated. For example, she states that the Peach-flower Woman and Boatman in part 1 represent the refreshing "primitive life force" of *zhonghua minzu,* and that the news clippings in part 3 "reflect Taiwan society" (Nieh 1980a, 3–4).

Indeed, bracketing for the moment the question of the novel's uncontainability, on one level one could decode an almost schematic design structuring the meticulously chosen details of the allegory. For example, each passenger on the refugee boat can be demonstrated to embody a type of response to the approach of "modernity" via the nation-state. Space limitations preclude a fully worked out exegesis of the novel; suffice it to say that, despite its deep investment in the last century or so of Chinese history, *Sangqing yu Taohong* also evokes a mythic *zhonghua minzu* based on a sense of primordial and continuous cultural membership predating and indeed transcending the modern nation-state. The most obvious example is the name *Sangqing,* the mulberry being a sacred tree symbolizing Chinese civilization (it feeds the silkworm that produces silk). *Taohong,* though associated with a primitive life force by Hualing Nieh herself, can hardly be construed as devoid of cultural connotations. Rather, the peach flower is no less Chinese than the mulberry, being replete with centuries of allusions ranging from the erotic (as in the phrase *taohuayuan* to the utopian (as in Tao Yuanming's *Taohuayuan ji*) to the tragic (as in Kong Shangren's *Taohuashan*). These and numerous other references to Chinese legend and folklore construct a sense of peoplehood endowed with far greater nobility and resilience than the modern nation-state, which, in being vulnerable to splitting at all, has betrayed its unsuitableness as a first principle. Yet for Nieh the latter still partakes of the inviolability of the former, both being enfolded in a notion of "Chineseness" capable of calling forth the most fervent passions.

Sinocentric Allegorical Readings from the Chinese Mainland

This equivocation about "Chineseness"—which, I again emphasize, is "ideological" and not a matter of Nieh's individual confusion—allows *Sangqing yu Taohong* to be shaped into nation-serving master narratives. It should come as no surprise that since the novel was published on the mainland, critics there have been well-nigh unanimous in reading the novel as solely or primarily a nationalist narrative.[26] Furthermore, since from the mainland's official point of view the nation means the People's Republic of China, Nieh's novel has been constructed by some as pro-People's Republic, well-intentioned if somewhat wanting in revolutionary class consciousness. Essays in an anthology dedicated to Nieh's works (Li and Chen 1990) are typical of this approach. Despite minor reservations, *Sangqing yu Taohong* is affirmed as a politically courageous and insightful work whose imperfections can be understood and tolerated given the author's obviously *ex-centric* location—outside the mainstream of Chinese history, here identified with the People's Republic of China.

The very fact that Nieh sacrificed part 4 of *Sangqing yu Taohong,* however reluctantly at heart, for the opportunity to publish it on the mainland betrays a belief that her "real" audience is the numerical majority of Chinese in "China proper."[27] In her 1980 preface to the expurgated edition, Nieh writes:

> I greatly admire *guonei* ["inside the nation," referring to those on the mainland] writers for their concern for the people; they write for the people. For me, a writer in exile, where could I find the people? I only had artistic demands to sustain me. Now that *Sangqing yu Taohong* can be introduced to *guonei* readers, I have begun to have doubts about myself. From now on, for whom should I write? What kind of works should I write? (Nieh 1980a, 6–7; my translation)

One gathers that for Nieh, at least at this point in her life and career, being ex-centric is considered an anomalous, pathology-inducing condition that must be redeemed by a return to the center, to within the borders of the nation, to *guonei.*

Sinocentric Allegorical Readings from Exilic/Diasporic Locations:

A Western-educated *haiwai* or "overseas" critic might detect a party-line predictability in the mainland interpretations of *Sangqing yu Taohong,* with their vulgar-Marxist and social realist, not to mention "patriotic," demands on the writer. By contrast, reception to *Sangqing yu Taohong* outside of the People's Republic might appear free of propagandistic freight. An examination of the book jackets of the various Chinese editions yields a thought-provoking contrast. The cover of the expurgated mainland edition shows a red background, a simplified map of southeastern China and Taiwan in black, and a white bird in flight over the Taiwan Straits, its right wingtip brushing the island. Evoked are both the dove of peace and the Princess Bird in the Epilogue, the latter's pebble-dropping now construed as a valiant effort to bring out reunification—the Sisyphean connotations of the labor would have to be brushed aside to make this heroic reading possible. On the other hand, the covers of the Youlian (Hong Kong), Huahan (Hong Kong), and Hanyi seyan (Taiwan) editions all have "neutral" graphic designs.[28] Thus the nonmainland publishers seem to perceive the book quite differently, more as an aesthetic object than as an instrument of partisanship.

It might be habitual for many nonmainland critics to rest the analysis on such a contrast. Yet I suggest that most haiwai criticism on *Sangqing yu Taohong,* notwithstanding its nonofficial discursive venues, its vocabulary of aesthetic autotelism, and its dissociation from an obvious nationalism, shares with its mainland counterpart a fundamental similarity: Sinocentrism.

Perhaps the best known and most widely cited piece of haiwai criticism on Nieh's novel is Pai Hsien-yung's 1976 essay, "The Wandering Chinese: The Theme of Exile in Taiwan Fiction."[29] Pai, himself a revered master of fiction, is among the first to appreciate the ambition and vision of *Sangqing yu Taohong*. Citing C.T. Hsia's oft-quoted phrase, "obsession with China," he contextualizes Nieh's novel in a centuries-old Chinese tradition of intellectuals exiling themselves from corrupt regimes, and observes that Nieh has designed the novel "as a fable of the tragic state of modern China, whose political schizophrenia is analogous to the chaotic world of the insane." The novel employs "personal dissolution as a paradigm for political disintegration"; "in creating the fragmented world of the schizophrenic, Nieh Hualing has allegorized the fate of modern China in all its tragic complexity" (Pai 1976, 210, 211). In short, the tragedy of the protagonist is homologous to the tragedy of China.[30]

Pai's "Wandering Chinese" essay has influenced a large number of haiwai critics (e.g., Li 1983; Yu 1993). But tellingly, it has also been cited, with equal admiration, by most of the mainland critics in the mainland collection referred to above (Li and Chen 1990)—people whose literary tastes, critical training and vocabulary, life experiences, and political beliefs could not have been more different from Pai's. Pai, son of a well-known Nationalist general, is staunchly anti-Communist; considers himself an exile from both Chinese nation-states; lives as a permanent resident and an academic in the United States; was trained as a critic in the United States in New Critical methods, among others; and has repeatedly denounced the intrusion of politics into art. Yet upon closer analysis, Pai is as obsessed as the (plainly nonexilic) mainland critics by *zhonghua minzu*'s fall. For both, the Chinese people have suffered a tragic slippage from the "natural" state of grace—the coterminousness of ethnocultural homogeneity, geographic dominion, and unitary political control.

The "literature of exile" under which Pai classifies *Sangqing yu Taohong*, far from transcending nation (as it may first appear to do), is very much a literature *about nation*. For the concept of exile is constituted by the concept of nation. It is the failures of the nation-state—to unify warring factions, to forge a tolerable form of government, to nurture and protect its citizens, to honor its cultural creators—that compel exile.[31] While Pai has never succumbed to the facile fantasy that return to the homeland will undo the exile's grief, neither has he considered putting down roots on non-Chinese soil—*luodi shenggen*, to cite L. Ling-Chi Wang's typology on Chinese American identity—a viable possibility (L. Wang 1994). In the exilic tradition, there is only the dichotomy between rootedness and deracination.

Let me add that, on the point of Sinocentrism, the term "diasporic," which some students of Asian diasporas prefer for its alleged flexibility and expansiveness, is actually quite similar to "exilic." The root meaning of "diaspora," the scattering of seeds, unavoidably privileges origin and descent. Diaspora too results from failures of the nation-state, although it does preserve the notion of "peoplehood" more aggressively than does the term "exile."

"Chineseness" Deconstructed: Some Asian American Readings

What happens when the notion of Chinese peoplehood becomes radically disjoined from the notion of the Chinese nation-state, whether the latter is considered to be in its "natural" state of plenitude, or in an interim of weakness and internecine strife? This is the question posed when *Sangqing yu Taohong*, translated as *Mulberry and Peach*, becomes incorporated into Asian American literature, which counts putting down roots where one resides—*luodi shenggen*—among its foundational principles. Established Asian American cultural criticism holds that once Asians move away from Asia for whatever reason, it is no longer tenable to fixate on Asia as center. Instead of preserving Asian cultures (a doomed enterprise anyway, given how the Asia left behind is not static but continues to change), they and their descendants can and should develop peculiarly Asian American identities and cultures that recognize the "here and now" of their historical particularities.[32]

From this perspective, a political exile is on the same footing as (that is, neither more noble nor more tragic than) an economic migrant seeking a better livelihood. Such an estimation is clearly at odds with Pai's sense of the self-banished intellectual's unique historical burden. An Asian American consciousness also wreaks havoc on the sacrosanct status of Asian origin, and for that reason might seem outlandish to the point of heresy to many Asians on Asian soil, especially to rulers with vested interests in expanding their political control or attracting economic capital. With regard to Chinese Americans, both the Communist and the Nationalist regimes have had a long tradition of treating them as *huaqiao*—Chinese sojourners—whose ultimate loyalty should be to the *zuguo*, or ancestral land (L. Wang 1995). When huaqiao do not show signs of returning to the center, the tendency is to construe them (compassionately) as having been prevented from doing so, or (reproachfully) as having been seduced by the materialism or spurious freedoms of their land of residence. *Wangben*, to forget one's origin, is among the most self-righteously deployed insults one person of Chinese ancestry could hurl at another.

Sinocentric sentiments are not shared by the students of Asian American literature whose work first forced, then inspired me, to rethink what kind of book Nieh's novel is. When they read *Mulberry and Peach* in the frame of the United States, a nation-state *other than* the People's Republic of China, the Republic of China, or else a posited unified China, patterns initially startling to me emerged. Furthermore, given the strong background in feminism of many of these young scholars, such a deconstruction is closely tied to the issue of gender.[33] The intertexts they deployed for Nieh's novel were not Qu Yuan or Lu Xun or Yu Li-hua, but Sui Sin Far, Frank Chin, and Theresa Hak Kyung Cha; their concerns were women's bodies, performativity of gender and ethnicity, women's madness and illness as fact and trope, and gothic images of decay and confinement (Nguyen 1997; Chen 1998; M. Chiu 1996; J. Chiu 1999). Such patterns eventually led me to a radical deconstruction of "Chineseness."

A fascinating case in point concerns part 4, set in the United States. In a Sinocentric reading, when Mulberry reappears as the wandering Peach, she can be said to have become a tragic symbol of the Chinese people in diaspora. A "stateless" illegal alien hounded by the U.S. immigration service, she sleeps around with an assortment of men (apparently making her living that way); her sexual restlessness may be a trope for the Chinese people's inability to replace their lost nation with a worthy and suitable object of allegiance. Her pregnancy, however (by a fellow Chinese), might be a sign of hope: despite her vacillations over abortion, the ending of the novel remains ambiguous, thus leaving room for some kind of future, however vaguely envisioned, for *zhonghua minzu,* that sense of abiding Chinese peoplehood on which exilic/diasporic consciousness depends as a last spiritual resort. In a Sinocentric frame, the United States functions as the backdrop to the Chinese protagonist's inner morality play, a mere signifier to an assortment of spiritual ills. It is thus an ahistorical "place," or rather nonplace. For all intents and purposes, when return to a Chinese center is foreclosed, Mulberry/Peach might have fallen off the face of the earth. (Which accounts for the very conceivability of excising part 4 altogether.)

Pai Hsien-yung again provides the exemplary statement: "With all her traditional values and ethics shattered, Peach Pink [Pai's translation of *Taohong*] plunges into moral and sexual anarchy, soon sinking to her spiritual nadir and becoming half-mad" (Pai 1976, 211). Madness and anarchy are here postulated as the opposite of having cultural values; if they take an American shape at all (in Pai's terms, "hitchhiking along the American freeways, getting picked up by whatever man comes her way"), it is incidental. In a similar vein, Li Li notes that by "going primitive," "Taohong becomes a liberated person, but then she is no longer a Chinese person or any other kind of person" (Li 1983, 408). That Peach might be an "Americanized" person is ruled out—her promiscuity is merely symbolic of reversion to a primeval state as an ineffectual solution to a Chinese spiritual crisis. "American" details like her hanging out with hippies are there to serve that symbolic end.

In contrast, in the "America-claiming" type of readings that some of the Asian American students engage in, it is China that fades into vagueness, while the United States clarifies into sharp focus as a place with its own history.[34] For example, when *Mulberry and Peach* was discussed in my seminar on transnational narratives by Asian American women, my interpretation (following Nieh) of Peach as a primitive life force was immediately challenged.[35] Students raised pointed questions along the following lines: If Peach symbolizes a primitive life force, are we saying it is prediscursive? Is such a thing even theoretically possible, considering how thoroughly one is interpellated from the moment of birth? If, for the sake of argument, we accept the idea of a primitive life force, a kind of tabula rasa, doesn't it ironically leave Peach more vulnerable to assimilation? Look at her participation in '60s counterculture and the sexual revolution, look at her acquisition of white feminist discourse about control over her own body (the abortion issue)—aren't these culturally inscribed, and once marked, how can they signify a primitive life force, which by definition transcends historical marking? In short, though at times their observations might have been articulated at the expense of *Chinese* historicity, it is clear that the students insisted on the availability, indeed inescapability, of alternative systems of value and behavior in diasporic locations, and refused to derive meaning solely from Chinese "origin." On this point, they would agree with David Palumbo-Liu's recent analysis of diasporic and ethnic identification: "Despite the diasporic subject's identification of the home it left behind, and despite any attempt to freeze time and fix space, the diasporic subject must give itself up to the temporal and historical as it is resituated in a new sociopolitical sphere." As Palumbo-Liu notes, it is no accident that the American narrative in *Mulberry and Peach* is propelled by the figure of the immigration agent: "It is his interrogation that marks the intervention of the state in the construction of ethnic identity and attests to its need to recuperate that fugitive subject into its political field" (1999, 347).

The contrast between Sinocentric and Asian American readings of part 4 raises a provocative possibility. The former, despite some critics' professions of distaste for nation-statist power, are premised on a yearning for the coincidence of such power with the Chinese people's mandate (however defined), such that just dominion over the "ancestral land" would render exile and diaspora unnecessary. On the other hand, without glossing over the extent to which some strands of Asian American criticism have played into U.S. nation-building myths (see critiques by, for instance, Campomanes 1992; Fujikane 1996), one might consider Asian American discourse by definition minoritarian. *Asian America,* a quasi-geographical term frequently used by Asian Americanists, refers to a cultural space with neither territorial claims nor state underwriting. To paraphrase that well-known aphorism on the distinction between a standard language and a dialect, one might say that Asian America is a "cultural nation" without an army and a navy. The validity of "Asian Americanness" as a culturally viable and vitalizing concept assumes—depends on—departure from the Asian origin and marginalization by its "official" culture, as well as minoritization by hegemonic American culture.[36] Asian American critical practices are sustained by the very lack of an army or a navy, whereas Sinocentric ones are informed by (or at least haunted by) the notion of an army and a navy, even if these happen to be absent or in the "wrong hands" at the moment. This statement is not about the relative powerfulness of individual critics, nor does it imply that Sinocentric critics are *personally* complicit in upholding the nation-state. Rather, the point is that the two groups' conceptualizations of "Chineseness" are quite distinct, emanating as they do from vastly disparate political situations.

When and Where Women Enter

Reading without the filtering lens of Sinocentric thematics, as some of my Asian American students do, one may find feminist issues readily foregrounded. Perhaps a mistrust of nation-state narratives encouraged by the notion of "Asian Americanness" has allowed gender-inflected details to emerge from the deeper shadow of "Chineseness." A host of intriguing questions then present themselves. For example, why has the author chosen a woman to be the representative Chinese subject, when the customary pattern in modern Chinese literature is to assign this role to a male, especially a male intellectual?[37] Is gender merely incidental, as implied by the majority of Sinocentric analyses positing a "universal" Chinese subject with unspecified gender? If the desired "natural" state of grace were restored, making the Chinese people and the Chinese nation one, would the female protagonist's insanity-inducing sufferings have been salved?

Textual details in *Sangqing yu Taohong/Mulberry and Peach* suggest an emphatic "no" to this question. When the protagonist's female gender is taken seriously, widely received views on the meaning of the novel begin to fracture. Both Pai Hsien-yung and a number of mainland critics begin their plot summaries with Sangqing's innocence (Pai 1976, 210; Li and Chen 1990, 339; 367; 375; 378; 396), but textual evidence paints no such picture.[38] Mulberry has never had an innocent childhood; rather, she is haunted by memories of abuse and violence, much of it caused by institutionalized oppression of women. Patriarchy-sanctioned promiscuity abounds (multiple concubines

and mistresses, legalized rape of maidservants, etc.); only it is not called promiscuity, a label reserved for condemning "loose women," but Confucian
tradition.

I read the critics' fabrication of an unblemished origin for Sangqing/
Taohong as bespeaking a desire to preserve the notion of an ideal *zhonghua
minzu* victimized by history (as if this *minzu* were not made up of people
who enact history, as if history were some inexplicable natural disaster).
On this point anti-Communist and pro-Communist readers converge: both
are silent about certain "unspeakable" aspects of history that would have
marred such a reassuring narrative. For the former, the "unspeakable" is
how the Nationalists lost the civil war despite massive U.S. aid; for the latter,
it is what kind of fate someone like Sangqing—from the gentry, with a
record of sexual misconduct, and indifferent to politics—would have met
had she stayed on the mainland. An all-purpose word, "tragedy," enables
one to fast-forward history, skipping the manifold reasons why contemporary Chinese subjects have been scattered. Perhaps Sinocentrism *needs* a
narrative of modern Chinese history as a coherent story of the fall, and such
a narrative can only be achieved by projecting innocence and health onto
Mulberry (the Virgin) while assigning sin and anguish to Peach (the Whore).

The question then arises of how the woman's body, especially the
woman's sexuality, has been used to serve the task of narrating nation—a
question that has been fruitfully explored by Lydia Liu in a "modern Chinese
literature" context (Liu 1994). Following Liu, I contend that in the vision set
forth in Nieh's novel, the interests of nation and the interests of women are,
more often than not, at odds with each other, and that the crises of nation
are typically a contest between patriarchal structures in which women have
no say. For example, in part 1, when the Refugee Student tries to rally his
fellow passengers with a stirring patriotic, anti-Japanese song, he raises one
of Peach-flower Woman's blouses, which the wind blows into a suggestive
shape like ample breasts. This image recalls Cynthia Enloe's analysis of how
women (and their sexuality) have typically functioned to support the nation-
state (Enloe 1989, 54).[39] Yet while Peach-flower Woman serves the meta-
phorical needs of nation, she has been excluded from its political structure
through imposed illiteracy: she can't even write her own name, and so can
never take part in the kind of signature campaign advocated by the Student. As part 1 is about to end with the news of the Chinese victory over
Japan, Nieh leaves us with the striking image of three generations of men
clinging to, and gratifying themselves on, Peach-flower Woman's reclining
body, her baby sucking noisily at her breast, and the Refugee Student and
the Old Man at her feet, each smoking a cigarette stuck between her toes.

In another inspired image (narrated by the Old Man) with the Rape of
Nanking as setting, a Chinese man and a naked Japanese soldier (a would-be

rapist) are shown tussling absurdly over a Chinese woman (the Chinese man's newly wedded wife). The former yanks at the latter's tiny penis while the latter bites the Chinese man's neck, but the fight is broken up by a German member of the International Relief Committee in Nazi uniform, whose sleeve insignia sends the Japanese soldier fleeing. Thus are the grand narratives of nation, stories capable of justifying world wars and rousing armies of patriots to action, reduced to a farcical scuffle between inept and insecure men, whose power is derived from accoutrements rather than from any inherent strength. Meanwhile, the woman in whose name the fight is fought is left out of the picture.[40] (She eventually becomes crazed from repeated trauma.)

In setting forth feminist interventions in an Asian American context, I am not arguing for an Asian American exceptionalism, suggesting that Asian American critics have a monopoly on feminist insights.[41] What I do want to submit is that for border-crossing texts like Nieh's novel, the concept of "Asian Americanness" might provide a catalyst for deconstruction by dislodging "Chineseness" from its place of honor, and that one result of such a process is to create the room for women's concerns to emerge. Of the critics of Chinese ancestry whose work I have consulted so far, only Leo Ou-fan Lee, as touched on above, has identified a productive potential for "decipher[ing]" and "deconstruct[ing]" "the master narrative of modern Chinese history" in the protagonist's border-crossings (Lee 1994, 230). He does not, like Pai, regard removal from Chinese soil as an unmitigable disaster. His outlook is, however, recognizably different from an Asian American critic's in that a shadowy Sinocentrism remains in his advancement of the notion of "Chinese cosmopolitanism"—a combination of "a fundamental intellectual commitment to Chinese culture and a multicultural receptivity . . . *beyond* the parameters of what is known as Chinese American ethnic or minority discourse" (Lee 1994, 229).[42] The suggestion is that in today's world, one might be in a better position to be a Chinese subject (i.e., have more freedom to practice the essential components of Chinese culture damaged by totalitarianism) or even be a better Chinese subject (i.e., be more equipped to be critical of a regime's excesses) away from Chinese-ruled nation-states. While Lee and the Asian American students both question the "natural" authority of the Chinese nation, he retains a belief in Chinese peoplehood not shared by them.

Conclusion

My necessarily brief essay has left many intriguing and important questions unexplored. For the purposes of this anthology, chief among them are two related issues: first, how precisely discursive activity is articulated with material conditions; and second, whether my analysis overlooks the possibility of some kind of rapprochement between Sinocentric, Asian American, and feminist critical practices.

I have highlighted an orientational commonality between the various Sinocentric readings of *Sangqing yu Taohong/Mulberry and Peach,* but to arrive at this focus I have had to simplify both Asian studies and Asian American studies, not to mention feminist studies (addressed in my essay only through the students' readings). As a number of scholars have reminded us (e.g., Hu-DeHart 1991; Mazumdar 1991; Chow 1993), the fields of Asian and Asian American studies have separate and complex institutional and discursive histories. I did not tease apart exactly how, under the Sinocentric rubric, critics variously located vis-à-vis "China" are embedded in—and have their readings made possible by—a matrix of economic relations and political/bureaucratic structures. Nor did I show how, within the Asian American context, changing demographics in the academy (both faculty and students) and in institutional job market forces have made for a time-lagged interest in Chinese-language works on American life such as Nieh's novel.[43] Perhaps examining the case of Nieh's novel alongside another well-known border-crossing text enjoying time-lagged critical attention, Theresa Hak Kyung Cha's *Dictée* (which is, however, in English), might foster more nuanced understandings of diaspora, postmodernism, globalization, postcoloniality, and a host of related notions currently interfacing with both Asian and Asian American studies.

The fact of existing interfaces raises the possibility of some sort of fusion or synthesis—of reconciling contradictions and eliminating all blind spots through an attempt to delineate, take into account, and respect as many critical practices as can be enumerated. To return to Elaine Kim's remark with which I began this essay, there have, after all, been many observable signs of increasing traffic between Asian and Asian American (identities, cultural productions, institutional entities, etcetera). Furthermore, theoretically certain combinations of interests are certainly entertainable; thus a Chinese-nationalist outlook and a feminist one need not be mutually exclusive, although at the present moment Sinocentric readings of *Sangqing yu Taohong/Mulberry and Peach* tend to be short on feminist subjectivity and long on Chinese subjecthood, and although the most trenchant feminist critiques I have encountered occurred in an Asian American context through the mediation of Anglo-American feminism.

Yet as I argued above, the tangled publication and reception history of the novel has already cast serious doubts on the concept of author as self-consistent artistic orchestrator, and the case of part 4 has demonstrated that the author herself may not be able to provide the ultimate authorized/authoritative analysis of what her work means. While in one sense *Sangqing yu Taohong/Mulberry and Peach* is an impeccably crafted allegory, in another sense it self-deconstructs relentlessly, its form (deliberately fragmented as it is in good high-modernist manner) inadequate to the task of ordering contending historical forces into a singular narrative. In addition to the factor of change over time, this unruliness of the material accounts for the shifts in Nieh's own focus from one preface to another of her various editions, highlighting now universality, transcendence, and the human condition; now the peculiar tragedy of Chinese history; now the hermetic purity of the dictates of art.[44] If the "source" of the novel herself, encapsulated in Nieh's single body, mind, and history cannot be unified, one might reasonably ask if diverse critical and pedagogical practices, each with its own material investments and corps of individual practitioners, could be. If nothing else, the selective, manageable, and "interested" focus required of any institutionalized endeavor would make an all-encompassing presentation impossible.

The case of part 4 even suggests that there might be some basic incommensurability between the Sinocentric readings and the Asian American ones, traceable to political differences between the respective discursive and material locations that subtend them. If so, this would be an incommensurability that could not be mitigated by soft-pedaling geopolitical anchorage for the concept of nation and by appealing to the transcendent, comprehensive, and difference-dissolving potential of transnationalism. Metaphorizing national boundaries, insisting that they need not be taken literally since what matter are *cultural* boundaries, would not allow one to arrive at a less contradiction-ridden reading of part 4. Nor could valorization of border-bursting multiplicity be taken as the final lesson: the protagonist is radically multiple but also in the end, by all accounts, mad.[45] The language of mutual exchange, support, understanding, and recognition is typically used to invoke the promise of Asian/Asian American intercourse. Yet while not dismissing the desirability of widening circles of acceptance, I would like to proffer the protean (and still metamorphosing) career of *Sangqing yu Taohong/Mulberry and Peach* as a case study in the need to attend to historical situatedness.

Notes

I am profoundly grateful to Hualing Nieh for generously allowing me to interview her extensively in March 1996 and for sharing with me her collection of various editions of *Mulberry and Peach,* reviews and critical essays, and documents related to its publication history. Special thanks are due the many colleagues who have provided astute and helpful comments on earlier drafts of this essay; among them, the editors of this volume, Kandice Chuh and Karen Shimakawa; Rachel Lee; Colleen Lye; David Palumbo-Liu; and the participants, too numerous to name, of the 1996 University of Washington workshop on the *Orientations* anthology project. Shu-mei Shih kindly shared her unpublished manuscript on Nieh's novel. I greatly appreciate the thoughtful comments made by students in my Spring 1996 seminar, especially Eliza Noh and Sandy Oh; and the compelling analyses offered by my former dissertation advisees (now esteemed colleagues) Tina Chen, Jeannie Chiu, Monica Chiu, and Viet Thanh Nguyen. Without their provocative insights this essay would not have been written.

1 Depending on the romanization system used, the author's surname is sometimes spelled "Nie"; the given name, hyphenated as "Hua-ling." The last name of her late husband, poet Paul Engle, is sometimes appended to her surname. In the reference list, only the Beacon Press paperback edition will appear; though now out of print, it is the last available English version in the United States. Other publication information will be provided and discussed in the text of the essay.

2 I am indebted to Shih for permission to quote from her unpublished paper.

3 The Chinese names literally mean "mulberry green" and "peach red" (or "peach pink"). For convenience, the English names of the protagonist will be used in the essay unless the context calls for Chinese.

4 Nieh was hired as a consultant by the Iowa Writers' Workshop in 1964. Nieh and Engle founded the International Writing Program at the University of Iowa in 1967. Nieh is still living in Iowa City (Engle passed away in 1991).

5 In 1988, *Sangqing yu Taohong* was published in full by Hanyi seyan chubanshe in Taiwan.

6 In Hong Kong, another edition of the full Youlian version was published by Huahan wenhua shiye gongsi in 1986.

7 At the time, all the mainland publishers were under direct government control. In her interview with the author, Nieh noted that given the political and cultural conditions in China at the time, it would have been impossible to publish *Sangqing yu taohong* at all if the cuts hadn't been made.

8 Published by Chunfeng wenyi chubanshe and Beijing's Huaxia chubanshe (as part of its "haiwai huawen zuojia xilie" or "overseas Chinese-language writers series"), respectively. Place of publication of Chunfeng not provided by author.

9 New World Press, which specialized in foreign language publications, was under government control, like all publishers on the mainland at the time.

10 Besides English, *Sangqing yu taohong* has been translated into many languages, among them Dutch, Hungarian, and Croatian. These lie beyond the scope of this essay and the limited compass of my literary knowledge, but would certainly make for a fascinating project in comparative reception studies.

11 Nieh added the subtitle out of a concern that Anglophone readers might find the terms "mulberry" and "peach" rather unintelligible, since these plants evoke entirely different associations in English than in Chinese.

12 For the purposes of this essay, a certain amount of "fudging" is tolerated for the sake of referential convenience. To refer to "the whole thing"—the collection of overlapping texts that constitutes the subject of this investigation—I say "Nieh's novel," or else link the Chinese and English titles with a slash. The unexpurgated Youlian edition in Chinese and the Feminist Press edition in English are considered the "default" versions.

13 Numerous scholars have studied the Chinese diaspora. A partial sampling of titles from recent years, both scholarly and journalistic, includes Cushman and Wang (1988), Pan (1990), G. Wang (1991), Skeldon (1994), Tu (1994), Seagrave (1995), Ong and Nonini (1997),

Suryadinata (1997), Wang and Wang (1998), and Ong (1999). Wang and Wang (1998) is based on the proceedings of the historic 1992 Luodi Shenggen: International Conference on Chinese Overseas, held in San Francisco. The ISSCO, or International Society for the Study of Chinese Overseas, was founded as a result of the conference and now has a large worldwide membership.

14 These include Pai Hsien-yung, Chang Hsi-kuo, Yu Li-hua, and others.

15 An additional indicator of interest: *Calyx,* a feminist journal in the United States, reviewed Nieh's novel (Lim 1990).

16 As examples of prima facie "empirical" support for this view, I point to not only the novel's publication by Beacon Press in its "Asian Voices" series (which includes both Asian and Asian American writers), but also its inclusion in Cheung and Yogi (1988), whose bibliography of Asian American literature is standard in the field, as well as the fact that the novel received a Before Columbus Foundation American Book Award in 1990, nominated by Shawn Wong, a veteran Asian American writer and anthologizer. For a related discussion on discursive placement, see Ma (1998).

17 Chinese American historian and activist L. Ling-Chi Wang must be credited with having the foresight and initiative to offer this course when he was chairman of the department in the early 1980s. I am deeply indebted to him for encouraging me to teach and study this body of literature at a time when it was considered inordinately marginal in the academy. Note that the prologue and part 4 are the excerpts from Nieh's novel selected in Li (1983), a key anthology on this body of literature.

18 This marginality was something of which the (at best moderately educated) early immigrant writers of the *Songs of Gold Mountain* were acutely aware; see Wong (1991).

19 The study of this body of work, by the way, still commands "mainstream" status in the field, compared to the study of Asian-language texts about American life.

20 For example, my colleague Professor Genaro Padilla of the English Department at the University of California at Berkeley offered a graduate seminar on the literature of border-crossing in which Nieh's novel was used. Two student papers on *Mulberry and Peach* generated by this course—Nguyen (1997) and Chen (1998)—are among those that provided the impetus for this essay.

21 I also thank University of California colleagues who have taught the book in both "Chinese" and "non-Chinese" contexts for contributing to my reconsideration of *Mulberry and Peach* by sharing their experiences with the novel—Professors Norma Alarcon, Lydia Liu, and Genaro Padilla (UC Berkeley) and Shu-mei Shih (UC Los Angeles).

22 Wise and prescient words, these, considering how such a view was contrary to received opinion in Asian American studies when the volume was being prepared in the mid-1980s.

23 Note the highly selective nature of this canon formation process. Translations of a number of works in the *liuxuesheng wenxue* ("literature of the sojourning students") category, such as short stories by Pai Hsien-yung and Chang Hsi-kuo, have been available for a long time, yet because their content does not fit into "cultural nationalist" emphases (e.g., recovering the voices of early immigrants, valorizing the working class and Chinatown), they have not been embraced by Asian Americanists.

24 See analysis below. This section of my essay focuses on Chinese-language analyses, of which more are in existence than English-language ones, but some English-language sources also display the approach I term "Sinocentric allegorical," such as Xiao Qian's blurb from *The People's Daily* on the cover of the New World/Sino-English translation, or Yu (1993). Pai, the foremost proponent of the exile thesis, has published essays on *Mulberry and Peach* in both Chinese and English.

25 Note that while I use the feminine pronoun here, in most Sinocentric allegorical readings the gender of the Chinese subject is unspecified. This will be examined in a later section of this essay.

26 Such a view of *Sangqing yu Taohong* is considerably bolstered by analyses of other pieces in Nieh's oeuvre, in particular, the short story *Wang Danian de jijian xishi* (The several blessings of Wang Danian) in the collection of the same name (Nieh 1980b); and the novel *Qianshan wai shui changliu* (the title is translated as *Lotus* or *Far Away: A River*) (Nieh 1984). Note that in the Li and Chen anthology of critical essays, Lu and Wang (1990), with their greater interest in gender issues, represent an exception to the celebration of nation.

27 Remember that the first edition appeared in Hong Kong, which at that time was not "Chinese soil" even though the population is overwhelmingly Chinese. (Hong Kong reverted to PRC rule in 1997.) Remember, too, that the ban in Taiwan against *Sangqing yu Taohong* was not lifted until eight years later.

28 They are, respectively, four wide, vertical bands of color, a photograph of green grass and pink flowers, and an all-over floral ground. Interestingly, the latest mainland edition (Beijing: Huaxia, 1996) seems to have adopted the "aesthetic" approach.

29 The widely cited English version was published in the United States in 1976; a Chinese version appeared in *Ming Pao Monthly* (Jan. 1970). In this essay quotations are from the English version.

30 In this essay, Pai makes a distinction between these modern Chinese exile writers, for whom "the individual's fate is inevitably bound up with the national destiny of China," and European exile writers who universalize the human condition (Pai 1976, 207). In a post-Tiananmen reassessment of the relevance of *Sangqing yu Taohong,* which has enjoyed an upsurge of interest, especially in Eastern Europe, Pai negates this difference somewhat by linking the Chinese tradition of *Shijing* and *Chuci* to the Western tradition of Mann, Hesse, Solzhenitsyn, Kundera, and others; his focus, as in Edward Said's essay "Reflections on Exile" (Said 1990), is now "the world" (Pai 1989). The larger scope of Pai's recent analysis will not invalidate my point about exilic literature's ultimate preoccupation with nation.

31 Denton notes that the literature of exile is "based on a paradox: the longing for freedom from one's past and the psychological need to define one's self in terms of that past" (Denton 1989, 137).

32 It should be noted that Asian American discourse, never monolithic even in its "cultural nationalist" period (late 1960s and early 1970s), has been undergoing intensive self-critique of late regarding its theoretical underpinnings, missions, and constituencies, especially in connection with changing demographics (about two-thirds of Asian Americans are now foreign-born) and globalization. See Aguilar-San Juan (1994), Omi and Takagi (1995), and Okihiro et al. (1995) for various engagements in this self-critique.

33 For the purposes of this paper I consider these students to be trained in Anglo-American feminism; some are versed in French feminist theory, but through American institutional mediation.

34 "Claiming America," a term originally used by Maxine Hong Kingston, is now taken in Asian American cultural criticism to refer to establishing the presence of Asian Americans in the United States.

35 I am indebted to the students in my spring 1996 seminar for their stimulating discussions of *Mulberry and Peach,* especially to Eliza Noh and Sandy Oh for their comments on part 4.

36 R. Radhakrishnan notes of the immigrant (in this case Indian): "Her naturalization into American citizenship simultaneously minoritizes her identity. She is now reborn as an

ethnic minority American citizen" (Radhakrishnan 1994, 221). His insight into minority status as the result of a process of minoritization can be applied, *mutatis mutandis,* even to immigrants without official American citizenship. Moreover, we can think of the descendants of immigrants defined as "ethnic" as then being born into a minoritized subject position rather than into an undifferentiated and egalitarian "Americanness."

37 Well-known examples, heroic or antiheroic, range from (late Qing) Liu E's Lao Can to (May Fourth) Lu Xun's Ah Q and Ba Jin's Gao brothers of the *Family* trilogy, to (more recently, in 1960s–1970s *liuxuesheng wenxue,* or "literature of the sojourning students," set in the United States) Pai Hsien-yung's Wu Hanhun and Yu Li-hua's Mou Tian-lei.

38 To simplify documentation, authors in the Li and Chen anthology will not be listed separately.

39 I am indebted to Rachel Lee for drawing my attention to this source.

40 In endowing the tangle of male bodies in the fight with overtones of sexual intimacy, Nieh brilliantly suggests the bond of power between men. This is a bond from which women are excluded.

41 As mentioned above, mainland critics Lu and Wang express concern for the protagonist as female rather than merely Chinese subject, while it was Anglo-American feminist presses that published two of the English editions.

42 Note for the record that the Asian American students cited in this essay didn't appear to have read Lee when they came up with their deconstructive readings.

43 Among the factors to consider are the growing presence of immigrant scholars in American higher education (especially those from mainland China after immigration from the People's Republic resumed in 1979); their need to carve out a niche in areas hitherto unclaimed by traditional East Asian studies; the demand for "diversity" in curriculum and faculty created by liberal multiculturalism; institutional preference for scholars who can give "more bang for the buck" by teaching more than one literature and serving at once traditional disciplines and "ethnic" constituencies; and an increase in biliterate immigrant students who can fill courses on diasporic issues.

44 For example, while Nieh (1980a) provides detailed historical readings, Nieh (1988b) speaks emphatically of the novel's relevance to the human condition in general, even appearing to find sensitivity to specific events in Chinese history reprehensible. The former preface implies that artistic concerns are solipsistic, but the latter adopts the tone of an uncompromising writer at the service of her art.

45 Proving through a mad protagonist that it is the world itself that is mad—a common literary device—does not negate the fact that Mulberry/Peach is in constant pain and not functioning well.

Biyuti *in Everyday Life:*
Performance, Citizenship, and Survival
among Filipinos in the United States[1]

MARTIN F. MANALANSAN IV

———┼———

You have to be a little savvy, a little wise. You are in America now. You must know
how to act accordingly.[2] These are the wise words of one of my Filipino informants, Celia, a Filipina who has been in the United States for twenty years,
almost half of which as an undocumented person.[3] She was admonishing
her niece who at that time had recently arrived from the Philippines. Celia
spoke of those years with pride, reflecting on how far she has been able to
go and how much she has accomplished. She insisted that she overcame
all of the hardships because she knew when to perform particular scripts at
different times.

Celia's words are echoed by Ernie, a gay Filipino immigrant who notes:

> Kung gusto mong maging biyuti ang buhay mo dito sa Amerika, kai-
> langan maintindihan mo ang iba't ibang drama dito. Kapag natutuhan
> mo na—biyuti ka!
> *If you want to have a beautiful life here in America, you have to understand the*
> *different dramas here. If you learn all these, then you will be beautiful.*

Ernie deploys the gay slang words of *biyuti* and *drama,* which at first glance
are merely phonetic transliterations of the English words "beauty" and
"drama," but, as will be shown below, enable a more interesting reading of
the everyday life of U.S. Filipinos.

Mang Kiko, a seventy-year-old Filipino immigrant slightly departs
from both Celia and Ernie:

> Tayong mga Pilipino, marunong tayong makipagkapwa-tao. Whether
> sa katulad nating Pilipino o sa mga Amerkano. Kahit wala na tayo sa

ating bayan, importante pa rin paggiging magalang at mabait. Alam natin ang ating lugar. Alam natin kung sino tayo.

We, Filipinos, we know how to interact with others. Whether it is with other Filipinos or with Americans. Even if we are no longer in our country, being respectful and being good is still important. We know our place. We know who we are.

Mang Kiko spoke these words when I asked him about his assertion that Filipinos are able to immigrate and survive successfully in the United States. His words depart from Ernie's and Celia's in the way he conceived performance as proper conduct and as indigenous habit. He argues that there is an implicit habitual script that guides our actions and shapes our views that persists even as Filipinos cross geographic boundaries.

These words from three Filipinos in various stations and divergent positions in America portray specific perspectives on the travails of living in the United States. They also engage the notion of performance in interesting ways. While many of these "acts," if one were to consider them as such, can be seen as instances of resistance, subversion, or contestation, many of my Filipino immigrant informants regard such performances as ways to survive. Survival in this sense is different from the notion of survival popular in ethnic studies social science literature, which traces a specific trajectory from movement, settlement, pathos, and victimization to fulfillment, assimilation, and attainment of the American dream.[4] Survival, at least in the way my informants and I deploy it, insists on polyvocal and multivalent forms that do not follow a singular path. Here, survival isn't about "adaptive" strategies that are biologically or socially rational; rather it is about quotidian struggles that may or may not "make sense," or routines or habits that become part of a daily living that is neither a celebration of resistance and contestation nor assimilation. Social action is steeped in the kinds of ambivalence that defy monolithic construction of either "free agency" or "finite social destiny."

I suggest that a useful way of apprehending and analyzing U.S. Filipinos' lives, ways of being and belonging, would be to focus on a notion of quotidian performance that takes into account emic notions, historical conditions, and structural positions. Social theorists have long recognized the efficacy of using dramaturgy in apprehending social situations. Erving Goffman and other sociologists, as well as Victor Turner and his cohort of anthropologists, have employed performance as an integral part of their theoretical and empirical explorations. Gender theorists such as Judith Butler have extended the discussion and analysis of performance in terms of the "acting out" of roles by men and women. In this paper, I want to explore critically the ethnographic and theoretical implications of utilizing a performative framework in a study of Filipinos in the United States, and by implication, investigate its utility to the fields of Asian and Asian American studies.

In my framework, performance acquires a quotidian dimension unlike most recent social and gender theories that focus on public spectacles and rituals. I investigate seemingly disparate spaces of Filipino diasporic life such as religion, family life, and leisure. To analyze the dynamics of these spaces, I utilize two pivotal idioms of Filipino gay men's argot, particularly their self-conscious valorization of theatrical or dramaturgical idioms. *Biyuti,* which is a loose transliteration of the word "beauty," is used not only to talk about the aesthetic qualities of things, people, and objects, but is also used to talk about the flow of daily life, countenance, feelings, and self (e.g., *Kumusta ang biyuti mo?* How is your beauty today? *May sakit ang biyuti ko.* My beauty is sick.). *Drama* not only refers to the theater or theatrical productions, but is used to talk about occupation, sexuality, personality, and personhood.[5] My gesture in deploying these two idioms is not so much a kind of "queering" of the Filipino diaspora as it is a strategic use of social idioms from a marginalized group of people as lenses through which to gaze and peruse the daily life of "mainstream" Filipinos. In other words, my use of these idioms, while rooted in Filipino gay men's aesthetic, is a compelling, useful, and artful way of apprehending U.S. Filipinos' lives, as well as an intervention into staid and uncritical renderings of Filipinos.[6]

I propose that family life, praying, and "having fun" among Filipinos in the United States are significant and signifying sites of negotiation and contestation. Through ethnographic fieldwork in Filipino communities in New York and California, I argue that inherent in these acts are particular "scriptings," or, more appropriately, "improvisations" of life trajectories and bodies in commonplace events and situations. Within a transnational context, such acts are circulated, scattered, and shifted according to various technologies and hegemonies. As such, "Filipino" bodies as the "literal texts" of such performances are rewritten and refigured in such moments as a karaoke sing-along, a block rosary group, and a family dinner.

On another level, this work is in part a critique of theorists such as Butler and Sedgwick on queer performativity and Bourdieu and Rosaldo on practice and habitus. By using performative idioms constructed by "natives" to read field events and conversations, I intend to subvert prevailing notions of performance analysis by centering the "actors/agents" not only as part of the "enactment" process, but also and simultaneously as part of the consumption or audience-related, scriptwriting, and autoethnographic processes. In addition, I want to explore the scope and limits of the performative paradigm to suggest how linkages and conversations between Asian studies and Asian American studies may be forged.

In the next section, I consider the efficacy of performance in its theoretical deployment in social science and humanities writings. In particular, I locate performance in relation to the everyday (as opposed to spectacle/theater), to nationhood/ethnicity (as opposed to gender/sexuality), and within the strictures of transnational and postcolonial processes. The next section consists of three vignettes or moments of quotidian performance that are not meant to be exemplary, but rather are specific engagements that shed some partial light on U.S. Filipinos' struggles to become citizens (in the broadest sense of the term) and to belong to specific communities. The final section is a critical consideration of U.S. Filipinos' lives, specifically in creating a poetics of survival and a politics of performance.

Positioning Performance

The basic stuff of social life is performance, "the presentation of self in everyday life" (as Goffman entitled one of his books). Self is presented through the performance of roles, through performances that break roles, and through declaring to a given public that one has undergone a transformation of state and status, been saved or damned, elevated or released. (Turner 1987, 81)

Performance-based research, or the use of the dramaturgical process and structure, has long been part of traditional social theory. Performance as the focus of analysis has emerged in social theory in general and in theorizing on gender and sexuality in particular as a reaction to the ideas that human behavior is predetermined and that individuals are nothing more than functional automatons following the "natural" course of social life. By performance, I mean the dynamic flow of behavior of individuals within a quotidian and/or "staged" production. A focus on performance therefore posits social behavior as a set of creative responses to situations. Schechner, speaking of Victor Turner's work, declared "[p]erformance is a paradigm of process" (1986, 8). Therefore, performance, as a key analytical concept, amplifies the processional nature of identity. Within this framework, identity is not only a state of being, but a matter of becoming and enacting. Identity then is conceptualized as contingent, unstable, and constantly being remade. The analytic of performance enables theorists and researchers to conceive of individuals and groups as imbued with agency and promotes the consideration of the complex and dynamic nature of social action.

Sociologists Garfinkel, Goffman, and other ethnomethodologists proposed that individuals in society are like actors on a stage. Goffman in particular advocated the view that in the everyday course of events, individuals "present" veiled or "managed" impressions of themselves to others depending on interests and situational constraints. Unlike most performance theorists both past and present, Goffman insisted on both the continuity and discontinuity of dramaturgical elements in everyday life. He noted:

> The legitimate performances of everyday life are not "acted" or "put on" in the sense that the performer knows in advance just what he is going to do, and does this solely because of the effect it is likely to have. The expressions it is felt he is giving off will be likely "inaccessible" to him. But as in the case of less legitimate performers, the incapacity of the ordinary individual to formulate in advance the movements of eyes and body does not mean that he will not express himself through these devices in a way that is dramatized and preformed in his repertoire of actions. In short we all act better than we know how. (1959, 32)

In anthropology, Victor Turner concentrated on the performative dimensions of ritual and public expressive forms from parades to actual theatrical productions. For Turner, performances provided a way of understanding the ritual process. Ritual, in a sense, was a way of resolving social and symbolic crisis. Anthropologists like Hymes, Ben Amos, and others concentrated on performance in relation to language and folklore.[7] This group examined oratory, public debates, and other forms of what is called "verbal art" (Bauman 1977).

Research on sexuality and gender has also used the performative paradigm in different ways. In sociology, the "sexual scripts approach" (following the symbolic interactionist school of thought) suggested that sexual conduct is constituted through a scripting process on societal, intergroup and intrapsychic levels (Simon and Gagnon 1984, 53). An individual's sexuality therefore is a performance of the proscriptions and prescriptions of the social environment. Esther Newton's (1972) pioneering work on female impersonators proposed the idea that gender is a "fabrication." Following Newton's formulation, Butler (1990) codified the notion of gender performance and suggested the processes of mimicry inherent in the process of "being" "female" or "male." Butler's emphasis on the primacy of surface while alluding to anthropological examples (primarily Newton's) fails to consider the kinds of cultural idioms, pleasures, and pains involved in the configuration of surface. In other words, Butler unwittingly robs the social "actors/actresses" of agency and instead relegates them into competent mimics.

Recent studies on performance from the humanities—namely, feminist, drama, gay and lesbian, and queer studies—have focused on the strictly textual genres of theater.[8] For example, the current fascination with cross-dressing has been focused on "staged" performances with very little regard to what happens outside and beyond the "stage." Most if not all of these works are focused on the aesthetic contours of a well-bounded performative text, be it a one-person monologue, a play, or a parade.

In this essay, I am concerned with the aesthetic dimension of performance only as it informs the narratives and behavior of my informants. I believe that performance as an analytical concept, despite Butler's attempts to extend its explanatory uses to issues of gender and sexuality, has remained largely confined to "staged" or theatrical genres. Following Morris's (1995, 585) lead, I want to push the discussion on performance into the still widely unexplored arena of ethnic and racial performances in everyday life. This is not to say that the everyday does not contain elements of spectacle and theater (in the strict sense). Rather, I am suggesting that in order to understand both extremes, the interpenetration of the everyday with spectacle and theater must be centered. Most importantly, by grounding the discussion of gender and sexual performance in the everyday life of a specific group, one can alleviate the pitfalls of turgid theorizing.

To accomplish this task, I utilize the concept of *positioned performance*. Positioned performance partakes of traditional theories on social behavior and recent theorizing on gender and power. With this concept, performance is structurally located within various hierarchical relationships and implies divergent engagements of actors with so-called scattered hegemonies. In other words, performance is constituted and contextualized by power and history. The concept of positioned performance is grounded not only from the vantage of theory, but more importantly, from the actors' point of view and cultural knowledge. I arrived at this theoretical stance from the consistent themes that arose from fieldwork with Filipino gay men. In many instances, informants' discourses and behavior presented a persistent performative view of the world. This is evident in the pivotal idioms of biyuti and drama that encapsulate a self-conscious "native" notion of performance. These idioms serve as a means of conceptualizing the world and more importantly, inform proper conduct and action.

Anthropological studies of island Southeast Asia suggest that performance is an important component in issues of power and gender.[9] Anderson's (1972) influential essay brilliantly interprets a Javanese conception of power into that of potency. Potency is not a matter of who owns what and how much. Material things are seen as "traces" or after-effects of potency, which is primarily invisible (Errington 1990, 143). One is able to demonstrate one's potency in terms of being able to command an audience's attention (Errington 1990, 143). Errington noted that:

The performing arts tend to be far more important through island Southeast Asia than are any silent plastic or visual arts. Dance, trance-dance, public curing rites through spirit possession, shadow puppet theater, public chanting of sacred texts—these are the characteristic and best-known expressive forms of island Southeast Asia. It is no accident that these performances attract audiences, that the performers . . . are regarded as capable of performing because they are spiritually potent, and that the degree of the performer's potency tends to be judged by the size of the audience they [sic] attract. . . . Attracting audiences is crucial to demonstration of potency, and therefore to the exercise of "power" such as it is, in both large hierarchical politics and smaller, more level politics. Individuals who aspire to tap potency and gain prestige must attract audiences. (Errington 1990, 43–44)

In matters of gender, Errington posited that in island Southeast Asia, "Differential access to power tends to be located in theory, not at the level of the 'person's' intrinsic gendered characteristic or anatomy analogue, but in practices" (Errington 1990, 40). This is not to say that women have the same access to power as men in this part of the world despite the fact that gender differences are less pronounced here than in other regions. Rather, it is to suggest that the few times when women do acquire prestige and power/potency, these factors are not seen as anomalous. The immediate concern has to do with being able to demonstrate potency through performance. Performance therefore is the crucible of power/potency in island Southeast Asia.

Moreover, ethnographies of Southeast Asian societies suggest that performance is the necessary template of proper conduct and is an index of a person's moral being. Central to this suggestion is the seeming preoccupation of Southeast Asian societies with "surfaces." Peacock's (1968) study of *ludruk,* a Javanese popular theatrical genre, suggests that performance is based on the principle of *alus,* or refinement. Alus is part of Javanese cosmological distinctions between refinement and crudeness (*kasar*) that permeate not only aesthetic performances but much of daily life. *Alus-kasar* distinctions can be perceived in terms of situations involving the difference between: high (court) and low Javanese language;[10] humans and animals; batik fabric and cheap cloth; and restraint in art or etiquette and unrestrained expression of impulses (Peacock 1968, 7). Ludruk therefore gives expression to a principal idiom of Javanese everyday life. Sally Ann Ness's (1992) study of *sinulog,* a dance practiced in Cebu City in the Philippines, indicated that its performance was in part an interested manipulation of surfaces or appearances of religious images and institutions. Ness suggests that the sinulog

performance enacts particular sector, class, gender, and other group interests indirectly, while Fenella Cannell notes that among the Bikolanos in
the Philippines the manipulation of appearances in various beauty contests
or church rituals provide pleasure and a means of negotiating with various
class, gender, cultural, and national hierarchies (Cannell 1991/1995).

Apart from its ethnographic foundation, the concept of positioned
performance is shaped by ideas on transnational movements and practices.
My Filipino informants, as mentioned earlier, are part of an increasing number of mobile people. U.S. Filipinos are "transmigrants," or people who
maintain relationships and other connections with both their country of origin and their country of settlement (Glick-Schiller et al. 1994). No longer
prone to "permanent rupture," these groups of peoples continually create, maintain, and transform circuits of articulation and exchange of ideas,
memories, objects, people, and technologies (Basch et al. 1994). Global and
transnational theorists have acknowledged the continuing permeability of
national and local borders and the increasing seamlessness of lives across
the world. Anthropologists Ulf Hannerz (1992) and Arjun Appadurai (1988;
1990; 1991) have in recent years attempted to theorize and codify the processes, practices, and identities that have arisen due to new transnational
structures.[11]

Appadurai had earlier noted that traditional ethnography's "incarceration of the native" or the native's territorialization to a specific place and
time is no longer viable in the present moment. He asserted that the global
ethnoscape, or the "landscape of persons who make up a shifting world
in which we live, tourists, immigrants, refugees, exiles, guestworkers, and
other moving groups," is the new terrain the anthropologist must confront
and argued that these new configurations have established a shifting cultural, economic, and political landscape that has made it imperative to create a new perspective or a new way of conducting anthropology (1991, 192).
No longer isolated, fieldwork locales have increasingly (and more obviously) linked to larger supranational structures and processes, and anthropologists must respond by focusing not on internal processes within the
group(s) s/he is studying, but rather on the interface and negotiations between different levels of interactions, ideologies, and practices. This transnational anthropology then would, in the words of George Marcus, "remake
the observed and the observer" (1992, 315–25).

Within this context, identities and processes must be analyzed in terms
of the circulation of ideas, practices, and structures because these social phenomena are no longer tied down to specific territories or spaces. As Gupta
and Ferguson noted, "[The transnational public sphere] . . . has enabled the
creation of forms of solidarity and identity that do not rest on an appropria-

tion of space where contiguity and face-to-face interaction are paramount" (1992, 9). Within what he called the "global ecumene," Hannerz noted the creation of "creolizing cultures." He argued against the tendency to look at the ongoing globalizing situation as tending toward homogenization of all cultures. Rather, he posits that such teleological thinking does not take into consideration the complex interaction and existing hierarchies of center and periphery.

Colonial and postcolonial histories, structures, and processes are instrumental in creating what can be seen as multiplex reactions and counterreactions to supralocal processes. The diffusion and reception of ideas, technologies, and other practices are not smooth, uncomplicated processes. Rather, they are marked by resistance, contestations, and lacunae. Positioned performance therefore is situated in what Rosaldo (1989) and Anzaldua (1987) call the "borderlands," which are busy intersections of race, sexuality, gender, class, and ethnicity and not so much specific geographic sites. Borderlands, as part of shifting populations and bodies, are important locations where negotiations and engagements for the creation and struggle for symbolic and biological survival are continually "staged."

Performance within this transnational era and on the global/local stage is particularly crucial for the former colonized peoples of the Third World. As May Joseph aptly puts it, the conjunction of performance and hybrid subjectivities in this context "make[s] possible competing epistemologies of mutually afflicted, dissonant and contesting narratives of empires, bodies, localities and nations" (1995, 6). Shohat and Stam argued that Third World transmigrants, or, as they call them, "hybrid diasporic subject[s]" are "confronted with the 'theatrical' challenge of moving, as it were, among the diverse performative modes of sharply contrasting cultural and ideological worlds" (1994, 42). The transmigrant is continually made aware of the performative aspects of survival, so much so that s/he is continually compelled to move or "travel" (albeit discomfittingly) between various codes of behavior. The transmigrant has a heightened consciousness of the importance of having a bricoleur's sense of the "right" or "appropriate" conduct. Such valuations of conduct continually change depending on who is (over)looking the situation, which could be anyone from an older family member to immigration authorities.

In most recent studies on performance, however, the emphases have been on the ways theatrical and/or spectacular productions shed light on the everyday. As stated above, I am interested in the way everyday life and the life narratives of U.S. Filipinos inform, and are informed, by the idioms and processes of theater and drama. In other words, I want to explore the dramaturgy of U.S. Filipinos' lives not so much as an aesthetic exercise, but as a way of understanding the articulation of their identities and the conditions under which they live. The primacy of the everyday provides an ethical basis for considering the theatrical aspects of social life. Performance, in this work, therefore is not a matter of just "acting" or "aesthetics," but rather of the struggle for survival.

Allegories of Survival in the Everyday

DINNER WITH THE DE LA CRUZ FAMILY

In 1994, I was invited to dine with the De La Cruz family. Oscar and Arlene De La Cruz and their three small children lived in a two bedroom apartment in Elmhurst, Queens. Oscar and Arlene were medical support professionals — Oscar a physical therapist, and Arlene a nurse. Their three children, ages three to seven, were all born in the United States.

Before we started dinner, Oscar was trying to calm the kids. They were busy screaming at each other while watching a television show. Oscar bemoaned the fact that these kids, having been born and raised here, have no sense of propriety. He said, "These kids don't know how to behave in front of guests. They are just too American."

Arlene called us into the dining room and presented us with an array of Filipino dishes. Arlene said, "We try to give the kids a sense of being Filipinos, at least through the food. They rarely speak to us in Tagalog. Oftentimes, when we speak to them in Tagalog, they respond in English."

Arthur, the eldest child, started whining and complaining. "Mom, you made adobo again. You know I don't like it." Arlene, who looked a little embarrassed at her son's outburst, said "Arthur, keep quiet and eat your food," to which Arthur answered with an emphatic "no" and stared back defiantly.

Oscar just sighed and complained that the kids acquire all these bad manners and habits from television. He said:

> *Dito sa* [Here in] America, you learn to be very independent even at an early age. I don't think it's appropriate *di ba* [isn't it]? If I spoke to my mother that way in Philippines, I would have been banished from the table and given a spanking. I am sure becoming independent and thinking for yourself is good, but at what expense?

Arlene chimed in to say that to become successful in America, one had to be aggressive and independent. She was also quite ambivalent about the material and emotional costs of raising a famiy in America as opposed to the Philippines:

> *Kung may pamilya ka sa Amerika napakahirap, lalo na kung may mga bata.*
> *Magastos. Kailangang ng baby sitter, kailangang ng ganito, ng ganoon. Pagkata-*

pos, nandiyan na iyong kung anu-anong mga kalokohan ang natutuhan ng mga bata. Iyang si Arthur, masyadong Amerkano na. Minsan hindi ko na maintindihan magingles. At kung sumagot sa akin, para akong kalaro niya.

It is difficult to have a family in America especially if you have kids. It is so expensive! You need a sitter, you need this, you need that. And then you have all the naughty things that the kids learn. Take Arthur. He is becoming too American. Sometimes, I can't even understand when he speaks in English. And when he talks to me, [it is] as if I am one of his playmates.

Dinner for the De La Cruzes was a way of maintaining a calm in an otherwise spiraling storm toward what they see sometimes as inevitable — the Americanization of their family. Oscar said, "I know that my kids will be Americans in their behavior, but Arlene and I will try hard to inject some Filipino traits." While the couple tries to rein in the effects and consequences of being immigrants, they nevertheless are happy to be in America. They acknowledge that they will never be able to live well materially in the Philippines. In the anxiety and ambivalence brought about by their children's "Americanized" behavior, they see their home and moments like dinnertime as ways to prevent a total capitulation to the ways and habits of Americans. As Oscar put it, "So once in a while we have *tuyo* [dried fish], the kids complain about the smell and cringe when they first taste it. Then they start eating it. Very soon, they will start asking Arlene to prepare it for every meal."

Small victories indeed, but is it resistance? Arlene and Oscar would not think so. Rather, they see it as one way to survive the unbridled onslaught of America into their homes. As Oscar has observed, as a parent, he can only try to "inject" a little of the Philippines whenever it is possible, and then sit back, maybe bite his lips, and hope for the best.

KARAOKE NIGHT AT THE NEW MANILA

I was invited to a gay beauty pageant in a small Filipino-owned restaurant in Woodside, Queens in 1993. Woodside is the site of a significant Filipino enclave in New York City. The pageant was organized by Miss Saudi, one of my gay informants. He said that Miss Java, one of my main informants and one who was very famous in the circuit of Filipino drag queens, was judging the contest. I arrived at 7:30 in the evening, more or less right on time. It was my first time at the New Manila and I was expecting to be confronted by a nightclub or pub-like atmosphere. Instead, I was surprised to see a family-style restaurant with big round tables and various families seated and eating Filipino food. Except for one or two Caucasians, everybody there was Filipino. In the middle of the din of people talking, eating, and walking around, I heard someone singing at one end of the stage. It was a middle-aged man singing a Frank Sinatra song with the tune coming out of a karaoke machine.

I thought I came on the wrong night and was turning around to leave when Miss Saudi called my name. He rushed over to me saying, "The pageant is a bit delayed. Tonight is Karaoke Night, also."

I asked if the pageant would be held later after the non-queer-looking clientele had left. He said that the pageant was part of the entertainment. He further said, "It's like being in the Philippines. Somebody lip-synching and then you have a drag beauty context. Somewhat like the *karnabal* [carnival]."

I looked back at the karaoke spectacle and noticed the interesting decor of the makeshift stage. While the sound equipment and karaoke occupied the central space of the stage, there were lights that surrounded its periphery. In addition, despite being in the middle of summer, there were miniature Filipino Christmas lanterns or *parols* hung from the ceiling, interspersed with small American flags.

The man who was singing the Sinatra ballad was receiving thunderous applause from the audience every time he sang the refrain to "My Way." One of the Filipino gay men who was waiting for the contest said, "He [the singer] could easily be the Frank Sinatra of the Philippines."[12]

When I mentioned that I found this public spectacle to be very amusing, Miss Saudi explained this event this way:

Alam mo ba, kahit na restaurant ito, parang bahay na rin ito. Biro mo, pagkaalis mo ng subway diyan sa sixty-first avenue, parang nasa Pipinas ka. Hindi ba sa atin, ordinaryo na lang ang manggaya tayo ng mga Afam na singers o movie stars. Dito sa Amerika, kailangan orig na orig ka. Bakit ba? Kung hindi natin type. At least magaling tayong manggaya. Mas biyuti tayo kapag lipsynching ang drama natin.

You know, even if this is a restaurant, this is like a home. Take note, once you leave the subway at sixty-first avenue, you are suddenly transported to the Philippines. Here in America, you have to be very original [to be appreciated]. But why not? If we don't like to be [original], at least we are good at imitating. We are more "beautiful" if lipsynching was our "drama."

Miss Saudi echoed several other Filipinos who were present there. One Filipino family man who was with his wife and three children emphasized how this was part of their weekly routine—to have Friday night dinner at this restaurant and be entertained by this specific spectacle. He said:

Pumupunta kami every week—kasama na sa aming weekly routine. Pagkatapos naming sunduin ang mga bata sa sitter, tumutuloy kami dito. Gusto nami dito kasi parang nakikita ko yong mga mukha at ingay ng Pilipino. At saka yang karaoke at contest ng mga bakla—hindi ba ordinaryo lang yan sa atin. Balewala yang nagdidisplay na mga bakla na nakadamit babae. Yung kalye namin sa Malate, araw-araw akala mo may parada ng mga bakla.

We come here every week—as part of our weekly routine. After we pick up the kids from the sitter, we go directly here. We like it here because you see familiar faces and hear sounds of Filipinos. And the karaoke and the contest of the *bakla* [Tagalog gloss for cross-dressers, homosexuals, and hermaphrodites], they are ordinary events in the Philippines. It is nothing to see bakla dressing up like women. In our street in Malate [a district in Manila] it always looked like a daily parade of bakla.

The spectacle or the public drama of the karaoke is in fact infused with a kind of "strategic banality." People insisted on how routine all these activities were, and yet the allure of the place in relation to the outside world of New York City was how its seemingly unique event provided potent memories of, and vibrant reliving of, the everyday and the commonplace back in the Philippines.

BLOCK ROSARY AND MOBILE FAITH

In a small apartment in the East Village, I was witness to a gathering of thirty Filipinos who come together to pray the rosary in front of a statue of the Virgin Mary. The statue stays in one place or residence for one week, and afterwards it is transferred to another house or apartment. In the Philippines, this practice of circulating religious icons usually occurs in neighborhoods. In New York, the statues may travel to different parts of the city, and sometimes cross over to either Connecticut or New Jersey.

During this particular moment, the group also had petitions to the Virgin Mary that they wrote down on pieces of paper and that were read during the rosary prayers. These petitions were wishes or needs of individuals that they were asking the Virgin Mary to address, and might include a wish that a green card be received, a sick friend or family member be healed, that a relative in the Philippines be granted a visitor's visa to the United States, or for financial help. These petitions were in fact no different from previous petitions in other locations, and reveal the kinds of crises immigrant Filipinos face. These otherwise private crises are publicly announced albeit without the names of the petitioners. Many of the people present felt a kind of affinity with many of the dilemmas about which petitioners wrote.

One of the participants said, "I came [to America] with my faith and I have kept it." Many of those present and others whom I interviewed looked at their membership in the Catholic Church and their observance of its rituals as a kind of safety net or buffer against the harsh realities of living in a new land. Rick, a forty-year-old man, said:

> *Kayod ka nang kayod. Kahit na may mga kamaganak ka sa states, ikaw pa rin ang bahala sa sarili mo. Kung wala kang green card o kaya mawalan ka ng trabaho, mahirap na. Puro stress din dito. Kaya dasal lang ako ng dasal.*
>
> You work hard. Even if you have relatives here in the States, you are the only one responsible for yourself. If you don't have a green card or if you lose your job, it will be difficult. There is so much stress, too. That is why I pray a lot.

Religion for many of them is a refuge not only from the realities of immigrant lives, but also from what they perceive to be the secular way of life in America. One informant said that he is amazed at the relatively insignificant role religion plays in American daily life.

> *Sa Pilipinas, palaging may dasalan. Ang linggo, maraming nagsisimba. Sa New York, noong nakaraan ang Semana Santa, parang walang nangyari. Kung sa Pilipinas yan, walang mga regular TV shows. Lahat nakasarado. Dito parang balewala.*
>
> In the Philippines, there are always opportunities for worshipping. On Sundays, many people go to Mass. In New York, Holy Week came and went as if nothing happened. If it [Holy Week] happened in the Philippines, there would be no regular TV shows. Everything would be closed. Here, it is insignificant.

Filipinos articulate their difference from "others" through their religion. In comparison with other Catholics, such as the Irish and Latinos, several Filipinos I interviewed seem to believe their performance of religious duties to be more authentic. Marta, who considers herself to be very religious, is suspicious of Catholics from different ethnic/racial groups. She said, "I pray everyday, but unlike many of these Catholics, I try to maintain a good virtuous life."

Many, however, are ambivalent about the strength of their faith and how sporadic their participation is in religious practices. A few even predicted their gradual falling away from the Church. For many of those present in the block rosary prayer, however, it was one way to feel a sense of continuity in the midst of a fragmenting life in America. As Marta, the pious informant puts it, "While there are many uncertainties in living in America, there is at least one constant thing in my life, which is my religion. I don't have to wonder what I will do on Sunday. I will be in church."

The stories or allegories I have presented suggest three important points. First, they portray the dramaturgy of survival of a marginalized group in their quest for citizenship (of various sorts) and identity. Second, they illustrate how performance can be a paradigm for understanding the lives of Filipinos in the United States. Finally, they demonstrate that performance can be an important node in the continuing dialogue between Asian and Asian American studies.

These allegories are somewhat unwieldy, unruly, or possess an unfinished quality to them. As Svetlana Boym elegantly notes:

> The everyday tells us a story of modernity in which major historical cataclysms are superseded by ordinary chores, the arts of working and making things. In a way, the everyday is anticatastrophic, an antidote to the historical narrative of death, disaster and apocalypse. The everyday does not seem to have a beginning or an end. In everyday life we do not write novels but notes or diary entries that are always frustratingly or euphorically anticlimactic. In diaries the drama of our lives never ends — as in the innumerable TV soap operas in which one denouement only leads to another narrative possibility and puts off the ending. Or diaries are full of incidents and lack accidents; they have narrative potential and few completed stories. The everyday is a kind of labyrinth of common places without monsters, without a hero, and without an artist-maker trapped in his own creation. (1994, 20)

The allegories, while containing the mundane events of eating, praying, and leisure or play, set forth a series of dilemmas about living through and despite the trauma and damage of displacement (Jan Mohamed and Lloyd 1991). These traumas occur in episodes such as the dilemma of locating established religion in the lives of immigrant Filipinos or imbuing the right values and habits in children. They are ways that on the one hand revivify ideas and memories of the homeland, while on the other problematically engage the harsh realities of living in America and its concomitant problems, such as acquiring a green card. In other words, the performance of particular quotidian tasks such as dinner or leisure betrays the doubleness of engaging "trauma," which includes the contrasting realities of erasure and preservation. The difficulties of living in America are partially erased and highlighted at the same time. As Jan Mohamed Lloyd further suggest, the trauma and damage are never completely forgotten nor completely acknowledged, but rather is always, whether wittingly or unwittingly, only partially resolved.

The allegories also paint the picture of the impossibility of total assimilation. Oscar and Arlene De La Cruz's situation of raising kids and the New Manila's not-so-new entertainment style show the implicit ambivalence present in the immigration experience. While the De La Cruz family seems to be biding their time until they witness their kids' total Americanization, they attempt to tame the seemingly wild force of American mores and values by orchestrating what could be seen by many as futile resistance. The awareness implicit in the couple's understanding of the assimilation problematic, in terms of proper conduct, provides a crucial view of how quotidian or everyday performance can be understood. In part, everyday routines such as the dinner are technologies for disciplining individual bodies. At the same time, however, and as the De La Cruz family has shown, bodies are neither passively nor completely inscribed with American or Filipino habits.

The karaoke and the block rosary events portray the ambivalence of attitudes and instability of events, particularly as Filipinos both publicly and privately re-cover the spaces of belonging in both the homeland and the land of settlement.[13] The drama of singing Frank Sinatra ballads and the biyuti of being a devout rosary crusader reflects in part geographic, moral, and cultural dissonance present in the performance of these two events. Thus the informants' words reveal and rehearse the travel and movement of bodies, ideas, and practices, and at the same time uncover the dynamic of nonmovement that immigrants need to create in order to survive.[14] Immigrants, while having physically traveled or moved, need also to root themselves in whatever way and however incompletely in the new land in order to live. Thus while there may be echoes or simulation of travel in particular moments, there are also, as in the petitions, moves toward some kind of rooting to the here and now—to such banal needs as passing a licensing exam to practice medicine in the United States.

These allegories uncover the strategic importance of the commonplace and the quotidian. While many performance theorists are actively involved in the analysis of the theatrical spectacle, the biyuti of everyday life, as in a daily meal, is founded on the drama of social actors/actresses struggling to survive routine oppressions and violence. The importance of such ritualistic yet mundane acts, which often escape the critical eye of many cultural studies scholars, is inherent in their ability to shed light on the rather tenuous connections between morality/ethical considerations and gritty survival. The instances of gratification and pleasure in the family meal or a restaurant drag show, as in the organized practice of religious beliefs suggest alternative modes of being and belonging. While many of these Filipinos recognize that they are in America for the long haul, these scenes from the everyday exhibit intentions and agency around what, to many of them, are good or moral ways of surviving.

More importantly, these quotidian acts highlight the eccentric locations of Filipinos in the United States, as Oscar Campomanes (1995) has so convincingly stated.[15] Despite the colonial and postcolonial political, military, economic, and cultural connections between the Philippines and the United States, Filipinos are not legibly memorialized or adequately represented in the U.S. national imagination. The very notion of "Filipinos in the United States" in fact dramatizes the ironic displacement that haunts Filipinos living, working, and trying to survive and "settle" between America's shores and borders. The scriptings of the lipsynching performances, the rosary sessions, and daily meals depart from the protocol of the nation by (re)staging alternative and multiple "origins." This is made clear by the fact that performances of the biyuti of being either Filipino or American are in flux, despite the persistence of particular icons and practices. The biyuti and drama of such events as the rosary ritual and the restaurant meal and entertainment do not rest solely on the evocation of one place or one original source. Rather, these events follow circuitous paths of connections and disconnections. As the insightful words of Miss Saudi suggest, Queens and Manila, the United States and the Philippines, mutually mimic each other. The boundaries between these disparate places blur on the levels of image and sound.

It is at this juncture that the performative paradigm acquires its importance to the task of apprehending the links and attempts at conversations between Asian and Asian American studies. Navigation of disciplinary and areal borders demands a positioning of the performance paradigm within bodies of knowledge that have long been consigned to and incarcerated within specific "culture areas" or "regions." Deploying this paradigm is a strategic way to offset such artificial demarcations. Positioned performance and the performative paradigms open up a space between these two "areas" of study by demonstrating how the popular idea of "traditional scripts" long ascribed to Asians living in Asia is no longer feasible. The linkages and routes made by postcolonial Third World migration implicitly demand a remapping of such frontiers. The allegories of positioned performance therefore describe and define the ways by which "new" traditions are being carved within and against hegemonic "national" traditions.

In many ways, Filipinos at the New Manila Restaurant and the goings-on at the De La Cruz household point to a more fruitful path for the scholarly examination of the dynamics of citizenship and survival in both "areas" of study. Positioned performance provides a mode of analysis that reconsiders social actors/actresses who are unable, for various reasons, to step into the "legitimate stage" of citizenship. Citizenship, as the quotidian performance of survival, then becomes the necessary weapon against the position of monolithic scripts of legal and cultural personhood and nationhood. For Filipinos in the United States, the biyuti of everyday life and the drama of engagement and struggle take place between place and nonplace, between boundedness and movement, and between competing visions of "America" and the "Philippines."[16]

Notes

1 I use "Filipinos in the United States" or "U.S. Filipinos" to put forward the kind of naming that my informants have chosen when they engaged me in discussions, as well as to portray and defy the maverick position Filipinos occupy in the American imagination.

2 Direct quotations are given to demonstrate the specific performative turns in verbal texts. More specifically, language is a vital tool in the process of scripting that I want to portray in this essay.

3 Names of informants have been concealed with pseudonyms and other identifying circumstances have been changed to protect their privacy.

4 For an example of such work, see Gordon 1964. Omi and Winant 1986 provide a cogent critique of Gordon and other similar theorists.

5 For an extended discussion of these idioms in the context of Filipino gay men's speech, see Manalansan 1995a and 1995b.

6 For the purposes of this paper, I will not rehearse the criticisms of Filipino and Filipino American scholars regarding the problems of representation. For further discussions, see Campomanes 1995; Aguilar-San Juan 1994; and Cordova 1983.

7 See Bauman and Briggs 1990 for a comprehensive review of the study of poetics and performance in anthropology.

8 Recent works of this kind that follow Butler's (1990) include Hart and Phelan 1993; Case, Brett, and Foster 1995; Case 1994; and Taylor and Villegas 1994.

9 The archipelagic formation that is part of the Southeast Asian region comprises the cultures and peoples of Malaysia, Indonesia, and the Philippines.

10 See Siegel 1986 for an incisive study of this linguistic situation.

11 See the following works for diverse viewpoints on global issues of diaspora, displacement, immigration, and exile: the essays of Wallerstein, Friedman, and others in Featherstone's (1990) edited volume on global theory; and *Cultural Anthropology* 7(1) for groundbreaking essays on space, identity, and difference; Basch, Glick-Schiller, and Szanton-Blanc (1994) focus on cases of transnationalism and attempt to present a coherent theory.

12 In Filipino popular entertainment, there are contests for being the best imitator of a Hollywood star or an American pop singer. Filipino movie stars were also traditionally praised and given such monikers as "The Audrey Hepburn of the Philippines."

13 Strategies of "recovery" and memory, with specific reference to Filipino American community press, are also discussed in Rick Bonus's Ph.D. dissertation, University of California, San Diego.

14 See Homi Bhabha's brilliant comments in the discussion of Clifford's 1991 essay, "Traveling Cultures."

15 I am grateful to Chandan Reddy for this insight and felicitous phrase.

16 Kandice Chuh and Karen Shimakawa were the most gracious hosts in a supportive and productive conference, and most patient editors. I would like to thank Chandan Reddy for his meticulous reading of the essay and consistent encouragement, and Rick Bonus for his astute comments and for suggesting relevant readings.

Missile Internationalism

KUAN-HSING CHEN

The Lack

As the only author positioned outside the geopolitical space of U.S. academia, ever since being invited to contribute to this volume, initially titled "Disciplining Asia," I have felt compelled to solve the puzzle: Who is the subject attempting to "discipline" Asia? Which parts of the disunified "Asia" are we talking about? If I understand correctly, this project is a programmatic move to forge a disciplinary space *between,* intended to *cross* or *disrupt* the boundaries of Asian and Asian American studies. What makes this negotiation possible seems to be on the surface a common *object:* the imaginary space of "Asia"—a product of imperialist mapping in history; and the hidden enunciating *subject* forging this link turns out to be the same as the one who attempts to "discipline Asia"—another putative positionality, the American/U.S., another result of European conquest. This lack of acknowledgment of the enunciating site has been the common practice for the self-claiming "intellectual" (oftentimes academics, in practice), living between the walls of American campuses. More deeply, whether diasporic or otherwise, it is an imperial nationalism—"We are the world," a political unconscious that blocks out reflexivity to utter its own geocolonial location in the nation-state.

To problematize this desire for convergence, one then has to mark out the historical conditions of possibility within which the desire for linkage takes place. The current vogue of "globalization" provides an all too easy answer. It not only loses specificities, but also erases the historical trajectories of colonial imperialism. Movement activists put the matter succinctly, in relation to the NAFTA and APEC formations, when they spoke out "Against Imperialist Globalization."[1] Nonetheless, the coming together of the two discursive fields (Asian and Asian American studies) does interestingly connect to the globalization question, even though these two institutions have been operating within the same national space. It seems to be true that what links Asian studies (growing out of the Cold War area studies formation) and Asian American studies (coming out of progressive human rights movements of the 60s, through a "transnational" alliance of nationality and ethnicity within the U.S. context) together is the concentrated direction of global capital flow into Asia and the changing relation of the nation-states in Asia with respect to the United States. One could easily cite the increasingly salient phenomenon of Asian diasporics, growing up and trained in the United States, who have become the frontal forces in the operation of transnational capital (TNC) in Asia, and who have also become middlemen mediating between the United States and Asian states through funding/donation. In other words, the forging of the necessary link between the two "disciplinary" fields is actually a "forced" response to the already established, if not intensified, alliance among the sectors of the state and capital.

As an "outsider," geopolitically and disciplinarily, I understand well the fluidity of the diasporic flow that has rendered the spatial stability of the inside/outside metaphor impossible; that is, "America" has been inside "Asia," just as "Asia" has been inside "America" throughout the 20th century, if not earlier, in the mid-19th century. Yet this very fact weighs and is structured differently on the level of the cultural imagination in diverse non-unitary sites and has to be problematized historically. For those of us doing critical cultural analysis, living in the so-called post-Cold War Asia, and disconnected from the aforementioned fields, to better understand "America's Asia" in our own context, there seems to be a logical necessity to also reconnect to these two communities, for intellectual as well as political reasons. At the same time, the desire for linking has to be cautiously measured against the all too easy ethnic-regionalist interpellation ("Asian" and "Asia") that springs the trap of reproducing that trait of colonial government categorization (whether by race, ethnicity, nationality, or regionality), and its continuing figure, transnationalism (of capital and state). Against this background, I shall reinvoke the pan-class based politics of internationalism, an almost buried tradition of the internationalist left. With the emerging paradigmatic shift toward the "postcolonial" episteme, internationalism is not simply a "return of the repressed," but a political response to push further the incomplete project of decolonization.

In the 1996 "Dialogues with Cultural Studies" Conference, held at

Tokyo University, Stuart Hall openly acknowledged the overprivileging of "English" experience in the current state of postcolonial studies. This over-privileging might have to do with the historical experiences of the key pro-ponents of postcolonial studies, who came out of the English (ex-)colonies, or with "English" being the hegemonic language, which has rendered publi-cation in other languages rather invisible.[2] Indeed, once the analytical focus is put on different geocolonial sites, such as the East Asia region, other im-perial forces will come to the forefront. Throughout the entire 20th century, two most critical imperial forces have come to shape local-national cultural formation in the East Asia region: Japanese colonialism in the first half of the century, and U.S. neoimperialism in the second. While literature on the historical experience of Japanese colonialism has been abundant, studies on U.S. imperialism seem to be relatively absent.[3] It is rather curious that in the current vogue of postcolonial studies, which has almost constituted a para-digm shift not only in the field of critical cultural studies but increasingly reconfigures other disciplinary formations, such as Asian and Asian Ameri-can studies within the U.S. academy, the question of U.S. imperialism has not been adequately posed. Perhaps the purpose of this essay is precisely to put the question back in, at least to begin to address the question of the culture of U.S. imperialism in the context of East Asia.

Yet how do we account for this "lack"? The easiest, but least satisfy-ing way, to answer the question is to deny the imperial status of the United States: the hegemony of the United States has been achieved through "lead-ership," by winning global consent rather than by imposing force, military and otherwise. This argument immediately crumbles if we bring in the obvi-ous U.S. military presence in Asia, not to mention the Gulf War or the recent missile attacks on Iraq. The denial can be more subtle. In the introduction to *Cultures of United States Imperialism,* an important intervention within the tradition of American studies, Amy Kaplan explains,

> Most current studies of imperial and postcolonial culture, however, tend to omit discussion of the United States as an imperial power. The history of American imperialism strains the definition of the post-colonial, which implies a temporal development (from "colonial" to "post") that relies heavily on the spatial coordinates of European em-pires, in their formal acquisition of territories and subsequent history of decolonization and national independence. How would this Euro-centric notion of postcoloniality apply to the history of American im-perialism, which often does not fit this model? (Kaplan 1993, 17).

That is, there is an epistemological break between Eurocentrism and Amer-icancentrism.[4]

The second way is to attribute the omission to the construction of the Cold War: the formation of an anti-Communist bloc and of anti-Communist ideology have effectively displaced the question of U.S. imperialism, and the arrival of the post-Cold War era (after the dismantling of the Soviet Union and Eastern Europe) has reopened the political space for the question's return. There might be limited truth to this argument. To secure governing power, political regimes in places such as Japan, Korea, and Taiwan have formed alliances with the United States to combat Communist enemies, and the effectiveness of interpellating anti-Communist fear has not allowed any possible discursive positionality to pose the question of imperialism to "Big Brother."[5] The danger of the Cold War determinist argument is the outward projection, and dumps the responsibility on the "outsiders" without confronting the nationalist desire of identification and disidentification with the culture of U.S. imperialism; it further exaggerates the radical discontinuity in so-called postwar politics.[6] Writing within the context of the 1948 Cheju Island massacre (also known as the "4.3 event"), Seong Nae Kim argues,

> The 4.3 Event and its violent closure in massacre prefigured the Korean War in 1950, the ideological battle of the Cold War which ended in stalemate with the loss of millions of lives. Although the Cold War has ended, anti-Communist ideology continues to dominate state politics in South Korea and has effectively silenced much of the memory of the 4.3 Event. . . . Since the end of World War II, it could be said that Koreans have lived under "the state of emergency" for national unity and identity. This profound sense of emergency has served to justify state violence in both separate regimes of south and north Koreas. . . . As it is described as "a microscope on the politics of postwar Korea," the 4.3 Event remains stigmatized as a primal scene in the acceleration of Korean modernity, that is closely related to political violence of the state. (S. N. Kim 1996)

Taking clues from Kim's warning not to exaggerate the post-Cold War discontinuity and not to dismiss the responsibility of the nationalist state, I shall argue that "colonial identification" accounts for the omission of U.S. imperialism in the context of East Asia. As studies of the cultures of U.S. imperialism are still emerging, it is precisely now that internationalist alliances among diverse intellectual communities can be formed to facilitate critical decolonization and to avoid ending up in the nationalism-on-nationalism discursive trap in the studies of "the culture of imperialism."

The third factor might be described as the problem of intellectual agency. It is really absurd that the proponents of postcolonial studies in the

U.S. academy have not properly taken up the question of U.S. imperialism. Are diasporic intellectuals complicit with imperial nationalism, and therefore unconsciously ignoring the question of imperialism? This problem, to be sure, is not limited to the Third World diaspora in the United States; it is also a problem for the Third World collaborator. Perhaps we could formulate the problem as one of diasporic opportunism and native collaborationism. The former term refers to those who reside in the imperial center space: not only selling their politically correct (multicultural) identity, they monopolize speaking positions to block voices coming from "home"; and the latter points to those "returnees" from the neocolonial empire, who have clearly projected a desire to "return" to the center. They become the native informant (drawing on theories produced in the empire, partly enunciated by the diasporic opportunists), to "report" local information, and become an academic broker in collaboration with the center powers, diasporic or otherwise, left or right. Various practices of nationalism are attacked by the two-in-one agent, but not U.S. imperial nationalism. Because self-interests are at stake, both parties are cautious about the question of U.S. imperialism and therefore are complicit in producing "the lack." This opportunism plus collaborationism obviously could not fully explain it. Why can't third world intellectuals in Asia who are not collaborating with U.S. imperial power take on the responsibility?

Historically, as a dominant cultural imaginary, "America" has never been outside "Asia," just as "Asia" has never been outside "America" since mid-19th century, as pointed out earlier. Japan was opened by the U.S. state and American capital in 1858 through the port treaty system. The impact of the system's economic and political forces should not be understated. By the 1930s, "America" had become a constitutive element in Japanese identity. The shocking passage uttered in Takanobu Murobuse's 1929 *America,* recently cited by Yoshimi Shunya, in considering " 'America' in Contemporary Japan," testifies to this point: "Where could you find Japan not Americanized? How could Japan exist without America? And where could we escape from Americanization? I dare to even declare that America has become the world, Japan is nothing but America today."[7] Obviously, the rise of the U.S. as a global power after World War I was not only felt in the imperial center in East Asia but also in European empires. As a newcomer to colonial power, the United States's strategy of "self-determination" proved to be effective not only in competition with the established power, but also in winning over the collaboration of colonized nationalist subjects. Aime Cesaire documented this sentiment in the 1940s: "I know that some of you, disgusted with Europe, with all that hideous mess which you did not witness by choice, are turning — oh! in no great numbers — toward America and getting used to looking upon that country as a possible liberator. . . . So, once again, be careful! American domination—the only domination from which one never recovers" (Cesaire 1950, 60). Here, Cesaire did not give us the detailed argument to explain why American domination would be the *only* form from which one could never recover; but Cesaire's intuitive formulation might well be to warn pro-American enthusiasts that a new form of imperialism without the older form of territorial colonization was emerging.

Indeed, the defeat of Japanese imperialism after World War II was immediately replaced by the U.S. occupation. In the context of Korea, "Americans found that they had to use Japanese systems . . . [the] military, the bureaucracy, or the policy" (Cumings 1984, 479–50). That is, there seems to exist a genealogical handover from Japanese to U.S. imperialism throughout the East Asia region. Since the Hiroshima/Nagasaki atomic bomb incident, the Japanese nation-state has been living under the permanent shadow of the United States; South Korea and Taiwan have been hailed as loyal allies. Even the People's Republic of China has seen the United States as the negative Other, the representative of the West. Ever since the 1950s, "America" has gradually become an "inside outsider" or an "outside insider" against which slices of (national) identity have been formed. Without having to go through an inventory listing, one would only have to point to the current popularity of the "X Can Say No" phenomenon to see "the U.S. complex." "Japan Can Say No," "China Can Say No," and even "Taiwan Can Say No." Unmistakably, the United States is the object-unity of this "no." [8]

This, then, is what I take to be a central problematic that might serve as a linking point for different disconnected fields. From my point of view, this undertaking has to depart from the earlier cultural imperialism thesis that sees that the new wave of imperialism no longer operates through territorial acquisition, but imposes its cultural product from the "outside" to "brainwash" the Third World subject, without explaining the inner logic of cultural imperialism. Instead, this undertaking might have to push seminal work such as Edward Said's *Culture and Imperialism* from the imperial centers to the colonized spaces of East Asia so as to open up the problematic of how imperialism generates long term effects. This happens not so much through cultural apparatuses such as transnational media intervention, but through negotiation and articulation of political-economic forces vis-à-vis local histories in various sites. In other words, the question becomes: how and through what processes and mechanisms are capitalist and imperialist globalizing forces dialectically articulated to the local cultural formation?

From the point of view of the history of a global decolonization movement, the contemporary moment of the (ex-)colonies in the East Asia context is still one of a process of decolonization, and in at least three convolutedly connected forms: nationalism, nativism, and civilizationalism. All three forms have been endorsed, but at the same time critically cautioned against, by earlier analysts: Fanon's critique of nationalism in the 1940s and 1950s during the peak points of the Third World independence movement; Memmi's questioning of nativism during the 1950s and 1960s; and Nandy's revitalization of a critical traditionalism (or what I describe as civilizationalism) some twenty years after the formation of India.[9] These interventions, though produced outside the East Asia region, might be helpful as anchoring points toward an understanding of the historical formation of psychocultural structures. It will become clear that, in positioning cultural studies as a decolonization movement that attempts to disarticulate colonialist and imperialist cultural imaginaries that are still actively shaping our present, this paper attempts to place the culture of U.S. imperialism within the problematic of colonial identifications so as to account for the lack of studies of U.S. imperialist cultures.

To be clear, this essay has a two-fold intention. First, it seeks to establish theoretically the imaginary relation of the "United States/America" to "Asia" through the discourse on colonial identification: the United States as the object of identification and disidentification. Second, it puts this theoretical analysis in the context of the question of internationalism through a concrete historical event. I hope the implications of my own dialogue with Asian and Asian American Studies will become clear in the process.

The United States/The Object

To be sure, the Fanonian problematic was set in a context of direct colonial encounter, where skin color distinction marked the Manichaean divide, where colonial language was imposed on the populace, where symbolic systems, economic resources, political positions, and the like were in the hands of the invaders. If Japanese colonialism can be more legitimately analyzed through Fanonian eyes, then the "remote control" of the United States has been more complex. I am attempting to argue that such remote control can even be more effective, less imposing, more acceptable.

Let me put forward a rather simple theoretical proposition: the postwar history of colonial identifications has set limits on the boundaries of the local cultural imaginary, consciously or unconsciously articulated by and through the institutions of the nation-state, which in turn has shaped our psycho-political geography. The United States in the postwar era has become that central figure of identification. We reevoke identification not so much to psychologize history, but precisely the reverse: the material history of imperialism has in effect established the neocolonial master as the object of identification and even disidentification through which neocolonial systems of representation and modes of living infiltrate the space of the national-popular cultural imaginary; the directions of the flow of psychic desire and energy operate under the rubric, and within the boundary, of the colonial and neocolonial cultural imaginary. This chain of movements traverses the social body. The power of the culture of U.S. imperialism has been precisely to insert itself into the geocolonial space by taking over the status of "Japan" as the imaginary figure of modernity and constituting itself as the object of identification. Not only has American English become the first foreign language to be acquired, that nation's institutional forms have been "copied." The United States gradually became the routinized, almost the only possible, space for "advanced" education; for both the state bureaucrat and the oppositional elites, "American" experiences have become the reference points of their own legitimation. The trickle-down effects have been unthinkable to the extent that things "foreign" in the popular imagination would largely come to mean "American"; in short, "America" has been the model with which to "catch up." I don't wish to go too far in directly applying Fanon's account, suggesting that "Japanese," "Korean," "Chinese," or "Taiwanese" wants to be "American," which would not be very different than saying "the black man wants to be white."

As an ascending form of nativism, civilizationalism has been gradually emerging. Cho Hae-Joang (1995) has succinctly analyzed the Confucian Revival movement in Korea; Chua Beng Huat (forthcoming) has pinpointed the Singaporean's redrafting of the identification as Asian; and Japan is obviously undergoing a re-Asianization phase. Of course, this "self-rediscovery" movement is connected to the regionalization of global capital, but its psychoanalytical drive is once again grounded in reaction to the long-term colonial history. The pronounced or unpronounced Other, against which this Asian civilizationalist identity is defined, is the "West," now represented by "America." Throughout the region, there is a weird sense of "triumphalism" with respect to the West, despite internal antagonisms: the 21st century is "ours," "we" are finally centered. Wherever one is geographically positioned, there is an emerging cliche-like formula: "Asia is becoming the center of the earth and we are at the center of Asia, so we are the world." This is where history comes in. Contrary to the now fashionable claim that we have entered the postcolonial era, the mood of triumphalism as reaction to, and reactionary formation from, colonialism indicates that we still operate within the boundary of colonial history, which has generated a whole set of what could be described as the colonial cultural imaginary. In the context of Taiwan, the independence versus unification, or integrationist versus separatist antagonism, can be understood in such interpellation. For the integrationist, unification with China does not necessarily mean an identification with the PRC communist state; to give up the sign "China" is to throw away one's entire cultural heritage, the five thousand years of a gigantic civilization, the unitary foundation without which "Chinese" could not survive its suffering on account of, and possible partition by, the "West" in the past two hundred years. Finally, in the foreseeable future, we can predict the rise of China, the only possible force on earth to combat America.

Disidentification is meaningless without the prior existence of identification; one has to identify with something first in order to launch one's disassociation. The above analyses have no sarcastic motive or wish to ridicule any of these, but to point out that both modes operate within the same space defined by the same object. By now, I hope I have provided one possible answer to "the lack": the United States/the Object. Perhaps the implication is too obvious: we have to recognize that America has not only been with us, but has rather been part of us, if we wish to honestly understand the cultural composite of our self or selves; that the United States has not merely defined our identities, but become the referent point of our cultural imaginary. Unless the temporal and spatial logic of this cultural imaginary can be deconstructed and exposed; unless objects of identification can be redirected and multiplied, we are doomed to the histories of colonialism taken over by the neocolonial structure. Unless the cultural imaginary we have been living with can be decolonized, the vicious circle of colonization, decolonization, and recolonization will continue to move on.

Missile Internationalism

If decolonization defines the task of a politically charged postcolonial studies, and this task can only be fulfilled collectively across borders, then internationalism might be a viable positioning. I have written about internationalism, or, more specifically, a new internationalist localism, in relation and response to two interrelated enterprises: nationalism and transnationalism, but never in relation to Asian and Asian American studies, as such (Chen 1992, 1997). The historical formation of these two enterprises, to be sure, have always been transnational in character, but I very much doubt whether there is a self-conscious internationalist component in the mainstream practices; at its best, it might be homologous to what I shall call the most powerful form of internationalism, that of the nation-state, predicated on the nationalist interpellation, or, to use the official term, national interests. This I shall call a "missile internationalism."

Prior to the 1996 Taiwanese Presidential election, a significant number of e-mail messages came to me from friends who, living outside Taiwan — not necessarily ethnically Chinese or Taiwanese — are concerned with the missile crisis. These friends seemed to be more nervous than we were. Once you were there, there did not seem to be much you could do. Life has to go on. This powerlessness or indifference was then interpreted as the maturity of the people of Taiwan to handle the crisis, despite the fact that the middle class had emptied out all of its savings to exchange for U.S. dollars (Citibank had shipped in cash to meet anxious demand). Locally, the election was hailed and celebrated as the first and finally accomplished democratic achievement in four hundred years of Taiwan's history or in the five thousand years of the Chinese history, contingent upon one's political stands on independence or unification.

Right after the election, a renowned diasporic intellectual historian living in the United States wrote a long piece in the bestselling newspaper, *China Times*. He argued that the first direct presidential election for the place under the missile attack was in fact a battle between two modern concepts: democracy and nationalism. Of course, Taipei won over Beijing, the Kuomintang (KMT) won over the Chinese Communist Party (CCP), or liberal democracy over communism; in short, good versus evil. More complexly, he viewed the situation historically and argued that Chinese nationalism has changed gears from the old defensive phase to the new offensive type; the object of its attack is the United States, the sole symbol of Western imperialism surviving today. The story is of course more convoluted than his narration suggests.

What he did not point out was that the "war game" involved not only one, but rather at least three state-mobilized nationalisms: Chinese, Taiwanese, and American. Of course it is difficult to evoke U.S. nationalism, since it's everywhere and nowhere. The "we are the world" trope of the political unconscious has saturated the American social body to the point of absurdity. More than ever, internally "Taiwan" is for the first time now unified, regardless of ambiguous ideological differences that emerged when confronting the Chinese missiles. The three political parties agreed on a huge increase in the national defense budget (the oppositional Democratic Progressive Party [DPP] which used to argue persistently against the size of the defense budget, took the lead). Anti-Communist rhetoric that had died down for years now resurfaced.

Historically, after 1949, "Communist China" has been consistently constructed by the KMT state as the imaginary other to maintain its political legitimacy, which in turn overshadowed and shaped the oppositional Taiwan independence movement, using the sign of China as the other to construct its own identity and to struggle for political power monopolized by the mainlander Chinese, the KMT. These oppositional energies, essentially ethnically charged and defined, were later swallowed by the Min-nan President Lee who came to power in 1988. Through a "silent revolution," a term used by his party staff member, he gradually took over the KMT party machine. Three years ago, once he had declared that the KMT had been a political regime "coming from the outside" as a "colonial state," the entire oppositional Taiwan Independence movement collapsed into a statist project. The Lee complex finally crystallized in this election; with four candidates running, he won over 54 percent (DPP votes dropped to 21 percent).

With Lee elected, an era of political turmoil ended; state power redistribution was over and done with. He announced that a new political situation was coming into being, and that there was even a possibility of forming a coalition government: As had been widely predicted, factions within the DPP would be incorporated into the new deal; the oppositional part would be split in reality, if not in form; and one faction of the DPP party leadership was even calling for dissolving the KMT and DPP into the New Taiwan Party. In short, Lee's success was partly consequent to the missile attack. The long-term imaginary other established since 1949 finally crystallized into a real enemy. A familiar banal logic is obviously at work here: nationalism is able to resolve its internal differences and become a unity by confronting the crisis coming from the external enemy.

The "centering" of Taiwan in the global media had less to do with "democracy" and more to do with the war game between China and the United States, but Taiwan obviously benefited from the free worldwide advertising, which the state had tried, by every means possible, to garner for itself in other instances, so as to promote its "joining the United Nations" campaign, but could not get anywhere. The missile war game finally put Taiwan on the world map. In this sense, Taiwan was obviously the big winner.

On the surface, the PRC became the loser in the international arena; but not really. Its leadership not only saved face through the missile maneuvering, but also was able to use the instance to reshape and recharge its nationalist energies, which had been compromised by the market economy. No form of regionalism or separatism was possible in this moment: separatism would become the target of attack. This served as a warning not only to Taiwan and Tibet, but also to the successful economic regions of the southeast and northwest where there had been secret calls for relative autonomy.

Interestingly enough, it was around this juncture that the connection between postcolonialism and nationalism was concretely manifested in the case of contemporary China. The CCP General Secretary Chiang Tser-ming, at the end of 1995, appropriated the concept of postcolonialism in the state-mobilized "Talking about Politics" campaign, to address "Western con-spiracy," warning that "colonialist culture is now penetrating China." As a result, anti-Western and nationalist sentiment became the two sides of the same coin. A scholar working at the Chinese Academy of Social Sci-ences, who had studied in the United States, was approached by Chiang's staff member, encouraging him to link the postcolonial "theory" he had learned in the United States to political reality. He came up with the con-clusion that the major enemy of China is transnational capital led by U.S. imperialism, which is now "slowly and surely" destroying China and erod-ing national sovereignty. This did not seem to be the subjective wish of the Chinese state; it had its echo in its other—the United States. There is no space here to rehearse the 150-year-old formation of Chinese nationalism that has been reactive to the imaginary enemy of the "West." This has been the material basis for Chiang's postcolonialism to interpellate the nation-alist subject. China's entry into the structure of global capitalism has in-dicated that, contrary to the will of the globalization theorist, nationalism has not been in decline, but has become a necessary political and economic instrument for state power in competition with other states and transna-tional corporations. The missile game has put the symbolic sign, China, in the center stage of the international power game—that is, the only possible and qualified enemy of the United States in the world.

This staging was more than welcomed by the United States, which has been desperately seeking an "other" to displace the fallen USSR. Conser-vative Republican nationalists immediately jumped at the chance to launch their frontal attack. Sending the U.S. fleet to the Taiwan Strait was only logi-cal. Across party lines, the move would: protect the "stability" of the Asian region, which is our long-term role as a world police presence; protect our loyal ally, Taiwan; and, more than anything else, maintain a strong mili-tary presence in Asia (and benefit the weapons industry), something that has long been proposed by leading scholars, such as Samuel Huntington; and finally displace our attention from economic problems, increased un-employment, and multicultural conflicts, by projecting discontent on the enemy. If one could not fire real missiles at the imaginary other, one could at least do it symbolically. Therefore, this humanist internationalism is fully justified.

In the middle of the missile crisis, "An Open Letter to the Social Elites in Taiwan" reached our mailbox at school. The letter was signed by an un-known organization, Club 51, with an English slogan, "Save Taiwan—Say Yes to America—Statehood for Taiwan." When we received the seven-page letter, we thought it was probably just in support of U.S. intervention in the Taiwan Strait to counter the PRC attack. No, it was more radical than that. Club 51 called for a "Taiwan State Building Movement" to join the United States as the 51st state, so as to "guarantee Taiwan's Security, Stability, Prosperity, Liberty and Democracy." The letter was actually well argued. It said, "National identity is neither based on blood genealogy nor on military forces. We have the right to choose to be American, we have the right to live in New York or San Francisco. . . . Any intelligent person would know that without the U.S. protection, it is difficult for Taiwan to survive" (Chou 1996). Overinflating the Club 51 sentiment is out of the question here; but in a crisis situation, it is not surprising to see the overflow of suppressed unconscious desire. In such instances, one could perhaps better understand that there is no point in even uttering the phrase "U.S. imperialism."

It is precisely here that we meet Seong Nae Kim's analysis of Korean postwar modernity, where the foundational narrative has been anti-Communism: the complaint of U.S. imperialism will be immediately translated as an identification with the Communist regime. The regulated binarism leaves no space to insert critical formulation. The hidden "parental guidance" built in the past fifty years thus resembles another widely circulated claim: "if Taiwan were still under the Japanese, we probably would be better off." At the risk of arousing the resentment of my friends, I will say, paraphrasing Fanon, that both Japan and America are *inside* of our cultural subjectivity. What could be the critical effect of such a recognition? A celebration of imposed hybridity? A retreat into nativist purity? I take such recognition as part of the decolonization in motion, a point at which reactive anxiety can be turned into active forces.

So, who was the winner of the "Missile game"? The three state machines involved all got what they wanted. Nationalism triumphed. Taiwan, for the first time in the postwar era, finally found a moment of solid unity; critical intellectuals knew too well in such an instance to be silent; if not, they would be silenced. China had occasion to shift gears and drop its socialist and communist doctrine, and to launch its nationalist postcolonialism against the West, so as to cover up its internal problems carried over by the formation of a new capitalism; indeed, to insert itself as the leader of the non-West. The United States was more than happy to find its imaginary "other."

Hiding behind these three versions of nationalism is the structure of global capitalism. I know this sounds too much like an economistic position: Can Taiwan survive without the Chinese market? Can the United States forsake its economic interest in China and dominance in the East Asia region? Can the CCP on the one hand enact strong expressions of resentment against the West (which binds itself to the enemy), and on the other hand continue to seduce capital investment to help its becoming another hegemonic global power? What I call a "missile internationalism" is effectively recognition that the war game became an alliance among the three nation-states to the benefit of each.

Who was the loser then? Us: those who had no way to intervene, to disrupt the state's mobilization, and who do not believe in the staging of nationalist unity to suppress everything else. In this process, we heard nothing from the progressive sector of U.S.-based intellectuals, be they Asian or Asian American studies scholars who were supposed to be best equipped to analyze and respond to the situation; even if there had been a response, the overflow of satellite TV images in the mainstream media would have prevented the voice from being heard. For those of us living in Taiwan, the situation was immediately clear: no one could disrupt nationalist unity and find a legitimate space to speak.

This crude analysis leads to a familiar conclusion. Unless one can think of ways to move beyond self-interest, the obsession with identity politics, we will run the risk of reproducing internationalism of the nation-state on any level of abstraction. Parallel to this form of internationalism of the state and capital, another line of internationalist solidarity grounded in local constituencies has to be formed. Only then, when the next wave of the missile crisis is being staged somewhere, we will hear alternative voices from alternative spaces.

Notes

1   See "Declaration of the People's Conference Against Imperialist Globalization," a conference held in Quezon City, Philippines, 21–23 November 1996.

2   For instance, in Japan, Iwanami Publishers (1993) has released an eight volume series on its former colonies. One could even push further to argue that (post)colonial studies has been one of the major trends of intellectual concern in the post-World War II Japan.

3   For recent useful studies of Japanese colonialism before the end of World War II, see Duus et al. 1984, 1989, 1996; Peattie 1988; Takeshi 1996; for local impacts and responses, see Cheng 1996; Kang 1996; Lee 1992; *Journal of Southeast Asia Studies* 1996; Kratoska 1995; for postwar studies, see Halliday and McCormack 1973, and Lo 1996.

4   To be sure, Kaplan is not trying to deny the imperial status of the United States, but struggles to rewrite the dominant historiography. Writing within the space of American historiography, Kaplan's strategy is to relink "United States nation-building and empire-building as historically coterminous and mutually defining" (Kaplan 1993, 17).

5   For a recent account of the Cold War and post-Cold War discursive structure, see Berger 1996. The fear of communism, mobilized after World War II, has been amazingly powerful. The Cheju Uprising in 1948 in Korea and the "white horror" in 1950s Taiwan are still not reclaimed by the states because of their "red" connections. See Seong Nae Kim 1996 for a detailed argument on how anticommunism is able to operate to suppress its "internal" enemies.

6 In a recent conference, "Cold War in East Asia and State Terrorism," held in February 1997, one of the presenters dumped the entire responsibility to U.S. imperialism.
7 The statement is cited in Yoshimi 1996.
8 See Sung et al. 1996 and Ker 1996. Interestingly, the objects of the "no" in Ker's account are multiple: the United States, Japan, and China.
9 For more detailed analyses, see Chen 1997 and forthcoming.

III   PARA-SITES, OR, CONSTITUTING BORDERS

Leading Questions

REY CHOW

⊥

Orientalism and East Asia:
The Persistence of a Scholarly Tradition

The sinologist Stephen Owen wrote a controversially negative essay about
"world poetry" not too long ago in the pages of *The New Republic*.[1] While ostensibly reviewing the English translation of the collection *The August Sleep-*
walker by the mainland Chinese poet Bei Dao, Owen attacks "third world"
poets for pandering to the tastes of Western audiences seeking "a cozy ethnicity" (Owen 1990, 29). Much of what is written by non-Western poets is, he
complains, no longer distinguished by a true national identity but is instead
"supremely translatable" (Owen 1990, 32):

> Most of these poems translate themselves. These could just as easily
> be translations from a Slovak or an Estonian or a Philippine poet. . . .
> We must wonder if such collections of poetry in translation become
> publishable only because the publisher and the readership have been
> assured that the poetry was lost in translation. But what if the poetry
> wasn't lost in translation? What if this is it?
>
> This *is* it. (Owen 1990, 31; emphasis in original)

As a sinologist, Owen's biggest concern is that contemporary Chinese
writers are sacrificing their national cultural heritage for a "translation" that
commodifies experiences of victimization. He warns: "And there is always a
particular danger of using one's victimization for self-interest: in this case,
to sell oneself abroad by what an international audience, hungry for political
virtue, which is always in short supply, finds touching" (Owen 1990, 29).

Like other "new poetries," such as new Hindi poetry and new Japanese poetry, the "disease of modern Chinese poetry" is that it is too Western-ized. For Owen, the most important question is therefore: "Is this Chinese literature, or literature that began in the Chinese language?" (Owen 1990, 30–31).[2]

In her criticism of Owen's essay, Michelle Yeh points out the obvious contradictions that underlie what appears to be an objective and scholarly discussion:

> On the one hand, he is disappointed at the lack of history and cul-ture that would distinguish China from other countries. On the other hand, the historical context essential to the writing and reading of con-temporary Chinese poetry is not taken seriously and is used only as an occasion for chastising the poet who writes "for self-interest". . . . The cynicism is oddly out of step with the high regard in which Professor Owen holds poetry, for it not only ignores personal and literary history but also underestimates the power of poetry as a vital means of spiri-tual survival, of affirming individual dignity and faith when virtually all else fails. (Yeh 1991, 8)[3]

For readers who know something about China, Owen's attitude is not a particularly novel one. It is typical of the disdain found in many rela-tively recent American scholarly reactions toward the liberalized China of the 1980s. Harry Harding (1982) has written informatively about this kind of "debilitating contempt" that succeeded the euphoric China fever of the 1960s and 1970s. But more is at stake here. What kind of cultural politics is in play when a professor from Harvard University accuses the men and women from the third world of selling out to the West? While he criticizes poets like Bei Dao for succumbing to the commodifying tendencies of transna-tional culture out of self-interest, what is absent from Owen's musings is an account of the institutional investments that shape his own enunciation. This *absence* constitutes a definite form of power by not drawing attention to itself and thus not subjecting itself to the harsh judgment of self-interest that is so useful in criticizing others. The elaboration and fortification of this kind of absence amounts to the perpetuation of a deeply ingrained Ori-entalism in the field of East Asian studies, of which Owen's practice is but one example. Because this is an Orientalism at which many East Asia schol-ars, both native and non-native, connive, it is of some urgency to mobilize criticism of it.

Colin MacKerras writes about Edward Said's *Orientalism:* "Although designed specifically as a critique of the Western study of West Asian civilizations, its main points are equally applicable to the study of China"

(MacKerras 1989, 3). Precisely because of this, the arguments against Said's work in the East Asian field are often similar to their counterparts in South Asian and West Asian studies. Critics like Said, it is often said, belittle and ignore the work that is being done by specialists of these non-Western cultures and that has produced knowledge about peoples whose traditions would otherwise perish. I have indicated elsewhere that we need to acknowledge the significance of this type of work as sharing an *episteme* with primatology (Chow 1991). It is, however, not enough simply to align a field like East Asian studies with primatology and compare the salvational motives of their respective practitioners. What needs to be foregrounded is the nature and extent of the self-interestedness involved in the disapproval of the critique of Orientalism as a transcultural phenomenon.

Although Owen in his piece is not directly criticizing Said's work, his arguments clarify many of the current feelings in his field. Basic to Owen's disdain toward the new world poetry is a sense of loss and, consequently, an anxiety over his own intellectual position. This anxiety can be understood in part through Sigmund Freud's analysis of melancholia (1959). For Freud, we remember, the melancholic is a person who cannot get over the loss of a precious, loved object and who ultimately introjects this loss into his ego. What Freud emphasizes throughout his discussion as the unique feature of the melancholic, who differs from other kinds of mourners, is that he exhibits the symptoms of a delusional belittling of himself. Because the nature of the loss remains unconscious to the patient, the loss is directed inward, so that he becomes convinced of his own worthlessness as if he has been unjustly abandoned.

In his essay, Freud is concerned with the relationship between the self and the lost loved object. Freud's construction involves two parties, subject and object, and does not go on to show how the melancholic acts in regard to other subjects. Postcoloniality here offers a use of Freud that necessitates a rethinking of his theory about the melancholic disorder. In the case of the sinologist's relationship with his beloved object, "China," melancholia is complicated by the presence of a third party—the living members of the Chinese culture, who provide the sinologist with a means of *externalizing* his loss and directing his blame. What Freud sees as self-directed denigration now finds a concrete realization in the denigration of others.

For Owen, the inferior poetic skills of Bei Dao are, ostensibly, what he considers to be signs of the third world poet's inability to rise to the grandeur of his own cultural past. But this moralistic indictment of the other's infidelity masks a more fundamental anxiety. This is the anxiety that the Chinese past, which he has undertaken to penetrate, is evaporating and that the sinologist himself is the abandoned subject. What this means, significantly, is that a situation has been constructed in which the historical relation between the "first world" and the "third world" is reversed: Writers of the third world like Bei Dao now appear not as the oppressed but as oppressors, who aggress against the first world sinologist by robbing him of his love. Concluding his essay sourly with the statement, "Welcome to the late twentieth century," Owen's real complaint is that *he* is the victim of a monstrous world order, in front of which a sulking impotence like his is the only claim to truth.

Characteristic of this Orientalist melancholia are all the feelings proper to nineteenth-century Anglo-German Romanticism: the assumption that literature should be about depth and interiority, that expression of emotional truth should be modest, if not altogether wordless, and that being cultured means being hostile toward any form of reification and exhibitionism. Notably, Owen is not insensitive to oppression and suffering (he repeatedly points to the injustice caused by Western imperialism and Western cultural hegemony), but such sensitivity demands that oppression and suffering should not be announced loudly or even mentioned too often by those who are undergoing it, for that would amount to poor taste and insincerity. Reading him, one has the sense that in order to be good, poetry must be untranslatable because any translation would be suspect of *betraying* the truth. By implication, human language itself is a prime traitor to preverbal phenomena/sentiments.[4]

Confined to a discursive space that is theoretically at odds with the comparative tenets of contemporary cultural studies, the sinologist holds on to the language of the nation-state as his weapon of combat. This is one of the major reasons why history, in the sense of a detailed, factographic documentation of the local, the particular, and the past (understood as what has already happened and been recorded), enjoys such a prioritized disciplinary status in East Asian cultural politics. The hostility toward the critique of Orientalism currently heard in some East Asian scholarly circles is a direct consequence of this language of the nation-state. But if the critique of Orientalism is rejected, as is often the argument, for its universalizing overtones, then the idea of China, Japan, or East Asia as distinct historical entities is itself the other side of Orientalism. In a discussion about how universalism and particularism reinforce and supplement each other, Naoki Sakai writes:

> Contrary to what has been advertised by both sides, universalism and particularism reinforce and supplement each other; they are never in real conflict; they need each other and have to seek to form a symmetrical, mutually supporting relationship by every means in order to avoid a dialogic encounter which would necessarily jeopardize their reput-

edly secure and harmonized monologic worlds. Universalism and particularism endorse each other's defect in order to conceal their own; they are intimately tied to each other in their accomplice [*sic*]. In this respect, *a particularism such as nationalism can never be a serious critique of universalism, for it is an accomplice thereof.* (Sakai 1989, 105; emphasis added)

Of Japan, for instance, Sakai writes specifically:

Japan did not stand *outside* the West. Even in its particularism, Japan was already implicated in the ubiquitous West, so that neither historically nor geopolitically could Japan be seen as the *outside* of the West. This means that, in order to criticize the West in relation to Japan, one has necessarily to begin with a critique of Japan. Likewise, the critique of Japan necessarily entails a radical critique of the West. (Sakai 1989, 113–14; emphasis in original)

What these passages indicate is that Orientalism and a particularism like nationalism or nativism are the obverse and reverse of the same coin, and that criticism of one cannot be made without criticism of the other. The tendency in area studies, nonetheless, is to play them off against each other with nationalism/nativism gaining the upper hand. This has led to what Gayatri Spivak calls a "new culturalist alibi," by which some seek to avoid the pitfalls of the earlier Orientalism simply by particularizing their inquiries as meticulously as possible by way of class, gender, race, nation, and geographical locale (1989, 281). We see this in a title construction such as "*Funu, Guojia, Jiating*" [Chinese women, Chinese state, Chinese family] (Barlow 1991). The use of "Chinese" as a specifier signals a new kind of care and a new kind of attentiveness to the discursive imperatives — "Always contextualize! Never essentialize!" — of cultural pluralism. But *funu, guojia, jiating* are simply words in the Chinese language that mean *women, state, family.* Had the title been "la femme, l'état, la famille," would it be conceivable to append a phrase like "French woman, French state, French family"? In the name of investigating "cultural difference," ethnic markers such as "Chinese" easily become a method of differentiation that precisely blocks criticism from its critical task by reinscribing potentially radical notions such as "the other" in the security of fastidiously documented archival detail. A scholarly nativism that functions squarely within the Orientalist dynamic and that continues to imprison "other" cultures within entirely conventional disciplinary boundaries thus remains intact.

At a conference on gender issues in twentieth-century China, my commentator, an American female anthropologist who has done pioneering work on rural Chinese women, told the audience that what I said about the relation between China studies and Western cultural imperialism made her feel politically uncomfortable. Instead, she suggested, we should focus on the "internal colonization" of Chinese women by Chinese patriarchy. This person was thus still illustrating, in 1991, the point G. Balandier made in 1951, namely that "out of a more or less conscious fear of having to take into consideration . . . the society of the colonial power to which they themselves belong," Western anthropologists persistently neglect the "colonial situation" that lies at the origin of their "field of research" in most parts of the world (Wallerstein 1966, 34–61).

These examples of pressures to focus on the "internal" and the specifically "Chinese" problems are examples of how what many profess to be cross-cultural study can remain trapped within a type of discourse that is geographically deterministic *and hence* culturally essentialist. "China," "Japan," and "East Asia" become signs of "difference" that reaffirm a sense of identity as originary self-identicalness. The problems posed by women and imperialism in the East Asian field are thus often subordinated, philosophically, to a local native tradition (in which any discussion of women alone would be guilty of coloniality) and, institutionally, to "area studies," where imperialism as a transnational phenomenon is dismissed as irrelevant. What this means is that, while plenty of work is done on East Asian women, much of it is not feminist but nationalist or culturalist; while plenty of work is done on the modern history of East Asia, much of it is not about East Asia's shared history with other orientalized cultures but about East Asia as a "distinct" territory with a distinct history. What is forgotten is that these notions of East Asia are fully in keeping with U.S. foreign policy in the post–World War II period, during which the older European Orientalism was supplanted by the emergence of the United States as the newest imperialist power with major military bases in countries such as Japan, Korea, Taiwan, the Philippines, and Vietnam.

What is also missed is that when we speak against Orientalism and nativism, we understand them as *languages* that can be used by natives and non-natives alike. A critique of the Orientalism in East Asian pedagogy neither implies that only "natives" of East Asian cultures are entitled to speaking about those cultures truthfully nor that "natives" themselves are automatically innocent of Orientalism as a mode of discourse.

The most crucial issue, meanwhile, remains Orientalism's general and continuing *ideological* role. Critics of Said in the East Asian field sometimes justify their criticism by saying that Said's theory does not apply to East Asia because many East Asian countries were not, territorially, colonial possessions. This kind of positivistic thinking, derived from a literal understanding of the significance of geographical captivity, is not only an instance of the ongoing anthropological tendency to deemphasize the colonial situation as I mention above; it also leaves intact the most important aspect of Orientalism—its legacy as everday culture and value. The question ought, I think, to be posed in exactly the opposite way: *not* how East Asia cannot be understood within the paradigm of Orientalism because it was not everywhere militarily occupied, but how, *in spite of* and perhaps because of the fact that it remained in many cases "territorially independent," it offers even better illustrations of how imperialism works—i.e., how imperialism as ideological domination succeeds best without physical coercion, without actually capturing the body and the land.

Here, the history of China vis-à-vis the West can be instructive in a number of ways.[5] Unlike India or countries in Africa and America, most parts of China were, in the course of European imperialism, never territorially under the sovereignty of any foreign power, although China was invaded and had to grant many concessions throughout the nineteenth century to England, France, Germany, Russia, Japan, and the United States. Major political movements in China, be they for the restoration of older forms of government (1898) or for the overthrow of the dynastic system (1911), be they led by the religious (1850–1864), the well-educated (1919), the anti-foreign (1900, 1937–1945), or Communists (1949), were always conducted in terms of China's relations with foreign powers, usually the West. My suggestion, however, is that the ability to preserve more or less territorial integrity (while other ancient civilizations, such as the Inca, the Aztec, India, Vietnam and Indochina, Algeria, and others, were territorially captured), as well as linguistic integrity (Chinese remains the official language), means that as a "third world" country, the Chinese relation to the imperialist West, until the Communists officially propagandized "anti-imperialism," is seldom purely oppositional ideologically; on the contrary, the point has always been for China to become as strong as the West, to become the West's "equal." Even though the Chinese communists once served as the anti-imperialist inspiration for other "third world" cultures and progressive Western intellectuals, that dream of a successful and consistent opposition to the West on ideological grounds has been dealt the death blow by more recent events such as the Tiananmen Massacre of 1989, in which the Chinese government itself acted as viciously as if it were one of its capitalist enemies.[6] As the champion of the unprivileged classes and nations of the world, Communist China has shown itself to be a failure, a failure that is now hanging on by empty official rhetoric while its people choose to live in ways that have obviously departed from the Communist ideal.

The point of summarizing modern Chinese history in such a schematic fashion is to underscore how the notion of "coloniality" (together with the culture criticisms that follow from it), when construed strictly in terms of the *foreignness* of race, land, and language, can *blind* us to political exploitation as easily as it can alert us to it. In the history of modern Western imperialism, the Chinese were never completely dominated by a foreign colonial power, but the apparent absence of the "enemy" as such does not make the Chinese case any *less* third world in terms of the exploitation suffered by the people, whose most important colonizer remains their own government. China, perhaps because it is an exception to the rule of imperialist domination by race, land, and language involving a foreign power, in fact highlights the effects of the imperialistic *transformation of value and value-production* more sharply than in other third world cultures. Unlike, say, India, where the British left behind insurmountable poverty, a cumbersome bureaucracy, and a language with which to function as a "nation," but where therefore the sentiment of opposition can remain legitimately alive because there is historically a clearly identifiable *foreign* colonizer, the Chinese continue to have "their own" system, "their own" language, and "their own" problems. The obsession of Chinese intellectuals remains China, rather than the opposition to the West. The cultural production that results is therefore narcissistic, rather than simply oppositional, in structure. Whatever oppositional sentiment there exists is an oppositional sentiment directed toward itself—"China," the "Chinese heritage," the "Chinese tradition," the "Chinese government," and variants of these.

To give to Chinese and East Asian studies the critical energy they need is therefore to articulate the problems of *narcissistic value-production within*— rather than in negligence of—the larger context of the legacy of *cultural imperialism*. Neither of these alone suffices for a genuine intervention. The work that has yet to be done on the subject of East Asia is not a matter of sidestepping the critique of Orientalism in order to talk about what are "authentically" East Asian historical issues. Instead, putting the myth of authenticity within the history of a mutually reinforcing universalism and particularism, we must demand: Why were questions of Orientalism not asked earlier, and why are they being avoided even now?

Sanctifying the "Subaltern": The Productivity of White Guilt

The Orientalist has a special sibling whom I will, in order to highlight her significance as a kind of representational agency, call the Maoist. Arif Dirlik, who has written extensively on the history of political movements in twentieth-century China, sums up the interpretation of Mao Zedong commonly found in Western Marxist analyses in terms of a "Third Worldist fantasy"—"a fantasy of Mao as a Chinese reincarnation of Marx who fulfilled the Marxist promise that had been betrayed in the West" (1983, 186). In the

1970s, when it became possible for Westerners to visit China as guided and pampered guests of the Beijing establishment, Maoists came back with reports of Chinese society's absolute, positive difference from Western society and of the Cultural Revolution as "the most important and innovative example of Mao's concern with the pursuit of egalitarian, populist, and communitarian ideals in the course of economic modernization" (Harding 1982, 939). At that time, even poverty in China was regarded as "spiritually ennobling, since it meant that [the] Chinese were not possessed by the wasteful and acquisitive consumerism of the United States" (Harding 1982, 941).

Although the excessive admiration of the 1970s has since been replaced by an oftentimes equally excessive denigration of China, the Maoist is very much alive among us, and her significance goes far beyond the China and East Asian fields. Typically, the Maoist is a cultural critic who lives in a capitalist society but who is fed up with capitalism — a cultural critic, in other words, who wants a social order opposed to the one that is supporting her own undertaking. The Maoist is thus a supreme example of the way desire works: What she wants is always located in the other, resulting in an identification with and valorization of that which she is not/does not have. Since what is valorized is often the other's deprivation — "having" poverty or "having" nothing — the Maoist's strategy becomes in the main a *rhetorical* renunciation of the material power that enables her rhetoric.

In terms of intellectual lineage, one of the Maoist's most important ancestors is Charlotte Brontë's Jane Eyre. Like Jane, the Maoist's means to moral power is a specific representational position — the position of powerlessness. In their reading of *Jane Eyre,* Nancy Armstrong and Leonard Tennenhouse argue that the novel exemplifies the paradigm of violence that expresses its *dominance through a representation of the self as powerless:*

> Until the very end of the novel, Jane is always excluded from every available form of social power. Her survival seems to depend on renouncing what power might come to her as a teacher, mistress, cousin, heiress, or missionary's wife. She repeatedly flees from such forms of inclusion in the field of power, as if her status as an exemplary subject, like her authority as narrator, depends entirely on her claim to a kind of truth which can only be made from a position of powerlessness. By creating such an unlovely heroine and subjecting her to one form of harassment after another, Brontë demonstrates the power of words alone. (Armstrong and Tennenhouse 1989, 8)

This reading of Jane Eyre highlights her not simply as the female underdog who is often identified by feminist and Marxist critics, but as the intellectual who acquires power through a moral rectitude that was to become the flip side of Western imperialism's ruthlessness. Lying at the core of Anglo-American liberalism, this moral rectitude would accompany many territorial and economic conquests overseas with a firm sense of social mission. When Jane Eyre went to the colonies in the nineteenth century, she turned into the Christian missionary. It is this understanding—that Brontë's depiction of a socially marginalized English woman is, in terms of ideological production, fully complicit with England's empire-building ambition rather than opposed to it—that prompted Gayatri Spivak to read *Jane Eyre* as a text in the service of imperialism. Referring to Brontë's treatment of the "madwoman" Bertha Mason, the white Jamaican Creole character, Spivak charges *Jane Eyre* for, precisely, its humanism, in which the "native subject" is not created as an animal but as "the object of what might be termed the terrorism of the categorical imperative" (1986, 267). This kind of creation is imperialism's use/travesty of the Kantian metaphysical demand to "*make* the heathen into a human so that he can be treated as an end in himself" (Spivak 1986, 267; emphasis in original).

In the twentieth century, as Europe's former colonies became independent, Jane Eyre became the Maoist. Michel de Certeau describes the affinity between her two major reincarnations, one religious and the other political, this way:

> The place that was formerly occupied by the Church of Churches vis-à-vis the stablished powers remains recognizable, over the past two centuries, in the functioning of the opposition known as leftist. . . .
> [T]here is vis-à-vis the established order, a relationship between the Churches that defended an *other world* and the parties of the left which, since the nineteenth century, have promoted a *different future*. In both cases, similar functional characteristics can be discerned. . . . (1984, 183; emphases original)

The Maoist retains many of Jane's awesome features, chief of which are a protestant passion to turn powerlessness into "truth" and an idealist intolerance of those who may think differently from her. Whereas the great Orientalist blames the living third world natives for the loss of the ancient non-Western civilization, his loved object, the Maoist applauds the same natives for personifying and fulfilling her ideals. For the Maoist in the 1970s, the mainland Chinese were, in spite of their "backwardness," a puritanical alternative to the West in human form—a dream come true.

In the 1980s and 1990s, however, the Maoist is disillusioned to watch the China she sanctified crumble before her eyes. This is the period in which we hear disapproving criticisms of contemporary Chinese people for liking Western pop music and consumer culture, or for being overly interested in sex. In a way that makes her indistinguishable from what at first seems a political enemy, the Orientalist, the Maoist now mourns the loss of her loved object—Socialist China—by pointing angrily at living third world natives. For many who have built their careers on the vision of Socialist China, the grief is tremendous.

In the cultural studies of the American academy in the 1990s, the Maoist is reproducing with prowess. We see this in the way terms such as "oppression," "victimization," and "subalternity" are now being used. Contrary to Orientalist disdain for contemporary native cultures of the non-West, the Maoist turns precisely the "disdained" other into the object of his/her study and, in some cases, identification. In a mixture of admiration and moralism, the Maoist sometimes turns all people from non-Western cultures into a generalized "subaltern" that is then used to flog an equally generalized "West."[7]

Because the representation of the other as such ignores (1) the class and intellectual hierarchies within these other cultures, which are usually as elaborate as those in the West, and (2) the discursive power relations structuring the Maoist's mode of inquiry and valorization, it produces a way of talking in which notions of lack, subalternity, victimization, and so forth are drawn upon indiscriminately, often with the intention of spotlighting the speaker's own sense of alterity and political righteousness. A comfortably wealthy white American intellectual I know claimed that he was a "third world intellectual," citing as one of his credentials his marriage to a Western European woman of part-Jewish heritage; a professor of English complained about being "victimized" by the structured time at an Ivy League institution, meaning that she needed to be on time for classes; a graduate student of upper-class background from one of the world's poorest countries told his American friends that he was of poor peasant stock in order to authenticate his identity as a radical third world representative; male and female academics across the United States frequently say they were "raped" when they report experiences of professional frustration and conflict. Whether sincere or delusional, such cases of self-dramatization all take the route of self-subalternization, which has increasingly become the assured means to authority and power. What these intellectuals are doing is robbing the terms of oppression of their critical and oppositional import, and thus depriving the oppressed of even the vocabulary of protest and rightful demand. The oppressed, whose voices we seldom hear, are robbed twice—the first time of their economic chances, the second time of their language, which is now no longer distinguishable from those of us who have had our consciousnesses "raised."

In their analysis of the relation between violence and representation,

Armstrong and Tennenhouse write: "[The] idea of violence as representation is not an easy one for most academics to accept. It implies that whenever we speak for someone else we are inscribing her with our own (implicitly masculine) idea of order" (1989, 25). At present, this process of inscribing often means not only that we "represent" certain historic others because they are/were oppressed; it often means that *there is interest in representation only when what is represented can in some way be seen as lacking.* Even though the Maoist is usually contemptuous of Freudian psychoanalysis because it is "bourgeois," her investment in oppression and victimization fully partakes of the Freudian and Lacanian notions of "lack." By attributing lack, the Maoist justifies the speaking for someone else that Armstrong and Tennenhouse call "violence as representation."

As in the case of Orientalism, which does not necessarily belong only to those who are white, the Maoist does not have to be racially white either. The phrase "white guilt" refers to a type of discourse that continues to position power and lack against each other, while the narrator of that discourse, like Jane Eyre, speaks with power but identifies with powerlessness. This is how even those who come from privilege more often than not speak from/of lack. What the Maoist demonstrates is a circuit of productivity that draws its capital from others' deprivation while refusing to acknowledge its own presence as endowed. With the material origins of her own discourse always concealed, the Maoist thus speaks as if her charges were a form of immaculate conception.

The difficulty facing us, it seems to me, is no longer simply the first world Orientalist who mourns the rusting away of his treasures, but also students from privileged backgrounds Western *and* non-Western, who conform behaviorally in every respect with the elitism of their social origins (e.g., through powerful matrimonial alliances, through pursuit of fame, or through a contemptuous arrogance toward fellow students) but who nonetheless *proclaim* dedication to "vindicating the subalterns." My point is not that they should be blamed for the accident of their birth, nor that they cannot marry rich, pursue fame, or even be arrogant. Rather, it is that they choose to see in others' powerlessness an idealized image of themselves and refuse to hear in the dissonance between the content and manner of their speech their own complicity with violence. Even though these descendents of the Maoist may be quick to point out the exploitativeness of Benjamin Disraeli's "The East is a career," they remain blind to their own exploitativeness as they make the East *their* career (1871, 141).[8] How do we intervene in the productivity of this overdetermined circuit?

Between Orientalism and nativism, between the melancholic cultural connoisseur and the militant Maoist—this is the scene of postcoloniality as many diasporic intellectuals find it in the West. "Diasporas are emblems of transnationalism because they embody the question of borders," writes Khachig Tölölyan (1991, 6). The question of borders should not be a teleological one. It is not so much about the transient eventually giving way to the permanent as it is about an existential condition of which permanence itself is an ongoing fabrication. Accordingly, if, as William Safran writes, "diasporic consciousness is an intellectualization of [the] existential condition" (1991, 87), of dispersal from the homeland, then "diasporic consciousness" is perhaps not so much a historical accident as it is an intellectual reality—the reality of being intellectual.

Central to the question of borders is the question of propriety and property. Conceivably, one possible practice of borders is to anticipate and prepare for new proprietorship by destroying, replacing, and expanding existing ones. For this notion of borders—as margins waiting to be incorporated as new properties—to work, the accompanying spatial notion of a field is essential. The notion of a "field" is analogous to the notion of "hegemony," in the sense that its formation involves the rise to dominance of a group that is able to diffuse its culture to all levels of society. In Gramsci's sense, revolution is a struggle for hegemony between opposing classes.

While the struggle for hegemony remains necessary for many reasons—especially in cases where underprivileged groups seek equality of privilege—I remain skeptical of the validity of hegemony over time, *especially if it is a hegemony formed through intellectual power.* The question for me is not how intellectuals can obtain hegemony (a question that positions them in an oppositional light to dominant power and neglects their share of that power through literacy, through the culture of words), but how they can resist, as Michel Foucault said, "the forms of power that transform [them] into its object and instrument in the sphere of 'knowledge,' 'truth,' 'consciousness,' and 'discourse'" (1977, 208). Putting it another way, how do intellectuals struggle against a hegemony that already includes them and can no longer be divided into the state and civil society in Gramsci's terms, nor be clearly demarcated into national and transnational spaces?

Because "borders" have so clearly meandered into so many intellectual issues that the more stable and conventional relation between borders and the field no longer holds, intervention cannot simply be thought of in terms of the creation of new fields.[9] Instead, it is necessary to think *primarily* in terms of borders—of borders, that is, as *para-sites* that never take over a field in its entirety but erode it slowly and *tactically.*

The work of Michel de Certeau is helpful for a formulation of this para-sitical intervention. De Certeau distinguishes between "strategy" and another practice—"tactic"—in the following terms. A strategy has the ability to "transform the uncertainties of history into readable spaces" (de Certeau 1984, 36). The type of knowledge derived from strategy is "one sustained and determined by the power to provide oneself with one's own place" (de Certeau 1984, 36). Strategy therefore belongs to "an economy of the proper place" and to those who are committed to the building, growth, and fortification of a "field" (de Certeau 1984, 55). A text, for instance, would become in this economy "a cultural weapon, a private hunting preserve," or "a means of social stratification" in the order of the Great Wall of China (de Certeau 1984, 171). A tactic, by contrast, is "a calculated action determined by the absence of a proper locus" (de Certeau 1984, 37). Betting on time instead of space, a tactic "concerns an operational logic whose models may go as far back as the age-old ruses of fishes and insects that disguise or transform themselves in order to survive, and which has in any case been concealed by the form of rationality currently dominant in Western culture" (de Certeau 1984, xi).

Why are tactics useful at this moment? As discussions about multiculturalism, interdisciplinarity, the third world intellectual, and other companion issues develop in the American academy and society today, and as rhetorical claims to political change and difference are being put forth, many deep-rooted, politically reactionary forces return to haunt us. Essentialist notions of culture and history; conservative notions of territorial and linguistic propriety, and the "otherness" ensuing from them; unattested claims of oppression and victimization that are used merely to guilt-trip and to control; sexist and racist reaffirmations of sexual and racial diversities that are made merely in the name of righteousness—all of these forces create new "solidarities" whose ideological premises remain unquestioned. These new solidarities are often informed by a *strategic* attitude that repeats what they seek to overthrow. The weight of old ideologies being reinforced over and over again is immense.

We need to remember as intellectuals that the battles we fight are battles of words. Those who argue the oppositional standpoint are not *doing* anything different from their enemies and are most certainly not directly changing the downtrodden lives of those who seek their survival in metropolitan and nonmetropolitan spaces alike. What academic intellectuals must confront is thus *not* their "victimization" by society at large (or their victimization-in-solidarity-with-the-oppressed), but the power, wealth, and privilege that ironically accumulate from their "oppositional" viewpoint, and the widening gap between the professed contents of their words and the upward mobility they gain from such words. (When Foucault said intellectuals need to struggle against becoming the object and instrument of power, he spoke precisely to this kind of situation.) The predicament we face in the West, where intellectual freedom shares a history with economic enterprise, is that "if a professor wishes to denounce aspects of big business, . . . he will be wise to locate in a school whose trustees are big businessmen" (Stigler 1984, 145). Why should we believe in those who continue to speak a language of alterity-as-lack while their salaries and honoraria keep rising? How do we resist the turning-into-propriety of oppositional discourses, when the intention of such discourses has been that of displacing and disowning the proper? How do we prevent what begin as tactics — that which is "without any base from where it could stockpile its winnings" (de Certeau 1984, 37) — from turning into a solidly fenced-off field, in the military no less than in the academic sense?

The Chinese Lesson

The ways in which modern Chinese history is inscribed in our current theoretical and political discourses, often without our knowing about them, are quite remarkable. I can think of at least three major instances. First, poststructuralism's dismantling of the sign, which grew out of a criticism of phonetic logocentrism from within the Western tradition and which was to activate interest in text and discourse across humanistic studies, began in an era when Western intellectuals, in particular those in France (Jacques Derrida, Julia Kristeva, Philippe Sollers, Roland Barthes, Louis Althusser, to name a few) "turned East" to China for philosophical and political alternatives. Chinese writing has been a source of fascination for European philosophers and philologists since the eighteenth century because its ideographic script seems (at least to those who do not actually use it as a language) a testimony of a different kind of language — a language without the mediation of sound and hence without history.[10] Second, the feminist revolutions of the 1960s and 1970s drew on the Chinese Communists' practice of encouraging peasants, especially peasant women, to "speak bitterness" (*suku*) against an oppressive patriarchal system. The various methods of "consciousness-raising" that we still practice today, inside and outside the classroom, owe their origins to the Chinese "revolution" as described in William Hinton's *Fanshen* (1966).[11] Third, the interest invested by current cultural criticism in the socially dispossessed rejoins many issues central to the founding ideology of the Chinese Communist party, which itself drew on Soviet and other Western philosophies.[12] As I indicate in the essay "Against the Lures of Diaspora," the one figure that is represented and discussed repeatedly in modern Chinese writings since the turn of the twentieth century has been none other than the "subaltern." [13]

To prioritize modern Chinese history this way—to say that modern China is, whether we know it or not, the foundation of contemporary cultural studies—is not to glorify "Chinese wisdom." Rather, my aim is to show how the "fate" of an ancient civilization turned modern epitomizes and anticipates many problems we are *now* facing in the West, which in many ways is condemned to a kind of belated consciousness of what its forces set in motion in its others, which usually experience the traumas much earlier. In this regard, the impasses long felt by modern Chinese intellectuals vis-à-vis "their" history, which not only comprises a language used by over a quarter of the world's population but also a long tradition of writing, printing, publishing, examinations, revolutions, and state bureaucracy, can serve as a model for the West's future in the negative sense, that is, a future whose disasters have already been written.

To give one example, the sanctification of victimization in the American academy and its concomitant rebuke of theory as intellectualist and elitist parallel, in an uncanny fashion, the treatment of intellectuals during the Chinese Revolution, when labels of "feudalist," "reactionary," "Confucianist," and the like led to murder and execution in the name of salvaging the oppressed classes. This alleged separation of intellectuals from life continues today, not so much in China, where intellectuals are poorly paid, as in places where part of the power enjoyed by intellectuals comes precisely from bashing themselves from an anti-intellectual position of solidarity with the masses. Terry Eagleton's recent diatribe against American intellectuals— even though his own publications are bestsellers in the American intellectual market—is a good example of this kind of Cultural Revolution thinking inside capitalist society. Eagleton's attitude is consistent with the typical European intellectual disdain toward America and with British intellectual disdain toward French thought. This is how he uses the Tiananmen incident to target *his own* enemies:

> Viewed from eight thousand miles off, [the new historicist] enthusiasm for Foucault has a good deal to do with a peculiarly American left defeatism, guilt-stricken relativism and ignorance of socialism— a syndrome which is understandable in Berkeley but, as I write, unintelligible in Beijing. The unconscious ethnocentrism of much of the U.S. appropriation of such theory is very striking, at least to *an outsider*. What seems on the surface like a glamorous theory of the Renaissance keeps turning out to be about the dilemmas of aging 1960s radicals in the epoch of Danforth Quayle. I write this article while the Chinese students and workers are still massing outside the Great Hall

of the People; and I find it rather hard to understand why the neo-Stalinist bureaucrats have not, so far anyway, moved among the people distributing copies of Derrida, Foucault and Ernesto Laclau. For the Chinese students and workers to learn that their actions are aimed at a "social totality" which is, theoretically speaking, non-existent would surely disperse them more rapidly than water cannons or bullets. (1990, 91; emphasis added)

The claim to being an "outsider" is a striking one, bringing to mind not only Jane Eyre's self-marginalization, but also nineteenth-century Britain's "splendid isolation." Needless to say, it remains the case that the "people" of the third world are invoked only in the form of an indistinguishable mass, while first world intellectuals continue to have names.

Growing up in the 1960s and 1970s in Hong Kong, that "classic immigrant city" and "junction between diaspora and homeland" (Pan 1990, 363, 373), I experienced Chinese communism differently from many of my colleagues in the American academy and as a result am incapable of drawing from it the sense of revolutionary conviction that still infuses the speeches of Marxist intellectuals in the West. If Gramsci writing in prison "might have been Mao announcing the Cultural Revolution" then the problem of Mao, for many Chinese, was precisely that he "did what Gramsci thought" (Dirlik 1983, 184, 203). My most vivid childhood memories of the Cultural Revolution were the daily reports in 1966 and 1967 of corpses from China floating down into the Pearl River Delta and Hong Kong harbor, of local political unrest that led to disruption of school and business, and of the brutal murder of Lam Bun, an employee of Hong Kong's Commercial Radio (a pro-British institution, as were many of Hong Kong's big financial enterprises of that time) whose work during that period involved reading a daily editorial denouncing leftist activities. On his way to work with his brother one day in 1967, Lam Bun was stopped by gangsters, who barred them from getting out of his car and burned them alive. There are also memories of people risking their lives swimming across the border into Hong Kong and of people visiting China with "the little red book" but also with supplies of food and clothing. This was a period of phenomenal starvation in China. Some people from Hong Kong were going in the hope that, if not searched by border authorities, they could leave behind the food and clothing for needy relatives. (One woman, I recall, wore seven pairs of pants on one of her trips.)

What I retain from these memories is not a history of personal or collective victimization but the sense of immediacy of a particular diasporic reality—of Hong Kong caught, as it always has been since the end of the

World War II, between two dominant cultures, British colonial and Chinese communist, neither of which takes the welfare of Hong Kong's people into account, even though both would turn to Hong Kong for financial and other forms of assistance when they needed it. This marginalized position, which is not one chosen by those from Hong Kong but one constructed by history, brings with it a certain privilege of observation and an unwillingness to idealize oppression. To find myself among colleagues from the United States, Europe, India, and Africa who speak of Chinese communism in idealized terms remains a culture shock. My point, however, is not that of denouncing communism as an error of human history.[14] With the collapse of communism in the Soviet Union and the waning of communism in China, it is easy to bash Marxists and Communists as "wrongdoers" of the past two centuries. This would be like saying that Christians and the Church misrepresent the true teachings of the Bible. To the contrary, I think an understanding of what went wrong would be possible only if we are willing to undertake what Foucault advocates as a historical analysis of "fascism," a term that, as Foucault said, has been used as a floating signifier with which we blame the other for what goes wrong.[15] The first step in this analysis is not, for instance, to show how the Soviet Union has woken up to its error of the past seventy-four years but to acknowledge that what happened in the Soviet Union and China are necessary events of a positive present of which we, living in the other half of the globe in "capitalistic freedom," are still a functioning part. To pose the "Gulag question," Foucault said, means:

> refusing to question the Gulag on the basis of the texts of Marx or Lenin or to ask oneself how, through what error, deviation, misunderstanding or distortion of speculation or practice, their theory could have been betrayed to such a degree. On the contrary, it means questioning all these theoretical texts, however old, from the standpoint of the reality of the Gulag. Rather than of searching in those texts for a condemnation in advance of the Gulag, it is a matter of asking what in those texts could have made the Gulag possible, what might even now continue to justify it, and what makes it [sic] intolerable truth still accepted today. The Gulag question must be posed not in terms of error (reduction of the problem to one of theory), but in terms of reality. (1980, 135)

The hardest lesson from Chinese communism, as with Soviet communism, is that it has *not* been an accident but a process in the history of modern global enlightenment. This is a process that strategizes on the experiences of the "subalterns" while never truly resolving the fundamental division between intellectual and manual labor, nor hence the issues of hierarchy, inequity, and discrimination based on *literate* power. What the Chinese Cultural Revolution accomplished in a simplistic attempt to resolve that fundamental division was a *literal* destruction of intellectuals (as bearers of the division). While actual lives were thus sacrificed en masse, literate power as social form and as class division lives on. If indeed the subalterns were revolutionized, then why, we must ask, are we still hearing so much about problems in China that obviously indicate the opposite, such as the sexual oppression of women, the persistent illiteracy of the peasants, the abuse of bureaucratic power by those in charge of the welfare of the people — all in all what amounts to continued class injustice in a supposedly classless society?

Writing Diaspora

Each of the preceding sections contains questions that are part of the "intellectualization" of a "diasporic consciousness." The history of Hong Kong predisposes one to a kind of border or parasite practice — an identification with "Chinese culture" but a distantiation from the Chinese Communist regime; a resistance against colonialism but an unwillingness to see the community's prosperity disrupted. The advantage of a continuous and complete institutional education, even when that education was British colonial and American, means that unlike many people who had no means of leaving Hong Kong before the Chinese Communist takeover in 1997, I have not been "subordinated." Even though my personal history is written with many forms of otherness, such otherness, when combined with the background of my education, is not that of the victim but of a specific kind of social power, which enables me to speak and write by wielding the tools of my enemies.

When its term of colonization by the British came to an end in 1997, Hong Kong was, in a way that makes it unique in the history of Western imperialism, handed over to a new colonial power called "its mother country." (It will share this peculiar condition with neighboring Macau, currently a Portuguese colony.) Squeezed between West and East, Hong Kong currently has a democracy that is as fragile as its citizens' ethnic ties to China are tenacious. As Martin Lee, the most outspoken leader for democracy in Hong Kong, describes it: "Imagine a paper door. Of course you can walk through it. It is only useful if you respect the people behind it, and open it and enter only after you've been invited. Democracy in Hong Kong is that paper door, hoping that China will respect us and will not therefore barge in" (reported in Branegan 1991, 27). While China already shows its will to exercise authoritarian rule—the leading example being that of imposing the building of a nuclear power reactor in Daya Bay, in close proximity to utterly unevacuable Hong Kong—Hong Kong citizens themselves remain fascinatingly contradictory in their diasporic consciousness.

The following are but two recent examples. First, during May 1989, more than half a million of Hong Kong's citizens took to the streets to give support to the student demonstrations in Beijing. We now know that many of the Chinese democracy leaders who escaped from China in subsequent months did so under the auspices of the "Yellow Bird Operation," a secret network of Hong Kong intellectuals who collaborated with the underground triad societies in Asia for the cause of their "compatriots." (The effect of the Beijing government's military violence was that civilians and criminals formed a united front.)[16] Second, in the summer of 1991, when an unprecedented flood disaster struck the majority of Chinese provinces, it was once again the citizens of Hong Kong who, by the end of that summer, had collectively donated more than HK$0.7 billion (approximately US$90 million) to China flood relief.[17]

My deliberate attempt to chronicle the major role played by Hong Kong in these happenings in China is not, however, an attempt to promote "Chinese" solidarity, which is what fueled and continues to fuel the recent events. And here I write as a kind of diasporic person in diaspora, a Hong Kong person in North America. Many in Hong Kong, like other Chinese communities overseas, are inspired by a sense of their "Chineseness"—many claimed, in June 1989, to have awakened to their "Chinese" identity, and the fundraising activities in 1991 were conducted under slogans such as "Blood Is Thicker than Water." In the absence of a national religion, a strong single political regime, an identity based on national unity, and, often, the possibility of ever living in China, the claims to ethnic oneness—sinicization—suffice as a return home and are as practically effective as they are illusory and manipulative. Like all myths of origin, sinicization is usually "exploited for a variety of political and social purposes by the diaspora, the homeland, and the host society" (Safran 1991, 91–92). David Yen-ho Wu defines it this way:

> For centuries the meaning of being Chinese seemed simple and definite: a sense of belonging to a great civilization and performing properly according to the intellectual elites' norm of conduct. This is what Wang Gungwu referred to as the Chinese "historical identity." The Chinese as a group traditionally believed that when a larger Chinese population arrived in the frontier land, Sinicization was the only possible course. It was inconceivable that any Chinese could be acculturated by the inferior non-Chinese "barbarians"; however, such acculturation has been a common course of development for Chinese in the frontier land and overseas, although people still insist that an un-

adulterated Chinese culture is maintained by the Chinese migrants. (1991, 176)[18]

I call the current political sentiments in Hong Kong "contradictory" because the forces of sinicization are unbelievably strong precisely at a time when Hong Kong's historical difference from China should stand as the most uncompromisable opposition to the mainland. While that difference is always invoked (even by the Chinese authorities themselves, who promised a "one country, two systems" rule after 1997), one has the feeling that the actual social antagonisms separating China and Hong Kong—such as a firmly instituted and well-used legal system, emerging direct elections, the relative freedom of speech, and so forth, all of which are present in Hong Kong but absent in China—are often overwritten with the myth of consanguinity, *a myth that demands absolute submission because it is empty.* The submission to consanguinity means the surrender of agency—what is built on work and livelihood rather than blood and race—in the governance of a community. The people in Hong Kong can sacrifice everything they have to the cause of loving "China" and still, at the necessary moment, be accused of not being patriotic—of not being "Chinese"—enough. (The same kind of logic was behind the guilt-tripping purges of the Cultural Revolution: sacrifice everything, including your life, to the party, but it remains the party's decision whether or not you are loyal.) Going far beyond the responsibility any individual bears for belonging to a community, "Chineseness," as I show in various other discussions, lies at the root of a violence that works by the most deeply ingrained feelings of "bonding" and that—even at the cost of social alienation—diasporic intellectuals must collectively resist.[19]

Part of the goal of "writing diaspora" is, thus, to *unlearn* that submission of one's ethnicity such as "Chineseness" as the ultimate signified even as one continues to support movements for democracy and human rights in China, Hong Kong, and elsewhere. Such support must be given regardless of one's ethnic roots. My goal is to set up a discourse that cuts across some of our new solidarities by juxtaposing a range of cultural contradictions that make us rethink the currently dominant conceptualizations of the solidarities themselves. If there is something from my childhood and adolescent years that remains a chief concern in my writing, it is the tactics of dealing with and dealing in dominant cultures that are so characteristic of living in Hong Kong. These are the tactics of those who do not have claims to territorial propriety or cultural centrality. Perhaps more than anyone else, those who live in Hong Kong realize the opportunistic role they need to play in order, not to "preserve," but rather to negotiate their cultural identity; for them opportunity is molded in danger and danger is a form of opportunity. Their diaspora is a living emblem of the cryptic Chinese term *weiji,* which is made up of the characters for "danger" and "opportunity," and which means "crisis."

Vera Schwarcz recently wrote that "contemporary Chinese intellectuals have become fractured vessels—broken-hearted witnesses to their own and their countrymen's suffering." But, she goes on to say, "Fidelity to historical memory . . . requires intellectuals to acknowledge their own complicity in China's long-standing autocracy. This is an important and also a rather bleak responsibility" (1991, 105). An essay of mine was written with the sense of this bleak responsibility.[20] This essay was presented in my absence at a major conference in late 1990. My discussant was someone who is a graduate from Harvard and a faculty member of a university in the United States. In the original essay I had made a mistake in my translation from the Chinese. On the basis of this mistake, my discussant trashed the entire essay, commenting to the audience that, after all, "she's from Hong Kong."[21] The question behind this statement of the *fact* of my geographical origin, I suppose, was: How can this Westernized Chinese woman from colonial Hong Kong, this cultural bastard, speak for China and Chinese intellectuals? Had it been my ambition to represent China or be authentically Chinese, I would have been shattered in shame. What remains useful from this episode in diaspora is its lesson about a persistent and pernicious form of centrism.[22] Like many of his contemporaries in mainland China, this person who attacked me lived through the hardships of the Cultural Revolution, which disrupted and hampered the institutional education process of the Chinese youths of that time. He should have been quicker than most to recognize the cultural violence in the words that spoke to him. That someone like he should survive the experience of such a vast oppression so politically, ethnically, and linguistically centrist and so adamantly devoted to the perpetuation of such centrism is a foremost example of the *strategized* realities challenging contemporary Chinese and all other intellectuals today.

Notes

This essay was originally published in 1993 as the introductory chapter to *Writing Diaspora: Tactics of Intervention in Contemporary Cultural Studies*, reprinted here with permission from Indiana University Press. Minor changes have been made in the essay to fit the purposes of the present volume.

1   The piece is a review of Bei Dao, *The August Sleepwalker* (see Owen 1990).

2   An indictment of contemporary Chinese poetry that is remarkably similar in its racist spirit to Owen's is another review of *The August Sleepwalker*, by W. J. F. Jenner. A few examples from Jenner: "great poetry can no longer be written in Chinese"; "Bei Dao's lines rarely have the inevitability, the weight, the structure, the authority of real poetry"; "[The modern Chinese poets] Wen Yidou and Xu Zhimo are not up there with Auden

and Yeats"; "translations of modern Chinese poetry into English . . . do not lose all that much, because there is not much in the original language to be lost . . ." (Jenner 1990, 193–195). I am grateful to Gregory B. Lee for this reference.

3   This essay has been published in Chinese in *Jintian* (Today). The page reference for the English version is taken from Yeh's manuscript.

4   The mutual implications between "translation" and "betrayal" as indicated in an expression like "*Traduttore, traditore*" and their etymological relations to "tradition" will have to be the subject of a separate study.

5   This paragraph and the next are taken, with modifications, from the chapter "Digging an Old Well," in Chow 1995. I am grateful to Teresa de Lauretis for telling me that I needed to clarify my point about "coloniality."

6   The official position in China today is that nothing of real significance happened in Tiananmen Square in May and June of 1989, and that it is best not to recall the demonstrations and the victims in public. In an interview with Chinese and non-Chinese reporters in early 1991, the Chinese Premier Li Peng responded to questions about the Tiananmen Massacre with the following kind of "rationality": "It has already been two years since the June Fourth incident; there is no need to discuss it any more. . . . Under the urgent circumstances of the time, had the Chinese government not acted decisively, we would not be able to have the stability and economic prosperity we see in China today." "Zhong wai jizhe zhaodaihui shang Li Peng huida wenti" (Li Peng's responses to questions at the press conference for Chinese and foreign reporters), *Ming Pao Daily News,* Vancouver Edition, April 11, 1991; my translation.

7   What Spivak criticizes as the "conflation of the indigenous elite women abroad with the subaltern" is but one prominent aspect of this current trend (1989, 273).

8   I am grateful to Prabhakara Jha for locating this reference for me.

9   For a discussion of the limits imposed by "field" and "fieldwork," see Clifford 1991, 96–116. In ethnography at least, Clifford advocates cross-cultural studies of travel and travelers as supplements to the more traditional notion of fieldwork.

10   Even though Derrida points out in *Of Grammatology* that Chinese writing "functioned as a sort of European hallucination" (1984, 80), his own project does not go beyond the ethnocentrism of a repeated reference to the other culture purely as a bearer—a sign— of the limits of the West. Gayatri Spivak puts it this way: "There is . . . the shadow of a geographical pattern that falls upon the first part of the book. The relationship between logocentrism and ethnocentrism is indirectly invoked in the very first sentence of the 'Exergue.' Yet, paradoxically, and almost by a reverse ethnocentrism, Derrida insists that logocentrism is a property of the *West*. He does this so frequently that a quotation would be superfluous. Although something of the Chinese prejudice of the West is discussed in Part I, the *East* is never seriously studied or deconstructed in the Derridean text. Why then must it remain, recalling Hegel and Nietzsche in their most cartological humors, as the name of the limits of the text's knowledge?" (1976, lxxxii; emphases in original). By insisting that logocentrism is "Western," Derrida forecloses the possibility that similar problems of the "proper" exist in similarly deep-rooted ways in the non-West and require a deconstruction that is at least as thorough and sophisticated as the one he performs for "his" tradition.

11   For an informative account of Western feminism's borrowings from the Chinese Communist Revolution, see Lieberman 1991.

12   For detailed critical discussions on this topic, see Dirlik 1978, 1989, and 1991.

13   See chapter 5 of *Writing Diaspora* (Chow 1993).

14　The danger of a book such as Nien Cheng's *Life and Death in Shanghai* (1988) lies precisely in its blindness to what is embraced as a heavenly alternative to Chinese communism — the United States of America.

15　"The non-analysis of fascism is one of the important political facts of the past thirty years. It enables fascism to be used as a floating signifier, whose function is essentially that of denunciation. The procedures of every form of power are suspected of being fascist, just as the masses are in their desires. There lies beneath the affirmation of the desire of the masses for fascism a historical problem which we have yet to secure the means of resolving" (Foucault 1980, 139).

16　Unofficially organized by a group of supporters for China's Democracy Movement in Hong Kong, the "Yellow Bird Operation" was aimed at assisting those persecuted by the mainland Chinese government to leave China. With over US$2 million collected from traders and major networking aid from the triad societies in Asia, they have arranged secret escapes to the West for over 130 Chinese opposition intellectuals since June 1989, including the student leaders Wuer Kaixi and Li Lu, the government consultant Chen Yizi, and the scholars Yan Jiaqi and Su Xiaokang. Because of an error in one of the arranged trips, Yellow Bird Operation's actions are now known to the Chinese National Security Department (the equivalent of a secret police). Some of its members revealed their identities and their work at an interview with the BBC's news program "Panorama" in mid-1991. My information is based on an account in *Xin Bao / Overseas Chinese Economic Journal* (the U.S. edition of the *Hong Kong Economic Journal*), 7 June 1991, 5. This account is a selected translation from a report on the "Yellow Bird Operation" in *The Washington Post*, 2 June 1991.

17　Donations from Taiwan were also enormous. A discussion of Taiwan's role in the China events will have to take into account the strong Taiwanese nativism that currently inspires political debates and artistic productions.

18　Wu's essay appears in a special issue of *Daedalus* entitled "The Living Tree: The Changing Meaning of Being Chinese Today."

19　See the chapters of *Writing Diaspora* (Chow 1993).

20　See Chow 1993, chapter 4, 73–98.

21　Participants at this conference can testify to this event.

22　Leo Ou-fan Lee recently criticizes what he calls the "'centrist' frame of mind" by defining it as "the elitist belief" that intellectuals "can ultimately influence the reformist leaders in the party to their way of thinking." Lee associates this centrist frame of mind with some of the intellectuals and writers who left China partly because of the Tiananmen Massacre. See Lee 1991, 219.

Modelling the Nation:
The Asian/American Split

DAVID PALUMBO-LIU

The impossibility of the actualization and stabilization of "Asian American" is directly linked to the distinction made between "Asian" and "American," the false premise of their mutual exclusion. This in turn may be read as an exemplary instance of the failure of interpellation that characterizes ideology, an inevitable failure because the "call" for the subject—what, exactly, the Other demands of its subjects—is impossible to discern. This impossibility is rooted in the inherent contradiction that informs the constitution of that Other—the dominant term must always finesse this contradiction by projecting its lack, its radical incompleteness, upon the subject. Here, the undecideable element is precisely the constitution of "America" under the pressure of race and ethnicity.[1] Asians are deemed inadequate to America, marginalized, or excluded in order to (re)consolidate the nation's image of its ideal self, which is nonetheless contradicted by its white supremacist ideology. Thus the constitution of "Asian-American" (as well as other hyphenated subjectivities) seems never able to be completed, for the very ontological status of "America" depends upon a tenuous, historicized, provisional, and contingent consolidation of nation against itself. The nation can only be named as a particular within an ideology that simultaneously claims universality: America is the corporate entity supposedly comprised of all American citizens, yet it is a *particularly* textured, nuanced, and functioning image of the nation that foregrounds certain of its elements and suppresses the rest.[2] In this scenario, it is better to view the "Asian/Asian American" split as a vacillating, multidirectional attempt at predication, rather than a teleologically predetermined and irreversible phenomenon: the contents of "Asian American" vary as the ratio of "Asianness" to "Americanness" is manifested in social practice. Yet despite such practices that have relegated Asian Americans to particularly delimited roles in the American imaginary, this repertory includes, not insignificantly, that of a "people" who, albeit marginalized, serve as *models* for Americans. How to read the contradiction of margin and model if not to re-evaluate the presumptions of the "center"?

In this essay I examine the deployment of the model minority myth as an exemplary instance of such negotiations of social and political subjectivity. I locate the model minority myth in the historical convergence of domestic civil rights activism and an emergent "Pacific Rim discourse." Both appearances of the myth are haunted by a sense of America's weakened position at home and globally, particularly in relation to East Asia.[3] It is crucial to understand that while the signified of the model minority myth certainly broadened to include, variously, East, Southeast, and South Asian groups, the specific group named by the term, the group whose particular characterization defines the nature of both the myth generated and its ideological functions, was Japanese Americans. Along with the focus on domestic educational and economic "success" (which has to be linked to a proliferation of studies claiming that Japanese Americans were the United States's most "exogamous" Asian group, thereby signaling both their biological infiltration of, and socioeconomic assimilation to, the nation), the particular attention given Japanese Americans was filtered through the optics of an international remapping of the Unites States's relation to the "Pacific Rim," in which Japan emerged as a newly hegemonic economic power. The genesis of the model minority myth, the "line" between Asian and Asian American, was indistinct, yet at the same time the myth was inseparable from a general and conflicted anxiety regarding the manner in which "America" could be preserved in the midst of both domestic economic and political upheaval and international renegotiations of power.

At "home," it is no wonder that the invention of the "modelling" function of Japanese Americans was deeply ambivalent. Addressed both to other racial minorities, who were told to emulate Japanese American assimilation, *and* to white Americans, who were seen to have lost the guiding ethical principles of America, the "domestic" model minority myth was to serve a salutary purpose. Yet this presented a problem: the very fact that a "model" had to be posited at all signaled a recognition of the weakening of the American state, a recognition that cast suspicion on its triumphalist ideology. Swerving to avoid the disclosure of any structural crisis, reactionary pundits made this "problem" part of a larger and more important solution. Conservatives needed a weapon to use against liberals who were pushing civil rights legislation—they found it in Japanese Americans, whose reputed success showed that urban poverty and violence were not the outcomes of institutional racism, but of constitutional weaknesses in minorities that might well be at least partially produced by the welfare state. In short, the model minority myth provided the opportunity for conservatives to situate the causes of these problems *outside* of a consideration of institutional racism and economic violence: the success of the Japanese Americans was used to dispute a structural critique of the U.S. political economy. Yet the very racism away from which conservatives tried to draw attention reappears strongly in the logic of the model minority myth.

What I wish to draw attention to here are the particular mechanisms whereby the "successful" predication of "Asian-to-Asian American" was diverted and destroyed. Ironically, the road to recovery was to be led by a people who, once that mission was accomplished, would literally self-destruct by virtue of the fact that they would have become *too* successful. That is, they had become Americans, but as such they were contaminated with exactly the weaknesses and complacency from which their marginal status had protected them. Asian Americans could show America how to be "great" again, but after so doing they were either remarginalized as "Asian" or brought down to a more pedestrian sphere: a "normal" American. It was left to white Americans to be inspired by, but ultimately surpass, Japanese Americans, aided by the resuscitation of "America" as an inherently *white* nation.

The international manifestation of the myth, which promoted Japanese business ethics and methodologies as the wave of the future, was equally ambivalent. While the domestic myth was deployed to contain and divert civil rights policymaking, neutralize activism, and promote a laissez-faire domestic urban policy, the international myth challenged the United States to modify its modes of economic operation. This variant of the model minority myth can be traced to early Pacific Rim discourse, which likewise emerged in the early 1960s, but it became most prevalent and anxious in the late 1970s, after the recognition of China, the fall of Saigon, and within deepening economic crisis. While the American business sector began to turn toward Japanese economic success as a model for a revision of American business practices, the interpolation of a "foreign" mode of business and production, no matter how benign the guise it might take ("synthesis," "adaptation," "selective borrowing") threatened to eliminate not only the weaknesses of the American way of business but also precisely those elements that had contributed for more than a century to the ideology of triumphant American exceptionalism. I will analyze these two articulations of the model minority myth within the context of their historical appearance.[4] These different contexts produce different modalities of the myth, yet what is most germane to our purposes is the way both texts reinstate "America" and contain and neutralize the model of Asia and Asian Americans.

A certain ressentiment informs both manifestations of the model minority myth, and led its adherents to cautiously reinstate the line between Asians and Americans. Admiration for the Japanese Americans and Japan was inextricably linked to self doubt. Yet ideologues adeptly contained this negativity in two ways. First, they placed the blame for the nation's troubles on minorities and liberal do-gooders and aligned themselves with the image of Japanese Americans they had constructed. This dynamic has had historically profound and far-reaching effects, for it has facilitated the splintering of Asian Americans from progressive political engagement, both by working to convince many Asian Americans themselves of their privileged status and the conservative logic that underwrites it and by aligning Asian Americans with the white middle class in the eyes of counterhegemonic activists. Second, they rationalized their resentment by pointing up the supposed limitations of Japanese Americans, their constitutional unfitness for Americanization.

Reaction to Japan as a potential model for corporate revitalization produced an equally important set of effects, most noticeably the surfacing of the inherent contradictions of a capitalist system ostensibly predicated upon laissez-faire policies. While some argued for the continuance of laissez-faire *domestic* policies, letting the "fittest" prove their worth and gain their rewards, speaking out against state intervention in the form of social reform and civil rights, these same individuals could be heard demanding that an *activist* U.S. government put in place tariffs and controls on Japanese goods.[5] The excuse for this inconsistency was that this had to be done only because Japan had a protectionist policy in place anyway. Yet this alibi did not provide a convincing distraction from the endemic problems of U.S. manufacturing and marketing in late capitalism. Rather, a way had to be found to resuscitate America from a position of strength. This essay explores the restorative strategies deployed to salvage America and distinguish it from Asia. Under these prerogatives, "Asian America" existed in a particular, liminal state.

Modelling Minorities

The first articulation of the model minority thesis was made in an article by social demographer William Petersen entitled, "Success Story, Japanese American Style," published in the *New York Times Magazine* on January 9, 1966, less than six months after the Watts riots in Los Angeles. Several other journalists and commentators quickly picked up this theme, which focused on high educational achievement levels, high median family incomes, low crime rates, and the absence of juvenile delinquency and mental health problems among Asian Americans, and juxtaposed this success against the failure of blacks in America. The message was clear—patient and quietly determined hard work brings success; welfare dependence and sheer "laziness" bring economic disaster. Scholars have since questioned the data from which this myth was created; nevertheless, the predominance of the image of the quietly hardworking Asian American has persisted in the popular imagination.[6] There is a substantial amount of scholarship on the model minority myth, both supporting and debunking its findings; however, none have remarked upon the inherently fatalistic and contradictory nature of Petersen's praise of Japanese Americans and his suggestion that they might act as models for other minorities. His conclusions, fueled by a comparative analysis, serve both to underwrite a conservative anti-civil rights agenda and, ironically, to isolate Japanese American "success" as an irrepeatable feat. Even as the line between Asian and Asian American seems to be drawn into a telos of Japanese American assimilation, we find the reinstantiation of nationally bounded identities. In this process, two possibilities emerge for Japanese Americans—either they are Americanized and lose their modelling function, or they are Japanized and isolated from America.

Petersen elaborated his argument in a book, *Japanese Americans: Oppression and Success* (1971), which was published as part of a series, "Ethnic Groups in Comparative Perspective." One of the core elements of Petersen's study is his unabashed admiration for a people who, faced with immense oppression, of which the internment was only the most explicit and dramatic instance, managed to become one of the most "successful" minorities in the United States. Petersen explains: "I started not with a feeling of identification or even particularly of empathy, but with an interesting analytical problem: why in the case of *this* colored minority past oppression had led to phenomenal economic and social success, contradicting the generalizations derived from the experience of Negroes, American Indians, Mexican Americans, and others" (ix). Although he includes American Indians and Mexican Americans in this list, it is clear that his main point of comparison is American blacks, who are seen as the primary motivation for civil rights laws and whose inability to succeed in American society is the "cause" of the Watts riots.[7] Petersen's "explanation" of Japanese American success must be read as a pointed rebuttal of Lyndon Johnson's belief that "the black experience was fundamentally different from that of other immigrants."[8] Not only was the black experience not exceptional, but insisting on its specificity prevented blacks from benefiting from the Asian American model, according to conservatives.

To dismiss the particular historical effects of slavery, Petersen chronicles a history of the prejudice and oppression faced by the Japanese, and their responses. Crucially, their ability to rebound, and even take advantage of oppression as a stimulus for success, is due not to the values of family or religion (since, under the force of assimilation, the influence of these things is modified), but rather to loyalty to something entirely particular and predetermined called a "subnation": "Except for their smaller size, subnations have the main features that we associate with nationality: an actual or putative biological descent from common forbearers, a common territory, an easier communication inside than outside the group, a sentimental identification with insiders and thus a relative hostility toward outsiders" (216).

Petersen gives example after example of the Japanese American "subnation" at work: "Their education has been conducted like a military campaign against a hostile world, with intelligent planning and tenacity. Their heavy dependence on the broader Japanese community was suggested in a number of ways" (115). The picture that emerges from this analysis is of a minority's success based on its maintenance of both a social and spatial separatism: segregation has its benefits *if* this social space enjoys a particular subnational profile. In other words, the very forces that kept Japanese Americans apart from the "mainstream" (as Petersen envisions things) allow them to maintain both the purity and strength of their subnation. To this he counterposes blacks: "Negroes shifted their reference group: once pleased to have risen above their fathers' status, now many blacks are aggressively dissatisfied that they have not yet achieved full equality with whites. One consequence of massive civil-rights programs has been to exacerbate racial conflict, to encourage the rise of black violence and white backlash" (218). He implies that by not accepting their status as separate (and unequal), blacks have signed their own death warrants. Yet that is not as disturbing to Petersen as the manners in which black discontent has breached the segregationist barrier between black subnation and white nation, manifesting itself in civil unrest, exposing America's legacy of racism and ideological contradiction.

While one reading of Petersen's book might be that Japanese Americans are successful because they "earned" their status as super-whites, there is a more profound and vastly more cynical element in his narrative. His reliance on the concept of a rather militant Japanese American subnation ("education conducted like a military campaign"), with its definitive elements of spatial, social, and psychic difference, isolates it and particularizes it so much that it can be an object of mimesis only by approximation or, more specifically, by *bricolage*. That is, other groups can only "model" themselves after the Japanese Americans by improvising with the elements

218 David Palumbo-Liu

indigenous to their own particular, predetermined subnation. This attempt at mimicry can only lead to failure, it seems, for no other group has the specific genetic material of *Japan* as a basis for their subnation.

Yet even as he celebrates this subnation he senses a waning of effect —assimilation has eroded (but not yet eradicated) the borders and inner strength of the subnation: "in many respects the Japanese Americans are now more American than Japanese—in political loyalty, language, and way of life. Let us hope, however, that the subnation is not to be completely melted into the melting pot" (232). The misfit between Japan and America, the impossibility of predicating a Japanese American subject that might retain its potency, is thus emphasized in Petersen's "discovery" that the more Americanized the Japanese in America become, the less "Japanese" they are, and the less able they become to succeed by drawing on that special sense of subnation. Petersen speaks of increased "social pathologies" that plague the Americanized generation: "They [Sansei] have grown up, most of them, in relatively comfortable circumstances, with the American element of their composite subculture becoming more and more dominant. Part of their full acculturation to the general pattern is that they are beginning to show some of the faults of American society that were almost totally lacking in their parents' generation" (141). Thus, after segregating and particularizing the success of the Japanese American subnation as something no other group can replicate because of its specific origins in the emergence of modern Japan, Petersen proceeds to argue that successful assimilation into American society paradoxically produces a *negative,* debilitating effect on the Japanese Americans. To maintain their success, then, Japanese Americans must remain locked in a liminal, segregated, detemporalized zone *between* Asia and America.[9] Indeed this zone is precisely the product of the pressures of the contradiction that underlies Petersen's argument: he is caught between his ideological allegiance to American democracy and his admiration for a Japanese success story that emerges only from a particular reading of a Japanese social system that, by his own account, thrives on authoritarianism and the absence of "even a word for civil rights."

To conclude this discussion of Petersen's thesis, it is crucial to examine what, exactly, he means by "Japan," for on investigation one finds a specific remapping of both the Japanese nation and the United States. Petersen traces the success of Japanese Americans to the emergence of Japan in modernity. He is particularly struck by its adaptation and modification of Western technology, economics, and military systems. Such adaptation characterizes an inherent ability of Japanese that will equip them for success under the specific conditions of modernity. Witness his discussion of an instance of Japanese modernization:

The intelligent pragmatism that suggested these choices dictated to absolute commitments. The army was reorganized by the French, but within a few months of France's defeat in 1871 Japan shifted to the German military organization. The banking system, based at first on the American model, was soon changed to include elements of British central banking, long-term credit institutions copied from the French, and some innovations particularly suited to the local scene. (157)

This ability to fabricate a modern Japan from the raw materials of the West points to a specific agency—that of a Japanese social subject that is distinctly adaptive to the conditions of modernity:

"The individuals caught up in this transformation were expected to both retain the old and acquire the new. The psychological type that resulted from such counterpressures, at least as seen from the outside, is an array of self-contradictions. In a sense that was even true of the traditional culture, in which ancient Chinese borrowings often lay side by side with half-antagonistic native traits, together forming a composite that struck every foreigner as inordinately complex." (161)

Petersen tracks the "best of old while retaining the new" to a primordial instance that makes the case of Japan exceptional and neutralizes the modelling function of Japanese Americans. Correlating his comments on the Japanese American subnation with his conception of the Japanese nation, one discovers again that one cannot *be* like them; one can only emulate particular *fragments* of a complex and irrepeatable (sub)national culture: "Virtually by definition, each nation is distinctive in its culture: and the inculcation of its specific beliefs, attitudes, and patterns of behavior, one can reasonably hypothesize, differentiates the modal national of each country from the rest of the world's population" (160). He discovers that: "Perhaps we should draw no greater conclusion than that Japanese were trained by their multilayered culture to live effectively with complexities; in this sense, even the villagers had an 'urban' cast, a readiness for industrialism" (162).

From this celebration of the success of Japanese modernization, a process that accessed an essential Japanese subjectivity so universal that even rural villagers, much less the "average Japanese," moved smoothly into industrialization and modern complexity, Petersen moves to his main point—a link between this revisionist history of Japan and contemporary American institutions:

The faults of such a social system, as seen by a Western democrat, have often been pointed out, and in any case they are obvious enough. Structural lines as strong and clear as those in Japanese institutions easily merge with authoritarian control; political democracy is possible, as several periods of modern Japanese history have demonstrated, but not easily achieved or maintained. American commentaries have less often stressed the virtues of the system. The lack of privacy, the *absence of even a word for civil rights,* are symptoms of an organic strength that, on the one hand, motivated each Japanese to contribute his utmost and thus, on the other hand, enabled the nation to jump from an almost pathetic weakness to parity with the greatest powers in half a century. [emphasis added] (165)

Petersen leaves the criticism of the negative effects of the "Japanese system" to the obvious, for his task is pointing out the positive. Yet even as he weakly implies the disjuncture between American democratic ideals and Japanese authoritarianism, he maintains his admiration for what such authoritarianism has produced. This contradiction between emulation and the admission of ideological difference (for instance, admiration for a success bred of "Asian" conformity and allegiance to "tradition" and simultaneous adherence to "American individualism") haunts the interstices of the concept of the model minority. It is intimately linked to the contradictions of democratic capitalism, which argues at once for egalitarianism and class distinction, and that of a racist ideology that must contain or neutralize any challenge to white supremacy, even while arguing for its assimilative powers. If Japanese Americans are to be assimilated, their economic and spiritual potency, derived from their subnation, must be left at the door. If not, they are to remain at a hallowed, but hollow, space at the exterior seam of the American state. Furthermore, the liaison between the United States and Japan is frustrated by the absolute difference that anchors Petersen's reading of the national, and this insistent difference is found again and again in the logic of the model minority myth, a logic intimately linked to the racist contradictions of the United States.

Differentiating the National

As we have seen, from its very genesis, the model minority myth contained, qualified, and restricted the movement of its model Asians into America. No matter how "ideal" a subject might be constructed around the figure of the Asian, there must be "flaws" or exceptions posited in the Asian as a way to reparticularize "America." By inventorying them we discover the specific compensatory strategies used to salvage American racist ideology. In a move that parallels the criticism that Asians applying to elite universities were not "well-rounded," and that Asians climbing the corporate ladder lacked essential top managerial qualities, critics responding to the success of Japan in the world economy particularized both Japanese and Americans in order to construct two types of "success" and thereby downplay Asian success and rehabilitate America. One of the most explicit examples of such a strategy of redefining and rehabilitating America via a comparative, exceptionalizing analysis of "America" and Asia is James Fallows's 1989 liberal polemic, *More Like Us: Making America Great Again*.

In a climate filled with talk about the demise of America as the world's greatest economic power and Japan's ascension to that position, a plethora of books appeared suggesting that U.S. businesses might emulate the Japanese business style. This prescription bled into one regarding the rescue of American society in general. "Confucianism" was perceived as a convenient signifier for an importable mode of authoritarianism that could substitute for all those moral codes that America had formerly relied upon for its cohesion and order: the business sector was simply one of the many spheres that would benefit from such discipline and loyalty; the private space of the family unit, especially of the lower classes and racial minorities, was also in need of a neo-neo-Confucianism that remained (and remains) altogether vaguely defined. In contradistinction, Fallows, drawing on both his own family's background and his experiences as a journalist in Japan, argues for American exceptionalism. He characterizes the emulative discourse of contemporary pro-Japan advocates thus:

> Since the publication, in 1979, of Ezra Vogel's *Japan as Number One,* the idea that America should be more like Japan has been a constant theme in American political and intellectual life. American industrial planning should be more like MITI's. American schools should be more rigorous, like Japan's. American labor relations should be more consensual. American companies should treat their employees more like family and take the long, strategic view. Since the American work ethic and American management values have let us down, we should emulate those of the Japanese. (46n)

This, according to Fallows, is a simplistic and unthoughtful reaction to America's weakened condition: the way to "make America great again" is to be "more like us"; that is, to reconnect with what has historically distinguished America and realize that the way of the future should not be along the Japanese path (which, Fallows, like Petersen, insists can actually only be taken by the Japanese), but along a road uniquely American: "The purpose of this book is to remind Americans of how unusual our national culture is, and of why it is important that we not become a 'normal' society" (1).

In the course of his narrative, it becomes clear that what Fallows means by "normal" is exactly a predictable, convention-bound society: "America will be in serious trouble if it becomes an ordinary country, with people stuck in customary, class-bound roles in life" (3). Of all the national cultures in the world, America's, claims Fallows, is characterized by a productive chaos, an element of unpredictability. In contrast to the "Japanese Talent for Order" (the title of his second chapter), he poses the "American Talent for Disorder" (that of the following chapter). Rather than emulate a nation of rigid bureaucracies and entrenched elites (as he describes in his seventh chapter, "Confucianism Comes to America"), Fallows argues that the American spirit has always flourished under a condition of radical freedom, free from government interference in social life, archaic allegiances to extended families and traditional ethnic identifications, free from the strictures of mandated religion. It is precisely such freedom that underwrites American mobility and guarantees that all vestiges of old world caste and class systems are jettisoned in the exhilarating rush to modernity.

Like Petersen, Fallows not only greatly admires the Japanese, but also argues that the very things that produce such seemingly successful social subjects like the Japanese are particular to their historical, racial, and cultural situation. Unlike the conservative Petersen, however, Fallows the liberal is careful to explain how the very things Americans admire in the Japanese run contrary to the true values of America: their sense of family loyalty and obligation creates uncreative conformists; their national pride is borne of deep-rooted racist chauvinism. While Petersen downplays such negative aspects of Japanese "culture," for Fallows they demarcate a radical and definitive difference, and this allows him to break out of the contradictory mode of the "model minority myth" that compromises Petersen's disquisition.

Fallows's greatest attention is not, however, to the American spirit, but to the national political economy, and, by extension, the global. He argues that America's economic well-being is dependent on what he (after Schumpeter) calls "the creative destruction" of its capitalist system: "'Capitalism' usually calls up images of big machines or powerful financiers or perhaps class war, but what capitalism really means is change" (52). Upon performing this romantic reduction of capitalism to mere "change," Fallows proposes perpetual revolution driven by each individual's challenge to the status quo according to his or her particular goals (which might, indeed, change frequently according to whatever wrinkles might appear). What distinguishes America is that it provides the most fertile ground for a creative capitalism that thrives on such ad hoc, inspirational intuitions. While the Japanese seem to have gained economic superiority over the United States, the American model has the advantage in the long run. Simply put, and de-

spite the fact that he never mentions the term, the American spirit of spon-
taneous, creative, capitalistic mobility conjoins perfectly with the flexible
character of late capitalism. While Japan will remain mired in nationalist priorities and overly orderly methodologies, American "individualism" (and
this individualism is but one step away from a *post*national individualism
that is consonant with late capitalism's transnational corporate view) will
carry America into the twenty-first century. In short, we have an argument
as to which national culture, America's or Japan's, is best equipped for a late
capitalist, globalized economy, the key terms vacillating between American "flexibility" (Fallows) and Japanese ability to synthesize and discipline
(Petersen).[10] By comparing the two terms we derive a clearer sense of the historical specificity of their critiques and their application to the redefinition
of "America."

Two things are crucial to recognize in Fallows's narration. First, as
we have noted, is his rationalization for the rehabilitation of America in
the face of Japanese economic power. "We" can only rebuild our economic
strength if we recognize what made America great in the past—this same
element will make it great "again" well into late capitalism. Second, even
as he differentiates Japan from America (order vs. disorder, etc.), there is
an implicit argument that echoes prior articulations of Asians as the model
minority: while "Asia," tied down to a bureaucratized Confucian system,
will be overtaken by a more vital and imaginative "West," Asian *Americans*
might well contain the perfect measure of both cultures. Specifically, rather
than relegate them to the margins of the state, as Petersen does, writing for
a conservative agenda in the 1960s, Fallows's late twentieth-century liberalism embraces Asian Americans as another successfully assimilated immigrant group.

Indeed, to the consternation of both liberals and conservatives, Fallows uses social Darwinism to rebuff arguments against increased immigration.[11] Brushing aside the notion that immigrants will breed fear and resentment, especially among racial minorities, Fallows remarks, "America's
long-term strategic secret is that it can get the most out of people by putting
them in surprising situations. Competition from other Americans is the
source of most of this ultimately healthful disruption, but a continual supply
of new competition is invigorating too" (204). This simplistic and euphe-
mistic passage would nonetheless seem to still place Asians at a disadvantage, since they would remain under the sway of their native country's
Confucianist strictures and traditional prejudices. Yet this is not so. Fallows
describes the case of "the Nguyen Family," whom he met in 1982. The father
worked hard at menial manufacturing jobs in Los Angeles after leaving the
refugee camps. Then, he had a "stroke of blind luck":

In the resettlement office he bumped into an American refugee official whom he'd known in the camp. She said they needed more office workers to handle new arrivals. Although Nguyen still did not speak English smoothly, she agreed to put him in language school while starting him at $660 a month.

From this point on, the Nguyen family saga had all the classic elements of the Cuomo or Dukakis family's rise: sacrifice, study, ambition, frugality, achievement based on family pride. (102)

This instance is steeped in a mystified notion of "luck" that is heavily reliant on the classic American narrative: ("he had a stroke of blind luck, like those in Horatio Alger novels"); yet Fallows is careful to point up that "luck" must be complemented by individual effort: "the Nguyen family saga had all the classic elements of the Cuomo or Dukakis family's rise . . ."). This, then, is the particular amalgam that distinguishes America.

On one hand, Fallows argues closely for the particularity of nation, history, and culture. America's particularism is underwritten by its portrayal as that space wherein all the specificities of an individual's *past* identifications are erased under the imperatives of "change":

> Certainly there is little evidence in Asia or Africa that people can rise above racial, ethnic, or tribal divisions. But, to return to the point on which this book began, America *is* abnormal. It faced the challenge of immigration in much more intense form a century ago; and instead of being weakened, it was enriched. . . . Many of those now considered part of "mainstream" white America are descended from people seen as totally alien when they poured in. (206)

This argument neatly slides by the question of race (opening with Asians and Africans, but using successfully assimilated white immigrants as his evidence) in order to validate Fallows's assertion that the new world of America should be precisely a class- and color-free realm of free competition and "fair play" that is distinct most particularly from a Japan of exclusionist trade policies, calcified caste prejudice, and insiderism. Asian "success" is neutralized and historicized particularly in order that a promising future for America can be articulated through a selective and highly revisionist reading of its past and contemporary history. Petersen deploys Japanese Americans as a group whose reputed success bears witness to the essential justness and logic of American ideology, yet once they have been exploited as evidence, they must be recontained and neutralized. Fallows addresses a different historical period and approaches the subject from a different ideological perspective. Nevertheless, he employs a similar strategy of containment.

Whereas Petersen argues against a liberal revision of public policy in order to retain a racist social and political system, Fallows shrewdly differentiates between Asian Americans, who are deemed worthy of emulation because they have adapted their talents and spirit to the American way, and those Asians in Asia, whose skills and ethic of hard work will always be mired in Confucian conformity and thus always be subordinated, ultimately, to the independent, individualistic spirit of America. Petersen's conservative vision has Asian American success brought back into the realm of the unexceptional, so as to allow whites to regain hope of yet matching and overstepping Asian American success; Fallows reasserts American exceptionalism over and against the rise of Japan as a major economic player. In both cases, we witness a careful manipulation of the ratio of Asian to Asian American, deeply informed by a desire to rehabilitate the American state. Yet both these manipulations are predicated upon the drawing of a particular line between "Asian" and "American" that insists upon their separateness. Ultimately, economic ideology gives way to a racial segregation of the two in the American imaginary.

When we ask, "What keeps Asians from ultimately rising above whites? How are newer immigrant groups excluded? Why does anti-Asian racism persist?," we must note that any theory of race must address the complex dialectic between a fatalistic notion of the deterioration and endangerment of the dominant race, a notion necessary to underwrite exclusionary and prejudicial acts, and an optimistic element that persists in arguing for the ultimate value of the "superior" race. The role of Asians in America is best seen as a transmutable set of positionings that perform various ideological tasks within this dialectic.

It may be that by tracking the various positionalities of Asians in America one can achieve a sense of precisely those contradictions that inform American racism. In order to celebrate the triumph of American democracy, it is necessary to have a racial Other whose success bears witness to the legitimacy of such basic notions as upward mobility. Yet even assimilation into the elite classes cannot erase the mark of racial difference and the psychic and cultural differences that are assumed to accompany it. Such differences are held in reserve, able to be activated and deactivated selectively for different purposes. Hence, any notion of "marginalization" must cope with the variable *functions* of extremely subtle positionings within the political economy. The particularization of Asian Americans is of utmost historical significance. At present, they are variously catalogued in the inventory of America in U.S. social discourse: either lumped together with other racial minorities and marginalized peoples, or found divided from these groups and adjoined to whites. Or, most significantly, "Asian American" does not appear at all. The listing of American peoples often enough names "whites, blacks, Hispanics." The invisibility of Asian Americans in such instances is qualitatively different from the elision of indigenous peoples. While the latter's absence is the product of the convergence of genocidal policies and the willed discursive erasure of "the disappearing Indian" from the American imaginary, the invisibility of "Asian American" is an index of the inability of the United States to situate Asians in America. The teleological narrative of Asian/American is yet incomplete and unsettled—the "mold" is broken; it is uncertain what it has produced.

Notes

This essay is further developed in my book, *Asian/American: Historical Crossings of a Racial Frontier* (Stanford University Press 1999).

1   See Žižek 1989, 120n.

2   See Balibar 1990, "Paradoxes of Universality." See also the special issue of *differences* (volume 7, spring 1995) on the politics of the universal.

3   See Connery 1995, "Pacific Rim Discourse," as well as the essays collected in Dirlik 1993 for good overviews of the emergence of the modern notion of a "Pacific Rim."

4   I would insist that, as similar as each evocation of the model minority myth may be to another, it is crucial to note the specific historical context of each evocation and the functions it serves.

5   See also Cumings 1993 (40), who notes "the inability of elites to do more than oscillate between free trade and protectionism, between admiration for Japan's success and alarm at its new prowess."

6   For a critique of this thesis and specific data that disaggregates and specifies "success," see works by Cacas, Chan, Grove and Wu, T.W. Hazlett, Hurh and K-C. Kim, B-L. C. Kim, Osajima, Sue and Okazaki, and Yun.

7   For an excellent discussion, see Orfield 1988, "Race and the Liberal Agenda: The Loss of the Integrationist Dream, 1965–1974."

8   Orfield 1988, 325.

9   John W. Connor's findings seem to confirm Petersen's notion that the more assimilated Japanese Americans become, the lower their academic achievement. See Connor 1975, "Changing Trends in Japanese American Academic Achievement." See also McLeod 1986, "The Oriental Express."

10 Among the many analyses of Japan's ready-made postmodern, global culture, see Robertson 1992, *Globalization*. Robertson argues that Japan's ability to think globally is predicated upon its historically "syncretic" religion. For a rebuttal to such culturalist explanations, see Tomoji Ishi 1993, who notes that "less a product of some mysterious Japan culture, Japanese corporate culture derives from historically concrete economic and political structures and conflicts" (122).

11 See Skerry's review of Fallows's book, "Individualist America and Today's Immigrants" (1991). For examples of the conservative argument for more immigration, see Wattenberg and Zinsmeister 1990, "The Case for More Immigration." One should note that this argument specifies that these new immigrants should be admitted *only if* they possess the specific skills and capital needed by the United States.

In-Betweens in a Hybrid Nation:
Construction of Japanese American Identity
in Postwar Japan

YOSHIKUNI IGARASHI

Japanese studies has generally refrained from discussing Japanese American issues on the ground that they belong solely to American society. Scholars in the field must be careful not to overstep disciplinary boundaries: to discuss Japanese American experiences uncritically within the context of Japanese studies is an appropriation of Japanese American identity back within the boundaries of Japan; and, since they are Americans, Japanese American experiences should be discussed against American social and historical contexts. These cautions are necessary and useful in order not to privilege biological categories as essential. Particularly, the emphasis on the Americanness or the otherness of Japanese Americans functioned to some degree as an antidote to the cultural discourse popular in 1970s and 1980s Japan that claimed essential Japanese traits. It is by now commonsensical that Japanese American experiences do not belong to the field of Japanese studies.

Yet the strict exclusion of Japanese Americans from inquiries in Japanese studies has perhaps merely privileged the national boundaries between the United States and Japan. Rather than biological races, the nation-state serves as the foundation of scholarly inquiry. Although such inquiry may excavate diverse experiences within national boundaries, these diversities inevitably converge as a national experience, i.e., Japanese experiences. Diversities are rendered visible only insofar as they lead to a resolution and unity under a nation-state. Diasporic experiences of Japanese Americans, which refused to be appropriated into the concept of Japaneseness, have safely been located outside of the national boundaries and delegated to American studies. Japanese American experiences thus became invisible to

Japanese studies that tacitly participated in the policing of national boundaries through the maintenance of their disciplinary identity. The presence of Japanese Americans has been registered in the popular consciousness of postwar Japan and claimed its place within Japan. Yet discussing Japanese American experiences within the Japanese social context risks racial determinism if it is done with no regard to the conditions that rendered their experiences invisible within those boundaries as well as to the question of what constitutes Japaneseness. In order to search for possible ways to open studies of Japan to history outside of national boundaries, I examine the strategies deployed in representing Japanese Americans in 1950s Japan and trace the process through which Japanese Americans became invisible in Japanese society as well as in the field of Japanese studies.

Recalling his reunion with his Japanese American friend right after World War II, literary scholar, Saeki Shōichi, acknowledged his lack of concern during the war years toward the hardship endured by Japanese Americans who remained in Japan. It is estimated that between fifteen and twenty thousand Japanese Americans were in Japan at the beginning of the Pacific War and could not return to the United States until the postwar years.[1] Without the support of close family members and their communities, Japanese Americans faced the difficult task of maintaining material subsistence during wartime scarcity. Anti-American sentiments among Japanese people did not help. Saeki also claims that his lack of concern for Japanese Americans in Japan reflected the general absence of interest in the plight of Japanese Americans in the United States: "the existence of Japanese Americans was almost completely out of our sight."[2]

This general absence of interest in Japanese Americans seems to have persisted in Japan at least until the mid-1960s, despite Japan's renewed interest in things American in the immediate postwar period. For instance, *Nichibei kaiwa techō,* a short textbook for English conversation, was one of the first bestsellers that announced the return of the United States to the Japanese popular consciousness.[3] Many Japanese turned their envious gaze to the material wealth of American society portrayed not only through popular media, such as the comic, "Blondie," and *Reader's Digest,* but also by the American occupation forces.[4] As American citizens, Japanese Americans in Japan had access to American material wealth; hence, they similarly became objects of envy to many Japanese. A number of Japanese Americans who were stranded in Japan during the war gained employment through the occupation forces in the immediate postwar years and rebuilt their lives in Japan until they were repatriated to the United States.[5] Some chose to stay in Japan seeking business opportunities. Also, nisei soldiers from the United States, serving as interpreters in the occupation forces, represented the United States to Japanese people in their daily contacts with them.[6] Yet even though reunion with his Japanese American friend immediately after the war reminded Saeki of Japanese Americans in Japan, hardly any writings, literary or otherwise, concerning Japanese Americans were produced in Japanese in the first twenty years of the postwar period.

It is easy to dismiss this lack of interest as the sign of sheer negligence since the number of Japanese Americans who stayed in Japan during the war was limited; moreover, the total number of 260 thousand Japanese Americans did not seem large in comparison to Japan's population of about seventy million at the end of the war.[7] However, numerical determinism does not explain the sudden albeit moderate attention paid to Japanese Americans in the early 1970s when Japanese writers began to represent the plight of Japanese Americans caught in the U.S.-Japan conflict. There has been a peculiar synchronicity in the United States's and Japan's response to Japanese American issues. During World War II, when Japanese Americans were physically removed from West Coast states, their presence was also, as Saeki testifies, rendered invisible in Japan. Shortly after a number of civil rights-era American authors began examining Japanese American wartime experiences in the relocation camps, publications dealing with Japanese American issues also began appearing in Japan.[8]

In postwar Japan, discussions of the Japanese American plight resonated with conservative discourses that posited Japan as a victim in its past and current relations with the United States. Japan's emergence as an economic superpower in the 1970s afforded it stature sufficient to begin to examine the treatment of Japanese Americans in the United States during the war years. For example, Yamazaki Toyoko's fictional trilogy on Japanese Americans focuses on the hardship suffered by Japanese Americans in the relocation camps in its first half and spends its entire second half analyzing the effects of the atom bomb on Japanese Americans and the "prosecution by the victor" in the Tokyo war crimes trials.[9] There is no compelling literary reason for Yamazaki's juxtapositions; the second half of the novel is merely a patchwork of historical accounts. Yet the effects of these juxtapositions are unmistakable: Yamazaki encourages the reader to understand the plight of Japanese Americans as Japan's own.

Yamazaki's novel confirms the need to historicize the representations of Japanese Americans: the images of Japanese Americans in the United States and Japan have been largely defined by the two countries' relations. Placed "in between" Japan and the United States, Japanese Americans in postwar Japanese texts often embody the problematic nature of the two countries' postwar relations. In this article, I will read the traces of Japanese Americans within the cultural nationalism of 1950s Japan, a Japan that was beginning to recover from the trauma of the war and the American occupation. At this particular juncture in Japanese history, the concern for Japanese Americans remained low; silence on the subject reflected a desire to redefine Japan in the new postwar international order. Kojima Nobuo's "Enkei Daigaku Butai" (Yanjing University Unit) and "Hoshi" (Stars), two stories about Japanese American characters, are exceptions to the overall silence about Japanese Americans in the 1950s.[10] By working from Kojima's short stories to the larger cultural silence with respect to Japanese Americans in 1950s Japan, I will show that the silence surrounding Japanese Americans during and after the war was far from vacuous.

As I begin my discussion of the two stories, I should provide a cautionary note about my intervention into postwar Japanese history: my readings do not necessarily intend to break the silence about Japanese Americans in Japan. As a historical condition, the silence already reduced the figures of Japanese Americans to mere traces; hence, in exploring these traces I am not attempting to reconstitute "genuine" Japanese American voices masked by this silence. Perhaps the traces do not speak of the lives of Japanese Americans per se; but they eloquently speak about the silence, on the surface of which they were inscribed.

In discussing the in-between characters that Kojima creates in his stories, it is important to make reference to the intellectual milieu of 1950s Japan, and in particular to the dominant discourses of the period on Japanese culture. The cultural critic Katō Shūichi's well-known thesis of the "hybridity" (zasshusei) of Japanese culture stands as a preeminent example of the intellectual responses to the new political conditions surrounding late-occupation and postoccupation Japan. During an extended stay in Europe in the early 1950s, Katō began to locate the essential characteristics of Japanese culture in its close intertwining with Western culture, despite his initial intention of isolating Japanese culture in its pure form. Katō posits certain Western and Asian cultures as the pure forms of cultures, against which he measures Japanese culture's hybrid quality. According to Katō, English and French cultures retained their pure forms as the pinnacle of European culture; likewise in Asia, India and China have only been superficially affected by their exposure to Western cultures.[11] In this dichotomy of the West and Asia, Japan is placed in a unique position as a hybrid, exterior to both cultural traditions. In this hybridity, Katō finds generative possibilities. Japan, he argues, will fulfill its potential not by pursuing the pure form of its culture, but by recognizing and reevaluating its hybridity.

By defining Japanese culture as a third term and by complicating the binary opposition of East and West, Katō attempted to reconstruct Japan's cultural uniqueness. The simplicity and optimism of his thesis had strong appeal in mid-1950s Japan, which had just emerged from six and a half years of foreign occupation and was experiencing the continuing waves of American culture. Japanese culture was ideologically liberated from the negative implications of its hybridity. Katō's thesis affirms the popular desire for the other, the West, expressed in the realm of cultural consumption, while it also claims the unique quality of Japanese culture as distinct from both the West and Asia.

It is noteworthy that another well-known postwar intellectual, Maruyama Masao, responded to Katō's thesis rather negatively; instead of the generative possibilities of hybrid culture, Maruyama emphasized the infertility of the intellectual climate of Japan, where various imported European traditions merely coexisted.[12] Yet Maruyama's presentation of the intellectual climate of Japan in his book, *Nihon no shisō* (1961), strikingly resembles Katō's vision of Japanese culture in terms of an emphasis on eclecticism. While Katō sees the possibilities of hybridity, Maruyama emphasizes what he perceives as a negative aspect of eclecticism in the Japanese intellectual tradition. According to Maruyama, the acceptance of foreign traditions only attests to the lack of an integral subjective position in the Japanese intellectual tradition.

Despite their disagreement, what Katō and Maruyama demonstrate is that, by the 1950s, Japan was no longer defined in simple oppositional terms to the West or the United States. According to Katō and Maruyama, Japan has become the third term in a binary opposition of East and West. This contrasts to prewar writing, such as Okakura Kakuzō's *The Ideals of the East,* in which Japan, along with Asia, serves as an oppositional category to the West.[13] The 1970s discourse on Japanese uniqueness emphasized Japan's ability to understand the West, and, conversely, the West's inability to understand Japan. This asymmetrical flow of knowledge stems from this categorization of Japan as a hybrid of West and East. Although the West might be able to understand the East through analogy—for example, Confucianism in the image of Christianity—the West had no way of understanding Japanese culture that defied such analogies. However, Japan, as hybrid of both, could easily understand both the West and the East.

In other words, during the 1950s, cultural discourse along these lines surreptitiously removed Japan from association with the East and located it in a position between East and West. This move reflects Japan's actual position in the 1950s: Japan became dependent for its security on U.S. military power and U.S. markets. Against this politico-economic backdrop, such claims of Japanese culture's hybridity had a highly ideological function in confirming the status quo. Through this ideological construction of Japan, memories of past conflicts with the United States and Europe, as well as the colonization of fellow Asian countries, received little attention, let alone critical discussion. The Japan that had aspired to represent the East against the West was abandoned in discussions of Japan's hybrid culture: Japan had always been hybrid, imbued with the West.

After making his literary debut in 1948 with the short story, "Kisha no naka" (On the train), Kojima Nobuo published a series of short stories that focused on daily life during and immediately after World War II. As the literary critic Etō Jun claims, Japan's problematic relationship with the United States received Kojima's creative attention in several of these stories.[14] Kojima uses Japanese American figures in "Enkei Daigaku Butai" (1952) and "Hoshi" (1954) to illuminate the power dynamics between the United States and Japan. Through presenting his Japanese American characters as figures occupying the in-between space of the two countries, Kojima excavates the conflicts and tensions between the two countries that had been largely repressed in Japan during the immediate postwar years.[15]

Kojima's short story needs to be historicized within and against this representation of Japan as hybrid. By consciously introducing the in-between figures of Japanese Americans into his stories, he participates in the debate regarding Japan's hybrid identity. Kojima's writing is more historicist (more so in his 1954 work) than Katō's and Maruyama's, as it explores the historical condition that led to eager acceptance of the conceptualization of Japan as hybrid. Kojima allegorically represents these conditions in the form of an army unit at the moment of the Japanese empire's collapse. In particular, languages become the loci for the struggles of Kojima's characters to recast their identities within the liminal space of the army unit. In "Enkei Daigaku Butai" ("Yanjing University Unit"), Kojima does not yet make forceful reference to postwar Japanese society, but he did lay a foundation for a more thorough pursuit of the topic in the 1954 story, "Hoshi" (Stars).[16]

In "Enkei Daigaku Butai," the author focuses on the everyday lives of the members of the army intelligence unit. In March 1944, the protagonist, named Kojima (same as the author's own), is transferred from a unit in the Shanxi province of northern China to an intelligence unit in Beijing. The army is seeking nisei soldiers and those who are fluent in English for the purpose of gathering information. Kojima volunteers for the unit in hopes of being sent back to Japan to do intelligence work. However, he discovers to his disappointment that the unit is stationed at Yanjing University in Beijing. In the unit, Kojima meets several strange characters, including the nisei soldier, Ahikawa, an illegitimate child of an American Marine and a Japanese woman. Ahikawa resents his American heritage and is emotionally invested in Japan's victory. In contrast, Corporal Hanawa Zenjirō, formerly a florist in Japan, is convinced that Japan will be defeated in the near future.

Instead of making reference to the actual combat taking place throughout China, the plot focuses on the interactions of these three characters. Even when the battles in the Philippines are mentioned, they are conveyed with no sense of immediacy. For example, Kojima remarks that "the Philippines are big islands and take time to be defeated. After getting used to the fact that these islands are being defeated, the soldiers in remote areas became accustomed to it, and maintained the psychological state in which they thought nothing of it" (89). The unit appears to be remote from any actual battles taking place in Asia; the enemy, the United States, appears only in the form of intercepted communications. Thus the characters in the story live in the amorphous, timeless space of the war and the military. The narrator continues: "When I think about my hometown, my heart aches. But what can I do? One gets bored with the conversations [with one's family] that one ruminates, and forgets even [familiar] faces. I even got totally bored with the fantasy that I will die" (89). Repressing all memories of the past and adapting oneself to the liminal space of the army seems to be the only way to survive.

This strategy of survival thoroughly alienates Kojima from that which was once so familiar to him, the Japanese language, while Ahikawa turns out to be best suited to the unit's mission due to his exceptional language skills. Interestingly, the contrast between Kojima's and Ahikawa's relations to languages prefigures the two opposing evaluations of Japan's hybrid culture forwarded by Maruyama and Katō in the 1950s. The story of Kojima's estrangement from his own identity, which unfolds metaphorically through his troubled relation with language in general and with his native tongue in particular, resonates with Maruyama's critique of the celebration of Japan's hybrid culture. For Maruyama, the foreign elements in the Japanese intellectual milieu lead to a degenerative state of confusion. In contrast, the hybrid figure of Ahikawa and his suitability for the unit's mission embody Katō's positive evaluation of Japan's cultural conditions. The hybrid constitution of Japanese culture—the presence of the other—provides the basis for its vitality. Ahikawa's linguistic adeptness easily resonates, moreover, with the story's portrayal of his marked sexuality, clearly pointing to the generative possibility that Katō saw in Japan's hybrid culture. Perhaps for this reason, the text of "Enkei Daigaku Butai" itself is split into two and based on the contrast between the two characters' relations with the unnamed other, the United States.

The United States enters into the quotidian consciousness of the unit only through the voice of intercepted communications; its presence is at once immediate and distant. By contrast, China remains silent despite its inescapable presence in the lives of the unit members. For example, the scenes at the nearby brothel attest to the linguistic redress of China through the medium of Chinese female bodies. At the brothel, Kojima uses a mixture of Japanese, English, and Chinese to converse with one of the Chinese prostitutes. However, this conversation remains "incoherent" (84). The woman embodies three languages since she has three names, one in each language: Toshiko, Julia, and a Chinese name that she writes on a wall in her room but never pronounces (84). The silence surrounding the Chinese name is salient: the name appears only as a trace among the other writings on the wall, a sign of the prostitute's past memories. The Chinese name is denied its synchronic presence and relegated to the past. Similarly, in Katō Shûichi's postwar discussion of Japanese culture's hybridity and in Maruyama's negative evaluation of Japan's intellectual condition, Asia—particularly China—disappears from the triad of Asia, Japan, and the West. Their discussion assumes that China occupies an oppositional position with regard to the West; yet China remains a silent signifier and the ahistorical other to the West. Japan's hybridity is described solely in relation to the West in both Katō's and Maruyama's postwar articulations. Thus tropes of hybridity and in-betweenness assisted postwar society in concealing Japan's experiences in wartime China. In Kojima's story, the silenced woman's Chinese name intimates that China was already absent in the minds of the unit members even before the end of the war. The mission of the intelligence unit to decipher American codes is, after all, wholly oriented toward the United States. The unit, with its strange dependency on the enemy country and slighting of China, prefigures postwar Japanese society.

In the prostitute's room, Kojima proceeds to efface China as the past by erasing all the writings on the walls. One morning he visits the prostitute while she is not in her room and he decides to stay there anyway. After getting bored simply lying there, Kojima begins to scrub off the graffiti left by soldiers. The graffiti exists as a record of Japan's war against China in the prostitute's everyday life; numerous Japanese soldiers have left their marks on the walls.

He does not know why he has started the task; yet he feels compelled to finish washing the walls, since the clean spots are more conspicuous than before. After he completes the job, the fatigue from the cleaning makes him fall asleep. He dreams that his parents, wife, and friends are washing his body before they place it in a coffin. When he wakes up from the dream, he realizes that what he did will annoy the woman since the graffiti constitutes "memorable letters" for her.[17] The image of the coffin suggests that washing the walls represents Kojima's departure from everyday life. Once he completes the process of both alienating himself from the past and its memories and losing contact with everyday life, the boundaries of his self disintegrate. Kojima begins to talk in another's voice: speaking like Hanawa, he identifies himself as him to a patrol officer. Kojima's irrational behavior illustrates Maruyama's critique of the hybrid condition of the Japanese intellectual tradition, a condition in which diverse elements simply remain fragmentary without a temporal axis. In the end, Kojima's dysfunctionality defies the generative possibility of hybridity: the intimate contact with the Chinese prostitute in the trilingual environment only leads to the erasure of the past and the disintegration of his identity.

By comparison, the Japanese American, Ahikawa, appears to be the only person in the unit who does not have a problematic relationship with language. Fluent in English, Japanese, and Chinese, he is ideally suited for the unit's mission. In contrast, Japanese soldiers have problems with English, while the Japanese of other nisei soldiers is rudimentary. Ahikawa's in-between quality—his Japanese and American parentage and his fluency in Chinese—centrally locates him in an ironic fashion in the liminal space of the intelligence unit. This securely placed identity sanctions his act of conviction: Ahikawa publicly demonstrates his contempt for Hanawa, the defeatist in the unit, and even threatens to kill him in theatrical, Kabuki-like fashion. Standing out against the noncommittal attitudes of his fellow unit members, Ahikawa ironically serves as the most outspoken "representative" of Japan. Ahikawa tries and succeeds in accentuating his Japanese identity in the marginal space of the intelligence unit, but his desire to be a loyal Japanese is perceived as excessive to this space, rendering him a somewhat comical figure. Within the unit, which has already repressed the reality of fighting, Ahikawa's desire is an excess, for it reminds the unit members of the war that surrounds them.

Kojima construes Ahikawa's presence in the liminal space of the intelligence unit as an excess of sexual desire. Ahikawa serves as a constant reminder of the desires entangled in the conflicts between the United States and Japan. His hybrid body, the product of such desires, represents contradictory feelings of fascination with and revulsion toward the other. His hybridity manifests itself through its exceptional language ability and his undiminished sexual appetite. After Kojima finds Ahikawa defecating in a bush, they strike up a conversation in which the latter comments: "Actually, I was having a hard time because I was also feeling the other urge in the bush. Let's go have fun tomorrow [in the brothel]. Yeah, Ahikawa is prepared to die as a Japanese. I just resent my American father who gave birth to me" (79). Ahikawa's sexual appetite is so persistent that he cannot exercise full control over his body. He cannot defecate because he has a sexual urge. Ahikawa's sexual desire leads to a declaration of his readiness to die as a Japanese, yet, in the end, he admits to his American heritage. Ahikawa's hybridity becomes articulated and circulates in the form of sexual desire; his hybridity in turn marks sexual excess, which circulates in the unit whose mission is to decipher the enemy's language. In this sexually charged, bilateral relation of the United States and Japan, China figures only as the medium through which these contradictory desires play themselves out. The sexuality of the unit members, and Ahikawa particularly, are thus mediated by the bodies of Chinese prostitutes. It is no accident that the lice infesting Ahikawa's crotch spread to other unit members through Chinese prostitutes: the imagined community of the unit emerges through Chinese female bodies and consequent infection with lice.

The author's critical insights into identity construction through language notwithstanding, his criticism of the military and postwar society in "Enkei Daigaku Butai" is limited to a description of the fictional order of these spaces. Their depiction appears strikingly similar to the Japan that Katō and Maruyama outlined in their 1950s writings: a strange, static space without reference to the specific historical context that has produced it. Although the intelligence unit could exist only in relation to the exterior world, the condition that created it—Japan's conflicts with China and the United States—simply disappear in the story. The presence of the other is figuratively acknowledged only through the sexual desires of the unit members for the Chinese prostitutes. Yet the protagonist of the story keeps erasing the memories and the community formed around the Chinese prostitutes, while the United States remains cryptically encoded. Kojima can only adapt to the liminal space of the unit by erasing the other in the external world.

Although the author's critique of this space is humorous and biting, it offers little insight into how the desires for the other circulate in the unit and postwar Japanese society. Kojima, two years later would intensify his pursuit of the shadow of the other through another Japanese American character in "Hoshi."

In "Hoshi," Kojima introduces the figure of Private Jōji Sugihara into the imagined community of the Japanese Army.[18] Jōji is trapped in this space by a historical accident: the war breaks out while he is in Japan visiting his grandfather. His hybrid identity is established through such details as his education and his name. Jōji began junior high school in Japan, but returned to the United States to attend college. His given name, Jōji, is itself a perfectly Japanese name that nevertheless translates easily into the American "George." His culturally hybrid identity determines his marginal existence in the army; this marginality in turn encourages him to embrace with intensity the fictive order of the army. This split of Jōji/George ultimately propels the narrative.

Although the story centers around Jōji's self-hatred and desire to find his own identity and community, it also deals closely with how other Japanese around him act out their own desires and anxieties through this identity. Jōji's hybrid identity triggers the contradictory and sexually charged responses of Japanese characters toward Japan's other, the United States. Although Jōji is eager to forgo his marked in-betweenness, he is constantly reminded of what he is—a nisei in the army. They even give him a nickname, "America." Senior soldiers use Jōji to express their simultaneous revulsion and desire for the United States. They force him to "answer all sort[s] of questions about California and American women" and demand that he speak English and sing jazz (119/116). When he refuses to comply with their demands, Jōji is rewarded with "Western-style cooking" (a beating from senior soldiers) and he becomes the subject of "American sightseeing" (soldiers watching him "double over in pain") (119–20/116). By beating Jōji, the unit members exorcise the very desire that their beating sessions bespeak, their own desire for the Western other. In this way, Jōji's hybrid identity thus functions as a suture that contains the tension of the community in the army unit, a suture that announces the existence of the wound itself. It simultaneously expresses and conceals the tension between desire and revulsion for the United States. Facing the contradictory process of repression and accentuation of his social identity, Jōji attempts to gain a Japanese self by reifying the abstract hierarchy of the army in the form of the stars on the insignia. The stars become the symbols assuring his place in the army. Jōji turns himself into an ardent admirer of the stars, finding the community that he longs for among them. The army to which Jōji is initiated exists as the liminal space in which the stars provide the only orientation. For example, when Kojima describes the death of some Chinese soldiers, their bodies are reduced to the symbolic signifier of their rank, the stars:

> One of the dead soldiers, dressed in a sky-blue padded uniform, lay face down at the side of the path. One of our men nudged the body over with his foot and stared at it. There, in the same location on his neck, the dead soldier wore a single white star against the black of his collar. The meagerness of that enemy star—though it wasn't an absolute meagerness—made me feel close to the dead man. Or was it just because he was now a corpse? (126/121)

Jōji Sugihara feels an affinity with the dead Chinese soldier through the "meagerness of that enemy star," an abstract sign that embodies the military hierarchy. The army for which Jōji serves is an imagined community through and through, separate from history and society. Sociohistorical memories are obliterated in the military, replaced by the latter's own sociality and temporality, which are symbolized by official rank. People are reduced to their stars, the signifiers of their rankings. The sheer materiality of the soldier's corpse, devoid of historical and social reference, ironically provides the basis on which the stars can communicate among themselves. Jōji's empathy toward the Chinese soldiers is explicitly couched as that from one star to another.

Jōji finds consolation by contemplating an existence more marginal than his own, that of Private Hikida. Hikida's inability to adapt to army life makes him a perfect object of abuse in his unit. Thanks to Hikida, Jōji is not only relieved from daily mistreatment, but he also creates situations in which Hikida is abused. Jōji then feels safe, as if he were wearing "a cloak of invisibility" (121/118). Hikida becomes a mirror through which Jōji reflects and externalizes his marginality in the army. In the following description of Hikida's ugliness, Jōji admits to knowing how he himself must appear to the others:

> His ugliness had little to do with his awkward posture, or the fact that his uniform was always in disarray because his spare time was all devoted to receiving upbraidings for his idleness. Rather I felt that the measly single star on his collar deserved a better setting than his tiny eyes and his long, pale, downcast face with its three moles. Indeed his looks were an insult to that star. Even one star was too exalted for him. He made me wish that someone had invented an even humbler insignia.
>
> I couldn't bear thinking about the way others viewed me. But vaguely I sensed they felt that I was a disgrace to my own star, too. By insulting one star I was insulting every other star. (120/117)

Jōji is deeply aware of and anxious about his low status in the unit and yearns for a more permanent way to differentiate himself from Hikida. He wishes there were a visual sign—"an even humbler insignia"—that would place Hikida lower in the military hierarchy. The absence of such an insignia, however, only makes Jōji fixate on Hikida's marginality. Thus, Jōji takes Hikida's ugliness as the sign of Hikida's marginality: Hikida's more marginal status renders Jōji's hybrid identity invisible to the other members of the unit.

Contact with the local Chinese people also provides Jōji with great comfort since they do not know that he is a nisei. After Jōji is promoted to Private First Class, he and Hikida (who remains buck private) are assigned to stand watch at the city gate. Although this assignment allows them to speak with the locals and thus quench their thirst for human contact, this "dream" assignment is short lived. After witnessing their lax security at the city gate, their senior soldier kicks Jōji to the ground, reminding him and the locals of the reality of the army. After this incident, Jōji grows to further resent Hikida for maintaining his sympathetic attitudes toward the Chinese locals. Hikida simply does not care about being part of the army hierarchy. When Jōji eventually beats Hikida atop the city wall, Hikida turns the tables by reminding Jōji of his marginal status: "Hikida, still huddled on the ground, muttered petulantly, 'You're not a Japanese after all. You aren't! You aren't!' " (132/126). Although Jōji wants to and does believe that the hierarchy of stars is the basis of the absolute order, Hikida reminds Jōji of his marginalized status outside of the army.

Soon after the incident, Hikida is transferred to a unit in Southeast Asia—Jōji loses the "indispensable" (128/123) man, or star. He has to face his own hybrid identity without the protection of "a cloak of invisibility." Jōji is assigned to be an orderly to Captain Inoma, who takes up the task of creating a loyal Imperial Army soldier out of Jōji. One of the first orders that Inoma gives Jōji is to erase his past: "PFC Sugihara Jōji! You're going to have one hell of a time becoming a Japanese soldier. You will consider today the last time you have any past whatsoever" (136/128). Jōji is ordered to conduct the double act of marking and forgetting his own past by writing a personal history and "Journal of Self-Examination" as the first part of his reeducation. Inoma simply tears up Jōji's personal histories, and Jōji has to contemplate his superior's acts in his journal. Inoma demands Jōji express his past in writing only to repress it. By learning to articulate and simultaneously repress his identity as a Japanese American, Jōji finds the way to be a loyal Imperial Army soldier.

Even more effective in inculcating army values in Jōji is the following assignment: "He came up with an unusual method of testing my loyalty. He had me prepare three separate collar insignia of captain's rank. While he slept at night, I was to rotate them on his uniform every now and then. By doing that, of course, I was unable to forget even in my sleep that he was a captain" (136/129). The captain's reeducation of Jōji is so successful that Jōji begins to see him as a star: "I let the notion grow in me that the captain was himself a star, and that stars had an innate grandeur about them" (136/129). Furthermore, Jōji begins to personify the three sets of Inoma's insignia as his brothers and sister; he finally finds his imagined community among the stars that he names Tom, Frank, and Kate. Note that he gives the stars his brothers' and sister's American names.

This equation between stars and individuals, including himself, completes his reeducation, yet Jōji discovers that bodies of individuals do not fit neatly into the equation. He is shocked to see Captain Inoma's naked body as he washes his back: the arbitrary relations between the signifier and the signified—Inoma's rank and his masculine body—throw Jōji. Jōji recalls his discovery of Inoma's body:

> One day when I was attending the captain in his bath, he climbed out of the tub and plopped himself down in front of me. I felt as though a powerful electric shock had run through me. I couldn't shake off the peculiar sensation that Kate was still clinging to the nape of his neck. Why should I be so stunned to see the captain nude, without his uniform? Who in fact was this naked man before me? He was muscular, to be sure, but was there such a great difference between me and this man with the close-cropped hair when both of us were in the buff? (137–38/129–30)

Although he manages to reregister the naked man in front of him as Captain Inoma, he has "a sluggish, uneasy feeling, as though a cog had slipped out of place" (138/130). The disjuncture between Inoma's naked body and his bodily existence in everyday life disturbs the sense of order Jōji found by matching individuals with stars. As a consequence, Jōji begins to notice that "there was something wrong with the way he snored in his sleep, and the way he spat out the window each morning" (138/130). Jōji is shaken when he finds living bodies of individuals beneath the abstract signs of stars.

Once he discovers the chasm between the signifier and the signified, he grows even more fixated on the stars. Indeed, when he sees a chief of staff in Beijing, he is mesmerized by the chief's stars and forgets to salute. Jōji even starts taking a few steps toward the chief until he is stopped by a "stentorian shout" (139/131). His disrespect toward the chief of staff enrages Inoma, who insists that Jōji commit suicide with a sword. Jōji's life, however, is saved by a comic discovery: both he and Inoma are surprised to discover that his navel is shaped like a star. Not only does Jōji find his ideal community among the stars, but he has always already been the star.

At the moment of his total identification with the stars, Jōji's self seems to disintegrate. After escaping Inoma's punishment for his irreverent behavior toward his superiors, Jōji wanders through the army compounds in a hallucinatory state. He even manages to escape even from the army compound, only to lose control over himself:

> In a frenzy I leaped a fence and came out on a road. I have no idea how long I walked, where my feet led me, what I did, or even if I was really in Peking. I had the feeling I had fallen off the planet altogether.

I dropped to the ground and cried out: "Army Private Sugihara Jōji! Where am I? Get me out of here!!" (145/135)[19]

Jōji's process of reeducation is complete: he totally internalizes the aura of the stars and cannot function outside of the army compound.

During the war, Jōji lives for a fictional life sustained in the army, a life that assumes the conflict of the United States and Japan. Yet the fictive hierarchy that Jōji grows to accept during the war suddenly disintegrates as the war comes to its conclusion. Following the defeat of Japan, one fiction is immediately displaced with another that promotes the mutual interests of the United States and Japan. During the war, the hybridity of Jōji's identity had to be repressed (yet marked as the trace of the tension) in order to maintain the fictive hierarchy of the army. In contrast, the newly imagined community of postwar Japan is eager, like the Japanese Imperial Army immediately after the war, to appropriate this hybrid identity in order to erase the memories of past conflicts with the United States. Jōji is once again placed at the site of tension, this time as an interpreter assigned to conceal the gaping wound inflicted by Japan's defeat. Although Jōji's prescribed role seems to change drastically once Japan is defeated, his function as the suture remains constant.

In Kojima's story, the aura of the stars tarnishes very quickly after Japan's defeat. Nevertheless, the army manages to maintain the semblance of order within itself. At the end of the war, the two stars that Jōji carries are "imbued with my memories, my experiences" (146/136). He vaguely desires to "continue living the sort of life in which stars would play a part" (147/136). Having learned to live in the self-enclosed community of the stars, life outside has become difficult to imagine. Yet the behavior of his superior officers, particularly that of Inoma, begins to disturb Jōji's sense of hierarchy in the army. Inoma orders Jōji to remember English again, the language that the officer had been so insistent on erasing from Jōji's memories. Jōji is appointed to the task of translation, interpretation, and teaching volunteer officers. Inoma also forces Jōji to wear an officer's civilian clothes and use just his given name when teaching English to his superiors, criticizing him for introducing himself to the class as "Army Private Sugihara Jōji." Inoma insists: "All you need tell them is the name your parents gave you—Sugihara Jōji. In fact, just plain Jōji is good enough" (148/137). In sum, Jōji's psychological problems stem from the reversal of the process that he had to go through to adapt to the "normalcy" of the army. Jōji has been deprived of the rank he has grown into and is once again thrown back on his origins; this time, however, the army is eager to appropriate his marginality.

For Jōji, the stars finally begin to recover an association with the world outside of the army, strange as it seems. Soon after the defeat, all of the members of the army are promoted one rank: such inflation of the rankings—an absurd motivation of his superiors—instill a degree of cynicism in Jōji. His secure relation to the army hierarchy is further challenged by Inoma's humiliating request for a job at his father's farm in the United States. All this perhaps prepares Jōji to rediscover the stars outside of the army:

> The autumn sunlight that shone through the trees from the vast Beijing sky make his platinum stars shimmer. The sight made me remember something I had forgotten for a long time—the stars and bells on a Christmas tree. I felt as though I could hear voices singing "Merry Christmas!" somewhere. What a bizarre association to make, I thought. (150–51/139)

The associations are "bizarre" to him since they are completely outside of the context of the army, the context in which he has buried himself. The United States returns to Jōji's mind as stars. It turns out that stars themselves are hybrid, imbued with Jōji's geohistorically specific experiences. Jōji looks at the stars as a Japanese soldier in Beijing and remembers Christmas in the United States.

On an LST (a type of military aquatic landing vehicle) for repatriation to Japan, Jōji's attitude toward the army hierarchy reverts back to ambivalence. It is clear that he is still emotionally invested in the hierarchy of the army, yet he is "incensed that even this man [the American staff sergeant] was caught up in the system of rank" (153/141). However, Jōji is quite unprepared for the incident that later takes place on the LST: just before the ship reaches the shore of Sasebo, American soldiers begin tearing off insignias from the collars of Japanese noncommissioned officers to collect as souvenirs. The hierarchy of stars in the Japanese army is displaced by the United States's military power. The scene that takes place on the LST that repatriates Jōji's unit and thousands of other soldiers is highly symbolic. Jōji has the following exchange with one of the American soldiers:

> "Do the repatriates always have their stars taken away like this?"
> "This is our first voyage. I don't know what anybody else does."
> "Does Sergeant Brown allow you to confiscate stars?"
> "He wants them more than anybody."
> "What happens if this leads to trouble among our men?"
> "This!" He pretended to be firing a machine gun. (156/143)

The authority of Japanese stars is gone, and they are reduced to quaint souvenirs for American soldiers. What replaces the order and hierarchy of Japanese stars is U.S. military superiority.[20]

The postwar Japanese society that Jōji anticipates is already shot through by the presence of the United States, and the community of stars Jōji once belonged to is displaced by sheer American military power. Similarly, on the American LST, the old stars lose their magic in the eyes of the Japanese soldiers: once the American soldiers retreat with their trophies, the Japanese in the hold begin ripping their own stars off from their uniforms. Jōji tries to stop them to no avail: even his own stars are ripped off and trampled by another soldier. Later, Jōji finds Inoma on deck wearing a pair of American army boots: an American officer has taken Inoma's boots and knapsack. Suddenly, Jōji makes a leap in his associations: he "recalled that his [Inoma's] feet were larger than average. . . . Inoma and the other soldiers were now looking for new stars" (158/144). Inoma's large feet give a sexual overtone to his desire for the other; though Inoma's large feet are momentarily deprived of their protection, they are immediately wrapped in a pair of American boots. Inoma's naked desire to wear new stars has already found a new object in the material presence of the United States.

When Jōji finally enters Sasebo Harbor, he is shocked to discover that "the hills were the color of the khaki uniform I wore" (158/144). The Japan to which he looked forward to returning is nothing more than an extension of the army and its vacuous space. Worse yet, there are no more stars. Historical and social memories of individuals were sacrificed in both the pre-1945 Japanese army and postwar Japanese society in order to maintain a fiction that these communities stood above history. The imagined communities of the army and postwar Japan share the same feature at the end of Kojima's fiction—the neutral color (*chūkanshoku:* literally, the "in-between" color) of khaki—into which all the stains and dirt of history have vanished. It turns out that the liminal space of the army that Jōji has experienced is not an exception, but rather the rule. He realizes that he will have to repeat his former experience all over again now that he has reached Japan. Jōji has to find a new set of stars within postwar Japanese society, which demands its members to repress past memories of the war. In order to embrace fully the stars of the American flag, postwar Japanese society needs to conceal the past conflict with the United States.

In "Stars," Japanese society after the war turns out to be the extension of the liminal space of the army; the army's response to the defeat prefigures the drastic change that Japanese society experienced. The difficult experiences of Japanese Americans during the war have gone unremarked since they are reminders of Japan's war against the United States. On the other hand, Japanese Americans remain inconspicuous within Japan despite the popular desire to cast Japan as a hybrid society. The perceived in-betweenness of Japanese Americans was appropriated by postwar Japanese society as a screen behind which to hide itself. After the surrender of Japan, Jōji's hybrid identity is resurrected in the army as a tool to conceal its principal role in the war and promote its newly found affinity within the United States.

It is important to reemphasize in this conclusion the historicity of the (non)representations of Japanese Americans in Japanese society. The images of Japanese Americans reflected the history of the two countries' contradictory relations: Japanese American identity became the locus where the tension of desire and revulsion was played out. Not surprisingly, strategies to represent them drastically shifted from the repression of their difference during the war to recasting Japan in the images of Japanese Americans in the 1950s. Kojima Nobuo's short stories illuminate this shift and the postwar representational strategy that appropriated Japanese American identity.

As a perfect illustration of this strategy at work, we can point to a 1950 criminal case. Many gruesome and media-worthy crimes occurred in immediate postwar Japan, but the armed robbery case that took place on 22 September 1950 in Tokyo acquired notoriety not because of what the robber accomplished but because of what he said to the police—"Oh, mistake"—when he was apprehended. After the perpetrator robbed a car that was transporting cash, he hid with his girlfriend at her apartment. When the police arrived two days later, the suspect pretended he was a nisei who did not understand Japanese, obviously trying to hide his criminal behavior by casting himself as Japanese American.[21] His one line of English, "Oh, mistake," immediately became the popular phrase of the year.[22] Such appropriation of Japanese American identity, as Kojima demonstrated, similarly constituted postwar Japan's desperate attempt to conceal its own criminal past. This minor criminal drama drew national attention precisely because it tapped a deep anxiety lying beneath the repression of the past, an anxiety about getting caught in the midst of pretense. The Japanese media were quick to label this case as a crime representative of postwar youth, the caricature of the postwar desire to emulate everything American. Ultimately, the embarrassment and humiliation that this case stirred—feelings that Kojima's antiheroic characters similarly invoke—touched on the anxieties (as well as the desire) of many Japanese about facing what was repressed in their postwar representations of Japan.

These anxieties required constant policing lest the pretense, that Japan had always been something else, would be brought under scrutiny. Japanese American identities served as a suture that concealed the disjuncture in Japan's modern history: Japanese Americans themselves appeared only as traces of conflicting Japanese desires toward the other. Even when they were visible, they manifested themselves only through a surrogate figure of a Japanese impersonator. A simple attempt at inclusion—announcing they have been there—is not a sufficient tactic in discussing Japanese American experiences within Japanese society when facing this tremendous exclusionary force. Perhaps only careful scrutiny of the conditions called "Japaneseness" that necessitated and enabled the exclusion process can assist in excavating Japanese American experiences from those of Japanese society.

Notes

I would like to thank Kandice Chuh, Teresa A. Goddu, Susan Hegeman, and Karen Shimakawa for their helpful comments and suggestions on earlier versions of this article. The Japanese names in this article are transcribed in the Japanese fashion—family names first, except for authors who publish in English (including myself). The names of Japanese Americans appear in American name order.

1   The Japanese government refused to recognize the American citizenship of nisei and their expatriation was denied, confirming the principle of *jus sanguinus*—those of Japanese extraction were automatically regarded as Japanese subjects. Robert G. Lee, "Introduction," in Mary Kimoto Tomita, 1995, *Dear Miye* (Stanford: Stanford University Press), 14–15. Mary Kimoto Tomita provides a rare glimpse of the hardship that many Japanese Americans experienced in wartime Japan. See *Dear Miye,* particularly 143–53.

2   It sold as many as 3.6 million copies in three months since its first printing in September 1945. Saeki Shōichi 1984, *Nichibei kankei no nakano bungaku* (Literature in U.S.-Japan Relations). Tokyo: Bungei shunjū, 306.

3   Asahi shinbunsha, ed. 1995. Nichibei kaiwa techo *wa naze uretaka* (Why has *Handbook for English Conversation* sold so well?). Tokyo: Asahi shinbunsha, 16–17.

4   For example, the Civil Information and Education Section in General MacArthur's headquarters actively circulated and showed films promoting American values throughout Japan during the occupation period. Although the films were about American values, often the visual presentations of American lives and material wealth left stronger impressions on the minds of many Japanese. See, Asahi shinbun gakugeibu. 1995. *Daidokoro kara sengo ga mieru* (Looking at the postwar period from kitchens). Tokyo: Asahi shinbunsha, 30–34. In 1946, *Shūkan Asahi* (Asahi weekly) and, in January 1949, *Asahi shinbun* began carrying Chic Young's cartoon, "Blondie," in which many Japanese looked upon the American way of life with envy. The postwar Japanese economy finally achieved its pre-1945 level in 1955.

5   The duration of time that Japanese Americans had to wait until they were repatriated varied. The process of repatriation began in 1946, with the number of repatriates peaking in 1948. For the issues involved in Japanese American repatriation, see Sodei Rinjirō. 1995. *Watashitachi wa teki dattanoka* (Were we enemies?) Tokyo: Iwanami shoten, 85–94.

6   Sadako Obata, who was born in the United States but had been living in Japan since 1939, recalls the reunion with her brother who visited her as an American soldier: "I was really happy since he was the only family member I had in Japan. Besides, he brought various things and food, and that changed the way people around me treated me" [my translation]. Sodei Rinjirō, *Watashitachi wa teki dattanoka,* 78.

7   In 1930, there were 139,631 people of Japanese extraction in Hawaii and 126,948 on the U.S. mainland. Brian Niiya, ed. 1993. *Japanese American History.* New York: Facts on File, 8.

8 The late 1960s saw an increase in Japanese publications on issues related to Japanese Americans. For instance, the 1960s and early 1970s publications in fields related to Japanese Americans included the following titles: Murayama Tadashi. 1964. *Amerika Nisei* Tokyo: Jijitsūshinsha; Karl Yoneda, 1967. *Zaibei Nihonjin rôdôsha no rekishi* (A history of Japanese workers in the United States). Tokyo: Shinnihon shinsho; Joe Koide 1967; 1970. *Aru zaibei Nihonjin no kiroku* (The record of a Japanese person in the United States) 2 vols. Tokyo: Yūshindō; Daniel Okimoto 1971. *Kamen no Amerikajin* (Masked Americans). Tokyo: Simul shuppankai; Wakatsuki Yasuo. 1972. *Hainichi no rekishi* (A history of anti-Japanese measures). Tokyo: Chūōkōronsha; Allan R. Bosworth. 1972. *Amerika no kyôsei shūyôjo* (America's Concentration Camps). Tokyo: Shinsensha.

9 Yamazaki Toyoko. 1986. *Futatsu no sokoku* (Two fatherlands) in *Yamazaki Toyoko zen sakuhin,* vol. 10. Tokyo: Shinchōsha. The novel was originally serialized in the weekly magazine, *Shūkan Shinchō,* for three years from June 1980 to August 1983. Yamazaki explains the motivation behind the work: "As Japan grew to be an economic superpower, I closely witnessed the situation where the mind of the Japanese became dilapidated [*kôhai*] and they even lost their natural feelings—love for their own country. I have had the desire to write on the theme of what is a fatherland for an individual, through [her Japanese American protagonist's] life in World War II." Yamazaki Toyoko. 1986. "Watashi no Sengo" (My postwar period) in "geppō 10," *Yamazaki Toyoko zen sakuhin.* Tokyo: Shinchōsha, 1 [My translation].

10 In 1946, the writer Nakayama Shirō wrote a short story about the lives of the Nisei in the ruins of Hiroshima. However, this work appeared in a minor literary journal and received little literary attention. Nakayama Shirō 1975; 1946. "Kumo no kageri" (Shades of clouds) in *Shinbi 13* (May 1946), reprinted in ed. Ogawa Kazusuke. 1975. *Waga 1945 nen* (My 1945). Tokyo: Shakai shisōsha, 113–59.

11 Katō Shūichi. 1974. "Nihon bunka no zasshusei" (The hybridity of Japanese culture) in *Zasshubunka.* Tokyo: Kōdansha, 28–32.

12 Maruyama Masao. 1961. *Nihon no shisō* (Japanese thought). Tokyo: Iwanami shoten, 63–64.

13 The book, which was first published in 1903, opens with the sentence: "Asia is one." Kakuzô Okakura. 1970. *The Ideals of the East.* Tokyo: Charles E. Tuttle, 1.

14 Etō Jun. 1973. *Seijuku to Sōshitsu* (Maturity and loss), in *Etō Jun Chosakushū, zoku,* vol. 1. Tokyo: Kōdansha, 65–92.

15 Kojima's contemporary, Ōe Kenzaburō, deploys a similar tactic by introducing Japanese interpreter, prostitute, and homosexual male as "in-betweens" (*chūkansha*) in his short stories. There are, however, differences in their readiness to name Japan's other. While Ōe identifies the United States and Europe as aggressive male figures in his stories to reveal an obsequiously positioned Japan vis-à-vis the United States and Europe, Kojima is extremely reticent about the power dynamics between Japan and the United States in "Enkei Daigaku Butai." When Kojima faces the presence of the United States by depicting the Japanese American figure in "Hoshi" two years later, he begins to articulate how deeply postwar Japanese society was defined by relations with the United States. Ōe Kenzaburō. 1958. *Mirumae ni tobe* ("Leap before look"). Tokyo: Shinchōsha. See particularly his Afterword, 251–52.

16 Kojima Nobuo. 1967. "Enkei Daigaku Butai," in *Amerikan sukūru.* Tokyo: Shinchōsha. The quoted text is my own translation.

17 Kojima Nobuo's desire to problematize the character's relations with languages is in contrast to another Japanese writer's attitude toward the Japanese language in relation to a Japanese American's figure. In his 1974 biography of a Japanese American navy offi-

cer, Yoshida Mitsuru contrasts the relative ease of deciphering Japanese codes with the practical impossibility of decoding the random coding system of the U.S. Navy. This crucial difference, according to Yoshida, lay in the peculiarities of the Japanese language. Yoshida claims that "Ōta, who was beginning to like the subtlety of expressions in written Japanese, felt tragic destiny in its limitation as a language of coding. For Yoshida, the Japanese language is burdened with the subtleties that defy the simple mechanical coding, and in turn the mastery of these subtleties assured the Japanese American, Ōta, a place within the hermeneutic circle of the Japanese society." Yoshida Mitsuru. 1974. *Chinkon Senkan Yamato.* Tokyo: Kōdansha, 193.

18 Kojima Nobuo, "Hoshi," in *Amerikan sukūru;* and, Kojima Nobuo. 1989. "Stars," trans. Van C. Gessel, *The Shōwa Anthology,* eds. Van C. Gessel and Tomone Matsumoto. Tokyo: Kodansha International. The first numbers in parentheses indicate the pages in the Japanese version and the second number, the translated version. I have modified the translation in some of the quoted passages.

19 "Where am I?" is my own translation. The original Japanese is "*Jibun wa dokoni irunoda.*"

20 American military power did not exactly displace the order and hierarchy of stars. The United States rather sought to legitimate its military presence through the emperor, who supported the order and hierarchy of stars, in postwar Japan. For a more detailed argument, see Igarashi 1998.

21 This case is listed in almost all popular chronologies published in the postwar period. See Sasaki Takeshi et al., ed. 1991. *Sengoshi daijiten.* Tokyo: Sanseidō, 14, 88, 761; Uno Shun'ichi et al., ed. 1991. *Nihon zenshi: Japan Chronik.* Tokyo: Kōdansha, 1098; Ishikawa Hiroyoshi et al., ed. 1994. *[Shukusatu ban] Taishūbunka jiten.* Tokyo: Kōbundō, 24, 111; Nishii Kazuo, ed. 1995. *Sengo 50 nen:* 50 years Postwar. Tokyo: Mainichi, 40; and Iwanami shoten henshūbu. 1991. *Kindai Nihon sōgō nenpyō.* Tokyo: Iwanami shoten, 380.

22 *Asahi shinbun,* 25 September 1925, 4.

Conjunctural Identities, Academic Adjacencies

R. RADHAKRISHNAN

To begin with an anecdote: the other day I had gone to a newly opened Thai restaurant with an Indian friend, a fellow Thai food enthusiast. The décor and atmosphere were excellent, and there was perceptible bonding among the owner, the waitress, and us as Asian-Americans of the diasporic-ethnic persuasion. The lunch itself was so-so; we had partaken of much better Thai lunches at comparable restaurants. As we asked for the check, there was further pleasant conversation; and then she, the owner, asked us: How was the food? After a fleeting mutual glance we responded, "Good, it was very nice." Both of us instantly felt we had been less than honest. My friend had even asked me during the meal if it would be within our mandate to suggest a few alterations to the chef: the vegetables a little crisper, the curry blended just a bit differently. Yet none of this was communicated, and, remember, we had been asked.

Why hadn't either of us offered our opinions, our critiques? Was it just the preference not to commit oneself, not to offend? Clearly, there was the question of who we were vis-à-vis Thai food: surely we had had Thai food on innumerable occasions; but we are not Thai, so how capable are we of evaluating the "authenticity" of Thai food? The fact that as impassioned cosmopolitan restaurant junkies we had had the Thai cuisine experience does not necessarily confer on us the kind of critical insider expertise necessary for an act of evaluation.[1] Moreover, where is the guarantee that cosmopolitanism is a desirable platform for comprehending ethnic nuances? Had this been an Indian restaurant, would we have felt more free to have been vocal?

I begin with this episode, and the questions that I have generated around it, with the intention of opening up a substantive thematic space where we can discuss the relationship between identity and expertise.[2] Is this relationship mutually constitutive, or hierarchically tilted toward either of the terms? What is the relationship between "Thai" as existential-ontological space and "Thai" as performative practice or category of expertise? It would seem that on the one hand "identity" exists as a specific and determinate anteriority that enables and legitimates certain expert representational practices; and on the other, it is these very expert practices that in effect constitute the anteriority-effect of identity.[3] Indeed, Thai or Indian practices of identity-styling can be evaluated with reference to a framework called "Indian" or "Thai," but at the same time this framework itself is nothing but the consolidated-negotiated effect of heterogeneous and contradictory practices. If identity itself is radically informed by heterogeneity, how then are distinctions to be made between one kind of heterogeneity and another?

When my friend and I refrained from critical comment, perhaps we were concerned that such a comment would call into question the very ethnic ontology of both the food and its maker. It would perhaps have amounted to an outsider saying: Your Thai practices have not added up to an authentic Thai identity. How then is the "other" to have a say in a situation where her expectations are simultaneously valid and irrelevant—valid since in a sense identity is always intended for the other, and irrelevant since the "other" is ontogenetically extrinsic to the "self"? The incommensurability that I am trying to adumbrate lies in the relationship between identity-practice as expertise, and therefore as something externalizable (whereby Self and Other become structural positions and locations, not essences), and identity-presence as something inherent and therefore irreducible, autochthonous and nongeneralizable.[4] What is open to question and criticism is the performative aspect of identity, but hiding behind the performative is the ontological authority of a name: the name and its agential control over the performance.[5] Between "being Indian" and "practicing Indian" there lies a space of semantic openness that is neither ideologically free nor ideologically consummate: a space where "name" and "agency" problematize each other. The issue that I am attempting to raise has to do with the relationship of identity to methodology, of constituency to epistemology, of macropolitical solidarity to micropolitical specialist practices, and of organic solidarity to specific intellectuality.[6]

Before I undertake to analyze Asian-American studies as project-and-formation, perhaps a little more is in order about "disciplinarity," "representation," and "production." When I was invited to be part of this project of envisioning a certain future for Asian-American studies, I felt delighted and honored as though I had been interpellated both with respect to my specific disciplinary formation (postcoloniality, poststructuralism, and the relationship between the two) and with reference to my larger and more inclusive solidarity with minority discourses in general and with Asian-America in particular. I am an Asian-American as well as a third world citizen, but I am not in Asian-American studies. My sense of ethnicity is based on my being an Asian-American *here* (though there is a lot more to me than can be covered under the rubric "Asian-American"), and yet I have theorized ethnicity at the intersection of poststructuralism and postcoloniality. So, who am I by virtue of my macropolitics of location, and who am I by virtue of my subject-positionality as a specific-academic and expert intellectual? Furthermore, how well do I understand the relationship between these two dimensions or mediations, and how can I clinch the two into one overarching sense of constituency? Do categories like "postcolonial," "poststructuralist," "Asian-American," "Pakistani," and the like all work in the same way? Do they belong to the same order of indexicality? When I call myself Asian-American am I making a representative identity claim on behalf of a certain group, or am I announcing the legitimacy of a certain institutional formation called Asian-American studies, or am I assuming that the institutional logic of Asian-American studies will be subsumed thoroughly, without remainder or contradiction, by Asian-American macropolitical identity? What is the difference between the statements, "I am a poststructuralist" and "I am an Asian-American"? How does the copula ("to be") work in each case? This fraught relationship of identity to methodology takes on an even sharper significance in the context of the institutional-academic production of knowledge.

A representational model is also a representative model. A representational model raises concerns such as adequacy, fidelity, authenticity, historical veracity, spokespersonship, inclusiveness, and so on. This move from the epistemological to the political is based on the reality of some unifying ideology that is presumed to have effected the generalization of *a* perspective by way of the ideological production of a collectivity. It is in this sense that the heterogeneous lived realities of peoples are mobilized and hegemonized *in the name of* nationalism, Hindutva, Islam, the proletariat, and the like. In other words, the representational model achieves success by way of the prescriptive singularity of the name that supposedly speaks for the "differences within." How is the One forged out of the many? Does the One speak for the many? These are questions that have been discussed with great passion in the impressive literature on nationalism.[7] There is no representation without "naming" (Asian-America as a name creates a certain interrelationship among the parts that constitute it), and "naming" as a process is symptomatic of a tension between epistemology and politics. If radical epistemology insists on a deconstructive and open-ended process, politics advocates strategic closure. As the Asian-American presence grows stronger in numbers, the question arises: How and in what forms should this presence be felt within the American body politic? Should Asian-America slip into all-America without tension, opposition, or friction in an exemplary "model minority" fashion, or should Asian-America raise its own questions and concerns even as it factors itself into the national equation called "America"?

Furthermore, isn't there the need to create a new and different language for the articulation of these concerns and issues? I would recommend that unless minority experiences are backed by their own independent epistemic claims, these experiences will get parsed coercively within the assimilationist syntax presided over by a dominant all-America. Unless minorities craft their experiences into their own forms of knowledge, they will always be vulnerable to cooptation by the epistemic categories of the dominant discourse. Clearly, minority knowledges are neither "pure" nor separatist; instead, they take the form of a double or multiple consciousness that dislodges the regime of the dominant One, which for my purpose here is the *Western* or the Eurocentric One.[8]

As specific-academic intellectuals, knowledge is our concern both in a specialist as well as in an organic sense. Minority intellectuals have to take the knowledge game very seriously and simultaneously sniff at it with rigorous suspicion. In an overall global context where the question "What is knowledge?" seems to have been settled definitively well before subaltern peoples and cultures were even asked to participate, subaltern/minority intellectuals need to play the knowledge game in a deconstructive "double-session": both reactively and proactively. They have to engage deconstructively with the fait accompli of dominant knowledges even as they legitimate their own subjugated knowledges. Rather than be seduced by the avant-gardism of metropolitan epistemologies, they need to develop criteria to differentiate between empowering and alienating knowledges, between knowledges that one can call one's own through the exercise of collective agency and those that call for the sacrifice of subaltern agency in the name of metropolitan success and acceptability. The institutional-academic formations of ethnic/minority knowledges will have to do better than merely canonize themselves and follow the road to success already paved by the dominant discourse: capitalist, patriarchal, Eurocentric. They will have to seek a different modality of knowledge (not just the usual winner-take-all, zero-sum games) and unless and until they revolutionize the rules by which the knowledge game is played, they will only serve to strengthen the regime of universal dominance undertaken in the name of the advanced and all-knowing West.

If knowledge is partly representation, it is also a production. The production model transgresses representational norms in the following ways: the authority of the original has no ontological primacy or priority over the actual production; the intelligibility of the object (such as Asian-America) is itself the constituted function of the act of production; the production adds something new that is not already there in the original object; the production model calls into question the synchronicity of the original object and thus opens it up to the differential plays of diachrony; and finally, the production model also raises the question of ideological perspectivity and interest and thus disallows the normative sovereignty of the original object. All these implications have a very special salience in the context of diasporan production that both acknowledges and problematizes "origins." To put it differently, diasporan projects can be mnemonic, provided the mnemonic itself is conceptualized as the product of a countermemory.

Will the ideology of Asian-America be single or plural? Will it be capitalist, nationalist, hybrid, hyphenated, Marxist, post-Marxist, ethnic or postethnic, gendered, sexualized? Whatever the eventual response, the historical reality of Asian-American studies cannot be thought of outside the framework of global asymmetry: the framework of a world structured in dominance. The fundamental issue confronting the conceptualization of Asian-America is that of ethnic hyphenation. Dwelling in the hyphen is not a matter of neutrality or of benign participation in the conjuncturality of "equal" histories. It is a mandate to acknowledge coevalness between two histories as well as a call to redress the existing imbalances between the two histories.[9] In other words, an activist-interventionist agency has to be coded into the very being of Asian-American studies. Dwelling in the hyphen is neither to be romanticized in the name of "free" individual choice, nor is it to be registered as a freefloating hybridity devoid of historical baggage. So, at the risk of sounding ideologically shrill, I will raise the question, "Which Asian-America?" in a theoretical vein, rather than as a bland descriptive query.

There is a need to make a distinction between "Asian-America" as a mere demographic census marker and "Asian-America" as a political-epistemic category. I am interested in the ideological production of Asian-America along certain lines, and not in Asian-America as a quietist, benign, and noninterventionist category that represents all Asian Americans. My emphasis here is that Asian-American intellectuals, scholars, and teachers should take up the responsibility of creating, molding, and bringing into being a certain kind of bloc known as Asian-America (here I am espousing a Gramscian model of the intellectual as leader/persuader/activist), and not throw up their hands in despair and/or neutrality. I realize Asian-Americans can be conservatives, Republicans, mainstream assimilationists, fierce capitalist-individualist-consumer fetishists, and all-American to the point of denying ethnic origins. Now, those are not my fellow Asian-Americans; the Asian-America that I am thinking of is neither nativist nor natalist, but an ideologist perspective that will have to be critical of mainstream America, of capitalist individualism, of Orientalism and Eurocentrism, and in deep solidarity with gay, lesbian, feminist, minority activist movements, and with the third world even though that world is not *here*. It is from such a point of view that I recommend that the hyphen-as-space be polemicized/militarized to call into question the motif of monothetic citizenship and render America vulnerable and accountable to the rest of the world.[10] Too often one hears the argument that since we have been *here* for generations now the significance of the *there* (wherever there might be in Asia or Africa, but Euro-America is a different matter altogether) dies, atrophies away for lack of context and relevance. It is as though Africa and Asia are not worthy epistemic domains in themselves; they can only be part of a traditional and nonmodern memory that can be obliterated in and through the process of Americanization.

It must be quite clear by now that I look on hyphenation in a favorable light. Not only am I contending that there are hyphenated identities, but also that such identities should produce knowledges that are hyphenated; for any other morphology does not have the capacity or the legitimacy to speak for hyphenated identities and hyphenated experiences. So, how does the hyphen speak, and how is the hyphen to be produced subjectively and agentially rather than be embraced and/or accepted as a given condition?[11] I begin with the assertion that the hyphen can speak only when it produces itself conceptually, theoretically, categorically. Ethnic hyphenation is indeed a cliché in the history of American identities. What I am suggesting, however, on behalf of the hyphen is something quite other. My point is that in the diasporan context, the hyphen should be produced as a theoretical category that is not to be owned by or normatively deployed by any one hyphenated constituency. In acknowledging the existential-epistemic alterity of the hyphen, both Asia and America are radically derealized in the name of an emerging heterogeneous historiography. The hyphen is also the *topos* that stages the ongoing differential conversation between the name-ability of the diaspora and the perennial namelessness of the *diaspora as such*.[12] The historicity of the hyphen warrants a different historiography, and dwelling in the hyphen, between identity regimes, necessitates a different narratology. Betweenness and conjuncturality ought to be enfranchised as modes of legitimate being before the hyphen can speak. How is the hyphen, whether graphically expressed or understood, in Asian-America to be historicized, to be produced? The *hyphen as such* in Asian-America has to do double duty and coordinate the Asian experience without resort to hierarchical maneuvers or identity coups. American identity is not something consummate to which an Asian flavor is being added, nor is Asia something more real than the mystifying and often discriminating contemporaneity of the United States of America. These options do not do justice to the complete coevalness of Asia with America as witnessed by the hyphen in all its double vision. There is indeed an America prior to hyphenation by the Asian immigrant experience, and indeed an Asia that has not traveled to America; but the hyphen both acknowledges these anterior relatives and de- and reterritorializes them in the context of the hyphen-as-relationality and relationality-as-hyphen.[13] The critical-semantic significance of the hyphen lies in its capacity to demand that so-called discrete, autonomous, or absolute histories be read and interpreted relationally, that is, with reference to other histories. Indeed relationality is so much at the heart of the hyphen that it represents relationality as such, and with the autonomous advent of the hyphen, there is no History, nor are there separate histories, but histories cross-hatched in relationality.[14] If the accountability of the hyphen to itself escapes the identitarian claims of both Asia and America (i.e., in a sense both Asia and America are reterritorialized given the emergent historicity of the hyphen), is the hyphen then neither an "insider" nor an "outsider" to either constituency, doubly "out" and doubly "in" in a Möbius-strip like dimensionless dimensionality? If from the point of view of hyphenation, America and Asia are "always already" mediated by each other, how do we get at any reliable and, need I say, "authentic" representations of and on either side of the hyphen? It would seem that here again the hyphen derails canonical notions of the One, and faithfulness to origins. From the point of view of Asian-America then, can Asia be invented and imagined at will, strategically or otherwise, and indiscriminately instrumentalized in the service of the history of the present, the history of the hyphen/the diaspora?

Sau-ling Cynthia Wong, in her essay "Sugar Sisterhood: Situating the Amy Tan Phenomenon" (1995) makes an excellent contribution to our understanding of the rhetoric of authenticity: what she calls "authenticity effects" and "authenticity markers."[15] Reading the Amy Tan phenomenon symptomatically, Wong situates "authenticity" between self and other, between the history of the self and anthropology. Making a distinction between authenticity-itself and authenticity markers, Wong problematizes any transparent valorization of authenticity. The questions raised are (as I travel with

Wong's insights into other related directions): Can there be authenticity without authenticity-effects and authenticity markers? Who is the authenticity for, the self or the other? Is authenticity-to-oneself a contradiction in terms, redundant, and is it different from authenticity-for-the-other? In a perceptive double-reading of Tan's use of Chinese "material," Wong tells us that certain features, whether these be the use of Chinese names or references to Chinese customs or lexical borrowings from Chinese, function for the white Western reader as "authenticity markers" whether or not they are reliable vehicles of authenticity. Driving a critical wedge between authenticity as content and authenticity as practice (for the other), between authenticity as verifiable and authenticity as autotelic style, Wong's essay knocks at an important question: Is identity thinkable/assumable/practicable without the normative notion of authenticity?

Authenticity functions on more than one level, the easiest to adjudicate being "facticity." In the essay, Wong corrects a few errors; and these are factual errors, literal misreadings of Chinese letters, words, etcetera. It turns out that even the evocative phrase "sugar sisterhood" is an instance of *meconaissance,* and yet it works, albeit erroneously. Thus, for example, an Asian-American scholar could be corrected, even reprimanded, by a Chinese specialist for getting a nuance wrong, and yet, I would not like to think that it is somehow intrinsic for the "insider" to "know it right." [16]

This issue has to do not just with facticity, however, but also interpretive authority. Yet how does one legislate interpretive authority given that the order of interpretation is not the same as the order of meaning or truth? One could of course say that certain modes of interpretation are specified within a tradition whereas certain others, though not without merit or interest, are not *within* that tradition. Thus we can distinguish among Confucian, Buddhist, and Taoist readings of Chinese texts, and say, postmodern or New Critical interpretations of the same texts. Besides, there have always been critical projects, from within a tradition, that have sought to revise, reform, and even revolutionize that tradition. [17] Battles among interpretations then are part of a constructivist epistemology where the relative merits and demerits of different constructions or constitutive interpretations cannot be settled through an appeal to the transcendent ontology of the Object. Yet choices are made, immanently perhaps, among different constructions based on interests, criteria, tastes, and the like.

Beyond the factual and the interpretive levels, there is a third level that has to do with the totality or the holistic integrity of any culture or tradition. Within a culture, there are all sorts of intricate metonymic and synechdochal relationships between qualities and states of being between parts and wholes; and these relationships are not "iterable" unless the entire structure is repeated either in the same context or in a different context. If it is a different context, then perhaps purists would expect the orthodox, normative canonical practice of that total structure, that is, the identical repetition of that structure, to nullify the alienating effect of a new and different context; by this logic one could say that Chinatown or Little India should be cultivated in active abeyance of their immediate American contemporaneity: but does this make sense, for why should a repetition be identical? Cannot iterability be dissipative rather than conservative of identity? Furthermore, what about the context in which the repetition is achieved? By holistic logic, details, such as the Japanese tea ceremony, or the Indian tradition that one should not stretch one's feet in the direction of elders, cannot be deracinated from their context and then derided or critiqued. While many of these caveats do have a protectionist purpose, i.e., protectionism against hostile misrecognition by dominant and/or antagonistic groups, they also serve to come down harshly, even punitively, against what I would like to call "the diasporization of identity." Chinatowns and Little Indias are interpellated by a double logic: on the one hand, the authority internal to the repetition and on the other, the dissemination of this very authority in alien and different contexts. The logic of dissemination is reducible neither to the value of the past, its rectitude within its own temporality, nor to the no-holds barred opportunism of the present moment: it can only be embodied as an ongoing form of historical noncoincidence of the "before" in the "after."

It is a little too naïve to expect that the "Asia" in Asian studies and the "Asia" in Asian-American studies are/should be identical. There are determining connections, and relationships between the two. Both "Asias" are constructed and not natural, and both carry historical density as well as urgency. The "Asian" in Asian studies is not necessarily authentic whereas the "other" Asia is merely "hybrid." My contention is that both "hybridity" and "authenticity" are forms of history, and neither is free of the taint of strategy and ideology: there are several morphologies of history, and no one morphology is by definition more historical than another. The diasporan take on Chinese nationalism, for example, has a historicity of its own and this sense of history within the diaspora should not be construed as any less dense, real, or representative than the resident Chinese nationalist production. We must also not forget that articulations from within ethnic/diasporan hyphenation propose a different object of study altogether. The interests that inform Asian studies and Asian-American studies are different. Built into the Asian-American experience of Asia is the diasporan context, the diasporan perspective: if you will, the historicity of the diaspora as well as the historicity of hybridity. This diasporan historicity is not something secondary or epiphenomenal that one can bracket off comfortably before proceeding to study Asia objectively, as though from its own perspective. Diasporic displacement is an autonomous theme in itself, *and* it acts as a critical/hermeneutic perspective from which the country of origin is seen in a certain light.

Diasporan historiography raises the second-order issue of mediation and mediatedness as an autonomous epistemological issue and thus complicates any attempt at enjoying an immediate relationship with whatever lies on either side of the hyphen: a pre-post-erous situation where the self-reflexive production of "mediation/mediatedness as meaning" postpones and problematizes the objective status of those realities and histories *of which* the diaspora is itself a *mediation*. I will allow myself to say, infelicitous as it may sound, that diasporan historicity functions in a double mode: as *mediation as such,* and as *mediation of.* The problem is to relate the two within a sense of constituency.

A term that comes to mind in this context is one that is often used in the Indian diasporan community: ABCD, that is, American-Born-Confused-Deshis (where "deshis" signifies national citizens of the country of origin). The assumption here is that these folks don't really know India except in the form of bits and pieces, rumors and myths, all resulting in confusion. There is then identity by birth (American), which does not seem to matter except as a matter of fact, and there is the deshi affiliation that is perhaps affective and value-laden, but an affiliation founded on confusion, half-knowledges, and putative values. The ABCD population sample is representative or expressive of a fatuous form of hybridity that is neither here nor there, anchored neither here nor there, clueless in superficial ambivalence.

As someone who values hybridity as a semantically rich state of being posited on the possibility of global heteroglossia, I would reformulate ABCD to spell "Americans Because Conjunctural Diasporans." [18] It is not America versus the diaspora and ethnic hyphenation, it is not ethnic separatism, and it is not American identity as the teleological resolution of the unfinished citizenship inherent in diasporic ethnicity. Most importantly, the purpose of the formulation is to read conjuncturality into the very heart of "identity." To state this in the context of my entire discussion of the identity politics of the hyphen, the ethic of the hybrid is to work on both sides of the hyphen, to divest itself of monoradical modes of belonging and inaugurate "ambi-valence" as a positive existential category. The Asian-American objective should be to announce and implement dialogism and reciprocity of influence such that the Asianization of America will be perceived as equally valuable as the reterritorialization of Asia in America. To live as an ABCD, then, is to realize the centrality of the conjuncture within the very heart of identity.

Whether it is Asian America or any other hyphenated community, the diasporan experience raises one big unsettling question that is rarely raised amidst the pragmatics of functional citizenship: Who are we? Diasporan theory does not emanate from a secure source of being, and it is not an attempt to consolidate through knowledge what is already obvious and axiomatic in the living experience. The living and the telling, the experiencing and the meaning-making happen simultaneously much like a radical existential script that begins to exist only when the screen is lifted and the lights turned on. The hyphen has to speak to exist, and given the ambi-valence of the diaspora, it is not always clear who the addressee is: all of America, Asia, only Asian-America? The identity question, "Who am/are I/we?" constitutes the diasporic epistemological domain; in other words, indeterminacy and the immanent undecidability of identity are the cornerstones of diasporic studies, as also the challenge, "how to proceed from 'I' to 'we.'" It is not a situation where epistemological investigations are authorized in the name of a preexisting identity secure in its normativity. The very reception and the production of identity are performed interhistorically and not within the representative plentitude of a single interpretive community. Might not an Amy Tan, as against a Chinese writer living in China and visiting the United States of America, say that the American audience that Sauling Cynthia Wong identifies as external to Chinese valences is very much internal to Amy Tan's sense of being? Furthermore, just as the "America" in "Asian-America" is not meant only for endorsement and celebration, so too with the "Asia." An Asian-American will and should have the intellectual freedom to dislike, reject, and critique aspects both of America and Asia. The ability to embody an identity and be part of a collectivity means nothing unless it also includes the capacity and the expertise to critique the very ground one occupies. Solidarity without critique is either a straitjacket or an empty shibboleth.

With this connection between critique and identity in mind, I reach the final segment of my essay that has to do with the adjacencies that have developed among the several disciplines that constitute the humanities. Should methodology be pure and totally intrinsic to the "truth" of the object of study? Or is it okay for methodology to be creatively interdisciplinary, even be nothing more than bricolage? Firmly grounded in the belief that methodologies should be broad-based, interdisciplinary, and heuristically open-ended, I would assert that the macrology (as well as the teleology) of Asian-American studies has room for a variety of practitioners. There is not and cannot be a single methodology that is immanently coextensive with the field called "Asian-American studies." As history tells us time and time again, even revolutionary knowledges and truths are not born with their own pristine ex nihilo modalities and procedures. Emergent knowledges take the "given" and shape it to their ends through the exercise of political will. Just as the political effectivity of an individual or group is measured both in terms of its ability to define itself and the effects of such self-definition on others who inhabit the social space, so too with academic formations.

Postmodernism and Asian-American studies. Following up on Cornel West's formulation that African-American postmodernism is not the same as Lyotardian, Baudrillardian, or Euro-postmodernism, I would say that Asian-American studies, too, has and can establish its own mediated relationship to postmodernity and not lose itself in the process. What are some of the themes in postmodernism that are germane and perhaps even helpful to Asian-American studies? Two motifs that on the surface seem hostile: the death of representation, and the death of authorial voice. Many minority theorists have noted (myself included) with indignation the cynicism with which Eurocentric "high theory" announces the end of representation and the death of the author at the very moment when subjugated and formerly colonized peoples have begun finding their voices and their modes of self-representation. Brilliant as this critique is, there is another side to this story. Distinctions need to be made between just and dominant representations. The postmodernist critique of representation is also a critique of dominance and of the inherence of dominance in erstwhile forms of so-called universalism—Eurocentrism in particular. Given the history of representation, minority and subaltern constituencies need to cultivate critical ambivalence toward the politics of representation: on the one hand, insist on the right for self-representation and on the other, resist programmatic univocality. Both postmodernism and poststructuralism produce deconstructive insights from within the dominant location, and with Edward Said, I would like to believe that there is a strong case to be made for cooperation across asymmetries between deconstructive knowledges of the West and the emerging knowledges of the Rest. The postmodern critique of univocity needs to be understood with its corollary: the celebration of multiplicity, heterogeneity, hybridity.

As for the death of the author's voice, again there is another side to it: the denaturalization of the voice opens up the meaning of the text/experience to its own imagined historicity. It also shows the way toward decanonization when the canon becomes dominant, and demonstrates usefully how "voice" and "canonicity" are not natural, but rather ideologically fraught. Equally useful is the manner in which the denaturalization of the voice promotes a critical attitude toward discourses of authenticity based on exclusion and the foreclosure of heterogeneity.

Poststructuralism and Asian-American studies. Poststructuralism at its best is informed by the Benjaminian insight that every document of civilization is also a document of barbarism. The fact that Asian-America or, for that matter, any constituency, is victimized or subjugated at a particular moment in history does not absolve it of the will to dominance. Subjugated cultures in particular are prone to internalizing dominance unless they are vigilant, and there is the practice of widespread dominance even within the solidarity of minority and subaltern groups. Asian-America is thus both outside dominant America even as it is part of that structure. The project of realizing itself in its own way is not disjunct from the project of "turning the dominant pages in a certain way."[19] Even in the case of minority formations where knowledge production is and should be closely related to the ideology of the politics of representation, every effort should be made to maintain both the heterogeneity as well as the openendedness of the thinking process so that political solidarity will not come in the way of the production of transgressive and autocritical knowledge.

Postcoloniality and Asian-American studies. It is ironic that the very dimension that has made postcoloniality unpopular with traditional Third World scholars is the very thing that makes it sympathetic to Asian-American studies, i.e., the focus on the diasporan location. Here are some overlapping concerns: hybridity and the politics of hybridity, the travails and attractions of metropolitan double-consciousness and ambivalence; a certain critical interest as well as distance from the development of discourses of "postality"; simultaneous attention to the intersectional nature of identity politics (race, class, gender, and sexuality); critique of nationalist discourses and the inadequacy of the "imagined community" of nationality; and finally, issues confronting "origins" and revisionist renditions of history. Also significant is the manner in which postcoloniality has succeeded in befriending and instrumentalizing varieties of poststructuralist practice (a theoretical alliance that already has spawned a number of controversies and anxieties) and in the process has served to highlight the issue of "traveling theory": of how theory in traveling can be renamed and reclaimed heterogeneously.

Finally, as one of the more recent entrants into the disciplinary areas called ethnic studies, Asian-American studies needs to do all it can to foster a coalitional mentality among minority formations.[20] As the African-American experience teaches us, many of these problems and crises have arisen before: the wheel does not have to be invented over and over again. I mention this only because there are occasions where, even in the field of theoretical productions, minorities skirmish over the questions of "who created the concept first?" and "who is bypassing whose prior authority?" and "who, in a blatantly cavalier fashion, is refusing to acknowledge prior contributions and prior battles?" At a time when multiculturalism is being invoked with such surpassing ease by administrators, corporations, and creators of commercials, it behooves Asian-American studies, along with other minority discourses, to wrest the initiative from these colonizing promoters and endorsers of multiculturalism and to empower the flow of heterogeneous knowledges as forms of persuasion that will transform the status quo and the "business as usual" mentality of the dominant corporate regime. Creating a space between discourses of a dehistoricized and superficial hybridity and the languages of essentialized authenticity, hyphenated knowledges have the honor as well as the hardship of elaborating an ongoing ethico-political coalition of what Lani Guinier (1994) calls "like minds, not like bodies." For it is to be hoped that minority knowledges as forms of persuasion will work differently from dominating knowledges and begin to imagine a relational world that has retired once and for all the model of "the winner take all" and the cultural politics of conquest.

Notes

1   For more on the nature of cosmopolitan identity, please see Robbins and Cheah 1998.
2   For a thought-provoking elaboration of the space between expertise and cultural identity, see Said 1983.
3   No one has theorized the performative more rigorously than Judith Butler. See in particular *Gender Trouble* (1990) and *Bodies That Matter* (1993).
4   I refer here to Lacanian psychoanalysis that posits that the unconscious is structured like language and effects the de-essentialization of the Self.
5   For more on the performative nature of identity in the context of nationalism and diasporan hybridity, see Bhabha 1994.
6   For a detailed discussion of the Foucauldian specific intellectual and the Gramscian organic intellectual, see my chapter, "Towards an Effective Intellectual: Foucault or Gramsci?" in *Diasporic Mediations* (Radhakrishnan 1996).
7   See in particular Parker et al. 1992; Bhabha 1992; and Chatterjee 1986 and 1993.
8   For a powerful inaugural statement of double-consciousness, see W. E. B. Du Bois's *The Souls of Black Folk* (1996; 1903) also, see Paul Gilroy's *The Black Atlantic* (1993). For a recent memorable application of Du Bois in the South Asian context, see Vijay Prashad, *The Karma of Brown Folk* (2000).
9   See Amin 1989 and Anzaldua 1987 for multilateral universalism and "betweenness," respectively. See Johannes Fabian, *Time and the Other* (1983), for an enabling evaluation of coevalness.
10   For a postcolonial critique of postmodernism, see my essay, "Postmodernism and the Rest of the World" (Radhakrishnan 1994).
11   This question is intended in the same register as Spivak's "Can the Subaltern Speak?" (1988).
12   For more on diaspora as a mode of intellectuality, see Rey Chow. Also see Sau-ling Cynthia Wong's influential essay, "Denationalization Reconsidered" (1995) and Kandice Chuh's "Transnationalism and Its Pasts" (1996).

13 See Deleuze and Guattari 1986 for notions of re- and deterritorialization.

14 See Mohanty 1989.

15 See Sau-ling Cynthia Wong 1995.

16 As Amitav Ghosh demonstrates brilliantly in *The Shadow Lines,* if facts and details are learnable any-where, they are also learnable every-other-where. Of course, the degree of immersion in the material may be of varying levels of intensity and organic belonging.

17 Chandralekha's ambitiously intellectual revisionist renditions of Bharata Natyam are a good example of an indigenous critique of one's own tradition.

18 For a powerful and persuasive theorization of hybridity, see Nestor Garcia Canclini, *Hybrid Cultures* (1995).

19 See Derrida 1981.

20 See Jan Mohamed and Lloyd 1991.

IV ASIAN/AMERICAN EPISTEMOLOGIES

Epistemological Shifts:
National Ontology and the New
Asian Immigrant

LISA LOWE

I begin this essay with the premise that the "new" Asian American—that is, the post-1965 Asian immigrant subject and community within the context of the United States—is an object of study that disrupts the disciplinary paradigms of Asian studies, American studies, and Asian American studies. The figure of the Asian American fractures the stability of "Asia" as an "area" for Asian studies; current Asian immigration forces into legibility the longer history of racialized Asian immigration for the field of American studies; and the post-1965 immigrations require rethinking the assumptions about the "racial formation" of Asian Americans within Asian American studies. Such discussions emerge at this historical moment, not because Asian immigrant settlement in the United States is a new phenomenon—we are well aware of a history dating back centuries—but rather because, since the Immigration and Nationality Act of 1965, the contemporary shift in the demographics of the Asian populations in the United States, and the international political, social, and economic forces of which those demographics are an index, currently initiates a reformulation of the objects and methods of study in the fields mentioned above.

In all three cases—Asian studies, American studies, and Asian American studies—the epistemological assumptions of fields that take as their objects a particular area, whether defined as a regional/cultural, national, or racialized community, are called into question by the "new" object "Asian immigrant" or "Asian American." To the extent that disciplinary fields simultaneously produce and manage their objects of study, the reckoning with the constitutive occlusion of the "Asian immigrant" within these fields would seem to be the necessary precondition for the forging of an adequate set of methods for the project of "mapping the Asian diaspora" set forth by this volume. Moreover, if the object "new Asian immigrant" is to become legible within these disciplines, it will also be important to situate these disciplines within the U.S. university, that is, as ideological state apparatuses for producing knowledge within and for the United States, whether the disciplinary foci are "Asia," "America," or "Asian America." By this I mean to observe that the emergence of the "post-1965 Asian immigrant" as an object of knowledge within the U.S. university holds the potential to displace a nationalist epistemology, not exclusively because such an object registers the emergence of international forces within the context of the national, but in the sense that each of the fields with which we are concerned must be understood as disciplines at the service of a U.S. nationalist ontology, disciplines that have traditionally produced knowledge providing for the established centrality and "being" of the United States.

From roughly 1850 until World War II, Asian immigration to the United States was a site for the eruptions and resolutions of the contradictions between the national economy and the political state, and from World War II onward, the locus of contradictions between the nation-state and the global economy. In the first period, the contradiction between the economic need for inexpensive, tractable labor and the political need to constitute a homogeneous United States was "resolved" through a series of legal exclusions, disenfranchisements, and restricted enfranchisements of Asian immigrants that simultaneously "racialized" these groups as "nonwhites" as it consolidated immigrants of diverse European descent as "white." In the latter period, the capital imperative has come into greater contradiction with the political imperative of the U.S. nation-state, with capitalism requiring an economic internationalism, and the U.S. state needing to be politically coherent and hegemonic in world affairs in order to determine the conditions of that internationalism.[1] The expansion that led from U.S. colonialism in the Philippines to wars in Korea and Vietnam violently displaced immigrants from those nations; the aftermath of the repressed history of U.S. imperialism in Asia now materializes in the "return" of Asian immigrants to the imperial center.[2] Yet despite this history, the fields of Asian studies and American studies institutionalized in the U.S. university emerged after World War II without a consideration of the phenomenon of Asian immigration to the United States. By the same token, Asia was the site for U.S. expansion—from the colonization of the Philippines to the military occupation of Japan to the wars in Korea and Vietnam—and the knowledges produced by Asian studies were crucial to U.S. national diplomatic, military, and economic projects in Asia during this period. Yet these involvements were themselves conspicuously, and perhaps constitutively, absent from the fields of Asian studies and American studies.

Asian American studies emerged in the late 1960s and early 1970s, in the context of the Civil Rights Movement and other ethnic studies initiatives, as a project for educational space in the university linking an epistemological critique with efforts for social transformation. It has been the concern of Asian American studies to address the legal and political economic history within which Asian immigrant laborers to the United States were racialized as nonwhites and ineligible for citizenship, and to study this history as constituting a racial formation specific to Asian Americans. Michael Omi and Howard Winant (1994) have argued that racial meanings within the United States are formed in the ongoing dialectic between the racial state's repressions and exclusions and the oppositional social movements that contest the state, such that race is "an unstable and 'decentered' complex of social meanings constantly being transformed by political struggle (55)." Asian American racial formation is thus understood as the result of a history in which, prior to World War II, Asian groups were racialized in relation to capital's need for low-wage noncitizen labor, and these state classifications were contested by Asian American communities and social movements. The series of Asian exclusion repeal acts passed between 1943 and 1952 set quotas limiting immigration from Asian countries, and lifted the bar to citizenship that dated back to 1790, permitting immigrants of Asian origins to become naturalized as citizens for the first time. The Immigration and Nationality Act of 1965 then abolished the quotas established by the repeal acts. Owing to the 1965 act, the majority of Asian Americans are today Asian-born rather than multiple-generation, and new immigrant groups from South Vietnam, South Korea, Cambodia, Laos, Thailand, the Philippines, Malaysia, India, and Pakistan have rendered more heterogeneous the already existing Asian American group comprising those of Chinese, Japanese, Korean, and Filipino descent. Thus the changing population of Asian immigrants can be said to constitute the newest racial formation of Asian Americans; this new immigrant formation has made it necessary for scholars in Asian American studies to think beyond a single racial paradigm or Asian racial identity toward a discussion of what Michael Omi has more recently termed "comparative racial formations" within "comparative racisms."[3]

Hence if the advent of this new immigration constitutes a new formation of Asian immigrants or Asian Americans, it has also initiated new questions that have ramifications for the research and study of "Asia" within Asian studies, the "America" within American studies, and the "Asian American" within Asian American studies. The task of "reading" the historical pasts and presents of these new formations are great: it requires not only critique and revision of the paradigms to address how each field's investment in an area establishes a constitutive blindness to the "Asian immigrant," but also necessitates connections between and across the fields, though these encounters will surely have to take account of the history of dissymmetry between the fields, the differences in their disciplinary imperatives and in the privileges of their institutional locations, as well as the large gaps between the subjects and knowledges posited by each field. This new interdisciplinary work is being undertaken in variously situated projects that seek to link epistemological critique with the historical, political, economic, and cultural shifts of the last thirty years.[4] Many forces have changed the questions we ask and the objects we ask about, but I would characterize some of the most significant as:

1. the "post-Fordist" restructuring of global capitalism employing "mixed production" and "flexible accumulation" that permits the exploitation of Asian workers both in Asia (in the "newly industrializing" countries of Hong Kong, Singapore, South Korea, and Taiwan, as well as the "free trade zones" in Thailand, Indonesia, Malaysia, India, and the Philippines) and in the United States;

2. the changed demography of the Asian American population as the result of the Immigration and Nationality Act of 1965 that has increased and diversified Filipino, Korean, Southeast Asian, and South Asian communities in the United States;

3. the colonial and neocolonial role of the United States in the Asian states from which these new Asian American communities immigrate;

4. the failure of citizenship and civil rights to guarantee equality of opportunity and resources to poor, racialized, and gendered communities in the United States; Glenn Omatsu (1994) has called it the "one-sided class war" of the 1970s and the "corporate assault on poor communities of color in the U.S.," both of which have made it so important to understand the racialization of Asians in relation to the racialization of other groups of color.[5]

In light of these shifts, we can appreciate the critical force of Asian migration to the West for area studies in the modern university. Asian migration to the West is one of the most concrete, illustrative indices of post-World War II globalization; the multiple effects of Asian migrations—on national cultures, global political economy, and finally, epistemology—are sources of evidence about the social formation of 21st-century globalization. Yet Asian migration to the West, as an object of study, has proven a highly unstable one. It exceeds disciplinary paradigms of Asian studies, American studies, and Asian American or ethnic studies, and reveals the limitations of these fields—each a modern epistemology for producing particular knowledges within a national ontology for which the United States is the referent.

Western modernity has persistently figured itself through Asian alterity—temporally and spatially distanced—but Asian migration to the West in the last half century presents a challenge to an earlier Orientalist epistemology. Within the context of U.S. engagements with China and Japan prior to and during World War II, "Asia" entered a national epistemology, emerging as a crucial object of study in the American university. Important area studies programs on South and Southeast Asia were established in the same period. Yet we can observe a decisive shift from the mid-century study of "Asia" to the attempts to apprehend "Asia," "Asian diaspora," and "Asian immigration" within the field of Asian studies today. While Asian studies has traditionally examined Asian civilizations, cultures, and languages, as distanced historically and geographically from the West, scholars have begun to examine the mobility and diversity of migrants from Asian national origins as an interruption of the proper object "Asia." Aihwa Ong's (1999) recent work has addressed the relationship between immigrant communities and the "homelands" in Asia within the framework of transnational capitalism, and Harry Harootunian (1993), Bruce Cumings (1999), and Vicente Rafael (1994) have criticized the role that Asian studies has played in U.S. foreign policy in Asia. The unstable nature of the object, "Asian migration to the West," presents challenges and opportunities to scholars in Asian area studies.

With respect to American studies, understanding Asian immigration to the United States is fundamental to understanding the racialized foundations of both the emergence of the United States as a nation and the development of American capitalism. The history of Asian immigrant formation highlights the production of *race* in the contradiction between national economy and the political state, as well as in the contradiction between the U.S. nation-state and the global economy, and it rewrites the history of the United States *as* a complex racial history. This is far from claiming that Asians are the only group to have been racialized in the founding of the United States, but rather to suggest that the history of the nation's attempt to resolve the contradictions between its economic and political imperatives through laws that excluded Asians from citizenship—from 1790 until the 1940s—may have something to say generally about race as a contradictory site of struggle for cultural, economic, and political membership in the United States. Like other racialized minority groups from Africa, the Caribbean, and Latin America, Asian American formation foregrounds for American studies the links between racial whiteness, nationalism, masculinity, and citizenship. At the same time, a focus on Asian Americans disrupts the usual racial binary of black versus white and, importantly, illuminates how this binary serves the perpetuation of racialized hierarchy within the history of the United States.

The exteriority of Asian Americans to national culture not only offers American studies critical insights into the role of national culture in the forming of citizens, but it also initiates a truly necessary inquiry into the *comparative* history of racialization: for example, the interrelationship of African American and Asian American racial histories. In the 1880s, as Chinese immigrants became "laboring subjects" yet were barred from political and social inclusion, in 1870 the Fourteenth Amendment to the U.S. Constitution admitted African Americans into citizenship as "American national subjects" but local ordinances barred them from working as laborers in the western United States. Helen Jun argues that while U.S. history has been constituted through a narrative privileging of the black and white racial crucible, the institutions and discourses that represent Asian immigrants as immutably foreign to the nation have not only constructed white national identity but they are also constitutive of, differentially, the history of black racial formation.[6] Grace Kyungwon Hong (1999) argues that, throughout the twentieth century, Japanese Americans and African Americans are not linked through a logic of identity, but through a relation of differential access to property rights by the state; she argues that the dispossessions that are a part of internment for Japanese Americans on the one hand, and segregation for African Americans on the other, are uneven, but linked, manifestations of the privileging of private property ownership that structures U.S. society.

Furthermore, the history of U.S. colonialism and war in the Philippines, Japan, South Korea, and Vietnam, and the racialized immigration from these sites obliges American studies to rethink the history of the United States as a history of empire. In discussing the relationship between U.S. empire and labor segmentation in the Southwest and western United States in the early twentieth century, Eleanor Jaluague argues that we must understand the interrelation and dependency of U.S. colonialism in the Philippines and the importation of Filipino laborers in California in order to understand the consolidation of "whiteness" and American citizenship during the New Deal era.[7] Asian American racial formation also brings a uniquely situated analysis of the intersections of race, gender, and sexuality to American studies. The history of Asian immigration exclusion and regulated settlement that has rendered Asian "masculinity" a "feminized masculinity," estranged from middle-class domesticity, also "hyperfeminized" Asian women and made them emblematic of feminized domestic space. As David Eng's (1997) work on Asian American sexuality and Gayatri Gopinath's (1997) discussions of "queer" South Asian diaspora have demonstrated, these racialized constructions of both Asian "masculinity" and Asian "femininity" have tended to elide non-heteronormative sexualities as threats to national integrity or to foreclose such sexualities by placing them outside the boundaries of the nation and the family. Chandan Reddy (1998a) has likewise argued that the marginalization of Asian immigrants from the historical emergence of middle-class domesticity in the United States makes Asian American formation a site from which to understand "family" and domesticity as racialized practices in the reproduction of the unevennesses of capitalist social relations.[8]

For Asian American studies, the influx of new Asian immigrants in the last two decades has made it more or less axiomatic to state that Asian Americans and Asian immigrants are a "heterogeneous" group, in terms of national origin, class, gender, sexuality, language, religion, and generation. This has led scholars within the field to be critical of racial essentialism and cultural nationalist formations of identity within the context of a single nation-state, and led activists to question whether ethnic identity always and in every instance leads to a progressive politics aimed at social and economic transformation. Yet it is imperative that Asian American studies push this critique even further in order to consider different Asian formations within the global or neocolonial framework of transnational capitalism; the object of this effort would be to supplement an Asian American studies notion of "racial formation" within one nation-state with an understanding of the multiple contexts of colonialism and its various extensions within the uneven development of neocolonial capitalism, in order to inquire into the significance of the "Asian American" within local situations and material conditions—in Asia, in the Asian diaspora in the West, as well as in the Asian diaspora in the non-West. To be quite concrete: Asians have served as both labor and capital within the emergence of the transnational economy. If we consider Asian racial formation within different Asian contexts, we understand that the earlier racialization of Asian immigrants through the exploitation of male noncitizen labor within the United States before World War II is rather different from the current use of neocolonized immigrant women in the global economy. It also differs from the current situation of Asian managers within Asian-owned factories in the Mexican and Central American export-processing zones, or *maquiladoras;* or that of Asian neocolonial capitalist development of the tourist industry in Hawai'i; or of middle-class Asian Americans in multiracial California, a state that has at once resegregated public education by banning affirmative action while it addresses populations of color through the buildup of what Ruth Gilmore

(1998) and Angela Davis (1997) have termed the "prison-industrial complex." In this situation, enfranchised middle-class Asian Americans are racialized in hierarchical terms with poor Asian immigrants and other groups of color. In the global expansion of the economy, the search for low-wage manipulable labor not only moves to Mexican maquiladoras, Southeast Asian factories, and immigrant manufacturing sites in Los Angeles or San Francisco, but it also moved unimpeded behind prison walls.

This said, the impossibility of a single Asian racial formation currently demands a redefinition of political project for Asian American studies, one that does not proceed from an assumption of the uniformity of the political subject along lines of racial, ethnic, or cultural identity. In the face of the radical nonidentity of Asian racial formations globally, Asian American studies must develop instead a shared language about exploitation within transnational capitalism, a language about economic and social justice rather than cultural or nationalist identity. This requires understanding that local specificities mediate and are indices of global conditions, and that while Asian migrancy is an index of the present social formation of transnational capitalism, it is dialectically linked with the forcible lack of migrancy of other groups in different parts of the world, whether women of the South, or the unemployed or incarcerated African American population within the United States. That is, transnational capitalism currently links the nonmigrant women who cannot escape the patriarchal violence of an authoritarian state or the local communities that have been dislocated from indigenous forms of economy—with the diasporic movements of Asian labor and capital. In a sense, these groups are "the other to the question of diaspora," as Gayatri Spivak (1996) has put it.[9] The subaltern women of the South, the incarcerated, or immobile nonworking racialized subject, are the "others" of the Asian American migrant. Within a global cartography in which capital is consolidated in the North through the exploitation of the South, the third world bourgeoisie becoming migrant in the West is a narrative of the consolidation of capitalism.[10] In this context, family reunification and cultural nationalist ties among Asian immigrant communities facilitate capital accumulation and the exploitation of others, that is, the "nondiasporic" (Reddy 1998b).

Since the 1980s, the profile of Asian immigration to the West has diversified, consisting of both low-wage service-sector workers and "proletarianized" white-collar professionals, a group that at once supplies laborers for services and manufacturing and that furnishes a technically trained labor force that serves as one form of "variable capital" investment in the U.S. economy.[11] Because Asian immigrants, in particular, are subject to the demotion and manipulation of skilled labor in the period of transition from entrepreneurial to corporate capitalism, the "white collar proletarianization" of Asian-educated immigrant engineers, scientists, or nurses can be distinguished from situations of U.S.-educated white middle-class "professionals; "variable capital" is one manner for understanding the use of lower-cost Asian immigrant professionals as one form of capital investment for the maximizing of surplus value. Thus transnational industries profit through the increased use of Asian immigrant women's labor, along with Third World and racialized immigrant women, as a "flexible" workforce in the restructuring of capitalism globally, and through the mobility of Asian professional and business classes.[12] Asian American studies is in the process of rethinking racial formation within this global context, and in terms of the comparative racialization of other immigrant and neocolonized groups.

New immigration from Asia disrupts disciplinary practices for the study of "Asia," "America," and even the "Asian American" that emerged in U.S. universities in the 1970s. To the extent that this new object exceeds the contours of the earlier paradigms, it may force a shift in the methods and objects of Asian studies, American studies, and Asian American studies, all of which furnished specific knowledges for the U.S. university and thus contributed to a U.S. nationalist ontology. At this point, it is still uncertain whether the figure of the post-1965 Asian immigrant will force a shift in the disciplines, or whether the disciplines will "renationalize" in the fixing and domestication of the Asian immigrant as an object of study, leaving their disciplinary paradigms, and the national ontology they maintain, substantially unrevised. We would be well served, indeed, if the discussions collected in this volume open the terrain for such shifts to take place.

Notes

1 This argument is elaborated in Lowe 1996.
2 On the post-1965 immigration from Asia, see Ong, Bonacich, and Cheng, eds. 1994.
3 Michael Omi, Annual Meeting of the Association for Asian American Studies, Honolulu, HI, 1998.
4 There are a number of new interdisciplinary projects that herald this epistemological shift, situating Asian immigrant racial formation within a global context, including: Shah (forthcoming); Eng (forthcoming); Laura Hyun Yi Kang 1997; Manalansan (forthcoming); Grewal (forthcoming); Chuh (forthcoming); Hong 1999.
5 See Lipsitz 1998, especially chapters 3 and 10.
6 Helen Jun, Ph.D. dissertation (in progress), Literature Department, University of California, San Diego.
7 Eleanor Jaluague, Ph.D. dissertation (in progress), Literature Department, University of California, San Diego.
8 See Reddy 1998a. See also Glenn 1983.

9 See Spivak 1996.

10 See also Spivak 1998.

11 On Asian immigrant communities in the United States following 1965, see Ong, Bona-cich, and Cheng 1994. See Bowles and Gintis 1976 on the "white collar proletariat." In discussing current transnational capitalist strategies for maximizing profits through ex-ploitative "flexible" reorganization and management of skilled and semi-skilled labor, Richard Appelbaum (1996) employs Marx's distinction between "constant capital" (in-vestment in machinery and equipment) and "variable capital" (the costs of living labor; variable capital is an important way of understanding the use of lower-cost Asian im-migrant professionals as a form of capital investment.

12 See Lowe and Lloyd 1997; Sassen 1991.

"Imaginary Borders"

KANDICE CHUH

In a recent conversation about undergraduate curriculum design, an Americanist colleague matter-of-factly asserted that because all American literature emerges from British literature, students must be compelled to take British literature courses in order to prepare them for the study of its U.S. counterpart. Arguably there is a certain value in reading British literature to American studies given the United States's historic transatlantic connections, but this formulation of what American literature *really* is clearly excludes the study of Asian American cultural formations, among others. Putting aside the use of the signifier "American" as referring only to the United States, this particular bounding of American literature, as synecdochic of "America" itself, essentially defines the nation in Anglocentric terms. Indeed, as demonstrated by Cathy Davidson and Michael Moon, American literature has largely been conceptualized by means of an overarching question of which social identities are and are not representative of the nation.[1] The master narrative of the nation, according to which "America" is a destined, natural result, relies on citizenship as its primary trope for conceptualizing who Americans are. The abstract citizen—she or he who successfully assimilates into and is assimilated by the national master plot—is the legitimate owner of the political space of the nation, whose past is (should be) irrelevant in light of the naturalized present. Unable, through official regulation and cultural disciplinization, to occupy fully that position of abstract citizen, Asian Americans and their cultural formations are excluded from the political and imaginary realm referenced by "America"/American literature. This enforced absence from the national literature, or more precisely, from the national literary curriculum, instantiates one way in which the cultural apparatuses of national identity formation come to be materially relevant.

For me, the consideration of how Asian studies and Asian American studies may and may not benefit from and work with each other is inextricably entangled in this struggle over the meaning of "America." This struggle metonymically references the reasons underlying a tradition of claiming a space in studies of U.S. cultural productions by Asian Americanist critics. While Asian American literature has successfully emerged as a coherent field of study over the past several decades, it remains nonetheless in some ways a peripheral appendage to American literature. Consequent to this kind of marginalization, Asian Americanists have fought to "claim America":[2] Institutionally and politically long-compelled to assert the Americanness of Asian American literatures, its study has in many instances come to all but deny any connection—historic, geographic, linguistic—to "Asia," in effect reproducing a seemingly immutable split between Asia and America.[3] There is a sense of temporality to this dissociation, an urgency driven by recognition of past and present injustices meted out by apparatuses of the nation to localize resistance within the boundaries of the nation in the here and now. By redefining the narratives constituting the U.S. nation to include, account for, and integrate Asian Americanness into the public domain of collective national memory, Asian Americanists have sought to actualize national belongingness in both the cultural and political realms. Indeed, it has been precisely this kind of work that has made possible the institutionalized, materially supported, study of Asian American cultures and histories.

At the same time, though, it seems that the logic organizing this work has overlooked an arguably first-order issue, and that is the imperialism of American ideology. Given that problematic characteristic, at what (or whose) expense are the rights and entitlements accruing to legitimized Americanness being materialized? By claiming ownership of U.S. national identity, Asian Americanists must also then claim responsibility for the cultural and material imperialism of this nation. To maintain some critical distance between possession of the nation and recognition of complicity in its deeply entrenched imperialist machinations, simultaneous to the work of realizing justice for Asian Americans must be confrontation of U.S. imperialism. This means, in part, conceptualizing the United States as contextualized in the global domain. It seems to me that it is therefore of vital importance for Asian Americanists to collaborate with practitioners of Asian studies in its myriad manifestations as one facet of this process. This is not to assume that the United States figures prominently or even at all in that work, but is rather to suggest that efforts to understand the functionalization of Asian American social subjectivities are hindered, for example and as discussed below, by ignorance of Japanese and Korean histories. It is, in other words, and following Dipesh Chakrabarty's dictum in his essay in this volume, to posit the critical importance of thinking through global historical specificities as instrumental to understanding the particularities and ideologies constituting local Asian Americanist sites of intervention.

The complex histories of relations between and among Japan, Korea, and the United States undergird my discussion here.[4] The role of those relations in the immigration experiences and patterns of Korean Americans, and its impact in conditioning Korean American formations throughout the 20th century, contextualizes the circumstances within and out of which Theresa Hak Kyung Cha's *Dictée* and Ronyoung Kim's *Clay Walls,* the texts anchoring discussion here, emerge. Kim's work, addressing as it does an earlier (pre–World War II) generation of Korean immigrants— many of whom left the peninsular nation as political refugees seeking to escape Japanese occupation—articulates that nexus of relations in a manner that bespeaks the particular conditions of the pre–World War II era. Cha's text, on the other hand, very specifically negotiates a different, arguably postmodern, set of circumstances within which the dynamics of relations among Japan, Korea, and the United States express themselves accordingly. In a sense offering a retrospective view of the pre–World War II era, Cha's work describes a contemporary form of Korean Americanness that remains firmly interconnected with that earlier history. Part of my goal here is to examine the ways in which these works, precisely because of their respective subject matters and methods of articulation, are and have been situated within Asian Americanist literary communities.[5]

Insofar as Asian Americanness in the U.S. public domain has been legally regulated along the vector not only of a nation-based racism, but also and simultaneously through racialized international relations between the United States and various Asian nations, to ignore those global historical specificities is tantamount to claiming the total irrelevancy of pastness to the present. By pastness, I mean to reference the narrative of U.S. citizenship that melts foreign identities into the national stock pot. What is external to the nation becomes, in effect, the past, even if those events are unfolding in current time. The only linkages to past time to remain integral to the U.S. National Symbolic are the American Revolution and its associated documents, defined as the founding event in the temporal life of the nation.[6] It is this interwoven texture of national time and identity formation that I examine here. Recognition of this quality in turn suggests a strategy for intervention in the processes of national identity formation that reads against the fabric of the national master plot. Reading, or critical analysis of textual formations constitutive of U.S. social subjectivities, anchors my project in this essay. Inasmuch as the concept of reading implies a dynamic and mutually constitutive relationship between text and reader and raises issues of epistemic authority integral to that relationship, it becomes a useful way of configuring an analogous relationship between nation and national subject. To read in a way that purposefully counters the exclusionary movements of national narrative thus argues for deliberate reframing of the objects of study—the nation and the national subject—from the field of the here/now to that of the also-there/then. Guided by the specific privileges, problems, and particularities of the here and now (this site of intervention), this interpretive strategy demands articulation of thereness to present time conditions.

The theories embedded in Asian American literatures drive this essay forward. That is, the internal coherencies of Asian American literary texts schematize particular modes of knowledge production—epistemic theories—that illuminate the organizing principles of not only those texts, but of the social subjectivities described in, and the system of circumstances external to, them. Asian American literature is, in other words, theory itself, self-reflexively critical of the function and effects of writing, and as such articulates interpretive paradigms integral to producing knowledge from what might be described as an Asian Americanist epistemological standpoint.[7] I try to sketch below what I will call the transnationalism of that theory, as inscribed in Cha's *Dictée* and Kim's *Clay Walls*. This is a transnationalism that refutes any notions of a natural and wholly bounded national identity while simultaneously iterating the historic and material power of the nation-state. Transnationalism in this sense is a critical methodology that mediates interpretation, counseling deliberate disruption of normative understandings of nationhood and social subjectivity, and that insists on recognizing the ideologies conditioning national identity formation.[8]

To be clear, the transnational instantiates in multiple forms specific to particular historical conditions. Cha's sense of transnationalism is one, as I suggest below, that emphasizes the inadequacy of conventional nationalist and narrative deployments of time in accounting for post-1965—the year marking the enactment of the Immigration Act that heralded the more recent wave of immigration from Korea—Korean American formations. That sense is one that resonates against David Harvey's and Fredric Jameson's respective explanations of the ways in which postmodern cultural productions are dynamically contextualized by contemporary conditions of globalized capitalism. On the other hand, the transnationalism that emerges from *Clay Walls* is one that is more concerned with configuring the tropes of immigration, exile, and settlement through which Korean Americanness of the earlier era might be understood. Precisely because of the differences between these texts in their uses and understandings of the interrelations among national, social, and political identities or identifications, their consideration together usefully highlights both the continuities and divergences among processes of cultural and social subjectivity formation.[9]

Transnationalist Time

U.S. nationalist ideology couches itself under cloak of naturalness and inevitability by maintaining strict control over the temporal logic of citizenship and nationhood. Cha's *Dictée* exposes this apparatus through its positing of a postcolonial identity that is fragmentary and never complete(d).[10] Interrogating the concept of citizenship—of the ways in which "naturalization" is a process of disciplining the individual into obedience to the nation—Cha concomitantly disrupts the notion that there is a confinable "then" and "now" correlating to a "foreign" past and a "citizen" present.[11] In *Dictée,* Cha demonstrates a metonymical rather than static relationship among past, present, and future. Its argument is made largely through its structure: it is a work that refuses developmental narration.[12] By its iteration of a non-narrative structure both in format and content, *Dictée* in effect proffers an understanding of nationhood and narrative that demands a suspension of temporal conventions. Paul Ricoeur's contention that, through *discourse,* the concepts of past, present, and future are made knowable is useful here.[13] Through discourse, "lived time"—that which is phenomenologically experienced—is made historical, and "cosmic time"—the historical sense of time—may be experienced phenomenologically. Sharing discourse, occupying the same linguistic time, enables collectivization of membership in the nation. *Dictée* rigorously interrogates such membership, discursively demonstrating disjuncture between the experiences of lived and cosmic time.

Cha's integration of Korean, French, and English languages in this text seems both necessitated by and consequent to the fragmentary, elusive subjectivity she describes. As Lisa Lowe points out, the notion of dictation functions as *Dictée*'s "emblematic *topos*" (1994, 38). The assimilation of language through dictation—the learning of "the vocabulary, idioms, and rules of grammar and syntax of the 'foreign' language through rendering an oral example into a written equivalent" (Lowe 1994, 38)—serves as the structuring metaphor of Cha's text. *Dictée* brings into the foreground the textuality of assumed and often invisible rules of linguistic correctness:

Aller à la ligne C'était le premier jour point Elle venait de loin point ce soir au dîner virgule les familles demanderaient virgule ouvre les

"Imaginary Borders"   281

guillemets Ça c'est bien passé le premier jour point d'interrogation
ferme les guillemets au moints virgule dire le moints possible virgule
la résponse serait virgule ouvre les guillemets Il n'y a q'une chose point
ferme les guillemets ouvre les guillemets Il y a quelqu'une point loin
point ferme les guillemets

Open paragraph It was the first day period She had come from a
far period tonight at dinner comma the families would ask comma
open quotation marks How was the first day interrogation mark close
quotation marks at least to say the least of it possible comma the
answer would be open quotation marks there is but one thing period
There is someone period From a far period close quotation marks (Cha
1995[1982], 1)

Both French and English are thus established as foreign, in close proximity
(i.e., transcribable) and yet not fully internalized (i.e., still textual), a quality
of knowable foreignness mirroring the subject of the passage, the "she"
from "a far" who is nonetheless "there," simultaneously distant and present.
For this "she," linguistic structure is textual and therefore interrogatable:
movement from "a far" requires movement into those textualities—a becoming a part of them—through transcription of self. "She" is disciplined
by rules of grammar, freed only by adopting them, when "The utter" becomes "Hers now" (Cha 1995[1982], 5). Cha thus frames the assumption of
language as a process involving the simultaneity of distance and proximity;
of a uniting through repetition of a third-person self with linguistic structure; of possession, both of and by language. "She" does not exist except as
she is transcribed through dictation. Disciplinization by the linguistic laws
of a language metaphorically represents the resignification of an individual
into a national identity. *Dictée* suggests, however, that this resignification
remains incompletely realized: "she" continues to recognize the textuality
of linguistic structure even as she enters into and participates in its disciplining activity.

Even, suggests *Dictée,* acquiescence and subsequent official acceptance
into foreignness does not complete a unitary subjectivity.

I have the documents. Documents, proof, evidence, photograph, signature. One day you raise the right hand and you are American. They
give you an American Pass port. The United States of America. Somewhere someone has taken my identity and replaced it with their photograph. The other one. Their signature their seals. Their own image.
And you learn the executive branch the legislative branch and the third.
Justice. Judicial branch. It makes the difference. The rest is past.

You return and you are not one of them, they treat you with indifference. All the time you understand what they are saying. But the papers give you away. Every ten feet. They ask your identity. They comment upon your inability or ability to speak. Whether you are telling the truth or not about your nationality. They say you look other than you say. As if you didn't know who you were. You say who you are but you begin to doubt. They search you. They, the anonymous variety of uniforms, each division, strata, classification, any set of miscellaneous properly uni formed. They have the right, no matter what rank, however low their function they have the authority. Their authority sewn into the stitches of their costume. Every ten feet they demand to know who and what you are, who is represented. The eyes gather towards the appropriate proof. Towards the face then again to the papers, when did you leave the country why did you leave this country why are you returning to the country. (Cha 1995[1982], 56–57)

The replacement of "my identity" with "their photograph" and in "[t]heir own image" in becoming American signals for "her" a pivotal point of differentiation at which the "rest is past." Cha again emphasizes the adoption of structure here: the three branches of government that literally define the structure of the nation must be learned in becoming American, and the learning of that structure "makes the difference" between present and past. Yet immediately following this appeal to a knowable, but "their," identity, comes a nonspecific description of a simultaneous embodiment of foreignness and nationality precipitated in part by "look[ing] other." The image of the uniform and of uniformity is enhanced by the repeated, militaristic interrogation of identity that occurs "every ten feet." The racialized immigrant, suggests Cha, is subordinated to all "true" possessors of nationality, who collectively have and deploy "their" authority to demand proof of identity. Cha recognizes the unnaturalness of even those who presumably have that authority, suggesting that the authority is "sewn into" a "costume." By placing these passages together, Cha structurally demonstrates that "the papers" both matter and are irrelevant: a constant redefinition, a repeated reassertion of identity-truth is necessary to maintaining the coherency of identity. The repeated request for assurance that the disciplining interpellation of nationalism is working itself indicates doubt about the absoluteness of that disciplinization.

In other words, *Dictée* not only describes the learning to possess, and possession by, a foreign past which is to become the naturalized present; it also interrogates the demands of an originary (national) identity. By emphasizing the links between and the narrativization of history and identity, Cha describes an originary subjectivity that is no more definitive than an immigrant identity, and often, no more familiar than the foreign. Passages offering Korean history are themselves fragmentary and discontinuous: "She" fades in and out as, for example, photographs, italicized meditations, transcriptions of historical documents, and narratives in epistolary form combine to offer an unevenly developed, rough topography of Korean history. She argues, in other words, against the ossification of thereness into a compact, completely knowable past that can be parceled out of identity in present time.

Simultaneous invocation of Korean and Japanese history brings with it acknowledgment of the fragmentary, mythological bases of both (national/self) identity and history:

> The "enemy." One's enemy. Enemy nation. Entire nation against the other entire nation. One people exulting the suffering institutionalized on another. The enemy becomes abstract. The relationship becomes abstract. The nation the enemy the name becomes larger than its own identity. Larger than its own measure. Larger than its own properties. Larger than its own signification. For *this* people. For the people who is their enemy. For the people who is their ruler's subject and their ruler's victory.
>
> Japan has become the sign. The alphabet. The vocabulary. To *this* enemy people. The meaning is the instrument, memory that pricks the skin, stabs the flesh, the volume of blood, the physical substance blood as measure, that rests as record, as document. Of *this* enemy people. (Cha 1995[1982], 32; emphasis original)

As names repeatedly resignify, so, too, do nation and national identity change meanings. Memory, or the remembering and rearticulation of the past, makes history immediate and reconfigures the present "she." National boundaries both gain and lose importance, seen at once as dramatically renameable and, in that recognition, all the more significant. Remembrance in *Dictée* becomes in this sense a re-member-ing of a nation. As Chung-hei Yun explains, "without the past, without the dismembered history to be remembered, the child of the present cannot redeem future or past. In retelling as a dictée/diseuse, the child born of exile is able to speak the words. The very act of retelling and re-membering the past emancipates her from the prison of stony and immobile silence" (1992, 93).

For Koreans ("*this* people"), Japanese imperialism's power to resignify overwhelms and disproves a definitive originary identity. The "enemy nation" subsumes "its own identity," reconstituting "*this* people" as "*this* enemy people." Japan's definition as language itself ("sign," "alphabet," "vocabulary") inscribes "*this* people" discursively, and articulation of self and nation is possible only through and as "the enemy." History is made through the conjoining of this past redefinition and a present memory of the past; history continuously invades and becomes the self/body/identity. Thus, for Cha, "the remnant is the whole," and "[t]he memory is the entire" (Cha 1995[1982], 38).

Coeval with the subsumption of "*this*" people's identity by the "enemy nation," "she" is invisible in *Dictée*'s description of the discursive economy of gender and sex. "She" comes into language only in and through "his" presence:

> He is the husband, and she is the wife. He is the man. She is the wife. It is a given. He does as he is the man. She does as she is the woman, and the wife. Stands the distance between the husband and wife the distance of heaven and hell. The husband is seen. Entering the house shouting her name, calling her name. You find her for the first time as he enters the room calling her. (Cha 1995[1982], 102).

"She" exists only insofar as she responds to his naming in this domestic space. As in the experience of entrance into a foreign discursive territory, "she" becomes a knowable entity—woman-wife—by being named by others. Cha writes:

> Being woman. Never to question. Never to expect but the given. Only the given. She was his wife his possession she belonged to him her husband the man who claimed her and she could not refuse. Perhaps that was how it was. That was how it was then. Perhaps now.
> It is the husband who touches. Not as husband. He touches her as he touches all the others. But he touches her with his rank. By his knowledge of his own rank. By the claim of his rank. Gratuity is her body her spirit. Her non-body her non-entity. His privilege possession his claim. Infallible is his ownership. Imbues with mockery at her refusal of him, but her very being that dares to name herself as if she possesses a will. Her own. (Cha 1995[1982], 111–12)

The disciplining interpellation of "the claim of his rank" while mocking a sense of "her" ownership of her self, nevertheless fails to complete its possession. "Her very being" denies his possession, "dar[ing] to name herself," to claim language for "her own." By drawing this parallel between the interpellative practices of discourse within public and private spaces, Cha describes the materialization of law into bodily possessions. Like Judith Butler's theorization of the ways in which bodies both literally and juridically come to "matter," Cha describes here a "process of materialization that stabilizes over time to produce the effect of boundary, fixity, and surface we call matter" (Butler 1993, 9). For "she," foreign/national/self identities are (not) enclosed by "*Imaginary borders. Un imaginable boundaries*" (Cha 1995[1982], 87; emphasis in original).

Understanding national identity formation in terms of time—understanding the trope of assimilation central to U.S. identity formation as embedded with the notion that there is a "right" time to be foreign, which is rightfully supplanted by the "right" time to identify with the nation—and by rejecting the linear chronology demanded by this national master plot, Cha in effect refuses the temporal logic of the master narrative.[14] Neither space—in her work, represented by Korea (variously a Korea that is at once itself and a possession of Japan) and the United States—nor time, the progression of identity ordered through a narrative of beginning, middle, and end, can be understood in terms of a single narrative of nation, according to *Dictée*. The time described is *transnationalist time,* which structures a narrative not developmentally but cornucopically. Distinctions between past and present, or foreigner and citizen, or outsider and insider, are maintained only through a deliberate erasure of the dynamic relations between the nation's exterior and interior. Transnationalist time references the fracture between historic and lived time for the Asian American subject, and thus reconfigures the relations between a nation and its citizen-subjects.[15]

The Trope of the Transnational

Cha's text calls attention to its transnationalist theorizing through its structure, demanding understanding of the impropriety of the organizational rules of the national master plot to account for its argument. In a more conventionally constructed work like Ronyoung Kim's *Clay Walls,* the aptness of transnationalism to contend with the national subjectification of racialized foreigners is evinced through the transnational trope that configures the story. At first glance, *Clay Walls* appears almost stereotypically representative of the "truth" of the promises inscribed in the American Dream so central to the master narrative of the United States. Visible in Kim's novel, however, is a struggle to articulate a Korean American subjectivity that is not the effect of a progressive Americanization, and is instead constituted by cornucopically intersecting vectors of Japanese imperialism, Korean nationalism and, U.S. racism, especially as the latter is articulated to American nationalism, and the materialities accruing to gender, class, and (hetero)sexuality. The conflicts and correspondences among these various interpellative ideologies and identificatory categories are demonstrated in *Clay Walls* as demanding a consistency of identity impossible to maintain.

Like Cha, Kim accounts for and traces Korean American subjectivity in multiple directions across national and temporal borders. Set largely in the time of the Japanese imperial occupation of Korea, this narrative of immigration is in many ways a story of exile: Chun, mistakenly identified as a student protestor against Japanese rule, is hurried into marriage to Haesu and forced to flee persecution by leaving for America. "In the days that follow" his departure from home,

> he found refuge with sympathizers, cast from one Korean patriot to another until he reached China. Even there he was in constant fear of his life. Posing as a Chinese, he was fearful that he would forget the warnings of his countrymen and turn his head at the shout of "*Yobo!*", a trick the Japanese secret police used to single out Koreans.
>
> He felt a measure of relief when he boarded the ship to America. Not until he stepped onto California soil did he feel safe. (Kim 1987, 156)

Having successfully evaded the hail (à la Althusser) of the Japanese police by assuming a Chinese persona, Chun arrives in California only to experience a different kind of alienation. Language here, in the face of identity in superficial physical characteristics, functions as the primary indicator of foreignness. That it is Chun's home language, Korean, that has the potential to facilitate his demise is significant to understanding Kim's interrelation of language and national identity. In the scenario of this passage, there is a collapse of distinction between language and identity that impels physical removal to another place. Chun's feelings of safety, found in contact with Californian soil, establishes the temporal sense of the narrative that gives rise to its most striking points of argument regarding the illusory nature of that safety. Racism bars Chun from fulfilling the promise of safety he feels upon arrival. *In* and *on* the nation, but repeatedly disciplined into remembrance that he is not *of* the nation, Chun falters in his efforts to find a place in the United States as he is drawn increasingly to gambling, a metaphor for his growing loss of control over his life, and finally dies in isolation, away from his family and from any connection to either an American or a Korean home.[16]

Kim points to an apparent emasculinization of Asian men associated with class identifications in transition across national borders: barred by racism from full participation in the U.S. public sphere and seemingly unable to accept his exile from Korea, Chun is seen as desperately grasping a sense of masculinity through sex and sexual violence. Unable to claim control over his life, Chun rapes Haesu, and "without a word, he turned his back to her to go to sleep":

> Haesu lay in the dark, humiliation crawled over her like damp moss. . . . She did not know the word for what he had done to her. "That thing" was how she referred to coitus. She didn't know the word for rape.

In the morning when Haesu awoke, Chun was gone. . . . All that lay on the kitchen counter was a crisp one hundred dollar bill.

Haesu had difficulty concentrating on her homework. Absent-mindedly, she recited the phrases assigned to her. "Good morning Mr. Smith. How are you? I am fine, thank you. Will you and Mrs. Smith join me for tea?" But her mind was on the events of the night before. She swore to herself that she would make Chun pay for debasing her. He would never have her respect, not after what he had done to her. (Kim 1987, 30)

The money left on the counter symbolizes both Haesu's and Chun's changed and changing class positions. Where in Korea, Haesu's position as a member of the *yangban,* or aristocratic, class provided her with a material safety net, in the United States she is economically even more vulnerable than Chun. Haesu's inability to articulate the experience marks an alienation of self from experience, and, as in *Dictée,* the coming into the language of America represents a transformation of subjectivity. On the other hand, for Chun, who later in the novel conducts an extramarital affair, the demonstration of masculinity through both rape and (hetero)sexual intercourse provides him with powerful and empowering pleasure: "For him, it was ecstatic" (Kim 1987, 146). Kim underscores the effect of national context on both gender and sexuality by contrasting these sexual experiences with one set in Korea during a visit to Haesu's family. While less violent in description, even then Haesu is left unsatisfied: "His murmurings ended abruptly and, with low uneven moans, he fell against her. She wanted him to go on, but he couldn't. He raised his head to brush his lips across her face. She turned away. 'No,' she said, denying him her lips" (Kim 1987, 129).

The occupation of stitchwork taken up by Haesu also functions as an illuminating node in the novel. That work, accomplished as it is within the literally domestic sphere of the home, implicates the practices of capital accumulation and disrupts simplistic notions of interiority and exteriority. The socio-political conditions of the public space that necessitate Haesu's choice of occupation are seen to figure centrally in affecting both the quotidian and profound elements constituting this family's life. In this very specific way, Kim brings into the field of vision the affective power not simply of "class" as an identificatory category, but of capital as an active player.

The irony that Chun's exile from Korea is the result of mistaken identity as a student protestor is emphasized by Haesu's corresponding exile. While Chun remains aloof to Korean patriotism, Haesu, who had not been accused of anti-Japanese demonstration, becomes increasingly active in U.S.-based Korean nationalism. Often as the only woman participant,

Haesu organizes and unifies the Korean patriotic organization of the small community of immigrants inhabiting this novel. For Haesu, the experience of exile coalesces her originary national identity, a process furthered by alienation from America. Haesu survives through a constantly changing and largely self-activated process of claiming agency. Her relative success in "claiming America" comes out of her ability to negotiate and shift the matrix of race, ethnicity, gender, class, and sexual identificatory effects; to, in other words, embody a permeability of borders.

Haesu's visit "home" to Korea makes clear that, as Benedict Anderson has written, "home . . . was less experienced than imagined, and imagined through a complex of mediations and representations" (1994, 319). Letters from Haesu's mother, combined with an idealized notion of an originary Korea fostered during nationalist meetings, support Haesu's nostalgic imaginings. Once there, she sees that "things have changed," as her mother repeatedly wrote, and in that realization, acknowledges change in her self. In the inexactness of the image in the mirror Haesu places between nation and self, she is forced to recognize the imaginary quality of her image of "home."

Haesu attempts throughout the novel to possess America as she once did Korea. Rejected by potential landlords who do not "want 'orientals,'" Haesu indignantly questions, "'I would certainly like to know why the Korean Declaration of Independence was modeled after the American Declaration.'" In sarcastic response to her friend's explanation that only certain areas are "unrestricted," "Haesu's lips opened with a smack. 'All men are created equal'" (Kim 1987, 21–22). Referencing the founding event of this nation's narrative life, Kim posits a disjuncture between lived and historic time for the Korean American subject. Neither desiring to reject Korea nor able in any case to do so, Haesu can only point to the discursive (i.e., the temporal and spatial) dislocation experienced in inhabiting the space of the transnational. That founding moment becomes meaningless as Haesu's narrative unfolds, and the concept of "home" is increasingly dissociated from yearning for national identification.[17]

Kim emphasizes even further the transnationality of Korean American subjectivity through her figuration of Faye, Chun and Haesu's daughter. A U.S. citizen by birth, Faye traverses a path of experiences that continually recollects Korean history both in Korea and the United States. Faye's friendship with Jane Nagano, a Japanese American schoolmate, highlights the intersecting vectors of past and present history. Waiting with Jane to sign up for a school activity, Faye learns of her newfound friend's connection to Japan: "Jane gave the teacher her full name and my heart sank into my shoes. Her last name was Nagano, a Japanese name. Every March First and just about every day in between, Koreans reminded each other to hate the Japanese" (Kim 1987, 208). The naming of Jane as Japan-identified abruptly transforms Jane from schoolmate to entity feared and hated, and, at the same time, causes Faye to question her own (Korean) identity and faithfulness to it. Caught in a discursive field that employs essential and definitive identifications, Faye worries about associating with Jane, and "trie[s] to forget that she [is] Japanese" (Kim 1987, 212).

Significantly, the Nagano family is responsible for Faye's introduction to Walt Whitman's poetry, which is literally performed for Faye by Jane's sisters. Kim parallels the experiences of first and second generation Korean Americans: as Japanese imperialism caused Faye's family to leave Korea and reside in the United States, in the next generation, Japanese Americans are responsible for Korean Americans' further integration into America. Kim demonstrates through this implicit comparison that nativity does not guarantee natural participation in the discursive time of the nation. It is rather through the National Literature—Willa Cather and Mark Twain, in addition to Whitman—that Faye learns what it means to "be" American.

Korea, represented nostalgically by and as Haesu, is seemingly at times at odds with the United States, as Faye comes to imagine the relationship. Yet as Lowe has argued, "interpreting Asian American culture exclusively in terms of the master narratives of generational conflict and filial relation essentializes Asian American culture obscuring the particularities and incommensurabilities of class, gender, and national diversities among Asians; the reduction of ethnic cultural politics to struggles between first and second generations displaces (and privatizes) inter-community difference into a familial opposition" (Lowe 1991b, 26). The privatization of these conflicts in other words enables a blindness to the systemic binary logic of national identity (us/them; United States/Korea) that in fact precipitates such conflict. Opening the field of interrogation to account for transnational connections through history posits a symbolic economy capable of accommodating a subjectivity (like Faye's and Haesu's) that is constituted not only or primarily by a process of dichotomization. Thus the conflicts between Faye and Haesu may be understood as preconditioned by a definitive bounding of the United States, rather than as consequent only or primarily to irreconcilable cultural differences.

Kim effectively redefines the notion of place and displacement with this text: in the face of the impossibility of achieving present time identification with America, she explicates through Haesu a mode of interpretation built on a foundation of multiplicity in origins, identities, and times. Permeability of time rather than pastness centrally organizes Haesu's and her family's existence in the United States. Unable and unwilling to reject wholly her past identification with Korea, Haesu sees and survives the United States through the trope not of assimilation, but of the transnation—through that position of being both and simultaneously *of* and *not of*. Boundaried progression from one place and time to another does not result in a wholly completed new national identity; instead, and like Cha, Kim explicates a condition of contingency and incompleteness as forming the relations between individuals and the nation.

Centering the Transnation

Reading these texts together not only highlights their deployment of transnationalism in their articulations of Korean Americanness, but also, and equally importantly, reveals the mutability of transnational horizons in configuring U.S. racialized identifications. In *Clay Walls*, the transnational emerges as a descriptor of narrative subjectivity. The novel's characters are transnational subjects insofar as the pressures and power of imperialisms and nationalisms together make impossible a comfortable *national* identification. The overt practices of Japanese imperialism, combined with those of U.S. racism characteristic of the pre-World War II era, underscore the need to focus on issues of identity and political subjectivity, as does Kim in this novel. While *Dictée* also takes up these kinds of interrelations among doctrines of power, the transnational in this later work nonetheless means something different. Seemingly more concerned with the process and the impossibility of achieving identity with a/the nation, Cha's work exemplifies the postmodern and postcolonial era's preoccupations with the characteristics of fluidity, boundary transgression, and self-reflexivity. Here, the transnational describes not so much a particular kind of subjectivity as it does an epistemology of the social subject.

These differences, too, correlate with contemporaneous concerns of Asian American studies. That is, the adoption of Kim's novel by early (i.e., 1970s) Asian Americanists arguably may be understood as correlating with the emphases placed on formulating the structures of identity and citizenship regulating Asian Americanness stressed by Asian American studies generally during that era. Likewise the current popularity of Cha's work may be understood in relation to the present commitments in Asian American studies to comprehend what racialized national identifications might mean in the global(ized) community. Together, these works testify to the ways in which the subject matter and the discourses of, as well as methodologies for, analyses of cultural works inform and resonate against each other.

While distinct in these and other ways, the two works share a common emphasis on the importance of history to transnationalism (or, the practice of seeing through national-global connections) in its multiple manifestations. As Cha and Kim argue, for example, the resignification of Korea from Japanese colony to excolony continue to matter in the here and now. Knowledge of that history is necessary to understanding the functionalization of Korean American social subjectivities.[18] Cha's and Kim's works counsel against interpretation through the identitarian lens of assimilation embedded in the master narrative of the nation. Instead, they call for a strategy of dis-simulation in the practice of interpretation, and correspondingly demand recognition of an epistemological transnational subject, rather than national subject. As Lowe argues in *Immigrant Acts: On Asian American Cultural Politics,* "immigrant," rather than citizen, most insightfully describes the epistemologies inhering in Asian American social subjectivities (1996, 7). The immigrant as descriptor rhetorically references that position of being both *of* and *not of*—that transnational space that cannot be singly located in space or time. By anchoring American cultural studies with the figure of the immigrant rather than that of the assimilated citizen, the orientation of such studies, while remaining specific to the U.S. cultural and political context, is reconfigured to accept axiomatically *difference and mutability* rather than *identity and fixity* as the default quality of the national character. Transnationalism in this sense becomes a strategy for recognizing the incompleteness of narratives of national identity formation.

This shift in orientation in one way answers the call to internationalize American studies put forth by Jane Desmond and Virginia Dominguez. Arguing that American studies has been problematically parochial in its privileging of work by U.S. scholars in residence in the States, Desmond and Dominguez "urge the development of a . . . kind of international scholarship on the United States . . . that truly decenters U.S. scholarship while challenging it with new formulations, new questions, and new critiques" (1996, 486). The liberal multiculturalist paradigms currently in place for "attending to diversity," they submit, are insufficient to "reveal how the terms of intellectual investigation and the generation of topics for debate are also an American product of American history" (1996, 485). In this light, the adoption of a transnationalist reading methodology may not only reorient the ways in which American literature and literary history are defined, but may also facilitate conversation across geographic and disciplinary areas that provide critique and insight previously unavailable. By reconfiguring assumptions of who has the authority to represent and speak of and for the nation, transnationalism has the potential to contribute to the project of, in Benjamin Lee's terms, developing a critical internationalism (Lee 1995).

For Asian Americanists, critical internationalism must involve reading practices responsive to the transnationalist tropes and temporalities exposed in Asian American cultural formations. What this means is that Asian Americanists must work within the frame of conceptualizing Asian America as but one node in a global network of Asian diasporic populations. By extension, this additionally implies the need to foster the understanding that Asian Americanist studies is a nodal point not only in studies of U.S. Americanness, but in those of Asianness, as well. That is, to defy the conventions of U.S. hegemonic epistemology, it is necessary to amplify purposefully the cross-geographic, cross-historical, and cross-discursive dynamics between Asianness and Asian Americanness in the critical methods of knowledge production.

Notes

My discussion in this essay grows out of the work of many of the contributors in this volume, in addition to that of others including Keith Aoki, Arjun Appadurai, Lauren Berlant, Homi Bhabha, David Eng, Inderpal Grewal, Susan Jeffords, Amy Kaplan, Elaine Kim, Caren Kaplan, Trinh T. Minh-Ha, Sangeeta Ray, Edward Said, and Leti Volpp among others, who respectively and in multiple, sometimes implicit ways, have argued for revisioning national boundaries and identity formations. I am also grateful for the responses received on a very early draft of this essay, offered by participants at the *Disciplining Asia* colloquium. Particular thanks to Lisa Lowe, both for providing insightful commentary on this essay as well as in light of the debt this argument owes to her work generally; to Karen Shimakawa for continuing and consistent intellectual and personal support; and to Susan Jeffords, who was instrumental in helping to formulate the broad ideas out of which this discussion emerges. Shawn Wong and Traise Yamamoto each offered excellent suggestions as to interpretation of Ronyoung Kim's novel. As always, endless gratitude to my family.

1   They write, "What constitutes a canon at a particular moment reflects current assumptions about what or who represents the nation" (Davidson and Moon 1995, 1).

2   Sau-ling Cynthia Wong attributes the phrase to Maxine Hong Kingston (Wong 1995).

3   Examination of the legal history surrounding Asian immigration to the United States acutely demonstrates the political need for Asian Americans to continue to work toward claiming that national identity. See Haney Lopez 1996; Hing 1993; and Lowe 1996.

4   For informative discussions on these histories, please see Takaki 1989; Choi 1993; Cumings 1981; Hing 1993; and S. Chan 1991.

5   This part of my argument is indebted to Lisa Lowe.

6   Regarding the U.S. National Symbolic, see Berlant 1991. See Ricoeur (1990, 106) for discussion of the ways in which time is made knowable through identification of a "founding event."

7   Please note that I am drawing a distinction here between Asian American and Asian American*ism*. The difference is an important one in order not only to avoid the pitfalls of essentialism, but also to emphasize the methodological rather than identity-based nature of the strategy I wish to describe. It seems to me that such emphasis contributes to the project of dislodging epistemic authority from the issue of authenticity—an issue that has plagued Asian American studies since its inception.

8   For illuminating discussions of transnationalism, see Appadurai 1993, Grewal and

Kaplan, eds. 1994, and Tölölyan 1991. Drawing on the work of these and other scholars, I have elsewhere defined the transnation as "a socio-political collectivity produced in diversely local and global articulations within an ever changing matrix of nationalisms and circumscribed by the flow of capital within and across national boundaries" (Chuh 1996, 96). More specifically, what I mean to reference by using the term here is an epistemological practice of centering the nexus of national and international cultural, political, and economic relations giving rise to the construction of Asian American social subjectivities.

9 Again, I am indebted to Lisa Lowe for her insights into the distinctions between these texts.

10 My discussion here is informed by the essays collected in *Writing Self, Writing Nation,* edited by Elaine Kim and Norma Alarcon (1992).

11 See R. Radhakrishnan's essay in this volume for an insightful discussion of the ways in which "here" versus "there" problematically structures knowledge about identity and identification.

12 As Lowe submits, "Neither developmental nor univocal, the subject of *Dictée* continually thwarts the reader's desire to abstract a notion of ethnic or national identity—originating either from the dominant culture's interrogation of its margins, or in emergent minority efforts to establish unitary ethnic or cultural nationalist examples" (1994, 36).

13 Ricoeur asserts that "temporality . . . [is] that structure of existence that reaches language in narrativity," and "narrativity . . . [is] the language structure that has temporality as its ultimate referent" (1981, 165). See Ricoeur 1990, 109: "The present is . . . indicated by the coincidence between an event and the discourse that states it. To rejoin lived time . . . we have to pass through linguistic time, which refers to discourse."

14 See Ricoeur's explication of Heidegger's concept of "within-time-ness": "It is because there is a *time to do* this, a right time and a wrong time, that we can reckon *with* time" (Ricoeur 1981, 169).

15 Cha's theoretical move here approximates Lisa Lowe's contention that "to focus on Asian Americans as 'immigrants' is not to obscure the understanding that almost half of Asian Americans are U.S.-born citizens. . . . It is not to draw attention away from the fact that most Asian Americans are now currently naturalized or native-born citizens and that Asian American struggles for inclusion and equality have significantly advanced American democratic ideals and their extension. It is rather to observe that the life conditions, choices, and expressions of Asian Americans have been significantly determined by the U.S. state through the apparatus of immigration laws and policies, through the enfranchisements denied or extended to immigrant individuals and communities, and through the processes of naturalization and citizenship" (1996).

16 As Yun explains, "Chun's desire to cling to the crumbling and ineffectual 'clay walls' also determines his attitude toward life. . . . Drifting from one place to another in search of work and exhausted from his futile wandering, he dies . . . an exile and homeless even in death" (1992, 88).

17 Yun has usefully summarized Haesu's shifting relationship to nations and nationality as an acceptance of an "alien land": "Human desire and the belief that a piece of land would make one's home a homeland turn out to be another human folly and illusion. Letting go of a corner of the remote land to which she has clung not only emancipates Haesu from crippling nostalgia but also impels her to accept the alien land as 'my country'" (1992, 89).

18 Moreover, U.S. (cultural and economic) imperialism's greater presence in Korea since

Japan's removal in 1945 bears directly on understanding Korean Americans in the U.S. public sphere. As Chungmoo Choi has persuasively argued, "assuming South Korea to be postcolonial eludes the political, social, and the economic realities of its people, which lie behind that celebrated sign 'post' of periodization" (1993, 78). She describes a "colonization of consciousness" characteristic of this era of neoimperialization: "By colonization of consciousness I mean the imposition by the dominant power of its own world view, its own cultural norms and values, on the (colonized) people so that they are compelled to adopt this alien system of thought as their own and therefore disregard or disparage indigenous culture and identity. Colonization of consciousness thus perpetuates cultural dependency and colonial subjectivity" (1993, 79). See also Choi 1993, 80–82; Cumings 1981; Takaki 1989, 53–57; and S. Chan 1991, 111.

"To Tell the Truth and Not Get Trapped":
Why Interethnic Antiracism Matters Now

GEORGE LIPSITZ

Scholars specializing in the study of race and ethnicity have been producing significant new works every year. Ethnic studies programs and departments are proliferating at an accelerated pace. At every level of instruction, lesson plans and curricula reflect an unprecedented attention to issues of identity and power. Yet while Ethnic studies is doing very well, ethnic people are faring very badly.

It has proven easier to desegregate libraries and reading lists than to desegregate college classrooms or corporate boardrooms. Ideas about ethnic people circulate widely, but many of the people themselves remain confined in ghettos, barrios, and prisons. The literature, art, and music created in communities of color frequently command more respect than the communities that created them. The dominant institutions of our society seem willing to make room for some version of "multiculturalism," but they remain unwilling to give members of aggrieved racial groups fair access to jobs and justice, to housing and healthcare, to education and opportunities for asset accumulation.

The contrast between the successes of ethnic studies and the crises facing ethnic communities is especially galling because academic ethnic studies emerged as a field precisely because of movements for social justice during the 1960s and 1970s. The institutional spaces we occupy exist because community activists and organizations won them through sustained collective struggle. Yet despite our best efforts the communities whose aspirations and grievances created us are faring badly.

Some of the disparity between the status of ethnic studies and the status of ethnic communities stems, in part, from the personal failings of individual scholars, from the elitism and ideological conservatism at the core of academic career hierarchies, and from the isolation of many ethnic studies scholars from the activities of actual social movements. The routine practices of training, employment, and evaluation in jobs that rely on "mind work" encourage a competitive individualism rooted in the imperative to surpass others in accomplishment and status. No one working in academia remains unaffected by those imperatives. We are allowed, and sometimes even encouraged, to take positions opposed to dominant power, but we are also pressured to separate ourselves from aggrieved communities and to confine our work within institutions controlled by the powerful and wealthy.

Yet the ethnic studies paradigm itself, as it has emerged historically, is also partly responsible for the problems we face. Competition for scarce resources among aggrieved groups and the success of our enemies in keeping us divided has often led to a one-group-at-a-time story of exclusion and discrimination rather than an analytic, comparative, and relational approach revealing injustice to be the rule rather than the exception in our society. The sense of sameness that holds ethnic groups together, builds organic solidarity, and makes ethnic mobilization logical and desirable can also encourage us to suppress differences and demand uniformity within our own groups. We have inherited much from the past, but some of it serves us poorly under present circumstances.

Malcolm X used to say that racism was like a Cadillac: they make a new model every year. There is always racism, but it is not always the same racism. Just as an owner's manual for a 1970 model would be little help in repairing a 1990s Cadillac, today's racism cannot be combated with theories, methods, and strategies from the 1970s. Global migration, the evisceration of the welfare state, and the increasing importance of new categories of "unfree" laborers unable to bargain about their wages and working conditions as a result of the growth of prison labor, undocumented immigrant labor, and welfare "reform" have led to a new era in racialized exploitation. The racism of postindustrial society proceeds through practices that produce differentiation rather than uniformity, pit outsider groups against each other, and give racialization distinctly different meanings for different groups. This new era demands new methods, theories, and strategies. It calls into question received wisdom and traditional ways of knowing.

Ethnic studies scholarship can play a progressive role in this context by exploring the interconnectedness of oppressions, by complicating the neoconservative and neoliberal paradigms that recognize only a "legitimate" civil rights paradigm advancing the interests of individuals and an "illegitimate" group politics paradigm based on "identity." At the present moment, many different groups suffer from racism, but it is not always the same racism. Gains made through the antiracist efforts of any one group might come at the expense of another aggrieved community. Conservatives ask Blacks to mobilize against bilingual education and social services for immigrants, while inciting Latinos and Asian Americans against affirmative action. Rather than being united into a coherent and unified polity by racial oppression, members of aggrieved racialized groups experience seemingly endless new forms of differentiation.

African Americans, for example, suffer especially harsh levels of housing segregation, unemployment, and political disenfranchisement. Consequently, a seemingly race-neutral reform like "term limits" for elected officials has especially disastrous consequences for their group. African American elected officials represented large population blocks even when voter turnouts were low, and consequently were able to channel resources through the state to communities deprived of access to private capital and intergenerational transfers of wealth because of racial discrimination in housing, employment, home loans, and education. By limiting the seniority that accrued to these officials, by making government weaker and therefore less able to compensate for racial discrimination in the private sector, and by denying African Americans the advantages that came from the block voting imposed on them by housing segregation, term limits seriously dilute the power of Black communities, further augmenting the privileges garnered by the already advantaged.

Latinos, in contrast, have been less successful than Blacks in turning demographic strength into political power. Consequently, they have been less damaged by term limits than Blacks have been. Yet educational inequality and segregation of students in low-income schools exact inordinate burdens on Latinos. Attacks on bilingualism and immigrant rights harm both Latinos and Asian Americans, but not in the same ways. The narrative of national decline most frequently used by neoconservatives to justify their policies has a special anti-Asian edge to it, in part because decline is traced to the U.S. defeat in Vietnam, but also because of the rise of economic competition from Japan and new industrializing countries in Asia, and the perceived threat to white privilege posed by immigrant Asian successes. The hate crimes that emanate from what Yen Le Espiritu (1997, 90) calls "the new yellow peril-ism" are racist and anti-immigrant in general, but have a specific meaning when carried out against Asian Americans because of the past and present roles played by Asia and Asians in the imagination of the United States. At the same time, the ways in which this narrative of national decline is often presented as a threat to white masculinity gives anti-Asian hate crimes an affinity to attacks on gays and lesbians and on women in a way that is not exactly parallel to hate crimes against other racialized or immigrant groups.

The generation of new low-wage labor jobs—and in some cases *no-wage* labor jobs—affects all communities of color, but especially women immigrants from Asia, Mexico, Central America, and South America. Unemployment has hit African Americans harder than it has hit Latinos or Asians. Welfare reform has been couched in directly racist and sexist terms through the use of images about excessive procreation among Black women and Latinas, even though these groups provide two of the largest sectors of hard working laborers while the majority of people receiving welfare are white. Discourses about crime focus attention on Black and Latino males who are incarcerated in numbers far greater than their percentage of the general and the criminal population, but this discourse consequently hides the rapidly increasing numbers of minority women incarcerated in penal institutions. Environmental racism hurts all aggrieved racialized populations, but Native Americans live in places that make them more susceptible to cancer than other racial groups. Latinos are more likely to breathe polluted air than Asian Americans are. Asian American and Pacific Islander babies in some cities are more likely to be born underweight and suffer malnutrition than babies from other groups are, while lead poisoning affects Black children more than children from any other group (Bullard 1993; Westra and Wenz 1995; Lipsitz 1998).

Yet precisely because no unified identity encompasses anyone's social world, interethnic antiracist activism offers an opportunity for new struggles for social justice as mobile, fluid, and flexible as the new forms of oppression, hierarchy, and exploitation generated by the current global balance of power. The panethnic concept of "Asian American" identity offers the quintessential model for interethnic antiracism in both activism and scholarship. Originating in a self-conscious strategy for maximizing resources in a specific historical moment, members of different Asian national groups worked together during the 1960s to build a movement emphasizing common concerns, even though they understood fully that many things also divided them. Created by people from different national backgrounds who spoke different languages, practiced different religions, and occupied very different places in the U.S. social order, the Asian American movement flaunted its constructedness in order to emphasize a common political project. The "identity" of being Asian American never presumed experiences that were identical. Yet for groups whose past rivalries had produced pernicious forms of disidentification with one another, coalescence on the basis of a common experience of racialization by the U.S. nation-state and economy served progressive political ends.

On account of this history, Asian American studies remains grounded in a politicized notion of identity. This grounding has enabled the field to raise unique questions about the nature of general concepts like citizenship and racial formation, rendering race less a matter of personal injury or personal affirmation than a shared social reality and structural social dynamic. Embodied individual experience counts for less in this constellation than does collective epistemological position. In a characteristically complex and insightful discussion, Lisa Lowe (1998) explains that Asian American studies emerges from specific historical realities and draws its determinate force from continuing engagement with them—from the recuperation of otherwise occluded histories of U.S. nationalism, gendered social stratification, labor exploitation, and racialized exclusion. The narratives and cultural practices of Asian immigrants and their descendants, according to Lowe, include displaced memories that become "refigured as alternative modes in which immigrants are the survivors of empire, its witnesses, the inhabitants of its borders" (1998, 30).

Asian American studies scholars do not simply "add on" previously ignored evidence about Asian Americans, but rather generate new ways of knowing by concentrating on objects of study that confound conventional modes of inquiry. Consequently, Asian American studies is not limited to the study of Asian Americans, but rather uses the specific historical experiences of Asian Americans to provoke comparative studies of the role of national culture in forming citizens and gendered subjects, in linking patriotism to patriarchy, and in disciplining and precluding alternative sexual and social identities. Rather than presuming a primordial homogenous, atomized, and discrete Asian American identity, Asian American studies encourages exploration of all the differences that define any group—ethnic differences within specific groups of national origin, differences caused by social identities and sexuality, by gender and generation, by class and religious conviction, by point of origin and political orientation (Espiritu 1996; Wei 1993; E. Kim 1982).

Asian American Studies also challenges scholarly and civic practices that define social identities within the confines of single nation-states. The historically specific experiences of people of Asian origin in the United States cannot be understood in isolation from the global history of empire building, war, transnational commerce, and migration that brought Asian America into existence in the first place (Okihiro 1994). Contemporary Asian American identities are part of a broader Asian diaspora that includes Asians in Africa, South America, Europe, Australia, the Caribbean, and Asia, as well as North America. Asian American culture reveals these links in clear and irrefutable forms, from the ruminations by composer Jon Jang on political repression in China to the blend of Filipino "folk" instruments with western avant-garde forms in the compositions of Eleanor Academia, from the country and western singer Neal McCoy who calls himself a "Texapino" to the hip-hop group the Boo-Yaa T.R.I.B.E., made up of Samoans from Carson, California, some of whom lived briefly with cousins in Japan before enjoying commercial success playing music based in African American aesthetic forms for largely Chicano audiences.

The model of interethnic antiracism pioneered with the Asian American movement is emerging as a tactical necessity for many people at the present time. Interethnic alliances do not erase purely national or racial identities, nor do they permanently transcend them. There is always room for more than one tactical stance in struggles for social justice, and ethnic nationalism especially will always be legitimate and meaningful under some circumstances. The current historical moment is generating new forms of struggle, forms eloquently described by Lisa Lowe as "alternative forms of practice that integrate yet move beyond those of cultural nationalism" (1997, 369).

There are many obvious reasons for interethnic antiracist activism, but the obvious reasons may not be the most important ones. Certainly alliances of this type produce strength in numbers. We are more powerful with allies than we would be alone. These alliances demonstrate solidarity in the present in order to reap its benefits in the future; if we are there for other people's struggles today, there is a greater likelihood that they will be there for us tomorrow. This solidarity also enables us to avoid the dangers of disidentification and disunity. By standing up for someone else we establish ourselves as people with empathy for the suffering of others. Common experiences in struggle also make it harder to play off aggrieved groups against one another. These experiences are a hedge against what John Okada (1957) described as "persecution in the drawl of the persecuted"—the tendency to defend oneself from unfair treatment by directing that unfairness onto someone else.

Yet some of the less obvious advantages of interethnic antiracism may be even more important to its logic at the present historical moment. Coordinated attacks against racist privilege enable individual racialized groups to move beyond defensiveness about their own specific identities and to make visible the new forms of racial formation being created every day in the present, not just those directly attributable to the history of slavery, conquest, genocide, immigrant exploitation, and class oppression. Interethnic antiracism shifts the focus away from a diagnosis of "minority" disadvantages to an analysis of "majority" advantages. Unlike most other kinds of antiracist work, it aims at peace and justice rather than at peace and quiet; attacking racism in order to face its consequences responsibly rather than merely trying to be free of the burdens that its long history imposes upon us. By proposing reallocation of resources and structural changes in institutions, it reveals racism to be about interests as well as attitudes, about finances rather than just feelings. By acknowledging the differentiated experiences of aggrieved racialized populations, it avoids the simplistic binary opposition that neoconservatives offer in response to racism — stupefied and uncomprehending "color blindness" versus primordial attachment to kin and kind.

Ultimately, the most important reason for interethnic antiracism is its epistemological value in enabling us to understand how power actually works in the world. Years ago, Toni Cade Bambara wrote a wonderful essay about the responsibility and privilege that cultural work entails because it requires us to see the world as others see it — to see what the factory worker sees, what the prisoner sees, what the welfare children see, what the scholar sees, what the ruling class myth-makers see. She argued our highest responsibility is "to tell the truth and not get trapped" (quoted in Deck 1993, 80). Bambara understood that we will misread our situatedness in the world unless we are able to view power from more than one perspective, unless we are able to look through multiple, overlapping, and even conflicting standpoints on social relations. In order to challenge the differentiated deployment of power in the contemporary world, we need to create places where our differences and our common interests remain in plain sight. We need places like those described by Patrick Chamoiseau in his epic novel about antiracist struggle in Martinique, "those places in which no one could foresee our ability to unravel their History into our thousand stories" (1998, 54).

In a recent interview, Angela Davis (1997) identified the epistemological importance of political activism that incorporates perspectives from different identities and experiences. She shows how the deep structural problems currently confronting African Americans become distorted by simplistic analyses based on single identities. To view the current crisis in the Black community as a crisis about Black manhood, for example, in some ways acknowledges the harm done to Black male employment and Black male wages by deindustrialization. Yet describing the crisis in terms of the declining value of Black manhood mistakes consequence for cause and leads to "remedies" that privilege the private sphere like rites of passage ceremonies, special schools for Black males, and condemnation of Black women for "succeeding" in ways that diminish the relative power of Black males. These responses all hide the broader structural causes of the crisis facing Black men and the Black community. They encourage Black men to seek more power *within* their community but not outside it, to seek redress from other aggrieved people rather than from those whose power has enabled them to engineer and profit from the decline in Black male wages. This approach hides the ways in which Black women and children have also been devastated by the effects of deindustrialization, and it renders invisible Black gays and lesbians.

Davis shows how a positive politics might still emerge from the specific experiences of Black men. They could, she argues, support the reproductive rights of women in their communities, could help Black lesbians adopt children, and could lead a struggle against violence against women. Yet these actions would require an intersectional and multiply positioned perspective on identity and social power. Similarly, Davis urges us to think of race and class as intersectional realities rather than competing categories. She praises the activist centers in Chinatown run by Asian Immigrant Women Advocates and other groups that combine lessons in literacy with legal advice about domestic violence, address issues about hours, wages, and working conditions, but refuse to detach the workers' lives as workers from their other identities as women, as racialized subjects, and as family members. In addition, these cross-class coalitions linking the concerns of immigrants with the struggles of ethnic women born in the United States also lead to interethnic antiracism since issues like low-wage women's labor and domestic violence cut across racial lines.

Davis's own role in mobilizing support among diverse populations for a garment worker-instigated boycott against a prominent garment maker exemplifies the positive possibilities of this kind of coalition work. Women of color often play prominent roles in these movements because their situatedness in relation to power has always required this kind of supple and creative thinking. As Lisa Lowe argues, "The Asian American woman and the racialized woman are materially in excess of the subject 'woman' posited by feminist discourse, or the 'proletariat' described by Marxism, or the 'racial' or ethnic subject projected by civil rights and ethno-racial movements" (1997, 362).

Solidarities based on identity are limited; solidarities based on identities are unlimited. People who have to see themselves as exactly the same in order to wage a common struggle will be ill-positioned for the ferocity of impending struggles, but those capable of connecting their own cause to the causes of others by seeing families of resemblance capable of generating unity will be much better positioned to make the kinds of unlikely alliances and unexpected coalitions that the differentiated struggles of the future will require. Battles to better the conditions of low-wage workers in the current context automatically entail connections with movements for immigrant rights, challenges to sexism, and historical traditions of anti-imperialism. Fights for better education for aggrieved populations quickly lead to questions about housing segregation and intergenerational transfers of wealth and opportunity through closed racial networks. Increasing incarceration of large numbers of minority youth raises questions about how property rights and legal rights have been increasingly racialized, just as concerns about the health and safety of children reveal the racialized and gendered encoding of such seemingly neutral social concepts as "the family." Mobilization by women against common grievances about sexuality and gender quickly bring into view the ways in which race inflects gender, but antiracist struggles waged by women also increasingly expose the sexualized and gendered qualities at the root of white supremacy.

Interethnic antiracist struggles for social justice bring together diverse populations in a way that makes visible previously hidden aspects of social relations. Within the structure of business unionism that prevails in the United States, it is hard for workers to win gains that do not hurt other workers. The concessions made to workers within individual labor-management negotiations are often passed on to consumers in the form of higher prices or, at the very least, still force unorganized workers to experience a new disadvantage in relation to workers who are organized. Davis notes that the demand for a shorter workday offers an alternative to this process, that it presents one demand that helps *all* workers by relieving the toil of some and opening up new jobs to unemployed and undocumented workers. By coming to this conclusion about the kind of demand capable of forging a unified struggle out of diverse identities, Davis reconnects us with the experiences of the past and shows that the "new social movements" are very much like the old. The original struggle for the "eight-hour day" in the late nineteenth century came about because of conditions very much like our own—a differentiated and divided workforce looking for common ground (Barrett and Roediger 1997).

Identifications within racial groups remain powerful for very understandable reasons. Shared experiences with discrimination and negative ascription by outsiders can build especially close bonds. A common language, religion, culture, or cuisine can make solidarity seem natural and inevitable. Yet this organic solidarity can come at a high price. It can make us expect to find more uniformity in our own groups than actually exists. It can encourage us to substitute ethno-sympathy and ethno-subjectivity for social analysis, and often leads to the politics described by Los Angeles activist Charlotta Bass as settling for "dark faces in high places" instead of struggling for substantive reallocations of social resources and social power.

All politics is about identity, but not all politics is identity politics. Political mobilization takes place when people share a common image of themselves as members of an identifiable group. Mutual identification (as citizens, workers, or subjects of any sort) takes place strategically, out of a perception that it makes sense for the moment to emphasize the things that build unity and to ignore temporarily the things that undermine it. In the year before his murder, Malcolm X used to argue that Black nationalism could serve as a unifying identity among African Americans with different religions, class positions, and political views because, in the final analysis, Black people in America "caught hell" because they were Black and for no other reason. Identity can be a unifying factor, but only if nonidentical people with diverse experiences agree politically that their common exclusion from power and opportunity on the basis of race matters more than their differences. For Malcolm X, at that stage in his life, a common "identity" could not guarantee political agreement, but a common political analysis could help produce a unified and progressive definition of identity. Black nationalism of the 1960s, like the American Indian Movement and the Chicano Movement, depended on winning adherents to a newly politicized definition of identity, not by presuming that common histories or physical features automatically guaranteed unity and solidarity.

Activists, artists, and scholars within ethnic studies today have created politicized notions of ethnic identity within and across ethnic lines. They have fashioned ways to be ethnic, but something more as well. For example, Glenn Omatsu details how scholarly research and community-based activism mutually reinforce one another within the Asian American activist movement. Community groups organizing among low-wage immigrant workers remain community-based in their mobilizations against racism, sexism, and class oppression, but they draw on the intellectual and material resources of Asian American studies programs, on theories of popular literacy and democratic pedagogy advanced by Paulo Freire and his followers, and on unexpected alliances and affiliations across class, race, and gender lines (Omatsu 1994). Important research by Laura Pulido (1996), Robert Bullard (1995), and Clarice Gaylord and Elizabeth Bell (1995) reveals how campaigns against environmental racism have promoted alliances among representatives of aggrieved communities of color, academic experts, and organized social movement groups.

Connections between academics and artists also play a vital role in the possible politics of the present moment. In his prophetic work, *The Wretched of the Earth,* Frantz Fanon described how artistic expressions sometimes anticipate political upheavals:

> Well before the political fighting phase of the national movement, an attentive spectator can thus feel and see the manifestations of a new vigor and feel the approaching conflict. He will note unusual forms

of expression and themes which are fresh and imbued with a power which is no longer that of invocation but rather of the assembling of the people, a summoning together for a precise purpose. Everything works together to awaken the native's sensibility of defeat and to make unreal and unacceptable the contemplative attitude or the acceptance of defeat. (1968, 243)

In our time, evidence of this cultural creativity exists in abundance. Community-based cultural production in Los Angeles exemplifies the potential of combining politics and culture. On one weekend in 1995, for example, college students from the California State University at Northridge chapter of the Moviemiento Estudiantil Chicano/a de Aztlan staged a "happening" to raise money to fund a suit against the University of California by a prominent Chicano professor. The evening's entertainment featured Chicano rap artists, comedians, musicians, and the Teatro Por La Gente (theatre for the people/community) performing what they described as "social/political/cultural Edu-drama-dies." On the same weekend, Chicano poets, visual artists, and singers joined with Japanese taiko drummers and The Watts Prophets, an African American spoken word/hip-hop ensemble, to stage a benefit at a warehouse loft owned by Chicano heavy metal musician Zach de la Rocha of the musical group Rage Against the Machine to raise money for the Los Angeles chapter of the National Commission for Democracy in Mexico, the support arm of the EZLN rebels fighting the Mexican government in Chiapas. Writing for the hip-hop magazine *Urb,* journalist Gerry Meraz described the weekend's events as "a new culture with roots in the old and appreciation for the art of people who need to be heard whether anyone likes it or not" (1995, 69). The broader culture of performance art, graffiti writing, and hip-hop from which these events emerged has been carefully catalogued, assessed, and encouraged in exemplary work by innovative scholars as well, especially C. Ondine Chavoya (1996), Michelle Habell-Pallan (1995), and Tricia Rose (1994).

Our time does not lack for activists or activism. Three decades of neoconservative and neoliberal assaults on the victories of the egalitarian movements of the past insure that the communities we come from and the institutions we inhabit will remain in crisis for the foreseeable future. Efforts to create new sources of private profit within the educational system through privatization, charter schools, vouchers, patent sharing, technology-based instruction, and schemes to turn universities into research and development arms of private corporations threaten the institutional future of education at all levels. It may be that, rather than serving as crucibles for a more democratic future, educational institutions will be phased out as useless anachronisms in a society devoted to making maximum possible profits out of all social endeavors. Yet intellectual and artistic work will remain important even if they largely take place outside of existing institutions, even if it is the work of social movements to recreate them in new sites. Similarly, social movements will remain under assault in a society that allocates resources and opportunities along group lines yet insists on structuring legal, educational, and political debates along individualistic lines — as if sexism, racism, class subordination, and other collective axes of power suppress us individually rather than collectively.

Many ethnic studies teachers, researchers, writers, and artists address political issues, but it is often difficult for contemporary intellectuals and artists to imagine how we could actually connect with social movements and play progressive roles in struggles for social change. One reason for this stems from the history of social movements during the past thirty years. As Toni Cade Bambara noted years ago, "it is difficult to maintain the faith and keep working toward the new time if you've had no *experience* of it, not seen ordinary people actually transform selves and societies" (1981, 160). For nearly three decades, the decisive social movements in the United States have come from the right, from mobilizations organized, funded, and guided by wealthy foundations and the public relations experts masquerading as scholars in their employ. A key goal of these movements has been to foreground private interests and obscure public concerns, encouraging people to think of themselves primarily as taxpayers and homeowners rather than as citizens or workers. This can be accomplished only by depicting the private property of white men as just rewards secured in fair competition in an open market, while dismissing demands for redistributive justice by aggrieved groups as the whining of special interests (see Plotkin and Scheurman 1994).

One of the biggest threats to this right wing view of the world is popular and scholarly memory of the democratic movements for change that shook society from the 1930s through the 1970s. Neoconservatives need to describe the antiracist social movements of the 1960s as simple struggles for desegregation and individual inclusion, erasing the broader critique of hierarchy and exploitation at the heart of mass mobilization in that era (Sniderman and Piazza 1993; Lipsitz 1998, 170–77). This is one place where the traditions of ethnic studies serve us well, because our connection to the social movements of the 1960s positions us uniquely to make distinctions between the *rhetorical* 1960s, as they appear in contemporary discourse, and the *historical* 1960s, as they actually unfolded within collective struggle.

In fact, the antiracist mobilizations of the 1960s did not view racism as an aberrant phenomenon in an otherwise just society, but rather identified racism as one of the key mechanisms for teaching, naturalizing, institutionalizing, and legitimating hierarchy, inequality, and exploitation. These "ethnic" movements realized that racism did not simply injure people of color, but that it provided the deep structure and legitimating logic for all forms of social, political, and economic exclusion. The movement had its share of integrationists, to be sure, but it also nurtured and sustained broad social critiques—not just of racist hierarchies, but of all hierarchies, not just of racist dehumanization, but of the broader dehumanization integral to a society where the lives of humans consistently count for less than the concerns of capital.

The only alternative to the civil rights paradigm within neoconservative ideology is "identity politics," which they caricature as a politics of entitlement based on skin color or gender. While sometimes giving grudging (although retrospective) recognition to the civil rights politics of the past as a once necessary response to Jim Crow segregation, the ideologues of contemporary racism dismiss "identity politics" as a simple expression of "tribalism," as a claim for special privileges in the present based upon past victimization that no longer exists (Schlesinger 1991). This caricature has little to do with the actual politics of racial nationalism, a politics mobilized during the 1960s not on unproblematic notions of "identity," but precisely the opposite—on efforts to give precise political meanings to being "Black," "Chicano," and "Asian American." These movements most often did not draw their politics from identities, but rather attempted to fashion new identities through politics. Of course, just as antiracist mobilizations included simple integrationists as well as complex social critics, racial nationalism sometimes included individuals rooted in identity politics. Yet the posters, publications, and pronouncements of nationalist groups from the past are also replete with internationalism, anti-imperialism and inter-ethnic antiracist alliances and affiliations.

No simple formula will suffice to conquer the contradictions we face. In political strategy as in scholarship no single solution will fit all situations. Still, we can draw creatively on the very contradictions we face to find solutions for ourselves and for others. Part of the racial problem today is a knowledge problem. The educational institutions in which we work are not irrelevant to the racialization of opportunities and life chances in our society today. In fact, they are important sites for the generation and legitimation of forms of knowledge that support and strengthen the racial status quo. Ethnic studies scholars are in an advantageous position to subject dominant regimes of knowledge to critical scrutiny, to identify and nurture activist sites where new knowledges are being created, and to play an active role in transforming social relations by helping to build the forms of knowledge and action capable of creating quite different kinds of social relations. The origins of ethnic studies scholarship in social movements serves to remind us that the academy and the community can help each other, that social movements can win institutional spaces in colleges and universities, but also that educational institutions can provide valuable resources to movements for democratic social change.

Social movements are proscribed in this culture precisely because they are so powerful, because we know more together than we know apart, because we are stronger collectively than we can ever hope to be as individuals. It is a burden—but also an honor and a responsibility to attach ourselves to the interethnic antiracist movements emerging in response to the increasing racialization of social services, opportunities, and life chances in the United States. Yet we can only do so if we devise new ways of knowing based on seeing what others see, on living out the admonition of Toni Cade Bambara "to tell the truth and not get trapped."

References

Abel, Richard L. 1995. *The Law and Society Reader.* New York and London: New York University Press.

Abelman, Nancy and John Lie. 1995. *Blue Dreams: Korean Americans and the Los Angeles Riots.* Cambridge: Harvard University Press.

Aguilar-San Juan, Karin, ed. 1994. *The State of Asian America: Activism and Resistance in the 1990s.* Boston: South End Press.

Aman, Alfred C. Jr. 1993. "Symposium: The Globalization of Law, Politics, and Markets: Implications for Domestic Law Reform. Indiana Journal of Global Studies: An Introduction." *Indiana Journal of Global Studies* 1 (fall): 1–8.

Amin, Shahid. 1995. *Event, Metaphor, Memory: Chauri Chaura, 1922–1992.* Berkeley: University of California Press.

———. 1989. *Eurocentrism.* New York: Monthly Review Press.

Anderson, Benedict. 1994. "Exodus." *Critical Inquiry* 20 (winter): 314–27.

———. 1972. *Java in a Time of Revolution: Occupation and Resistance, 1944–1946.* Ithaca: Cornell University Press.

Anzaldua, Gloria. 1987. *Borderlands/La Frontera: The New Mestiza.* San Francisco: Aunt Lute Books.

Aoki, Keith. 1996. "The Scholarship of Reconstruction and the Politics of Backlash." *Iowa Law Review* 81 (July): 1467–88.

Appadurai, Arjun. 1998. "Dead Certainty: Ethnic Violence in the Era of Globalization." *Development and Change* 29: 905–25.

———. 1996a. "Diversity and Disciplinarity as Cultural Artifacts." In *Disciplinarity and Dissent in Cultural Studies,* eds. Cary Nelson and Dilip Gaonkar. New York: Routledge. 23–36.

———. 1996b. *Modernity at Large: Cultural Dimensions of Globalization.* Minneapolis: University of Minnesota Press.

———. 1993. "Patriotism and Its Futures." *Public Culture* 5(3): 411–29.

———. 1991. "Global Ethnoscapes: Notes and Queries for a Transnational Anthropology." In *Recapturing Anthropology.* Ed. R. Fox. Santa Fe, NM: School of American Research Press.

———. 1990. "Disjuncture and Difference in the Global Cultural Economy." *Public Culture* 2 (2): 1–24.

———. 1988. "Putting Hierarchy in Its Place." *Cultural Anthropology* 3 (February): 37–50.

Appelbaum, Richard. 1996. "Multiculturalism and Flexibility. Some New Directions in Global Capitalism." In *Mapping Multiculturalism,* eds. Avery Gordon and Christopher Newfield. Minneapolis: University of Minnesota Press.

Armstrong, Nancy and Leonard Tennenhouse. 1989. "Introduction: Representing Violence, or 'How the West Was Won.'" In *The Violence of Representation: Literature and the History of Violence,* eds. Nancy Armstrong and Leonard Tennenhouse. London: Routledge.

Associated Press. 1993. "Changing the Face of America." *Chicago Tribune* (29 September), section 1, 1.

Association for Asian Studies. 1997. 1997 Annual Meeting Report. *Asian Studies Newsletter* 42 (spring): 39.

Association of American Colleges. 1964. *Non-Western Studies in the Liberal Arts College: A Report of the Commission on International Understanding.* Washington, D.C.: Association of American Colleges.

Balandier, G. 1996. "The Colonial Situation: A Theoretical Approach (1951)," trans. Robert A. Wagoner. In *Social Change: The Colonial Situation,* Immanuel Wallerstein. New York: John Wiley & Sons, Inc.: 34–61.

Balaoing, Michael John. 1994. "The Challenge of Asian Pacific American Diversity and Unity: A Study of Individual, Ethnic Bar Associations Within the Asian Pacific American Community of Los Angeles." *Asian Pacific American Law Journal* 2 (fall): 1–37.

Balibar, Etienne. 1990. "Paradoxes of Universality." In *Anatomy of Racism,* ed. David Theo Goldberg. Minneapolis: University of Minnesota Press: 41–49.

Balibar, Etiene and Immanuel Wallerstein. 1992. *Race, Nation, Class: Ambiguous Identities.* London & New York: Verso.

Bambara, Toni Cade. 1981. "What It Is I Think I'm Doing Anyhow." In *The Writer on Her Work.* Ed. Janet Sternberg. New York: W. W. Norton.

Barlow, Tani. 1995. "Introduction." *positions: east asia cultures critique* 3(2): v–vii.

———. 1991. "Theorizing Woman: *Funu, Guojia, Jiating* [Chinese women, Chinese state, Chinese family]," *Genders* (spring): 132–60.

Barrett, James R. and David Roediger. 1997. "Inbetween Peoples: Race, Nationality, and the 'New Immigrant' Working Class." *Journal of American Ethnic History* 16 (spring): 3–44.

Basch, Linda G., Nina Glick-Schiller, and Cristina Szanton-Blanc. 1994. *Nations Unbound: Transnational Projects, Postcolonial Predicaments, and Deterritorialized Nation-States.* New York: Gordon & Breach.

Bauman, Richard. 1977. *Verbal Art as Performance.* Rowley, MA: Newbury House Publications.

Bauman, R. and C. L. Briggs. 1990. "Poetics and Performance as Critical Perspectives on Language and Social Life." *Annual Review of Anthropology* 19: 59–88.

Behar, Ruth and Deborah A. Gordon, eds. 1995. *Women Writing Culture.* Berkeley: University of California Press.

Bei, Dao. 1990 [1988]. *The August Sleepwalker.* Trans. by Bonnie S. McDougall. London: Anvil Press.

Bennett, Wendell C. 1951. *Area Studies in American Universities.* New York: Social Science Research Council.

Berger, Mark T. 1996. "Yellow Mythologies: The East Asian Miracle and Post-Cold War Capitalism," *positions: east asia cultures critique* 4(1): 90–126.

Berlant, Lauren. 1991. *The Anatomy of National Fantasy.* Chicago: University of Chicago Press.

Bernstein, Richard. 1990. "The New Tribalism." *New York Times* (2 September).

Berson, Misha, ed. 1990. *In Between Worlds: Contemporary Asian American Plays.* New York: Theatre Communications Group.

Bhabha, Homi K. 1994. *The Location of Culture.* London and New York: Routledge.

———. 1992. "Postcolonial Authority and Postmodern Guilt." In *Cultural Studies,* eds. Lawrence Grossberg, Cary Nelson, and Paula Treichler. New York and London: Routledge. 56–66.

Bonus, Rick. In "Locating Filipino-American Identities: Ethnicity and the Politics of Space in Southern California." Ph.D. diss. Department of Communications, University of California, San Diego.

Bowles, Samuel and Herbert Gintis. 1976. *Schooling in Capitalist America.* New York: Harper.

Boym, Svetlana. 1994. *Common Places: Mythologies of Everyday Life in Russia.* Cambridge, MA: Harvard University Press.

Branegan, Jay. 1991. "Fighter for a Paper Door." *Time.* (27 May): 27.

Brecher, Jeremy and Tim Costello. 1994. *Global Village: Economic Reconstruction From the Bottom Up or Global Pillage.* Boston: South End Press.

Breckenridge, Carol. Forthcoming. "The Global Modern." *Public Culture.*

———, ed. 1995. *Consuming Modernity: Public Culture in a South Asian World.* Minneapolis: University of Minnesota Press.

Bullard, Robert. 1995. "Decision Making." In *Faces of Environmental Racism: Confronting Issues of Global Justice.* eds. Laura Westra and Peter Wenz. Lanham, MD: Rowman and Littlefield. 3–28.

Bullard, Robert, ed. 1993. *Confronting Environmental Racism: Voices From the Grassroots.* Boston: South End Press.

Bunch, Charlotte and Niamh Reilly. 1994. *Demanding Accountability: The Global Campaign and Vienna Tribunal for Women's Human Rights.* New York: Center for Women's Global Leadership and UNIFEM.

Butler, Judith. 1993. *Bodies that Matter: On the Discursive Limits of "Sex."* New York: Routledge.

———. 1990. *Gender Trouble.* New York: Routledge.

Cacas, Samuel P. 1992. "Relative at Best: Asian American 'Success' and Its Social Impact on Filipino Americans." *Journal of Filipino American Historical Society* 1(2): 35–40.

Cain, Maureen and Christine B. Harrington, eds. 1994. *Lawyers in a Postmodern World: Translation and Transgression.* New York: New York University Press.

Campomanes, Oscar V. 1995. "The New Empire's Forgetful and Forgotten Citizens: Unrepresentability and Unassimilability in Filipino-American Postcolonialities." *Critical Mass* 47 (September): 145–200.

———. 1992. "Filipinos in the United States and Their Literature of Exile." In *Reading the Literatures of Asian America.* eds. Shirley Geok-lin Lim and Amy Ling. Philadelphia: Temple University Press. 49–78.

Canclini, Nestor Garcia. 1995. *Hybrid Cultures.* Minneapolis: University of Minnesota Press.

Cannell, Fenella. 1991. "The Power of Appearances: Beauty, Mimicry and Transformation in Bicol." In *Discrepant Histories: Translocal Essays on Filipino Cultures.* ed. Vicente Rafael. Philadelphia: Temple University Press.

Caputo, John D. 1993. *Demythologizing Heidegger.* Bloomington: Indiana University Press.

Caplan, Arthur L. 1992. *If I Were a Rich Man, Could I Buy a Pancreas? And Other Essays on the Ethics of Health Care.* Bloomington: Indiana University Press.

Case, Sue-Ellen, ed. 1994. *Performing Feminisms: Feminist Critical Theory and Theatre.* Baltimore: Johns Hopkins University Press.

Case, Sue-Ellen, Philip Brett, and Susan L. Foster, eds. *Cruising the Performative: Interventions into the Representations of Ethnicity, Nation and Sexuality.* Bloomington: Indiana University Press.

Cesaire, Aime. [1950] 1972. *Discourse on Colonialism.* New York: Monthly Review Press.

Cha, Theresa Hak Kyung. [1982] 1995. *Dictée.* New York: Tanam Press.

Chakrabarty, Dipesh. 1998. "Modernity and Ethnicity in India." In *Multicultural States* ed. David Bennett. London: Routledge.

———. 1996. "Subaltern Studies and Its Attachment to the Nation-Space." Presented at "Disciplining Asia" symposium, University of Washington, Seattle (May 1–4).

Chakravarty, Anita. 1995. "Writing History." *Economic and Political Weekly* (23 December): 3320.

Chamoiseau, Patrick. 1998. *Texaco.* New York: Vintage International.

Chan, Jeffrey Paul, Frank Chin, Lawson Fusao Inada, and Shawn Wong, eds. [1974] 1991. *Aiiieeeee! An Anthology of Asian American Writers.* New York: Penguin Books.

Chan, Sucheng. 1991. *Asian Americans: An Interpretive History.* Boston: Twayne.

Chang, Robert. 1993. "Toward an Asian American Legal Scholarship: Critical Race Theory, Post-structuralism, and Narrative Space." *California Law Review* (October): 1241.

Chang, Tisa. 1995. "Artistic Vision." *Pan Asian Repertory Theatre: 1994–1995, 18th Season Program.*

Chatterjee, Partha. 1993. *The Nation and Its Fragments: Colonial and Postcolonial Histories.* Princeton: Princeton University Press.

———. 1986. *Nationalist Thought and the Colonial World: A Derivative Discourse.* London: Zed Books.

Chavoya, C. Ondine. 1996. "Collaborative Public Art and Multimedia Installation: David Avalos, Louis Hock, and Elizabeth Sisco's 'Welcome to America's Finest Tourist Plantation.'" In *The Ethnic Eye: Latino Media Arts.* Eds. Chon Norriega and Ana M. Lopez. Minneapolis: University of Minnesota Press. 208–27.

Chen, Jim. 1994. "Unloving." *Iowa Law Review* 80: 145–74.

Chen, Kuan-Hsing. Forthcoming. "Watch out for the Civilizationalist Interpellation: Huntington and Nandy," in Lee You-cheng, ed. *History and Theory of Cultural Studies.* Taipei: Academia Sinica.

———. 2000. "The Imperialist Eye: The Cultural Imaginary of a Subempire and a Nation-State." *positions: east asia cultures critique* 8(1): 9–76.

———. 1997. "The Decolonization Effects: The Internationalization of Cultural Studies." *Journal of Communication Inquiry* 21(2): 79–98.

———. 1992. "Voices from the Outside: Toward a New Internationalist Localism." *Cultural Studies* 6(3): 167–83, 192–96, 238–48.

Chen, Tina. 1998. "Sights Unseen: Acts of Impersonation in Contemporary Asian American Representation." Ph.D. diss., University of California, Berkeley.

Cheng, Nien. 1988. *Life and Death in Shanghai.* London: Penguin.

Cheng, Weng-Liang. 1996. "Anti-Colonial City during the Japanese Occupation Period: A Cultural History." Master's thesis. Graduate Institute of Building and Planning, National Taiwan University, Taiwan.

Cheung, King-Kok and Stan Yogi. 1988. *Asian American Literature: An Annotated Bibliography.* New York: Modern Language Association.

Chew, Pat K. 1996. "Asian Americans in the Legal Academy: An Empirical and Narrative Profile." *Asian Law Journal* 3 (May): 7–38.

Chin, Daryl. 1991. "Interculturalism, Postmodernism, Pluralism." In *Interculturalism and Performance.* Eds. Bonnie Marranca and Gautam Dasgupta. New York: PAJ Publications. 83–95.

Chin, Frank. 1973. "Roland Winters Interview." *Amerasia Journal* 2: 1–19.

Chin, Gabriel, Sumi Cho, Jerry Kang, and Frank Wu. 1996. *Beyond Self-Interest: Asian Pacific Americans Toward a Community of Justice, a Policy Analysis of Affirmative Action.* Affiliation of LEAP Asian Pacific American Public Policy Institute and UCLA Asian American Studies Center.

Chiu, Jeannie. 1999. "Uncanny Doubles: Nationalism and Repression in Asian American Literature and African American Literature." Ph.D. diss., University of California, Berkeley.

Chiu, Monica. 1996. "Illness and Self-Representation in Asian American Literature." Ph.D. diss., Emory University.

Cho, Hae-Joang. 1995. "Constructing and Deconstructing 'Koreanness' in the 1990s South Korea." Photocopy.

Choi, Chungmoo. 1993. "The Discourse of Decolonization and Popular Memory: South Korea." *positions: east asia cultures critique* 1 (spring): 77–102.

Chon, Margaret. 1995. "On the Need for Asian American Narratives in Law: Ethnic Specimens, Native Informants, Storytelling and Silences." *UCLA Asian Pacific American Law Journal* 3. 4–32.

Chou, Wei-ling. 1996. "An Open Letter to the Social Elites in Taiwan." (March 6).

Chow, Rey. 1995a. "The Dream of a Butterfly." In *Human, All Too Human.* Ed. Diana Fuss. New York: Routledge. 61–92.

——. 1995b. *Primitive Passions: Visuality, Sexuality, Ethnography, and Contemporary Chinese Cinema.* New York: Columbia University Press.

——. 1993. "The Politics and Pedagogy of Asian Literatures in American Universities." In *Writing Diaspora: Tactics of Intervention in Contemporary Cultural Studies.* Bloomington: Indiana University Press. 120–43.

——. 1991. "Violence in the Other Country: China as Crisis, Spectacle, and Woman." In *Third World Women and the Politics of Feminism.* Eds. Chandra Talpade Mohanty, Lourdes Torres, and Ann Russo. Bloomington: Indiana University Press. 81–100.

Chua, Beng Huat. Forthcoming. "Culture, Multiracialism and National Identity in Singapore." Ed. Kuan-Hsing Chen. *New Trajectories of Cultural Studies: Nation/State and Movements of Decolonization in the Asia-Pacific.* New York and London: Routledge.

Chuh, Kandice. Forthcoming. *Imagine Otherwise: Envisioning America through Asian Americanist Critique.* Durham, NC: Duke University Press.

——. 1996. "Transnationalism and Its Pasts." *Public Culture* 9(1): 93–112.

Chung, Tommy and Russell Valparaiso. 1973. "Interview by Lowell Chun-Hoon." *Amerasia Journal* 2: 130–48.

Clifford, James. 1991. "Traveling Cultures." In *Cultural Studies,* eds. Lawrence Grossberg, Cary Nelson, and Paula Treichler. New York and London: Routledge. 96–116.

Connery, Christopher. 1994. "Pacific Rim Discourse: The U.S. Global Imaginary in the Late Cold War Years." *boundary 2* 21 (spring): 30–56.

Connor, John W. 1975. "Changing Trends in Japanese American Academic Achievement." *Journal of Ethnic Studies* 2: 95–98.

Constantino, Renato. 1988. *Nationalism and Liberation.* Quezon City, Philippines: Karrel, Inc.

Cordova, Fred. 1983. *Filipinos: Forgotten Asian Americans.* Seattle, WA: Demonstration Project for Asian Americans.

Crenshaw, Kimberle, Neil Gotanda, Gary Peller, and Kendall Thomas, eds. 1995. *Critical Race Theory: The Key Writings that Formed the Movement.* New York: The New Press.

Cumings, Bruce. 1999a. *Parallax Visions: Making Sense of American-East Asian Relations.* Durham, NC: Duke University Press.

——. 1999b. "The End of History or the Return of Liberal Crisis?" *Current History* (January): 9–16.

——. 1993. "Rimspeak; or the Discourse of the 'Pacific Rim.'" In Arif Dirlik, ed. *What is in A Rim?: Critical Perspectives on the Pacific Region Idea.* Boulder, CO: Westview Press. 29–47.

———. 1984. "The Legacy of Japanese Colonialism in Korea." In Peter Duus, Roman H. Myers, and Mark R. Peattie, eds. *The Japanese Colonial Empire, 1895–1937*. Princeton, NJ: Princeton University Press. 478–96.

———. 1981. *The Origins of the Korean War: Liberation and the Emergence of Separate Regimes*. Princeton, NJ: Princeton University Press.

Cushman, Jennifer and Wang Gungwu, eds. 1988. *Changing Identities of the Southeast Asian Chinese since World War II*. Hong Kong: Hong Kong University Press.

Dasgupta, Gautam. 1991. *"The Mahabharata:* Peter Brook's Orientalism." In *Interculturalism and Performance,* Bonnie Marranca and Gautam Dasgupta, eds. New York: PAJ Publications. 75–82.

Davidson, Cathy and Michael Moon. 1995. "Introduction." In *Subjects and Citizens: Nation, Race, and Gender from Oroonoko to Anita Hill*. Durham, NC: Duke University Press.

Davis, Angela. 1997. "Interview with Lisa Lowe. Angela Davis: Reflections on Race, Class and Gender in the USA." In Lisa Lowe and David Lloyd, eds. *The Politics of Culture in the Shadow of Late Capital*. Durham, NC: Duke University Press. 303–323.

Davis, Michael C., ed. 1995. *Human Rights and Chinese Values: Legal, Philosophical, and Political Perspectives*. Hong Kong: Oxford University Press.

Deale, Frank. 1996. "Affirmative Action and Human Rights." *International Policy Review* 6(1): 76–83.

de Certeau, Michel. 1984. *The Practice of Everyday Life*. trans. Steven Rendall. Berkeley: University of California Press.

Deck, Alice B. 1993. "Toni Cade Bambara (1939-)." In *Black Women in America: An Historical Encyclopedia*. Eds. Darlene Clark Hine, Elsa Barkley Brown, and Rosalyn Terborg-Penn. Bloomington: Indiana University Press.

Deleuze, Gilles. 1994. *Difference and Repetition,* trans. Paul Patton. New York: Columbia University Press.

Deleuze, Gilles and Félix Guattari. 1987. *A Thousand Plateaus: Capitalism and Schizophrenia*. Translation and foreword by Brian Massumi. Minneapolis: University of Minnesota Press.

Deng, Francis M. 1993. *Protecting the Dispossessed: A Challenge for the International Community*. Washington, D.C.: The Brookings Institute.

Denton, Kirk. 1989. "Review of *Mulberry and Peach: Two Women of China* by Hualing Nieh." *Journal of the Chinese Language Teachers' Association* 24(2): 135–38.

Derrida, Jacques. [1985] 1988. *The Ear of the Other: Otobiography, Transference, Translation*. Trans. Peggy Kamuf. New York: Schocken Books.

———. 1981. *Positions*. Trans. Alan Bass. Chicago: University of Chicago Press.

———. 1976. "Translator's Preface." *Of Grammatology*. Baltimore: Johns Hopkins University Press.

Desmond, Jane and Virginia Dominguez. 1996. "Resituating American Studies in a Critical Internationalism." *American Quarterly* 48(3): 475.

DeWitt, Howard A. 1978. "The Filipino Labor Union: The Salinas Lettuce Strike, 1934." *Amerasia Journal* 5(2): 1–22.

Dirlik, Arif. 1996a. "Asians on the Rim: Transnational Capital and Local Community in the Making of Contemporary Asian America." *Amerasia Journal* 22(3): 1–24.

———. 1996b. "Reversals, Ironies, and Hegemonies: Notes on the Contemporary Historiography of Modern China." *Modern China* 22:3 (July): 243–284.

———. 1994. "The Postcolonial Aura: Third World Criticism in the Age of Global Capitalism." *Critical Inquiry* 20 (winter): 328–56.

———. ed. 1993. *What Is in A Rim?: Critical Perspectives on the Pacific Region Idea.* Boulder, CO: Westview Press.

———. 1991. *Anarchism in the Chinese Revolution.* Berkeley: University of California Press.

———. 1989. *The Origins of Chinese Communism.* New York: Oxford University Press.

———. 1983. "The Predicament of Marxist Revolutionary Consciousness: Mao Zedong, Antonio Gramsci, and the Reformation of Marxist Revolutionary Theory." *Modern China* 9 (April): 186.

———. 1978. *Revolution and History: Origins of Marxist Historiography in China, 1919–1937.* Berkeley: University of California Press.

Disraeli, Benjamin. 1871. *Collected Editions of the Novels and Tales by the Right Honorable B. Disraeli, vol. IV — Tancred or The New Crusade.* London: Longmans, Green.

Douzinas, Costas and Ronnie Warrington. 1995. "A Well-grounded Fear of Justice: Law and Ethics in Postmodernity." In Jerry Leonard, ed. *Legal Studies as Cultural Studies: a reader in (post)modern critical theory.* New York: State University of New York Press. 197–229.

DuBois, W. E. B. [1903] 1996. *The Souls of Black Folk.* New York: Penguin.

Duus, Peter, Roman H. Myers, and Mark R. Peattie. 1996. *The Japanese Wartime Empire, 1931–1945.* Princeton, NJ: Princeton University Press.

———. 1989. *The Japanese Informal Empire in China, 1895–1937.* Princeton, N.J.: Princeton University Press.

———. 1984. *The Japanese Colonial Empire, 1895–1937.* Princeton: Princeton University Press.

Eagleton, Terry. 1990. "Defending the Free World." In *Socialist Register 1990,* ed. Ralph Miliband, Leo Panitch, and John Saville. London: The Merlin Press.

Eng, David. 2001. *Racial Castration: Managing Masculinity in Asian America.* Durham, NC: Duke University Press.

———. 1997. "Out Here and Over There: Queerness and Diaspora in Asian American Studies." *Social Text* 52–53 (fall–winter): 31–52.

Eng, David L. and Alice Y. Hom, eds. 1998. *Q & A: Queer in Asian America.* Philadelphia: Temple University Press.

Enloe, Cynthia. 1989. *Bananas, Beaches and Bases: Making Feminist Sense of International Politics.* Berkeley: Univ. of California Press.

Errington, Shelly. 1990. "Recasting Sex, Gender and Power: Theoretical and Regional Overview." In *Power and Difference: Gender in Island Southeast Asia,* eds. Jane Monnig Atkinson and Shelly Errington. Stanford, CA: Stanford University Press. 1–58.

Espiritu, Yen Le. 1997. *Asian American Women and Men: Labor, Laws, and Love.* Thousand Oaks, CA: Sage Publications.

———. 1996. "Colonial Opression, Labour Importation and Group Formation: Filipinos in the U.S." *Ethnic and Racial Studies* 19 (January): 29–45.

Fabian, Johannes. 1983. *Time and the Other: How Anthropology Makes Its Object.* New York: Columbia University Press.

Fallows, James. 1989. *More Like Us: Making America Great Again.* Boston: Houghton Mifflin.

Fanon, Frantz. [1963] 1968. *The Wretched of the Earth.* New York: Grove.

———. [1952] 1967. *Black Skins, White Masks.* New York: Grove.

Farrior, Stephanie. 1997. "The International Law on Trafficking in Women and Children for Prostitution: Making It Live Up to Its Potential." *Harvard Human Rights Law Journal* 10 (spring): 213–55.

Featherstone, Mike, ed. 1990. *Global Culture: Nationalism, Globalization, and Modernity.* London: Sage.

Ferguson, James and Akhil Gupta, eds. 1992. *Cultural Anthropology* 7(1). Special issue on "Space, Identity, and the Politics of Difference."

Ferguson, Russell. 1990. "Introduction: Invisible Center." In *Out There: Marginalization and Contemporary Cultures.* Eds. by Russell Ferguson, Martha Gever, Trinh T. Minh-Ha, and Cornel West. New York: The New Museum of Contemporary Art. 9–14.

Foucault, Michel. 1980. "Power and Strategies." In *Power/Knowledge: Selected Interviews and Other Writings 1972–1977 with Foucault,* ed. Colin Gordon, trans. Colin Gordon, Leo Marshall, John Mepham, and Kate Soper. New York: Pantheon Books.

———. 1977. "Intellectuals and Power: A Conversation between Michel Foucault and Gilles Deleuze." In *Language, Counter-Memory, Practice: Selected Essays and Interviews,* ed. by Donald F. Bouchard, trans. by Donald F. Bouchard and Sherry Simon. Ithaca, NY: Cornell University Press.

Frankenberg, Ruth and Lata Mani. 1996. "Crosscurrents, Crosstalk: Race, 'Postcoloniality,' and the Politics of Location." In *Contemporary Postcolonial Theory,* ed. Padmini Mongia. London: St. Martin. 347–364.

Fraser, Nancy. 1989. "Singularity or Solidarity? Richard Rorty between Romanticism and Technocracy." In *Unruly Practices: Power, Discourse, and Gender in Contemporary Social Theory.* Minneapolis: University of Minnesota Press. 92–110.

Freud, Sigmund. 1959. "Mourning and Melancholia," *Collected Papers, vol. 4,* trans. Joan Riviere. New York: Basic Books, 152–70.

Fujikane, Candace Lei. 1996. "Archipelagos of Resistance: Narrating Nation in Asian American, Native Hawaiian, and Hawaii's Local Literatures." Ph.D. diss., University of California, Berkeley.

Fujitani, Takashi. 1995. "Nisei Soldiers as Citizens: Japanese Americans in U.S. National Military and Racial Discourses." Conference on the Politics of Remembering the Asia/Pacific War, East-West Center, Honolulu, Hawaii, 8 September.

Furnas, Joseph C. 1937. *The Anatomy of Paradise.* New York: William Sloan Associates.

Fuss, Diana. 1994. "Interior Colonies: Frantz Fanon and the Politics of Identification," *Diacritics* 24 (2–3): 20–42.

Garner, Stanton. 1994. *Bodied Spaces: Phenomenology and Performance in Contemporary Drama.* Ithaca, NY: Cornell University Press.

Gauhar, Altaf. 1987. "Asia: The Experience of the Sub-continent." In Bruno Kreisky and Humayun Gauhar, eds. *Decolonization and After: The Future of the Third World.* London: Southern Publications. 51–61.

Gaylord, Clarice and Elizabeth Bell. 1995. "Environmental Justice: A National Priority." In Laura Westra and Peter Wenz, Eds. *Faces of Environmental Racism: Confronting Issues of Global Justice.* Lanham, MD: Rowman and Littlefield. 29–39.

Gilmore, Ruth Wilson. 1998. "Globalization and U.S. Prison Growth: From Military Keynesianism to Post-Keynesian Militarism." *Race and Class* 40 (2/3): 170–88.

Gilroy, Paul. 1993. *The Black Atlantic: Modernity and Double Consciousness.* Cambridge: Harvard University Press.

Glendon, Mary Ann. 1994. *A Nation Under Lawyers: How the Crisis in the Legal Profession is Transforming American Society.* New York: Farrar, Straus, and Giroux.

Glenn, Evelyn Nakano. 1985. "Racial Ethnic Women's Labor: The Intersection of Race, Gender, and Class Oppression." *Review of Radical Political Economics* 17:3: 86–108.

Glick-Schiller, Nina et al., eds. 1994. *Nations Unbound: Transnational Projects, Postcolonial Predicaments, and Deterritorialized Nation-States.* New York: Gordon and Breach.

Goffman, Erving. [1959] 1963. *Stigma: Notes on the Management of Spoiled Identity.* New York: Simon and Schuster.

Gopinath, Gayatri. 1997. "Nostalgia, Desire, Diaspora: South Asian Sexualities in Motion." *positions: east asia cultures critique* 5 (fall): 467–89.

Gordon, Michael Wallace. 1994. "Hamburgers Abroad: Cultural Variations affecting Franchising Abroad." *Connecticut Journal of International Law* 9 (spring): 165–84.

Gordon, Milton. 1964. *Assimilation in American Life: The Role of Race, Religion and National Origins.* New York: Oxford University Press.

Gotanda, Neil. 1999. "Citizenship Nullification: The Impossibility of Asian American Politics." Lecture delivered at the University of Maryland, College Park, 8 December 1999.

———. 1995. "Critical Legal Studies, Critical Race Theory, and Asian American Studies." *Amerasia* 21:1/2: 127–35.

Gotanda, Philip Kan. Telephone interview. 9 May 1995.

Gray, Whitmore. 1995. "The Challenge of Asian Law." *Fordham International Law Journal* 9(1): 1–8.

Greenough, Paul. 1995. "Nation, Economy, and Tradition Displayed: The Indian Crafts Museum, New Delhi." In Carol Breckenridge, ed. *Consuming Modernity: Public Culture in a South Asian World.* Minneapolis: University of Minnesota Press. 216–48.

Grewal, Inderpal. Forthcoming. *Transnational America: Gender, Class, and Ethnicity in South Asian Diasporas.* Durham, NC: Duke University Press.

Grewal, Inderpal, and Caren Kaplan, eds. 1994. *Scattered Hegemonies: Postmodernity and Transnational Feminist Practices.* Minneapolis: University of Minnesota Press.

Grove, John and Jiping Wu. 1991. "Who Benefitted from the Gains of Asian-Americans, 1940–1980?" In *Racism and the Underclass: State Policy and Discrimination against Minorities,* eds. George W. Shephard Jr. and David Penna. New York: Greenwood Press. 99–111.

Guha, Ramachandra. 1995. "Subaltern and Bhadralok Studies." *Economic and Political Weekly* (19 August): 2056–58.

Guha, Ranajit and Gayatri Chakravorty Spivak, eds. 1988. *Selected Subaltern Studies.* New York: Oxford University Press.

Guinier, Lani. 1994. *The Tyranny of the Majority: Fundamental Fairness and Representative Democracy.* New York: Free Press.

Gupta, Akhil and James Ferguson. 1992. "Beyond 'Culture': Space, Identity, and the Politics of Difference." *Cultural Anthropology* 7 (February): 6–22.

Habell-Pallan, Michelle. 1995. "No Cultural Icon."

Halberstam, Judith. 1994. "The Making of Female Masculinity." In *The Lesbian Postmodern,* ed. Laura Doan. New York: Columbia University Press. 210–28.

Hall, Robert B. 1947. *Area Studies: With Special Reference to Their Implications for Research in the Social Sciences.* Social Sciences Research Council Pamphlet no.3. New York: Social Sciences Research Council.

Hall, Stuart. 1992. "The West and the Rest: Discourse and Power." In *Formations of Modernity,* eds. Stuart Hall and Gram Gieben. Cambridge: Polity Press.

Halliday, Jon and Gavan McCormack. 1973. *Japanese Imperialism Today.* New York: Monthly Review.

Haney Lopez, Ian. 1996. *White by Law.* New York: New York University Press.

Hannerz, Ulf. 1992. *Cultural Complexity: Studies in the Social Organization of Meaning.* New York: Columbia University Press.

Harootunian, H. D., and Masao Miyoshi, eds. 1993. *Japan in the World.* Durham, NC: Duke University Press.

Harding, Harry. 1982. "From China, with Disdain: New Trends in the Study of China," *Asian Survey* 22 (October): 934–58.

Hart, Lynda and Peggy Phelan. 1993. *Acting Out: Feminist Performances.* Ann Arbor: University of Michigan Press.

Hazlett, T. W. 1992. "Mything the Point." *Reason* (October): 66.

Hellwig, David. 1979. "Black Reactions to Chinese Immigration and the Anti-Chinese Movement: 1850–1910." *Amerasia Journal* 6(2): 25–44.

Hing, Bill Ong. 1993. *Making and Remaking Asian America Through Immigration Policy, 1850–1990.* Stanford, CA: Stanford University Press.

Hinton, William. 1966. *Fanshen.* New York: Vintage Books.

Hom, Marlon K., trans. 1987. *Songs of Gold Mountain: Cantonese Folkrhymes from San Francisco Chinatown.* Berkeley: University of California Press.

Hom, Sharon, ed. 1999. *Chinese Women Traversing Diaspora: Memoirs, Essays, and Poetry.* New York: Garland Publishing.

———. 1996. "Commentary: Re-positioning Human Rights Discourse on 'Asian' Perspectives." *Buffalo Journal of International Law* 3(1): 251–76.

———. 1994. "Engendering Chinese Legal Studies: Gate-keeping, Master Discourses, and Other Challenges." *Signs: Journal of Women in Culture and Society* 19 (summer): 1020–47.

Hom, Sharon K. and Xin Chunying, eds. 1995. *English-Chinese Lexicon of Women and Law* (Yinghan funu yu falu Cihuishiyi). Beijing: UNESCO and China Translation and Publication Corporation.

Hom, Sharon K. and Eric K. Yamamoto. 2000. "Re-Forming Civil Rights in Uncivil Times: The Struggles Over Collective Memory and Internationalizing Domestic Rights." *UCLA Law Journal* 47(6): 1747–802.

Hondagneu-Sotelo, Pierette. 1995. "Women and Children First: New Directions in Anti-Immigrant Politics." *Socialist Review* 25(1): 169–90.

Hong, Grace Kyungwon. 1999a. "'something forgotten which should have been remembered': Private Property and Cross-Racial Solidarity in the work of Hisaye Yamamoto." *American Literature* 71 (June): 291–310.

———. 1999b. "The History of the Propertyless." Ph.D diss., University of California, San Diego.

Hsu, Ruth. 1996. "A Conversation with Joy Kogawa." *Amerasia Journal* 22:1, 191 (1996).

Hu-DeHart, Evelyn. 1991. "From Area Studies to Ethnic Studies: The Study of the Chinese Diaspora in Latin America." In Shirley Hune et al., eds. *Asian Americans: Comparative and Global Perspectives.* St. Louis: Washington University Press. 5–16.

Hune, Shirley, ed. 1989. *Amerasia Journal* 15(2). Special issue, "Asians in the Americas."

———. 1989. "Expanding the International Dimensions of Asian American Studies." *Amerasia Journal* 15(2): xix–xxiv.

Hune, Shirley et al., eds. 1991. *Asian Americans: Comparative and Global Perspectives.* St. Louis: Washington University Press.

Huntington, Samuel P. 1993. "The Clash of Civilizations?" *Foreign Affairs* 72(3): 113–38.

Hurh, Wom Moo and Kwang Chung Kim. 1989. "The 'Success' Image of Asian Americans: Its Validity and Its Practical and Theoretical Implications." *Ethnic and Racial Studies* 12 (October): 512–38.

Hutchinson, Allan. 1995. "Calgary and Everything After: A Postmodern Re-Vision of Lawyering." *Alberta Law Review* 33 (August): 768–86.

Hwang, David Henry. Telephone interview. 10 April 1995.

Ichioka, Yuji. 1971. "A Buried Past: Early Issei Socialists and the Japanese Community." *Amerasia Journal* 1(2): 1–25.

Igarashi, Yoshikuni. 1998. "The Bomb, Hirohito, and History: The Foundational Narrative of Postwar U.S.-Japan Relations." *positions: east asia cultures critique* 6(2): 261–302.

Ishi, Tomoji. 1993. "Adjusting to the Rim: Japanese Corporate Social Responsibility in the United States." In Arif Dirlik, ed. *What Is in A Rim? Critical Perspectives on the Pacific Region Idea.* Boulder, CO: Westview Press. 121–34.

Ivy, Marilyn. 1995. *Discourses of the Vanishing: Modernity, Phantasm, Japan.* Chicago: University of Chicago Press.

Iwamoto, Gary. 1993. "History and Significant Achievements." In *Dreams and Promises: Northwest Asian American Theatre 20th Anniversary Commemorative Program.* 2–3.

Iwanami Publisher. 1993. *The Colonies of Modern Japan.* 8 volumes.

Jaluague, Eleanor. n.d. Ph.D diss., University of California, San Diego (forthcoming).

JanMohamed, Abdul and David Lloyd. 1991. *The Nature and Context of Minority Discourse.* Cambridge: Oxford University Press.

Jean, François. 1995. *Populations in Danger 1995: A Médicins Sans Frontières Report.* Translated by Iseult O'Brien. London: Médicins Sans Frontières.

Jenner, W. J. F. 1990. "Review of *The August Sleepwalker* by Bei Dao." *The Australian Journal of Chinese Affairs* 23 (January): 193–95.

Joseph, May. 1995. "Diaspora, New Hybrid Identities, and the Performance of Citizenship." *Women and Performance: A Journal of Feminist Theory* 7(2)/8(1): 3–13.

Journal of Southeast Asian Studies. 1996. Special Issue, "The Japanese Occupation in Southeast Asia."

Jun, Helen. n.d. Ph.D. diss., Department of Literature, University of California, San Diego (forthcoming).

Kandel, Randy Frances. 1993. "Whither the Legal Whale: Interdisciplinarity and the Socialization of Professional Identity." *Loyola of Los Angeles Law Review* 27 (November): 9–24.

Kang, Laura Hyun Yi. Forthcoming. *Compositional Subjects: Enfiguring Asian/American Women.* Durham, NC: Duke University Press.

——. 1997. "Si(gh)ting Asian/American Women as Transnational Labor." *positions: east asia cultures critique* 5(2) 403–438.

Kang, Min Jay. 1996. "Urban Transformation and Adaptation in Banka, Taipei: Marginalization of a Historical Core." Ph.D. diss. University of Washington.

Kaplan, Amy. 1993. "'Left Alone with America': The Absence of Empire in the Study of American Culture." In *Cultures of United States Imperialism,* eds. Amy Kaplan and Donald E. Pease. Durham, NC: Duke University Press. 3–21.

Ker, Rey-ming. 1996. *Taiwan Can Say No.* Taipei: Yeh-Chiang.

Kiernan, V. G. 1980. *America: The New Imperialism: From White Settlement to World Hegemony.* London: Zed Press.

Kim, Bok-Lim C. 1973. "Asian Americans: No Model Minority." *Social Work* 18 (May): 44–53.

Kim, Elaine H. 1992. Foreword. In Shirley Geok-lin Lim and Amy Ling, eds. *Reading the Literatures of Asian America.* Philadelphia: Temple University Press. xi–xvii.

——. 1982. *Asian American Literature: An Introduction to the Writings and Their Social Context.* Philadelphia: Temple University Press.

Kim, Elaine H. and Norma Alarcon. 1992. *Writing Self, Writing Nation: Essays on Theresa Hak Kyung Cha's Dictée.* Berkeley: Third Woman Press.

Kim, Helen and Jessica McClintock. 1993. "Two Points of View." *Korea Times* (15 December).

Kim, Ronyoung. 1987. *Clay Walls.* Seattle: University of Washington Press.

Kim, Seong Nae. 1996. "Mourning Korean Modernity: Violence and the Memory of the Cheju Uprising."

Kojma, Nobuo. 1989. "Stars." In *Shōwa Anthology,* eds. Van C. Gessel and Tomone Matsumoto. Tokyo: Kodansha International.

——. 1967. *American sukūru.* Tokyo: Shinchosha.

Kondo, Dorinne. 1997. *About Face: Performing Race in Fashion and Theatre.* New York: Routledge.

——. 1990. *Crafting Selves: Power, Gender, and Discourses of Identity in a Japanese Workplace.* Chicago: University of Chicago Press.

Koshy, Susan. 1999. "From Cold War to Trade War: Neocolonialism and Human Rights." *Social Text* 58 (spring): 1–32.

Kratoska, Paul H. 1995. *Malay and Singapore During the Japanese Occupation.* Singapore: Singapore University Press.

Kreisky, Bruno and Humayun Gauhar, eds. 1987. *Decolonization and After: the Future of the Third World.* London: Southern Publications.

Kronman, Anthony. 1993. *The Lost Lawyer: Failing Ideals of the Legal Profession.* Cambridge, MA: Belknap.

Kubiak, Anthony. 1991. *Stages of Terror: Terrorism, Ideology, and Coercion as Theatre History.* Bloomington: Indiana University Press.

Kureishi, Hanif. 1986. *My Beautiful Laundrette and the Rainbow Sign.* London: Faber and Faber.

Lai, Him Mark, Genny Lim, and Judy Yung. 1980. *Island: Poetry and History of Chinese Immigrants on Angel Island 1910–1940.* San Francisco: HOC DOI (History of Chinese Detained on Island).

Lambropoulos, Vassilis. 1996. "Nomoscopic Analysis. Special Issue of Ethical Politics." *The South Atlantic Quarterly* 95 (fall): 855–879.

Lee, Benjamin. 1995. "Critical Internationalism." *Public Culture* 7(3): 559–92.

Lee, Geok Boi. 1992. *Syonan Singapore under the Japanese, 1942–1945.* Singapore: Singapore Heritage Society.

Lee, Leo Ou-fan. 1994. "On the Margins of Chinese Discourse: Some Personal Thoughts on the Cultural Meaning of the Periphery." In Wei-Ming Tu, Ed. *The Living Tree: The Changing Meaning of Being Chinese Today.* Stanford, CA: Stanford University Press. 221–38.

Lee, Robert G. 1995. "Introduction." In Mary Kimoto Tomita ed., *Dear Miye.* Stanford: Stanford University Press.

Lee, Tahirih V., ed. 1997. *Chinese Law: Social, Political, Historical, and Economic Perspectives.* New York: Garland Publishing.

Lentricchia, Frank and Thomas McLaughlin eds. [1990] 1995. *Critical Terms for Literary Study.* Chicago: University of Chicago Press.

Leon W., M. Consuelo. 1995. "Foundations of the American Image of the Pacific." In *Asia/Pacific as Space of Cultural Production.* eds. Rob Wilson and Arif Dirlik. Durham, NC: Duke University Press. 17–29.

Leonard, Jerry, ed. 1995. *Legal Studies as Cultural Studies: a reader in (post)modern critical theory.* New York: State University of New York Press.

Leong, Andrew L. S. 1994. "A Practical Guide to Establishing an Asian Law Clinic: Reflections on the Chinatown Clinical Program at Boston College Law School." *Asian Pacific American Law Journal* 2 (fall): 83–100.

Leong, Russell C. 2000. *Phoenix Eyes and Other Stories.* Seattle: University of Washington Press.

Leong, Russell. 1996a. "Paper Houses." In *Race: An Anthology in the First Person,* ed. Bart Schneider. New York: Crown Books. 57–63.

——. 1993a. *The Country of Dreams and Dust* (Albuquerque, NM: West End Press).

——. 1993b. "Geography One." In *Charlie Chan Is Dead: An Anthology of Contemporary Asian American Fiction,* ed. Jessica Hagedorn. New York: Penguin. 215–229.

——. 1991. *Moving the Image: Independent Asian Pacific American Media Arts* (Los Angeles: UCLA School of Film and Television and Visual Communications).

——. 1990. *Why is Preparing Fish a Political Act: Poetry of Janice Mirikitani* (video, UCLA School of Film and Television).

——. 1974. "Rough Notes for Mantos." In Jeffrey Chan et al., eds. *Aiiieeeee! An Anthology of Asian American Writers.* New York: Penguin Books. 197–205.

Leong, Russell, ed. 1996. *Asian American Sexualities: Dimensions of the Gay and Lesbian Experience.* New York and London: Routledge.

Li Kailing and Chen Zhongshu, eds. 1990. *Nie Hualing yanjiu zhuanji* [An anthology of studies of Nieh Hualing]. N.p.: Hubei jiaoyu chubanshe.

Li Li, ed. 1983. *Haiwai huaren zuojia xiaoshuo xuan* [Selected fiction by overseas Chinese writers]. Hong Kong: Sanlian.

Lieberman, Sally Taylor. 1991. "Visions and Lessons: 'China' in Feminist Theory-Making, 1966–1977." *Michigan Feminist Studies* 6 (fall): 91–107.

Lim, Shirley Geok-lin. 1990. "Review of *Mulberry and Peach: Two Women of China,* by Hualing Nieh." *Calyx: A Journal of Art and Literature by Women* (summer 1990).

Lim, Shirley Geok-lin and Amy Ling, eds. 1992. *Reading the Literatures of Asian America.* Philadelphia: Temple University Press.

Linowitz, Sol M. 1994. *The Betrayed Profession: Lawyering at the End of the Twentieth Century.* New York: Scribner.

Lipsitz, George. 1998. *The Possessive Investment in Whiteness: How White People Benefit from Identity Politics.* Philadelphia: Temple University Press.

Liu, Lydia. 1994. "The Female Body and Nationalist Discourse: The Field of Life and Death Revisited." In Inderpal Grewal and Caren Kaplan, eds. *Scattered Hegemonies: Postmodernity and Transnational Feminist Practices.* Minneapolis: University of Minnesota Press. 37–62.

Lo, Hui-wen. 1996. "A Historical Analysis of the Importation of the Japanese Visual Products in Taiwan (1945–1996)." Master's thesis, Graduate Institute of Journalism, National Cheng-Chi University, Taiwan.

Loescher, Gilbert. 1993. *Beyond Charity: International Cooperation and the Global Refugee Crisis.* New York: Oxford University Press.

Lowe, Lisa. 1998. "The International Within the National: American Studies and Asian American Critique." *Cultural Critique* 40 (fall). 29–47.

———. 1997. "Work, Immigration, Gender: New Subjects of Cultural Politics." In Lisa Lowe and David Lloyd, eds. *The Politics of Culture in the Shadow of Late Capital.* Durham, NC: Duke University Press. 354–74.

———. 1996. *Immigrant Acts: On Asian American Cultural Politics.* Durham, NC: Duke University Press.

———. 1994. "Unfaithful to the Original: The Subject of *Dictée.*" In *Writing Self / Writing Nation: Essays on Theresa Hak Kyung Cha's Dictée.* ed. Elaine Kim and Norma Alarcon. Berkeley: Third Woman Press. 35–69.

———. 1991a. *Critical Terrains: French and British Orientalisms.* Ithaca, NY: Cornell University Press.

———. 1991b. "Heterogeneity, Hybridity, Multiplicity: Marking Asian American Differences." *Diaspora* 1(1): 24–44.

Lowe, Lisa and David Lloyd, eds. 1997. *The Politics of Culture in the Shadow of Late Capital.* Durham, NC: Duke University Press.

Lu Shiqing and Wang Jinyuan. 1990. "*Lun Sangqing yu Taohong.*" In Kailing Li and Chen Zhongshu, eds. *Nie Hualing yanjiu thuanji* [An anthology of studies of Nieh Hualing]. N.p.: Hubei jiaoyu chubanshe. 522–34.

Lubman, Stanley B., ed. 1996. *China's Legal Reforms.* New York: Oxford University Press.

Luban, David and Michael Millemann. 1995. "Good Judgment: Ethics Teaching in Dark Times." *Georgetown Journal of Legal Ethics* 9(1): 31–87.

Lye, Colleen. 1995. "*M. Butterfly* and the Rhetoric of Antiessentialism: Minority Discourse in an International Frame." In David Palumbo-Liu, *The Ethnic Canon.* Minneapolis: University of Minnesota Press. 260–89.

Ma, Sheng-mei. 1998. "Immigrant Subjectivities and Desires in Overseas Student Literatures: Chinese, Postcolonial, or Minority Text?" *Immigrant Subjectivities in Asian American and Asian Diaspora Literatures.* Albany: State University of New York Press. 93–129.

Macherey, Pierre. 1978. *A Theory of Literary Production.* London and Boston: Routledge and Kegan Paul.

MacKerras, Colin. 1989. *Western Images of China.* Hong Kong: Oxford University Press.

Mako. Telephone interview. 11 May 1995.

Manalansan, Martin F. 1995a. "In the Shadows of Stonewall: Examining Gay Transnational Politics and the Diasporic Dilemma." *GLQ: A Journal of Lesbian and Gay Studies* 2–4: 425–38.

——. 1995b. "Speaking of AIDS: Language and the Filipino Gay Experience in America. In *Discrepant Histories: Translocal Essays on Filipino Cultures,* ed. Vicente V. Rafael. Philadelphia: Temple University Press. 199–223.

——. Forthcoming. *Global Divas: Filipino Gay Men in the Diaspora.* Durham, NC: Duke University Press.

Mann, Patricia S. 1994. *Micro-Politics: Agency in a Postfeminist Era.* Minneapolis and London: University of Minnesota Press.

Mannoni, O. [1950] 1965. *Prospero and Caliban: The Psychology of Colonization.* Ann Arbor: University of Michigan Press.

Marcus, George, ed. 1992. *Rereading Cultural Anthropology.* Durham, NC: Duke University Press.

Marranca, Bonnie and Gautam Dasgupta, eds. 1991. *Interculturalism and Performance.* New York: PAJ Publications.

Matsuda, Mari. 1995. "Looking to the Bottom: Critical Legal Studies and Reparations." In Kimberle Crenshaw et al., eds. *Critical Race Theory: The Key Writings that Formed the Movement.* New York: The New Press. 63–79.

——. 1990. "Pragmatism Modified and the False Consciousness Problem." *Southern California Law Review* 63 (September): 1763–82.

Mazumdar, Sucheta. 1991. "Asian American Studies and Asian Studies: Rethinking Roots." In Shirley Hune et al., eds. *Asian Americans: Comparative and Global Perspectives.* St. Louis: Washington University Press. 29–44.

McLeod, Beverly. 1986. "The Oriental Express." *Psychology Today* (July): 48–52.

McClain, Charles J. 1996. *In Search of Equality: The Chinese Struggle Against Discrimination in Nineteenth Century America.* Berkeley: University of California Press.

McClintock, Anne. 1992. "The Angel of Progress: Pitfalls of the Term 'Post-Colonialism.' " *Social Text* 31–32 (spring): 84–98.

McDonnel, Patrick J. 1996. "Hotel Boycott is a High-Stake Battle for Union." *Los Angeles Times* (3 February).

Mehta, Uday. 1999. *Liberalism and Empire: A Study in Nineteenth-Century British Liberal Thought.* Chicago: University of Chicago Press.

——. 1997. "Liberal Strategies of Exclusion." In *Tensions of Empire: Colonial Cultures in a Bourgeois World,* ed. by Frederick Cooper and Ann Laura Stoler. Berkeley: University of California Press.

Memmi, Albert. [1957] 1965. *The Colonizer and the Colonized.* Boston: Beacon Press.

Meraz, Gerry. 1995. "Culture for the Cause." *Urb* 42 (May): 69.

Messer-Davidow, Ellen, David R. Shumway, and David S. Sylvan, eds. 1993. *Knowledges: Historical and Critical Studies in Disciplinarity.* Charlottesville: University Press of Virginia.

Minda, Gary. 1995. *Postmodern Legal Movements: Law and Jurisprudence at Century's End.* New York and London: New York University Press.

Minh-Ha, Trinh T. 1989. *Woman Native Other*. Bloomington: Indiana University Press.

Minow, Martha, Michael Ryan, and Austin Sarat, eds. [1993] 1995. *Narrative, Violence and the Law: The Essays of Robert Cover*. Ann Arbor: University of Michigan Press.

Miyoshi, Masao. 1993. "A Borderless World? From Colonialism to Transnationalism and the Decline of the Nation-State." *Critical Inquiry* 19 (Summer): 726–51.

Mochizuki, Ken. 1993. "Too Legit to Quit." In *Dreams and Promises: Northwest Asian American Theatre 20th Anniversary Commemorative Program*. 8–11.

Mohanty, Chandra Talpade. 1991. "Cartographies of Struggle: Third World Women and the Politics of Feminism." In Chandra Talpade Mohanty, Ann Russo, and Lourdes Torres, eds. *Third World Women and the Politics of Feminism*. Bloomington: Indiana University Press, 1–47.

Morris, Rosalind. 1995. "All Made Up: Performance Theory and the New Anthropology of Sex and Gender." *Annual Review of Anthropology* 22: 567–92.

Murphy, Peter. 1991. "Postmodern Perspectives and Justice." *Thesis Eleven* 30: 117–32.

Nakagawa, Martha. 1995. "Former Sweatshop Slaves Sue Manufacturers." *Rafu Shimpo* (26 October).

Nakanishi, Don T. [1976] 1981. "Minorities and International Politics." *Counterpoint: Perspectives on Asian America*. Los Angeles: UCLA Asian American Studies Center, 81–85.

——. 1973. "The Visual Panacea: Japanese Americans in the City of Smog." *Amerasia Journal* 2: 82–129.

——. 1971. Publisher's note. *Amerasia Journal* 1(1): ii.

Nakanishi, Don T. and Russell Leong. 1978. *Amerasia Journal* 5(1): 1–19.

Nandy, Ashis. 1994. *The Illegitimacy of Nationalism: Rabindranath Tagore and the Politics of Self*. Delhi: Oxford University Press.

Ness, Sally Ann. 1992. *Body, Movement, and Culture: Kinesthetic and Visual Symbolism in a Philippine Community*. Philadelphia: University of Pennsylvania Press.

Newton, Esther. 1972. *Mother Camp: Female Impersonators in America*. Englewood Cliffs, NJ: Prentice Hall.

Newton, Judith and Judith Stacey. 1995. "Ms. Representations: Reflections on Studying Academic Men." In *Women Writing Culture*, ed. by Ruth Behar and Deborah A. Gordon. Berkeley: University of California Press. 287–305.

Nguyen, Viet Thanh. 1997. "Writing the Body Politic: Asian American Literature and the Contradictions of Democracy." Ph.D. diss., University of California, Berkeley.

——. Interview with author. Iowa City, Iowa, 22–23 March 1996.

Nieh, Hualing. 1988a. *Mulberry and Peach: Two Women of China*. Translated by Jane Parish Young with Linda Lappin. New York: The Feminist Press at the College University of New York.

——. 1988. "*Sangqing yu Taohong liufang xiaoji (dai xu)*" [A brief account of *Sangqing yu Taohong*'s exile (in lieu of a preface)]. In *Sangqing yu Taohong*. Taipei: Hanyi seyan chubanshe.

——. 1984. *Qianshan wai, shui changliu*. Sichuan: Renmin chubanshe.

——. 1980a. "*Langzi de beige (qianyan)*" [The Wanderers' Lament (Preface)]. In *Sangqing yu Taohong*. Beijing: Zhongguo qingnian chubanshe. 1–7.

——. 1980b. *Wang Danian de jijian xishi*. Hong Kong: Haiyang wenyishe.

Nihei, Judith. Telephone interview. 28 April 1995.

Northwest Asian American Theatre (NWAAT). 1996. Ford Foundation Grant Proposal.

Okakura, Kakuzô. 1970. *The Ideals of the East*. Tokyo: Charles E. Tuttle.

Okihiro, Gary Y. 1994. *Margins and Mainstreams: Asians in American History and Culture*. Seattle: University of Washington.

——. 1973. "Japanese Resistance in America's Concentration Camps: A Re-Evaluation." *Amerasia Journal* 2: 20–34.

Okihiro, Gary Y. et al., eds. 1995. *Privileging Positions: The Sites of Asian American Studies.* Pullman: Washington State University Press.

——. 1988. *Reflections on Shattered Windows: Promises and Prospects for Asian American Studies.* Pullman: Washington State University Press.

Omatsu, Glenn. 1994. "The 'Four Prisons' and the Movements of Liberation: Asian American Activism from the 1960s to the 1990s." In Karin Aguilar-San Juan, ed. *The State of Asian America: Activism and Resistance in the 1990s.* Boston: South End Press. 19–70.

——. 1989. "Salute to the 60s and 70s Legacy of the San Francisco State Strike." *Amerasia Journal* 15(1): xv–xxx.

Omatsu, Glenn, ed. 1990. "Power to the People: The Don Nakanishi Tenure Case at UCLA." *Amerasia Journal* 16(1): 63–159.

Omi, Michael and Dana Takagi, eds. 1995. "Thinking Theory in Asian American Studies," Special Issue of *Amerasia Journal* 21 (1–2).

Omi, Michael and Howard Winant. 1994. *Racial Formation in the United States, from the 1960s to the 1990s.* 2nd ed. New York: Routledge.

——. 1986. *Racial Formation in the United States, from the 1960s to the 1980s.* New York: Routledge.

Ong, Aihwa. 1999. *Flexible Citizenship: The Cultural Logics of Transnationality.* Durham, NC: Duke University Press.

Ong, Aihwa and Donald Nonini, eds. 1997. *Ungrounded Empires: The Cultural Politics of Modern Chinese Transnationalism.* New York: Routledge.

Ong, Paul, Edna Bonacich, and Lucie Cheng, eds. 1994. *The New Asian Immigration in Los Angeles and Global Restructuring.* Philadelphia: Temple University Press.

Orfield, Gary. 1988. "Race and the Liberal Agenda: The Loss of the Integrationist Dream, 1965–1974." In *The Politics of Social Policy in the United States.* Ed. by Margaret Weir, Ann Shola Orloff, and Theda Skocpol. Princeton, NJ: Princeton University Press. 313–55.

Osajima, Keith. 1988. "Asian Americans as the Model Minority: An Analysis of the Popular Press Image in the 1960s and 1980s." In Gary Y. Okihiro et al., eds. Reflections on Shattered Windows: Promises and Prospects for Asian American Studies. Pullman, WA: Washington State University Press. 165–74.

Owen, Stephen. 1990. "The Anxiety of Global Influence: What Is World Poetry?" *The New Republic* (19 November): 28–32.

Pai, Hsien-yung. 1989. "*Shiji de piaobozhe: zhongdu Sangqing yu Taohong.*" *Jiushi niandai yuekan* 12: 93–95.

——. 1976. "The Wandering Chinese: The Theme of Exile in Taiwan Fiction." *Iowa Review* 7(2–3): 205–12.

Palumbo-Liu, David. 1999a. *Asian/American: Historical Crossings of a Racial Frontier.* Stanford, CA: Stanford University Press.

——. 1999b. "Awful Patriotism: Richard Rorty and the Politics of Knowing." *diacritics* 29 (spring): 37–56.

——. 1995. *The Ethnic Canon.* Minneapolis: University of Minnesota Press.

Pan, Lynn. 1990. *Sons of the Yellow Emperor: A History of the Chinese Diaspora.* Boston: Little, Brown and Co.

Parker, Andrew, Mary Russo, Doris Sommer, and Patricia Yeager, eds. *Nationalisms and Sexualities.* 1992. New York: Routledge.

Patel, Sujata. 1990. "Review of Ranajit Guha and Gayatri Chakravorty Spivak, eds., *Selected Subaltern Studies.*" *Contributions to Indian Sociology* 24(1): 137–38.

Peacock, James. 1968. *Rites of Modernization: Symbolic and Social Aspects of Indonesian Proletarian Drama*. Chicago: University of Chicago Press.

Peattie, Mark R. 1988. *Nanyo: The Rise and Fall of the Japanese in Micronesia, 1885–1945*. Honolulu: University of Hawaii Press.

Perkins, David. 1992. *Is Literary History Possible?* Baltimore: Johns Hopkins University Press.

Petersen, William. 1971. *Japanese Americans: Oppression and Success*. New York: Random House.

———. 1966. "Success Story, Japanese American Style." New York Times Magazine. 9 January 1966.

Phelan, Peggy. 1993. *Unmarked: The Politics of Performance*. New York: Routledge.

Picciotto, Sol. 1993. "International Business and Global Development." In Sammy Adelman and Abdul Paliwala, eds. *Law and Crisis in the Third World*. London: Hans Zell Publishers.

Plotkin, Sidney and William E. Scheurman. 1994. *Private Interest, Public Spending: Balanced Budget Conservatism and the Fiscal Crisis*. Boston: South End Press.

Potter, Pitman, ed. 1994. *Domestic Law Reforms in Post-Mao China*. Armonk, NY: M. E. Sharpe.

Prashad, Vijay. 2000. *The Karma of Brown Folk*. Minneapolis: University of Minnesota Press.

Pulido, Laura. 1996. "Multiracial Organizing Among Environmental Justice Activists in Los Angeles." In *Rethinking Los Angeles*. Ed. by Michael J. Dear, H. Eric Shockman, and Greg Hise. Thousand Oaks, CA: Sage. 171–89.

Radhakrishnan, R. 1996. *Diasporic Mediations: Between Home and Location*. Minneapolis: University of Minnesota Press.

———. 1994a. "Is the Ethnic 'Authentic' in the Diaspora?" In Karin Aguilar-San Juan, ed. *The State of Asian America: Activism and Resistance in the 1990s*. Boston: South End Press. 219–33.

———. 1994b. "Postmodernism and the Rest of the World." *Organization* 1–2: 305–340.

Rafael, Vicente. 1994. "The Cultures of Area Studies in the United States." *Social Text* 41 (winter): 91–111.

Ramaswamy, Sumathi. 1997. *Passions of the Tongue: Language Devotion in Tamil India, 1891–1970*. Berkeley: University of California Press.

Ratcliffe, Michael. 1991. "The Greeks, With an Accent on the French." *New York Times*, 28 July.

Reddy, Chandan. 1998a. "Home, Houses, Non-identity: Paris is Burning." In *Burning Down the House: Recycling Domesticity*. Ed. Rosemary Marangoly George. Boulder, CO: Westview Press.

———. 1998b. "Queer Racial Formations in the Global City." Presented at Modern Language Association Annual Convention. San Francisco (December).

Redfield, Robert. [1953] 1968. *The Primitive World and Its Transformations*. Ithaca, NY: Cornell University Press.

Rich, Frank. 1992. "Taking the Stage to Some of Its Extremes." *New York Times*. 6 October.

Ricoeur, Paul. 1990. *Time and Narrative*, vol. 3. Chicago: University of Chicago Press.

———. 1981. "Narrative Time." In *On Narrative*. Ed. by W. J. T. Mitchell. Chicago: University of Chicago Press.

Robbins, Bruce. 1997. "Sad Stories in the International Public Sphere: Richard Rorty on Culture and Human Rights." *Public Culture* 9(2): 209–232.

Robbins, Bruce and Pheng Cheah, eds. 1998. *Cosmopolitics*. Minneapolis: University of Minnesota Press.

Robertson, Roland. 1992. *Globalization: Social Theory and Global Change*. London: Sage.

Rosaldo, Michelle Zimbalist and Louise Lamphere, eds. 1974. *Woman, Culture and Society*. Stanford, CA: Stanford University Press.

Rosaldo, Renato. 1994. "Whose Cultural Studies?" *American Anthropologist* 96 (September): 524–28.

———. 1989. *Culture and Truth: The Remaking of Social Analysis.* Boston: Beacon.

Rose, Tricia. 1994. *Black Noise.* Hanover, NH: Wesleyan; University Press of New England.

Rouse, Roger. 1992. "Making Sense of Settlement: Class Transformation, Cultural Struggle, and Transnationalism among Mexican Migrants in the United States." *Annals of the New York Academy of Sciences* 645: 25–52.

Sachs, Wolfgang. 1992. *The Development Dictionary: A Guide to Knowledge and Power.* London: Zed Books.

Safran, William. 1991. "Diasporas in Modern Societies: Myths of Homeland and Return." *Diaspora* 1 (spring).

Said, Edward. 1993. *Culture and Imperialism.* New York: Alfred A. Knopf.

———. 1990. "Reflections on Exile." In *Out There: Marginalization and Contemporary Cultures,* ed. by Russell Ferguson et al. New York: The New Museum of Contemporary Art and Cambridge, MA: The MIT Press. 357–66.

———. 1983. *The World, the Text, and the Critic.* Cambridge, MA: Harvard University Press.

Sakai, Naoki. 1997. *Translation and Subjectivity: On "Japan" and Cultural Nationalism.* Minneapolis: University of Minnesota Press.

———. 1989. "Modernity and Its Critique: The Problem of Universalism and Particularism." In *Postmodernism and Japan,* ed. by Masao Miyoshi and H. D. Harootunian. Durham, NC: Duke University Press. Previously in *South Atlantic Quarterly* 87 (summer 1988).

Samuels, Steven and Alisha Tonsic. 1996. "Theatre Facts 1995." *American Theatre.* 13 (April).

San Juan, E. 1994. *Allegories of Resistance: The Philippines at the Threshold of the Twenty-first Century.* Diliman: University of Philippines Press.

Sarkar, Sumit. 1994. "Orientalism Revisited: Saidian Frameworks in the Writing of Modern Indian History." *Oxford Literary Review* 16, 1–2. Special Issue, "On India: Writing History, Culture, Post-Coloniality." Guest edited by Ania Loomba and Suvir Kaul: 205–224.

Sarkar, Tanika. 1993. "A Book of Her Own, a Life of Her Own: Autobiography of a Nineteenth-Century Woman." *History Workshop Journal* 36: 61.

Sartori, Andrew. Forthcoming. "Robert Redfield's Civilizations Project: An Intervention in the Political Imagination of Post-War America." *positions: east asia cultures critique.*

Sassen, Saskia. 1991. *The Global City: New York, London, Tokyo.* Princeton, NJ: Princeton University Press.

Schechner, Richard. 1986. "Magnitudes of Performance." In *The Anthropology of Performance.* Victor W. Turner and Edward M. Bruner, eds. Urbana: University of Illinois Press. 344–72.

Schlesinger, Arthur, Jr. 1991. *The Disuniting of America: Reflections on a Multicultural Society.* New York: Norton.

Schwarcz, Vera. 1991. "No Solace from Lethe: History, Memory, and Cultural Identity in Twentieth-Century China." *Daedalus* 120 (spring): 105.

Seagrave, Sterling. 1995. *Lords of the Rim: The Invisible Empire of the Overseas Chinese.* New York: G. P. Putnam's Sons.

Sequoya, Jana. 1996. "Trope Tricks: The Symbolic Functions of the Figure of the Indian for the Modern Imagination." Ph.D. diss. Modern Thought and Literature, Stanford University.

Seyd, Richard. 1987. "Song of a Sansei Playwright: An Interview with Philip Kan Gotanda and Richard Seyd." *West Coast Plays* 21/22: 166–74.

Shah, Nayan. Forthcoming. *Lives at Risk: Epidemics and Race in San Francisco's Chinatown.* Berkeley: University of California Press.

Shankar, Lavina and Rajini Srikanth, eds. 1998. *A Part, Yet Apart: South Asians in Asian America.* Philadelphia: Temple University Press.

Siegel, James. 1986. *Solo in the New Order: Language and Hierarchy in an Indonesian City.* Princeton, NJ: Princeton University Press.

Shih, Shu-mei. 1992. "Re-membering a Self: Nieh Hualing's *Mulberry and Peach* and Theresa Hak Kyung Cha's *Dictée.*" Presented at the University of California, Los Angeles. 8 April.

Shohat, Ella. 1992. "Notes on the 'Post-colonial.'" *Social Text* 31–32 (spring): 99–113.

Shohat, Ella and Robert Stam. Eds. 1994. *Unthinking Eurocentrism: Multiculturalism and the Media.* New York: Routledge.

Simon, William and Jophn Gagon. 1984. "Sexual Scripts." *Society* 22: 53–60.

Singer, Milton. 1976. "Robert Redfield's Development of a Social Anthropology of Civilizations." In *American Anthropology: The Early Years,* ed. by John V. Marra. St. Paul, MN: West Publishing Co.

Skeldon, Ronald. 1994. *Reluctant Exiles: Migration from Hong Kong and the New Overseas Chinese.* Armonk, NY: M. E. Sharpe.

Skerry, Peter. 1991. "Individualist America and Today's Immigrants." *Public Interest* 102 (winter): 104–118.

Sniderman, Paul M. and Thomas Piazza. 1993. *The Scar of Race.* Cambridge, MA: Harvard University Press.

Social Science Research Council (SSRC). 1948. *Area Research and Training: A Conference Report on the Study of World Areas.* Social Science Research Council Pamphlet no. 6. New York: Social Science Research Council.

Soley, Lawrence C. 1995. *Leasing the Ivory Tower: The Corporate Takeover of Academia.* Boston: South End Press.

Solomon, Jon. 1997. "China and the 'Discourse of National Spirit': Toward a Politics of Dislocation." Ph.D. diss. Cornell University.

Spivak, Gayatri Chakravorty. 1998. "Cultural Talks in the Hot Peace: Revisiting the 'Global Village.'" In *Cosmopolitics,* eds. Bruce Robbins and Pheng Cheah. Minneapolis: University of Minnesota Press.

———. 1989. "Who Claims Alterity?" In *Remaking History,* ed. Barbara Kruger and Phil Marian. Seattle: Bay Press.

———. 1986. "Three Women's Texts and a Critique of Imperialism." In *"Race," Writing, and Difference* (formerly *Critical Inquiry* 12:1 and 13:1), ed. Henry Louis Gates Jr. Chicago: University of Chicago Press.

———. 1988. "Can the Subaltern Speak?" In *Marxism and the Interpretation of Culture.* Ed. Cary Nelson and Lawrence Grossberg. Urbana, IL: University of Illinois Press.

———. 1996. "Diasporas Old and New: Women in the Transnational World." *Textual Practice* 10 (summer 1996): 245–69.

Steward, Julian H. 1950. *Area Research: Theory and Practice.* New York: Social Science Research Council.

Stigler, George J. 1984. *The Intellectual and the Marketplace.* Enlarged edition. Cambridge, MA: Harvard University Press.

Su, Julie A. 1997. "Critical Coalitions." Plenary Remarks, Critical Race Theory Conference Plenary Session. Yale Law School, 13 November.

Sue, Stanley and Sumie Okazaki. 1991. "Explanations for Asian American Achievements: A Reply." *American Psychologist* 46 (August): 878–80.

Sung, Chiang et al. 1996. *China Can Say No.* Taipei: Jeng-Jiang.

Suryadinata, Leo. 1997. *Ethnic Chinese as Southeast Asians.* Singapore: Institute of Southeast Asian Studies.

Symposium on Accreditation. 1995. *Journal of Legal Education* 45 (September): 415–56.

Symposium: International Law, Human Rights, and Lat Crit Theory. 1996–1997. *Inter-American Law Review* 28 (winter).

Symposium: Picturing Justice: Images of Law and Lawyers in the Visual Media. 1996. *University of San Francisco Law Review* 30 (summer).

Symposium: Popular Legal Culture. 1989. *Yale Law Journal* 98 (June): 1548.

Symposium: Teaching and Learning Professionalism. 1996. ABA Section of Legal Education and Admissions Committee and the Standing Committees on Professionalism and Lawyer Competence of the ABA Center for Professional Responsibility. Oak Brook, Illinois, 2–4 October.

Takaki, Ronald. 1989. *Strangers from a Different Shore*. New York: William Morrow.

Takeshi, Komagome. 1996. *Japanese Colonial Empire and Cultural Unity*. Tokyo: Iwanami.

Taylor, Diana and Juan Villegas. 1994. *Negotiating Performance: Gender, Sexuality and Theatricality in Latino/a America*. Durham, NC: Duke University Press.

Ting, Jan C. 1995. " 'Other Than a Chinaman': How U.S. Immigration Law Resulted from and Still Reflects a Policy of Excluding and Restricting Asian Immigration." *Temple Political and Civil Rights Law Review* 4 (spring): 301–315.

Tölölyan, Khachig. 1991. "The Nation-State and Its Others: In Lieu of a Preface." *Diaspora* 1 (spring).

Trask, Haunani-Kay. 1990. "Politics in the Pacific Islands: Imperialism and Native Self-Determination." *Amerasia Journal* 16(1).

Tsing, Anna. 1993. *In the Realm of the Diamond Queen: Marginality in an Out-Of-the-Way Place*. Princeton: Princeton University Press.

Tu, Wei-ming, ed. 1994. *The Living Tree: The Changing Meaning of Being Chinese Today*. Stanford, CA: Stanford University Press.

Turner, Victor W. 1987. *The Anthropology of Performance*. New York: PAJ Publications.

Umemoto, Karen. " 'On Strike!' San Francisco State College Strike, 1968–1969: The Role of Asian American Students." *Amerasia Journal* 15(1): 3–41.

United Nations Development Programme (UNDP). *Human Development Report*. 1995. New York: Oxford University Press.

———. *Human Development Report*. 1999. New York: Oxford University Press.

Utset, Manuel A. 1995. "Back To School with Coase: The Production of Information and Modes of Knowledge Within and Across Academic Disciplines." *Boston University Law Review* 75: 1063–96.

Uyeda, Clifford. 1978. " 'The Pardoning of Tokyo Rose': A Report on the Restoration of American Citizenship to Iva Ikuko Toguri." *Amerasia Journal* 5(2): 69–93.

Visweswaran, Kamala. 1994. *Fictions of Feminist Ethnography*. Minneapolis: University of Minnesota Press.

Waire-Post, Deborah. 1994. "Critical Thoughts About Race, Exclusion, Oppression, and Tenure." *Pace Law Review* 15 (fall): 69–110.

Wallerstein, Immanuel M., ed. 1966. *Social Change: The Colonial Situation*. New York: John Wiley and Sons.

Wang, Chenguang and Zianchu Zhang, eds. 1997. *Introduction to Chinese Law*. Hong Kong: Sweet and Maxwell Asia.

Wang, Gungwu. 1991. *China and the Chinese Overseas*. Singapore: Times Academic Press.

Wang, Ji-shihs, ed. 1995. *Civilization and International Politics: Chinese Scholars on Huntington's Theory of the "Clash of Civilizations."* Shanghai: People's Publisher.

Wang, L. Ling-Chi. 1995. "The Structure of Dual Domination: Toward a Paradigm for the Study of the Chinese Diaspora in the United States." In Michael Omi and Dana Takagi, eds. "Thinking Theory in Asian American Studies." Special Issue of *Amerasia Journal* 21(1–2): 149–69.

———. 1994. "Roots and the Changing Identity of the Chinese in the United States." In Wei-ming Tu, ed. *The Living Tree: The Changing Meaning of Being Chinese Today*. Stanford, CA: Stanford University Press. 185–212.

Wang, Ling-Chi and Wang Gungwu, eds. 1998. *The Chinese Diaspora: Selected Essays*. volumes 1 and 2. Singapore: Times Academic Press.

Wattenberg, Ben and Karl Zinsmeister. 1990. "The Case for More Immigration." *Commentary* 89 (April): 19–25.

Weber, Carl. 1991. "AC/TC: Currents of Theatrical Exchange." In *Interculturalism and Performance*, eds. Bonnie Marranca and Gautam Dasgupta. New York: PAJ Publications. 27–37.

Wei, William. 1993. *The Asian American Movement*. Philadelphia: Temple University Press.

Westra, Laura and Peter Wenz, eds. 1995. *Faces of Environmental Racism: Confronting Issues of Global Justice*. Lanham, MD: Rowman and Littlefield.

Williams, Patricia. 1991. *The Alchemy of Race and Rights: Diary of a Law Professor*. Boston: Harvard University Press.

Williams, Raymond. 1989. *The Politics of Modernism: Against the New Conformists*. London: Verso.

Wing, Adrienne, ed. 1997. *Critical Race Feminisms*. New York: New York University Press.

Wong, Sau-ling Cynthia. 1995a. "Denationalization Reconsidered: Asian American Cultural Criticism at a Theoretical Crossroad." *Amerasia Journal* 21(1–2): 1–27.

———. 1995b. " 'Sugar Sisterhood': Situating the Amy Tan Phenomenon." In *The Ethnic Canon: Histories, Institutions, and Interventions,* ed. David Palumbo-Liu. Minneapolis: University of Minneapolis Press. 174–210.

———. 1993. *Reading Asian American Literature: From Necessity to Extravagance*. Princeton: Princeton University Press.

———. 1992. "Ethnicizing Gender: An Exploration of Sexuality as Sign in Chinese Immigrant Literature." In Shirley Geok-lin Lim and Amy Ling, eds. *Reading the Literatures of Asian America*. Philadelphia: Temple University Press. 111–29.

———. 1991. "The Poetics and Politics of Folksong Reading: Literary Portrayals of Life under Exclusion." In *Entry Denied: Exclusion and the Chinese Community in America, 1882–1943,* ed. Sucheng Chan. Philadelphia: Temple University Press. 246–67.

———. 1989. "What's in a Name? Defining Chinese American Literature of the Immigrant Generation." In *Frontiers in Asian American Studies: Writing, Research, and Commentary,* ed. by Gail M. Nomura et al. Pullman, WA: Washington State University Press. 159–67.

———. 1988a. "Teaching Chinese Immigrant Literature: Some Principles of Syllabus Design." In *Reflections on Shattered Windows: Promises and Prospects for Asian American Studies,* ed. by Gary Y. Okihiro et al. Pullman: Washington State University Press. 126–34.

———. 1988b. "Tales of Postwar Chinatown: Short Stories of *The Bud,* 1947–1948." *Amerasia Journal* 14(2): 61–79.

———. 1987. "*Huamei zuojia xiaoshuo zhong de hunyin zhuti*" [The marriage theme in the fiction of Chinese American writers]. *Guangdong Shehuikexue Jikan* 11(1): 116–25.

Woo, Margaret Y. K. 1999. "(Un)Fracturing Images: Positioning Chinese Diaspora in Law and Culture." In Sharon Hom, ed. *Chinese Women Traversing Diaspora: Memoirs, Essays, and Poetry*. New York: Garland Publishing.

———. 1993. "Biology and Equality: Challenges for Feminism in the Socialist and the Liberal State." *Emory Law Journal* 42: 143–195.

World Bank. 1996. *Poverty Reduction and the World Bank*. Washington, D.C.: World Bank.

Wu, David Yen-ho. 1991. "The Construction of Chinese and Non-Chinese Identities." *Daedalus* 120 (spring): 176.

Yamamoto, Eric K. 1999. *Interracial Justice: Conflict and Reconciliation in Post-Civil Rights America*. New York: New York University Press.

——. 1995. "Rethinking Alliances: Agency, Responsibility and Interracial Justice." *UCLA Asian Pacific American Law Journal* 3 (fall): 33–74.

Yeh, Michelle. 1991. "The Anxiety of Difference—A Rejoinder." *Jiantian* [today] 1: 94–96.

Yen, Alfred C. 1996. "A Statistical Analysis of Asian Americans and the Affirmative Action Hiring of Law School Faculty. *Asian Law Journal* 3 (May): 39–54.

Yoshimi, Shunya. 1996. "'America' in Contemporary Japan: From Symbol to System," Presented at the conference "Patterns of Consumption of Asia's New Rich," Murdoch University, Australia.

Yu, Shiao-ling. 1993. "The Themes of Exile and Identity Crisis in Nie Hualing's Fiction." In *Nativism Overseas: Contemporary Chinese Women Writers,* ed. by Hsin-sheng C. Kao. New York: State University of New York Press. 127–56.

Yun, Chung-hei. 1992. "Beyond 'Clay Walls': Korean American Literature." In Shirley Geok-lin Lim and Amy Ling, eds. *Reading the Literatures of Asian America*. Philadelphia: Temple University Press. 79–96.

Yun, Grace, ed. 1989. *A Look Beyond the Model Minority Image: Critical Issues in Asian America*. New York: Minority Rights Group.

"Zhong wai jizhe zhaodaihui shang Li Peng huida wenti" [Li Peng's responses to questions at the press conference for Chinese and foreign reporters] 1991. *Ming Pao Daily News* Vancouver Edition (11 April).

Žižek, Slavoj. 1989. *The Sublime Object of Ideology.* London: Verso.

Contributors

DIPESH CHAKRABARTY teaches history and South Asian studies at the University of Chicago. He is a founding member of the editorial collective of *Subaltern Studies* and is the author of *Provincializing Europe: Postcolonial Thought and Historical Difference* (2000).

KUAN-HSING CHEN is Professor of Cultural Studies at the Center for Asia-Pacific Culture Studies, National Tsing Hua University, Hsin-chu, Taiwan. He is coeditor of the *Trajectories: Inter-Asia Cultural Studies*, and has edited numerous volumes including *Locating Political Society: Modernity, State Violence and Postcolonial Democracies* and *Cultural Studies in Taiwan*.

REY CHOW is Andrew W. Mellon Professor of the Humanities at Brown University. She is the author of a number of books, the most recent of which is *Ethics after Idealism: Theory, Culture, Ethnicity, Reading* (1998). She is also the editor of *Modern Chinese Literary and Culture Studies in the Age of Theory: Reimagining a Field* (2000).

KANDICE CHUH is Assistant Professor of English at the University of Maryland, College Park. She is currently at work on a manuscript entitled *Imagine Otherwise: Envisioning America through Asian Americanist Critique*.

SHARON HOM is Professor of Law at the City University of New York School of Law at Queens. From 1986 to 1988, she was a Fulbright scholar in the People's Republic of China. She has been active for the past 16 years in U.S.-China legal training exchanges and Chinese women's studies work. Her book publications include a coauthored text and workbook, *Contracting Law* (1996), a coedited *Chinese-English Lexicon on Women and the Law* (Yinghan funu yu falu cihuishiyi) (1995), and an edited volume, *Chinese Women Traversing Diaspora: Memoirs, Essays, and Poetry* (1999). In the summer of 2000 she was a scholar in residence at the Rockefeller Foundation's Bellagio Center in Italy.

YOSHIKUNI IGARASHI is Associate Professor of History at Vanderbilt University. He is the author of *Bodies of Memory: Narratives of War in Postwar Japanese Culture, 1945–1970* (2000).

DORINNE KONDO is Professor of Anthropology and American Studies and Ethnicity, and the Director of Asian American Studies, at the University of Southern California. She is the author of *Crafting Selves: Power, Gender, and Discourses of Identity* (winner of the J. I. Staley Prize, for a book having an impact on the field of Anthropology) and *About Face: Performing Race in Fashion and Theatre* (winner of a Cultural and Literary Studies Award from the Association for Asian American Studies). She was a dramaturge for Anna Deavere Smith's *Twilight: Los Angeles 1992* in its world premiere in 1993 at the Mark Taper Forum in Los Angeles, and for the film *Twilight: Los Angeles* for PBS, and is a playwright.

RUSSELL C. LEONG is the editor of UCLA's *Amerasia Journal*. He is the author of *Phoenix Eyes and Other Stories* (2000), which was chosen as the best book of fiction by the *Los Angeles Times*. He edited *Asian American Sexualities: Dimensions of the Gay and Lesbian Experience* (1996) and *Moving the Image* (1991). Leong is an adjunct professor of English in the Department of English at UCLA.

GEORGE LIPSITZ teaches Ethnic Studies at the University of California, San Diego. He is the author of *The Possessive Investment in Whiteness: How White People Profit from Identity Politics* and *A Life in the Struggle: Ivory Perry and the Culture of Opposition*.

LISA LOWE is Professor of Comparative Literature at University of California, San Diego, where she is affiliated with the programs in Ethnic Studies and Critical Gender Studies. She is the author of *Critical Terrains: French and British Orientalisms* (1991) and *Immigrant Acts: On Asian American Cultural Politics* (1996), and is coeditor with David Lloyd of *The Politics of Culture in the Shadow of Capital* (1997), and with Elaine Kim of *New Formations, New Questions: Asian American Studies*, a special issue of *positions: east asia cultures critique* (fall 1997).

MARTIN F. MANALANSAN IV is an Assistant Professor of Anthropology and of Criticism and Interpretive Theory at the University of Illinois, Urbana-Champaign. He is the editor of *Cultural Compass: Ethnographic Explorations of Asian America* (Temple University Press, 2000), and is currently at work completing a manuscript entitled *Global Divas: Filipino Gay Men in the Diaspora* for Duke University Press.

DAVID PALUMBO-LIU is Professor of Comparative Literature and Director of the Program in Modern Thought and Literature at Stanford University. He has published in journals such as *Amerasia Journal, Cultural Critique, diacritics, differences, New Literary History, positions: east asia cultures critique, Public Culture,* and others. His latest book is *Asian/American: Historical Crossings of a Racial Frontier* (1999).

R. RADHAKRISHNAN is Professor of English at the University of Massachusetts Amherst, where he teaches critical theory, poststructuralism, postcoloniality, and diasporan literature and theory. He is the author of *Diasporic Mediations: Between Home and Location* (1996) and *Theory In an Uneven World* (forthcoming). His essays have appeared in numerous collections and in journals such as *boundary2, Cultural Critique, Social Text, positions, Callaloo, MELUS, Transition, Differences,* and *Rethinking Marxism*. He is currently working on a book-length project on epistemology, ethics, and the politics of persuasion.

KAREN SHIMAKAWA is Assistant Professor in the Department of Theatre & Dance and the Asian American Studies Program at the University of California, Davis. She is currently at work completing a book-length manuscript entitled *'made not born': National Abjection and the Asian American Body on Stage*.

SAU-LING C. WONG is a Professor in the Asian American Studies Program, Department of Ethnic Studies, University of California, Berkeley. Born and raised in Hong Kong, she holds a Ph.D. in British and American literature from Stanford University, and has published extensively on various aspects of Asian American literature, including Chinese-language immigrant writing. She is the author of *Reading Asian American Literature: From Necessity to Extravagance* (1993); editor of *Maxine Hong Kingston's* The Woman Warrior: *A Casebook* (1999); coeditor with Stephen H. Sumida of *A Resource Guide to Asian American Literature* (forthcoming); and a founding editor of *Hitting Critical Mass: A Journal of Asian American Cultural Criticism*.

Index

Asian American studies, 9–10; activism in, 59, 253, 305; and coalition formation, 261–62; emergence of, 41, 57–58, 135, 269; epistemic claims of, 252; gender/sexuality studies in, 63–65, 272; global or neocolonial frameworks in, 273; "indigenization model" of, 41; as model for interethnic antiracism, 299–301; and postcolonialism, 261; and postmodernism, 260; and poststructuralism, 261; professionalization of, 58–59

Asian American theater, 28, 41–56; and activism, 42–43

Asian diaspora, 6; and Asian American studies, 293, celebratory readings of, 37–39; eccentric perspective of, 7; as epistemological object, 7; in performance, 52–55; and transnational capital, 173. *See also* Northwest Asian American Theatre (NWAAT)

Asian immigrant: as object of disciplinary study, 267–70; and white collar proletariat, 276 n.11. *See also* American studies; Asian American studies; Asian studies

"Asianness": as epistemological object, 7

Asian studies: and Asian immigration, 271; as crucial to U.S. militarism, 268; and U.S. foreign policy, 271. *See also* Area studies; South Asian studies

Asiatic racialization, 1–2; reified in area studies, 9–10

Bambara, Toni Cade, 302, 309
Bei Dao, 189–92
Bennett, Wendell C., 108
Biyuti, 155
Bradwell v. Illinois, 87
Brontë, Charlotte: *Jane Eyre,* 197–98
Brook, Peter: *The Mahabharata,* 49–50

Campaign finance scandal, 1–2
Capitalism: liberal capitalist world order, 2; U.S. capitalist ideology, 3. *See also* Globalization; U.S. imperialism
Cha, Theresa Hak Kyung. See *Dictée*
Chang, Robert, 96
Chin, Gabriel, 97

China, 1–3; anti-Chinese sentiment, 1–2; human rights discourse and, 3, 79, 82, 89; Most Favored Nation status and, 3
Chinese Exclusion Act of 1882, 87
Chinese legal studies, 87, 90–92; crossover with Asian American critical jurisprudence, 92
Chon, Maggie, 96
Citizenship: in *Dictée,* 281, 286; as master narrative of nation, 270–76
Clay Walls (Ronyoung Kim): 286; Japanese colonialism in, 287–90; Korean nationalism in, 288–89; language and national identity in, 287–88; sex and sexual violence in, 287–88; and the transnation, 290–91; U.S. racism in, 288–90
Clinton administration, 1
Coalitional formations, 261
Colonial identification, 178
Communitarian discourses, 95
Connery, Christopher, 3; and "Pacific Rim" discourse, 21 n.5
Cover, Robert, 77
Crafting Selves. See Kondo, Dorinne
Critical race theory, 77
Cultural imperialism, 177, 196. *See also* U.S. imperialism
Cultural studies, 31
Cumings, Bruce, 2–3, 21 n.3

Davis, Angela: epistemological effects of political action, 302–3; and prison-industrial complex, 274
de Certeau, Michel: strategy versus tactic, 202
Delhi, 113–14
Diaspora, 10, 34, 36
Dictée, 281–86; citizenship in, 281, 286; foreignness in, 282–84; gender/sex in, 285; language in, 281–82; memory in, 284; transnationalist time in, 286
Disciplinarity, 7, 11, 16; and Asian American studies, 250–51; and the "new Asian immigrant," 267–70. *See also* Area studies, American studies; Asian American studies; Asian studies
Discourse communities, 14, 110–19, 123–28
Drama, 155

East Asian studies: critiques of Orientalism in, 191, 194; melancholia and, 191–92; Orientalist legacy of, 26–27, 32, 191. *See also* Area studies; Asian studies

East West Players, 41–43

Embodiment: in Asian diasporic experience, 10; and globalization, 11; in theatrical performance, 43–46, 54–55

Eng, David, 10

"Enkei Daigaku Butai." *See* Kojima Nobuo

Ethnic studies, 296–309; and activism, 306–7; Asian Americans and the Law, 81; contrasted with ethnic communities, 296–97; institutionalization of, 9

Exploratory Committee on World Area Research, 7–8. *See also* Hall, Robert

Fallows, James: *More Like Us: Making America Great Again,* 222–27

Feminism, 6

Feminist conjuncturalism, 38

Feminist legal studies, 77

Frankenburg, Ruth. *See* Mani, Lata

Freud Sigmund: on melancholia, 191–92

Garner, Stanton: theater as occlusion, 44–45

Gay and lesbian studies: in Asian American studies, 6

Globalization, 2, 4, 20 n.2, 101–2 n.12, 172; academic globalization, 5, 10; and Asian immigration, 270; epistemological object formation, 10; as extension of U.S. capitalism, 21 n.3; Japanese, 277 n.10; as twenty-first-century formation, 270. *See also* Transnationalism

Gotanda, Neil, 1

Gotanda, Philip K.: on Asian American theater and activism, 42–43; on multicultural theatre, 48

Guha, Ranajit: as editor of *Subaltern Studies,* 111–12

Hall, Robert, 7–8, 128 n.1

Hall, Stuart: critique of postmodernism, 34

Harris, Angela, 96

Hawai'i: capitalist development of tourism industry in, 273

Hom, Alice, 10

"Hoshi." *See* Kojima Nobuo

Hwang, David Henry: on multicultural theater, 48, 56 n.6

Hyphenation, 254

Identity politics, 304–8

Immigrant literature, 135, 136; as "literature of exile," 140

Immigration and Nationality Act of 1965, 35, 267, 269–70

Immigration law, 77, 87; post-1965, 267

Interactive multiculturalism, 63, 122. *See also* Multiculturalism

Intercultural performance, 49–52; critiques of, 50–51

Interethnic antiracism, 299–306; as alternative to minority/majority discourse, 301; Asian American studies and, 299–301; and cultural production, 305–6; epistemological value of, 302; and identity politics, 304–8

International Artists Program (IAP), 53–55. *See also* Northwest Asian American Theatre (NWAAT)

Internationalism: critical, 292–93; missile, 180–85; and transnationalism, 173

Jameson, Fredric: cognitive mapping, 6; postmodernist nostalgia of, 34

Jane Eyre. See Brontë, Charlotte

Japan: and colonialism, 179, 287–91; and exceptionalism, 220; as hybrid, 231–33; "Japan bashing," 4, 32; modernization in, 219

Japanese Americans: absent in Japanese area studies, 228–30; in *Clay Walls,* 289–90; in postwar Japanese fiction, 230–46; as subnation, 218–19; wartime relocation of, 32, 87

Japanese Americans: Oppression and Success. See Petersen, William

Japanese area studies: absence of discussion of Japanese Americans in, 228–30; progressive formations within, 32–33. *See also* Asian studies; East Asian studies

Rafael, Vicente: critique of area studies, 8–9
Redfield, Robert, 108
Ricoeur, Paul, 281, 294 n.13
Rights-based discourses, 95
Román, David: critical generosities, 34
Rushdie, Salman, 118

Sakai, Naoki: translation as a social function, 10; universalism and particularism, 192–93
Sangqing yu Taohong. See *Mulberry and Peach: Two Women of China;* Nieh Hualing
Sinicization, 208–9
Smith, Anna Deveare: *Twilight: Los Angeles 1992,* 29
Social Text, 107, 109
South Asian diaspora studies, 119–22
South Asian studies, 109–28
Spivak, Gayatri Chakravorty: on *Jane Eyre* as imperialist, 198; and *Subaltern Studies,* 110
Su, Julie, 96
Subaltern Studies, 109–28; critiques of, 111, 114; globalized conditions of production, 113
"Success Story, Japanese American Style." *See* Petersen, William

Taiwan: Club 51, 183–85; 1996 Presidential election, 181–85
Theater: and activism, 42–43; Asian American, 28, 41–56; presentation versus representation, 44–45; as "terror," 43
Third World Movement, 7
"Trafficking": in cultural studies, 76; in legal studies, 76–77, 94–100
Translation (as social relation), 10–11, 14;

and academic globalization, 14; homolingual and heterolingual address, 14
Transnationalism, 5–6, 36–39; in Asian American studies, 290–91; emblematized by diaspora, 201; history in, 291–92; as methodology, 280, 292; transnation, 291–93, 294 n.8
Tsing, Anna: postcolonial theory and de-essentialism, 38
Turner, Victor, 157
Twilight: Los Angeles 1992. See Smith, Anna Deveare

U.S. colonialism, 270; and American studies, 272
U.S. Filipinos, 170 n.1; and quotidian performance, 153–70; and religion, 165–66; as transmigrants, 160–70
U.S. imperialism, 174; absence of discussion of, in postcolonial studies, 174–76; ideological imperialism, 278–79; supplanting Japanese colonialism in Asia, 179

Vanguardism, 35–36, 39
Visweswaran, Kamala: critique of Appadurai's transnationalism, 36–37; on race in anthropology, 40 n.2

Wagley, Charles, 108
Williams, Patricia, 84
Wong, Sau-ling C.: "authenticity effects," 255–56

Yamamoto, Eric, 96
Yamazaki Toyoko, 230

Library of Congress Cataloging-in-Publication Data
Orientations : mapping studies in the Asian diaspora / Kandice Chuh
and Karen Shimakawa, editors.
Includes bibliographical references and index.
ISBN 0-8223-2729-5 (cloth : alk. paper) — ISBN 0-8223-2739-2 (pbk. : alk. paper)
1. Asian Americans — Study and teaching. 2. Asia — Study and teaching. 3. Asian
Americans. 4. Cold War. I. Chuh, Kandice II. Shimakawa, Karen
E184.06 075 2001 973'.0495'007 — dc21 2001023150